The Essential Academic Dean

The Essential Academic Dean
A Practical Guide to College Leadership

Jeffrey L. Buller

JOSSEY-BASS
A Wiley Imprint
www.josseybass.com

Published by Jossey-Bass
A Wiley Imprint
989 Market Street, San Francisco, CA 94103–1741   www.josseybass.com

Jossey-Bass books and products are available through most bookstores. To contact Jossey-Bass directly call our Customer Care Department within the U.S. at 800-956-7739, outside the U.S. at 317-572-3986, or fax 317-572-4002.

Jossey-Bass also publishes its books in a variety of electronic formats. Some content that appears in print may not be available in electronic books.

Library of Congress Cataloging-in-Publication Data

Buller, Jeffrey L.
  The essential academic dean : a practical guide to college leadership / Jeffrey L. Buller.
     p. cm.
  Includes bibliographical references.
  ISBN 978-0-470-18086-0 (pbk.)
  1. Deans (Education) 2. Universities and colleges—Administration. I. Title.
  LB2341.B743 2007
  378.1'11—dc22

2007030432

Printed in the United States of America
FIRST EDITION
HB Printing 10 9 8 7 6 5 4 3 2 1

Table of Contents

About the Author

Jeffrey L. Buller is dean of the Harriet L. Wilkes Honors College at Florida Atlantic University. He began his administrative career as honors director and chair of the Department of Classical Studies at Loras College in Dubuque, Iowa, before going on to assume several administrative appointments at Georgia Southern University and Mary Baldwin College. Dr. Buller is the author of *The Essential Department Chair: A Practical Guide to College Administration* (Anker, 2006) and *Classically Romantic: Classical Form and Meaning in Wagner's Ring* (Xlibris, 2001), as well as numerous articles on Greek and Latin literature, 19th- and 20th-century opera, and college administration. Serving from 2003–2005 as the principal English-language lecturer at the International Wagner Festival in Bayreuth, Germany, he is widely known as an entertaining and popular speaker on such topics as international culture, music, literature, and higher education.

Introduction

If academic deans were actually like their depictions in the movies, few of us would willingly show our faces in public. Consider, for instance, the following role models:

- Dean Peter Morgan, Sr. (Charles Coburn) in *Vivacious Lady* (1938)

- Dean Vernon Wormer (John Vernon) in *Animal House* (1978)

- Dean Martin (Ned Beatty) in *Back to School* (1986)

- Dean Walcott (Bob Gunton) in *Patch Adams* (1998)

- Dean Carl Cain (Obba Babatundé) in *How High* (2001)

- Dean Gordon "Cheese" Pritchard (Jeremy Piven) in *Old School* (2003)

- Dean Van Horne (Anthony Heald) in *Accepted* (2006)

You can probably add a few more of your favorite fictional deans to this list. Every single one of them is either stuffy, stupid, or mean—or all three at once. The dean in most American movies is the person who stands in the way of the hero's desire to fulfill a dream, represents a hidebound tradition that undermines the true spirit of higher education, and ends up a figure of ridicule because he (and only very rarely *she*) was completely wrong about absolutely everything.

This is a book about how *not* to become that sort of dean.

Like its companion volume, *The Essential Department Chair: A Practical Guide to College Administration* (2006), this book focuses not on elaborate theories of administrative leadership but on real-life situations that deans face day in and day out. Inevitably, I've duplicated some of the topics that appear in *The Essential Department Chair.* (After all, deans and department chairs face some common administrative challenges.) On the whole, however, *The Essential Academic Dean: A Practical Guide to College Leadership* examines administrative issues that arise at a higher institutional level. I've tried to combine basic principles of good academic leadership with time-tested solutions to problems that deans will know well. You will find that recommendations to become stuffy, stupid, or mean appear nowhere in the pages that follow.

The book has been designed so that you can use it in either of two ways:

- You can read straight through from cover to cover because later topics build incrementally on the principles introduced in earlier chapters.

- Or you can consult this volume as a reference book, picking it up from time to time when you want to get some advice on how to deal with a particular challenge or to make best use of a special opportunity. If you decide to use the book in this manner, you'll find numerous cross-references throughout the text, guiding you to where each technical term was first defined or where a certain concept was discussed in greater detail.

I've also made each chapter as brief and self-contained as possible. My goal has been to provide you with all the clear, concise information that you can absorb in 10 minutes when time is of the essence.

A special feature of this book is the scenario analysis that concludes each major section. In a scenario analysis, you will be confronted with a hypothetical case study designed to apply the principles explored in previous chapters, several considerations that may cause you to reevaluate the situation, and some recommendations about how to handle the problem. It can be particularly informative to discuss a scenario analysis with a fellow dean or a trusted mentor to learn how different administrative approaches might be brought to bear on the same complex issue.

Scattered throughout the book you will find several essential principles that are formatted as follows:

> *Essential principles are the key ideas that can help you succeed in a variety of administrative situations. These are the principles to which you'll want to give particular attention when you face your own administrative challenges.*

Essential principles are designed to be short and easily remembered, but they are not mere platitudes. All of them have been tested in actual administrative situations and have proved their value. Even if you end up disagreeing with one or two of them, they deserve your serious and thoughtful attention.

This book is dedicated to my colleagues on the Council of Deans at Florida Atlantic University: J. Dennis Coates, Barry Kaye College of Business; Gary W. Perry, Charles E. Schmidt College of Science; Michael L. Friedland, Charles E. Schmidt College of Biomedical Science; Anne Boykin, Christine E. Lynn College of Nursing; Rosalyn Carter, College of Architecture, Urban, and Public

Affairs; Gregory F. Aloia, College of Education; Karl K. Stevens, College of Engineering and Computer Science; and Sandra Norman and Leslie M. Terry, who served in 2006–2007 as the acting deans of the Dorothy F. Schmidt College of Arts and Letters and the Office of Graduate Studies, respectively. These nine academic leaders taught me more about effective college administration, strong collegial support, and holding an institution's best interests as the highest priority than I could have learned in years of graduate seminars. I hope that each reader of this book may be fortunate enough to find colleagues as encouraging and talented as these.

Whether you are hoping someday to serve as an academic dean, have recently accepted such a position, or are already well into your administrative career, I also hope that you will discover that administrative leadership continues to offer you exciting, constantly evolving opportunities to apply your creativity, initiative, and problem-solving skills. Although this book focuses on the essential, day-to-day nuts and bolts of serving as a college dean, remember that it is only by mastering these details that you will have the opportunity to become a visionary. What you will find in the chapters that follow is advice on how to make your vision for the college a reality. But the *substance* of that vision is entirely up to you.

Each day in our administrative careers may be regarded as merely a step along an extended pilgrimage of self-discovery. As you continue your voyage, I hope that, wherever your personal journey takes you, it proves to be amazing and fruitful.

1

The View from the Middle

The responsibilities of an academic dean vary widely from institution to institution. At some schools the academic dean serves as the institution's chief academic officer, filling a role that combines aspects of being the provost, vice president for academic affairs, dean, and department chair all at the same time (see Chapter 54, "The Dean as Chief Academic Officer"). At other schools the dean may work almost exclusively with department chairs or division directors, each of whom has direct line authority over the faculty members in his or her unit. Other differences may include multiple levels of reporting relationships above and below the dean or just one level on either side of the deanship (the president as the dean's direct supervisor and the faculty as the dean's direct reports). Regardless of how different deans' job descriptions may be, they have one common feature: The dean serves in a middle management position. Although the dean may have a great deal of autonomy in budgetary matters and policy implementation, he or she ultimately reports directly to *someone*—usually a president, provost, or academic vice president—rather than to a board. At the same time the dean has several people to supervise, evaluate for performance reviews and recommend for salary adjustments, and unite effectively as an academic team. Hundreds of books have been written about the principles of leadership or how to get things done from the top. There is even literature on how to serve most effectively as an employee and the techniques of *followership,* a term coined by Robert Kelley (1992) and elaborated on in more comprehensive studies by Atchison (2004), Chaleff (2003), and Seteroff (2003). But how can deans be expected to lead from the middle?

As a way of answering this question, it might be useful to begin by recognizing that deans have always had a view from the middle. The word *dean* comes to English via Norman French from the Latin word *decanus,* which refers to an officer in charge of 10 people (cf. Latin *decem* or Greek *deka,* "ten"). A dean thus had far less authority, in etymological terms at least, than a *centurion,* who was in charge of 100 people, but far more than any of the 10 people who reported to the dean. Throughout the Middle Ages the word ceased to have a military connection and adopted various ecclesiastical connotations, such as the member of clergy who supervised 10 monks in a monastery, the head of a chapter in a cathedral, or a member of the religious hierarchy through whom a group of priests reported to an archbishop. With the religious missions of such academic institutions as Oxford and Cambridge, the word required only a very slight shift from an ecclesiastical to an academic perspective, placing the dean in charge of the behavior and academic progress of students in a college. As administration of colleges and universities developed, deans then became elected faculty members who provided administrative guidance, management, and vision. By the 20th century, deans in the United States were rapidly being hired as administrators rather than as teachers, individuals who almost always had strong academic backgrounds but who were appointed (and less frequently elected) because they had demonstrated a significant amount of talent or potential for making their colleges and schools run effectively.

From their origin, therefore, deans have always been individuals whose responsibilities drew them in two directions simultaneously: They were advocates for and supervisors of the people over whom they had authority; they reported to and served as the representatives of some higher official who set the limits within which they could operate. Performing both of these responsibilities effectively is continually one of the dean's challenges. Nevertheless, few aspects of the dean's tasks are as essential as the ability to see the institution's needs from the middle and to address those needs adequately. So how do you do that? Here are five general principles to keep in mind as you begin developing your own approach to providing leadership from the middle.

Explore ways of developing an atmosphere of collegial candor.

As a dean, you want your supervisor to treat you with respect, to give your views a fair hearing even if they are not ultimately accepted, and to share information with you freely, particularly in cases where having that information is essential to performing your job effectively. Is it unreasonable, therefore, to expect that those who report to you may be looking for many of the same considerations from your office? Your method of interacting with the department chairs, division directors, and faculty members in your unit should be a reflection of the role that you wish to play in the larger institutional structure; in fact, how you treat others may even help shape that role.

Developing an atmosphere of collegial candor means two things. First, it requires creating a working environment in which individuals feel safe to provide their perspectives on various issues and understand that you will agree or disagree with these views according to the argument's merits, not according to the individual advancing it. Second, it requires fostering an environment where the overall mission of the institution, rather than the personal convenience of its individual members, is the guiding principle behind all deliberations. You have an obligation, therefore, to apply this philosophy to all your discussions with your president, provost, or vice president of academic affairs. And you have no less of an obligation to exercise the same approach when dealing with members of your school or college.

The person who reports to you relies on you as a sounding board for ideas and insights, even if that person's behavior does not always appear open to alternative views. Disagreements with one's boss do not have to be confrontational, and job security rarely results from blindly concurring with every suggestion or perspective that your superior advances. When phrased in a collegial manner ("Now, that might be true, but another way of looking at it could be . . ." or "Perhaps, though, we should also consider whether . . ."), disagreements can broaden the perspectives brought to the discussion and may even help your supervisor avoid making a serious mistake. Administrators may be frustrated when those who report to them constantly and inconsiderately disagree with every idea that is advanced, every suggestion that is made, or every improvement that is proposed. But it can also be frustrating when people agree for the sake of agreeing and never fully engage with the merits of a proposal as it applies to the situation being discussed. Strive to be a dean who speaks freely when it is important to do so but who also understands how to provide alternatives in a constructive, consensus-building manner.

Creating an open atmosphere in your unit involves making it clear that department chairs and faculty members are free to express points of view that differ from yours—even in open meetings—as long as the discussion is conducted civilly and focuses on the college's central educational mission, not on personalities or private disputes. You should not tolerate grandstanding or outright insubordination, just as you would not expect your superior to tolerate that sort of unprofessional conduct. Nevertheless, you should try to promote an open exchange of ideas with those both above you and below you in the institutional hierarchy. Only by doing so are you likely to gain access to the information you need to perform your job effectively. Open channels of communication are also the sole way for the institution to avoid embarking on a disastrous endeavor because no one felt free to say that the proposal was unsound.

Seek ways of clarifying or crystallizing a vision.

Your institution's upper administration is likely to have articulated a vision for the future direction of your college or university; perhaps these ideas are contained in a strategic plan or in a vision statement endorsed by the president and governing board. Your faculty members also have a vision of how they would like their academic areas to develop, their students to learn, and their research to progress. None of those visions can be realized, however, without your view from the middle. The upper administration will need assistance in determining how its overarching goals for the institution are best realized and measured in your academic unit. The faculty will need assistance in seeing how their individual goals stand amid the institution's larger priorities and how they can play a significant role in making the strategic plan a reality.

The dean's job can thus be to serve as a catalyst in clarifying or crystallizing these visions. If one of the president's strategic goals is, for instance, to develop more undergraduate research at the same time that students improve their understanding of global issues, how can these two issues be combined in the curricula of the disciplines represented by your area? Can you lead your college or school toward adopting a new capstone experience for students that will include a substantial component of original research? Can you spearhead a review of all course curricula to strengthen international perspectives? Can you suggest alternative requirements for majors so that students who study abroad are less likely to be delayed in their progress toward graduation? As a dean, you understand the individual needs, methods, and philosophies of your disciplines far better than many of your upper administrators. As a result, you are in a unique position to shape the institution's larger vision into a plan that fits the ways in which disciplines actually work in your area.

Similarly, faculty members in your school or college may be interested in greater flexibility in their workload, revisions to evaluation procedures to more adequately suit their jobs, better compensation, or improved facilities. You have an opportunity to serve as an advocate for these needs—when you, in your professional judgment, see them as valid—by clarifying how they might advance the institution's strategic plan. If, for instance, improved student advisement, enhanced civic engagement, and collaborative endeavors between academic affairs and the student life office are institutional goals, are initiatives in these areas being properly rewarded under your current faculty evaluation structure? Institutions tend to get more of what they specifically measure and reward; you can help bridge the upper administration and the faculty by finding points of connection where strategic goals can justify faculty needs. If you implement a reward structure in which promotions, tenure, and annual increases are based, at least in part, on advancing the institution's strategic goals, you are more likely to see those goals achieved in a timely manner.

Remember that the dean's job is to serve neither as a lackey nor as a shop steward.

As a dean, you are likely to be asked, "Whose representative are you: the upper administration's or the faculty's?" This question really poses a false dichotomy, and it is usually asked by someone who is trying to bait you (to see perhaps whether your response will end up on the wrong side of his or her personal litmus test) or who is not particularly knowledgeable about college and university administration. Your most important duty as dean is to advocate for your unit's academic programs. At times, this advocacy will consist of making the case, as forcefully and eloquently as you can, for the needs of certain programs or individuals who report to you. At times, however, the best advocacy for your unit is clarifying for your department chairs and faculty members why certain of their perceived needs cannot or should not be addressed. Good deans sometimes have to say no. They are neither the upper administration's lackeys (serving merely as a conduit for the decisions made by the president and other senior administrators) nor their faculty's shop stewards (pressing for the adoption of every request made by those who report to them). Your view from the middle requires you to be both your own person *and* responsive to the perspectives of those above and below you. Knowing when one of these must take precedence over the other is a demonstration of good judgment.

Be consistent without becoming inflexible.

Both your supervisor and the faculty members in your area want to know what you stand for. They want to know your core beliefs, what is nonnegotiable with you, and your sense of vision for the school or college. In most cases people actually feel more comfortable when they believe that a program is headed in the wrong direction than when it is not headed in any direction. For this reason, you will be expected to speak regularly about your values and vision for your area. Be as consistent as possible in responding to these requests; deans who seem enamored of every new trend that arises in academia or every new initiative begun by their professional organizations seem as aimless as those who cannot find any particular cause to get behind. Both your president and your department chairs want to know that they can predict the general direction of your views on a subject. They will feel a greater sense of purpose in your unit if you develop clear priorities and act on them in a consistent manner.

It is important to be reasonable as well as consistent, however. Deans who never change their minds can be as destructive to an institution as deans who change their minds whenever they are presented with an alternative point of view. Reliability is far different than stubbornness. People will excuse you when you occasionally change direction or rescind a decision as long as they know the reasons for the change and you are candid about the process that led to the new decision. Avoid giving the impression that you simply caved in to pressure. Be clear about why the new course is necessary and how it still fits with the overall plan for your area. Nevertheless, if you find yourself having to explain these changes too often, it is time for you to reconsider the soundness of your original plan.

Try to find ways of seeing the big picture, the details, and the view from your own office simultaneously.

Everyone at your institution has a different perspective based on his or her individual role. The president will want you to see how your college or school fits into the big picture. Your faculty members will want you to see things from their vantage point, to understand the challenges of providing an active learning environment while producing scholarship and performing institutional service, and to help them achieve parity with a peer group that always seems to have a lighter workload and better pay. The key to being a successful dean is the ability to see all these points of view at the same time and to act on them with the best possible judgment. The issue cannot always be solely about the university; there are times when your individual school or college is going to have to come first in a decision. But your perspective cannot always be determined solely by your individual unit; sometimes your students will be better served if another dean receives a new faculty line or a major new facility. Being a team player means knowing the right moment to claim the glory and the right moment to share it.

You will also need to demonstrate within your programs an ability to think of the good of the whole and the good of its individual parts. Just as not every issue is about the whole university, not every decision you make is about the whole college. Too much equality can end up not being equitable at all. There will be times when one of your programs—or even one individual in your program—will receive more space, equipment, or resources because there is a need for more. It is not regarded as inequitable in a community when hospital patients receive significantly more resources than the healthy; at the moment, the greater needs of the sick or injured argue for greater care. The same is true with academic programs: At times, one department or individual will have greater needs than others. It will be a test of your judgment to recognize when those occasions arise.

The dean's view from the middle is thus an essential perspective for the efficient administration of a college or a university. Every institution needs to have people who avoid being so close to the details that they cannot see the overall pattern. As a dean, you are in the right place to understand the specifics of day-to-day activities in the classroom, laboratory, and studio so that you can appreciate the impact that administrative decisions have on people's lives. You can keep others' vision from becoming distorted and help implement the ideas that bring distinction to your institution.

Resources

Bright, D. F., & Richards, M. P. (2001). *The academic deanship: Individual careers and institutional roles.* San Francisco, CA: Jossey-Bass.

Ehrle, E. B., & Bennett, J. B. (1988). *Managing the academic enterprise: Case studies for deans and provosts.* New York, NY: American Council on Education/Macmillan.

Krahenbuhl, G. S. (2004). *Building the academic deanship: Strategies for success.* Westport, CT: Praeger.

Martin, J., Samels, J. E., & Associates. (1997). *First among equals: The role of the chief academic officer.* Baltimore, MD: Johns Hopkins University Press.

Tucker, A., & Bryan, R. A. (1991). *Academic dean: Dove, dragon, and diplomat* (2nd ed.). Phoenix, AZ: American Council on Education/Oryx Press.

Wolverton, M., & Gmelch, W. H. (2002). *College deans: Leading from within.* Westport, CT: Oryx Press.

Wolverton, M., Gmelch, W. H., Montez, J., & Nies, C. T. (2001). *The changing nature of the academic deanship* (ASHE-ERIC Higher Education Report Vol. 28, No. 1). San Francisco, CA: Jossey-Bass.

References

Atchison, T. (2004). *Followership: A practical guide to aligning leaders and followers.* Chicago, IL: Health Administration Press.

Chaleff, I. (2003). *The courageous follower: Standing up to and for our leaders* (2nd ed.). San Francisco, CA: Berrett-Koehler.

Kelley, R. (1992). *The power of followership.* New York, NY: Doubleday/Currency.

Seteroff, S. S. (2003). *Beyond leadership to followership: Learning to lead from where you are.* Victoria, BC: Trafford.

2

Preparing for the Dean's Role

Although, as we'll see in the next chapter, there's no one type of person who is "perfect" for every deanship, there are certain qualities that tend to be found in effective deans. A good dean should be able to cope with a large amount of detailed information while not becoming bogged down in insignificant matters. In other words, effective deans know an amazing amount about every single tree but never lose sight of the forest. A good dean should be able to delegate effectively, valuing others' contributions and understanding the implications of the following essential principle:

> *Delegation always implies a certain loss of control. The report or decision that is delegated to someone else is unlikely to be exactly like your own.*

Effective deans don't mind that loss of absolute control and, in fact, discover the value in having different perspectives brought to an issue. A good dean is the advocate not just of his or her own academic discipline but of all the disciplines represented by his or her unit. Many times, the dean will even serve as an advocate for areas outside his or her unit, understanding the needs of the institution as a whole. A good dean will be aware of recent trends in higher education but will avoid jumping on the bandwagon of every single new initiative. In other words, effective deans selectively respond to new ideas and emerging best practices, realizing that some hot new developments are mere fads and that others may not be appropriate in every situation. A good dean is capable of making hard decisions, defending them, and acknowledging when past decisions may have been wrong. A good dean is an excellent communicator, realizing that communication goes both ways and that it is just as important to listen well as it is to speak and write well.

People are attracted to deanships for all kinds of reasons, not all of them well considered or appropriate. Deanships almost always bring with them a higher salary and certain benefits—like a larger office, a designated parking space, membership in various clubs or professional organizations, opportunities to travel to interesting places, and free admission to certain events. Although these perquisites are undeniably attractive, they should never be the primary reason for seeking the position. Individuals who are attracted to deanships by the benefits rather than by the position itself frequently become frustrated by the long hours, 12-month contracts, complex problems to solve, numerous constituencies to satisfy, and realization that the benefits are really not as great as they had hoped. Similarly, individuals who are attracted to deanships because there is one burning issue that they wish to solve—the inadequacy of faculty salaries, the decline of academic standards, the lack of respect given their discipline, the wastefulness of the upper administration—are likely to discover that the problem is both more complicated and resistant to solutions than they had initially believed and that their lack of interest in other issues is making them ineffective in the overall challenge of serving as dean.

If you are considering seeking a deanship, it is time to conduct a critical self-analysis of your reasons for wanting to assume this responsibility, what you hope to gain by it, and what you envision offering others through this position. Ask yourself these questions, and answer them honestly:

- If I were offered a dean's position but only at my current salary, benefits, and perquisites, would I still be interested?

- How would I really feel if, for whatever reason, I found myself facing a great deal of anger and hostility at a meeting of faculty, students, or administrators who were directing their rancor at me personally?

- Am I a caregiver? How do I feel when I'm on the receiving end of a seemingly endless series of complaints, requests, demands, and needs day after day?

- Do I enjoy solving problems, even when the vast majority of those problems may be very difficult to address or, at the other extreme, so minor that the time required to solve them seems inefficient?

- How do I feel about attending meetings? Do I get bored easily when matters not directly related to my academic field are discussed at great length? Do I feel that numerous meetings and appointments take me away from my "real work"?

- When I think of the most important things that my institution does, what immediately comes to mind? Do I only think of faculty concerns and academic issues, or do I also think more broadly in terms of student development and student life issues, the institution's overall strategic direction, the school's relationship with external constituencies (trustees, legislators, advisory groups, donors, and so on), staff needs and concerns, and other such matters?

- Can I let things go easily when a decision is finally made and it hasn't gone my way? Do I need continually to revisit issues and to justify my perspectives?

- How do I handle isolation (i.e., not really being part of a group)?

If, after answering these questions, you still want to seek a deanship, how do you begin preparing for such a position? Although there are degree programs in higher education administration, most deans rise to their positions through the faculty, with little or no advance preparation for the work that they'll have to do. This chapter offers advice to help you prepare to be a successful dean.

Seek leadership roles.

One of the most important steps you can take in preparing to be a dean is to gain a variety of experiences that teach you about leading different kinds of groups. Look for opportunities to serve on curriculum committees both inside and outside your academic area. Volunteer for challenging committee assignments that will give you an opportunity to develop your leadership skills. Don't limit your exposure to easy successes or areas that you already know reasonably well. Rather, seek out new opportunities—particularly experience in conducting promotion and tenure reviews, grievance hearings, reviews of complex programs outside your area (even nonacademic programs, if possible), large-scale curriculum reforms (revisions to the general education program, conversion to or from the semester system, implementation of new standards across the curriculum), and the like. Try to get elected to your faculty senate or your institution's equivalent body that addresses matters of importance to the whole school. Volunteer to serve on committees in other colleges that require outside representation. Then, once you have sought out these leadership roles, begin to assess as candidly as you can your success and satisfaction in fulfilling the assigned duties. Are you able to find areas of common ground where others see only discord? Do you find it easy to look beyond the immediate needs of your discipline or area and see the big picture? If your work consisted mostly of this type of leadership—with significantly less time allocated to teaching, scholarship, and advising students—would you be satisfied? Can you provide evidence that you would be good at it?

Seek support roles.

In addition to seeking opportunities for developing your leadership potential, you may wish to prepare for the deanship by learning as much as possible about the issues that deans are asked to address. Support roles for the dean's office—such positions as assistant or associate dean, director of faculty development, special assistant for strategic planning—can provide you with a great deal of information about how deans do their work and what their assignments involve. At the same time that you improve your ability to address the many technical details of the dean's job, you may also have an opportunity to work with a mentor, a senior administrator who can provide you with on-the-job training. As the dean's office is called on to solve issues or problems, you can compare what you would have done or how you would have handled the situation with the decision that was made. In cases where you would have chosen a radically different course of action, discuss with your mentor how you would have approached the situation and why. Use your support role in the dean's office to determine which aspects of administrative work you have particular talent for and which may require additional training or experience. In certain cases you might find a particular niche—"the budget guru," "the strategic planning expert," "the curriculum authority"—that you can parlay into a deanship either at your own institution or elsewhere.

Volunteer for accreditation review committees.

Both regional accrediting bodies (such as the Southern Association of Colleges and Schools, the Middle States Association of Colleges and Schools, and the Western Association of Schools and Colleges) and specialized bodies that offer accreditation or certification in individual disciplines (e.g., the National Council for Accreditation of Teacher Education, the Association to Advance Collegiate Schools of Business, and the National Association of Schools of Music) are continually seeking qualified individuals to review applications for accreditation. Some of these opportunities involve an off-site review of the documentation that institutions have submitted for a new or renewed accreditation status. Other opportunities may involve travel to the institutions themselves to determine the accuracy of their self-studies, compliance reports, or responses to concerns that have been raised. In either case the experience will provide you with a great deal of information about current issues in higher education policy, the ways in which various institutions address the challenges that arise in offering high-quality academic programs, and the individuals at other institutions who can serve as good resources for you as you develop your administrative expertise.

Learn in detail how your institution works.

Although you probably already have a good sense of how your institution works in general, as a dean you will need detailed insight into how and by whom various decisions are made. Aside from curricular matters and other issues vital to your school's academic programs, who is responsible for which functions in such areas as student life, institutional advancement, public relations, security, the registrar's office, and the physical plant? You may be right to assume that the dean's office does not become involved in such issues as disputes between roommates, concerns about residence hall safety, off-campus programming, and corporate fundraising, but you need to have a very clear conception of who *does* handle these matters on your campus. Deans' offices frequently become clearinghouses for information. Students don't delineate between the academic side of their experience and other aspects of college life, such as paying their bills, engaging in cocurricular activities, and balancing the demands of their job and their studies. They will expect you not necessarily to know all the answers but to know where the answers can be found. Similarly, parents with concerns about charges for services or the behavior of a child's roommate are not going to call the central switchboard and ask for the bursar, the provost, or the residence life office. They're going to say, "Get me the dean!" And you will need to know how a variety of problems can be solved, even if you are not expected to solve them. Besides, the better you understand how your institution operates, the better you'll be able to function as dean.

Stay apprised of ongoing issues in academia.

No institution functions in a vacuum. The challenges that you face at your institution have parallels at literally dozens of other schools across the country. The best practices of these peer institutions can help inform your own decisions, and the problems they are addressing may well arrive at your own college in a year or two. As a result, you need to know what trends are emerging in higher education. Are the students who are enrolling in colleges in the next few years more likely to be focused on a career or interested in serving the greater good? Are there implications of federal law that will need to be addressed on your campus? What are some of the recent developments in the areas of academic freedom, intellectual property, students and faculty members with various disabilities, and similar issues? To extend your expertise in these areas, get acquainted with such publications as *The Chronicle of Higher Education, Dean & Provost, Change,* and *Peer Review.* Browse the web sites of major publishers in the field of academic administration—such as Jossey-Bass (www.josseybass.com), Magna (www.magnapubs.com), and ACE/Praeger (www.greenwood.com/praeger/ace.aspx) —to learn about current, important administrative topics.

Promote interdisciplinary work.

One way of practicing problem solving, building ties between different departments, and developing a vision for the future is to become active in interdisciplinary programs. Interdisciplinary studies frequently provide clear administrative challenges—because they belong to multiple departments, they often are seen as belonging to no one—that can give you an opportunity to polish your administrative skills while filling a genuine institutional need. They will also give you the chance to work with other departments on a wide variety of administrative challenges (developing new courses, achieving equity in load, securing funding, drafting written proposals, etc.) that you will need if you become a dean. In addition, success in promoting interdisciplinary programs can garner achievements outside your own academic department that can serve you well as you make the case that you are qualified to accept the challenges of a deanship.

Attend a wide range of events.

Another way of increasing your knowledge of different disciplines and how institutions work is to attend events across campus. Everyone has his or her own interests, and there are likely to be lectures, concerts, athletic events, seminars, discussions, and gatherings that you ordinarily would not attend, although you have been invited, because they are not closely related to your field or areas of concern. As a dean, however, you will be expected to understand the role that scholarship and cultural activities play in a wide variety of disciplines. You'll be expected to demonstrate support not just for your own academic department or field of specialty but for all the areas under your supervision. Therefore, the sooner you begin to attend campus events, the sooner you will begin to appreciate the complex contributions of different fields. You will also begin to be seen as an individual who has a broad view of what's important at your institution. Of greatest value to you, however, will be the expanded network of contacts and perspectives that you will gain through your increased campus activity.

Develop budgetary experience.

One area that deans can never master too thoroughly is planning and supervising budgets. If your institution or your discipline's professional organization offers budgetary workshops, enroll in them regularly. If workshops are not available to you, begin reviewing some reference works or surveys that deal with academic budgeting—such as Buller (2006), Mathews (1999), and Meisinger (1984)—and be certain that you are familiar with the basic terminology and principles of academic budgeting.

Attend workshops for deans.

Many organizations provide training sessions for deans, several of which are open to department chairs and other individuals who are interested in exploring the possibility of a deanship. These workshops will expose you to a large number of current best practices in higher education while also allowing you to ask specific questions about the dean's role. The web site of the American Council on Education (www.acenet.edu) can guide you to several leadership-training workshops. Seeking out training opportunities will help put you in contact with much of the information that you will need in your future role as dean. In addition, your participation in administrative workshops will announce to others who may be able to help that you are interested in a deanship. You will also begin forming a network of alliances who can support you in your administrative work.

Reorganize your résumé.

An administrator's curriculum vitae is likely to be organized differently than a faculty member's. Whereas a faculty member is likely to emphasize scholarly achievements, success in teaching, and service activity on his or her résumé, an administrator is more likely to give precedence to important accomplishments in leading an institution, managing resources, and supervising employees. Review your CV, therefore, and ask yourself, "What picture emerges from its pages?" Is it clear that the person whose work is reflected in that document has the experience needed to serve as an academic leader? If not, how could you reorganize your material in a way that calls attention to your administrative achievements?

Perhaps the best advice for prospective deans comes from John McDaniel, dean of liberal arts at Middle Tennessee State University, who, when asked about what he had learned in many years of successful academic administration, said: "It all comes down to humility, integrity, humor, perspective, and service. A good dean can figure out how to do the 'best' thing when it's just not possible to do the 'right' thing because resources, politics, and personalities are what they are. This is the perennial challenge for deans."

Resources

Bryant, P. T. (2005). *Confessions of an habitual administrator: An academic survival manual.* Bolton, MA: Anker.

Buller, J. L. (2006, Spring). Advice for future department chairs. *The Department Chair, 16*(4), 1–3.

Buller, J. L. (2006). Career planning for department chairs. In J. L. Buller, *The essential department chair: A practical guide to college administration* (pp. 178–185). Bolton, MA: Anker.

Middlehurst, R. (1993). *Leading academics.* Maidenhead, UK: Society for Research into Higher Education & Open University Press.

Walker, D. E. (1979). *The effective administrator.* San Francisco, CA: Jossey-Bass.

References

Buller, J. L. (2006). What every department chair needs to know about budgeting. In J. L. Buller, *The essential department chair: A practical guide to college administration* (pp. 144–153). Bolton, MA: Anker.

Mathews, K. W. (Ed.). (1999). *Administrative procedures for small institutions* (2nd ed.). Washington, DC: National Association of College and University Business Officers.

Meisinger, R. J. (1984). *College and university budgeting: An introduction for faculty and academic administrators.* Washington, DC: National Association of College and University Business Officers.

3

What Kind of Dean Are You?

Every now and then someone will ask, "What kind of dean are you?" This question may arise in a wide range of contexts. For instance, in an interview the person asking the question may be trying to ascertain whether you see yourself more as a catalyst for innovation (a change agent); a strong advocate for your area even when—or particularly when—its needs conflict with the rest of the institution's (a shop steward); a conduit of information from the upper administration to the faculty (a lackey); or an obsessively detail-oriented supervisor who will want to have a voice in every aspect of your college's operation (a micromanager). Fogarty (2006) even identifies four major types of "bad deans":

- *The indecisive dean:* who has difficulty making any kind of decision

- *The clueless dean:* who really doesn't understand academic administration as a whole or the local culture

- *The hoarder:* who cannot delegate authority

- *The shaker:* who promotes change simply for the sake of change, not because change is needed

In other contexts the questioner may be trying to learn whether you view yourself primarily as an administrator who happens to have academic responsibilities or an academic who happens to have administrative duties. Still others may be wondering whether you're a carbon copy of the former dean (who may have been much loved, universally detested, or something in between) or a new type of boss whom they will have to spend endless hours figuring out. There will even be those who ask this question because you have just done or said something that surprised, shocked, or dismayed them. This last case tends to have a recognizable inflection of its own, something along the lines of "What kind of dean *are* you?" Ending this question with "anyway" is optional but extremely common.

Because you will be regularly asked about your approach to being a dean—not to mention your management style and your administration philosophy—it pays to have a very clear understanding of who you are, what you are trying to accomplish as a dean, and how you view your role in the institution's overall structure. Although this self-assessment may at first appear extremely easy, it is actually quite challenging to develop and may only be reached after several years in the position. Too often, our concept of what we want others to think we are clouds our understanding of who we really are. We may even start to deceive ourselves about our true strengths, preferences, and ways of coping with stressful situations.

To develop a clearer understanding of your administrative style, it may be useful to perform an inventory of your individual strengths and preferences. The inventory that we'll conduct will be familiar to you if you've ever played the party game *Would You Rather . . . ?* where you must choose between two difficult alternatives. As you perform this self-assessment, be sure to answer honestly, not how you "should" answer. Responses such as "I don't know" or "The two choices seem equally (un)pleasant" are not allowed, and you may not invent your own third choice (such as a compromise between the two alternatives). In each case record which of the two statements you are most inclined to agree with and how difficult it was to make your choice. Score 1 for an extremely easy choice and 10 for an almost impossible choice; rank the other possibilities in between.

1. Would you rather . . .

   a. Retain every one of your department chairs, with no option to replace them in the future, for the rest of your tenure as dean?

   b. Have a system where you must replace every one of your department chairs each year (i.e., no chairs are permitted to succeed themselves or extend their terms)?

2. You must offer a new full-time faculty position to one of the following two departments. Which do you choose?

   a. The department with the largest number of majors.

   b. The department that produced the highest number of student credit hours (perhaps because it offers a large number of service or general education courses).

3. Enrollment at your institution is undergoing a massive, but temporary, increase. Which of the following do you do?

   a. Enforce existing maximum enrollment limits per section (maintaining a hard-won level of instructional quality, but compelling students to take courses from other colleges or schools or even to transfer to other institutions).

    b.   Open the floodgates in all courses (meeting student demand, but significantly increasing student-to-faculty ratios).

4.   You receive an unexpected telephone call about a serious problem. You are told that the caller is extremely angry, and when you learn the caller's identity, you become very anxious. Which caller is more likely to make you nervous?

    a.   The president of your institution.

    b.   A parent of one of your students.

5.   Would you rather . . .

    a.   Maintain the same curriculum for all the disciplines in your area for the rest of your career with no changes whatsoever (i.e., no new courses, no new programs, no syllabi alterations except for updated editions of current textbooks)?

    b.   Be required to replace every course, major, and requirement with a radically new approach, curriculum, and syllabus every five years?

6.   You are lured away from your current position by one of the following career opportunities. Which is it?

    a.   Serving as the founding dean of a college where there will be serious and unpleasant birth pangs but an opportunity to be innovative.

    b.   Serving as dean of a well-established, well-funded college that has most of its difficult decisions behind it.

7.   Which of the following scenarios would make you more uncomfortable?

    a.   Arriving at your office in the morning to find it taken over by a delegation of angry students.

    b.   Finding out that your office was taken over by students while you are traveling outside the country.

8.   Would you rather . . .

    a.   Have your duties revised so that all you did all day, every day was to check and recheck each unit's actual expenditures against its annual budgetary allocation to be certain that it was within budget?

b. Have your job constantly judged on your ability to successfully and creatively develop a never-ending series of innovative academic programs that are not offered by any other institution in the country?

9. You just learned that the chief academic officer of your institution and one of your fellow deans have had a serious disagreement. One side is clearly in the right; the other side is clearly in the wrong. Your gut reaction is that the person who is most likely to be at fault is . . .

a. The chief academic officer.

b. Your fellow dean.

10. There are only a few hours left before you have to leave campus for the summer to engage in a series of training sessions for deans. You can devote your time to only one of the following. Which do you choose?

a. Solving a serious problem that arose only today.

b. Launching a major new initiative that has the possibility of significant long-term benefits for your college.

11. A new facility will soon be ready for one of your disciplines to occupy. This project has been one of your most important goals for several years, the endeavor with which you had hoped to leave your mark. Unfortunately, you have learned that you must be away from campus on crucial business for more than a month after the building is completed. Which of the following alternatives would you choose?

a. Delegating the new facility's unveiling to someone else at your institution.

b. Delaying the opening until you can be present.

12. You learn that a student and a faculty member are in a dispute. With no other information to go on than that, which side do you believe is more likely to be at fault?

a. The student.

b. The faculty member.

13. There is a severe budget crisis, and you are forced to do one of the following. Which option do you choose?

    a.   Make substantial salary cuts for all employees.

    b.   Terminate the faculty member with the least seniority in each department.

14. Would you rather . . .

    a.   Spend an entire week involved in one very unpleasant, angry confrontation after another?

    b.   Have no other work to do for a month but the one activity that bores you the most?

15. Following a national search, one of your departments presents you with the names of two highly recommended candidates for a faculty position. Do you hire . . .

    a.   The applicant who is demonstrably the better teacher?

    b.   The applicant whose teaching ability is weaker but who will immediately bring your institution substantial research income?

16. A problem arises in your college. There is an 80% chance that it will fix itself and that if you intervene, your actions would only make the problem much, much worse. There is a 20% chance, however, that if you don't intervene now, the problem will quickly escalate into an extremely severe situation. What do you do?

    a.   Intervene now, even though there is an 80% risk that you will make matters worse, agreeing with Carl von Clausewitz that "it is better to act quickly and err than to hesitate until the time of action is past."

    b.   Wait and see, even though there's a 20% chance that you will end up with a disaster on your hands, agreeing with Lewis Thomas that "the great secret of doctors, known only to their wives, but still hidden from the public, is that most things get better by themselves; most things, in fact, are better in the morning."

17. You have an opportunity to leave your position for a new job with a significantly higher salary in a better location. But this new position is at an undistinguished institution, and your new title is so unimpressive that most of your current colleagues will view the new opportunity as a demotion. Which do you choose?

a. The higher salary, better location, and superficially less desirable position.

b. Your current position, which has more prestige but a lower salary.

18. Someone in your area arrives at your office visibly distraught. You find out that the employee is desperate to talk to you about a severe personal problem. But you are scheduled to appear before your governing board to make a major presentation; in fact, the board members are already waiting for you. What do you do?

a. Keep your commitment to the governing board, even though it means temporarily abandoning the distressed employee.

b. Help your employee, even though it means keeping the board waiting and possibly making the members angry.

19. Two problems have arisen in your college. Because of their severity, both must be addressed immediately. You have a trusted associate dean who can help you with one problem. So which issue do you take on yourself, and which do you delegate?

a. A messy but not particularly challenging personnel problem.

b. A more critical but not particularly difficult report that must be completed for your president.

20. It is your first meeting on an important new project for your college. To which of the following two activities do you devote the most of your meeting time?

a. Charging the committee, giving a great deal of attention to the result that you want members to create.

b. Discussing the best procedures to use in doing the committee's work, developing an action plan, and setting a meeting schedule.

Once you have answered each question in the inventory, review your choices to all 20 items and see whether you can summarize what your reactions to these dilemmas tell you about the following:

• *Where your sympathies tend to lie in the administrative hierarchy* (items 4, 9, 12, 18, and 19): While serving as deans, all of us assume other roles (consciously or not): friend of the faculty, defender of the student, aspiring provost or president, star scholar, and so on. You need to know how you instinctively see yourself so that you can compensate for this perspective's limitations when necessary and adopt this role more intentionally when appropriate. After all, knowing your bias in specific situations may encourage you to go out of your way to hear the other side when you need to, which will make you a better dean.

- *Whether you are most comfortable with innovation or change* (items 1, 5, 6, 8, and 16): People feel varying levels of comfort in a shifting and ambiguous environment. Some administrators thrive on change; they may even love it too much, unnecessarily altering policies and programs. Other administrators are overly averse to change; they will stick to a decision even when it's apparent that the decision is not working or has been counterproductive. It is important to be aware of what kind of dean you are when it comes to tolerating change. You can then compensate for your tendency at those times when greater change or stability may be needed.

- *Whether a significant part of your job satisfaction is derived from personal recognition* (items 11 and 17): A dean is motivated by many things: money, praise, the delight of solving a thorny problem, the excitement of creating something new, personal recognition, and so on. Because so much that a dean accomplishes is, by nature, less a personal achievement than a success for the college as a whole or for some part of the college, it is important for you to know whether this situation will provide you with the personal fulfillment you need. Many a dean has been left feeling dissatisfied because faculty members in the college, not the dean, have received prestigious fellowships, teaching awards, and book contracts. It is important for you to be aware of how you might feel should such a situation occur.

- *Your individual priorities:* Several of the items in this inventory compel you to choose between competing priorities, much in the way that academic units must struggle to rank their various needs and most pressing concerns. As a dean, you will be asked whether you place greater importance on the total number of majors in a discipline or the department's contribution to credit hour production at all levels (item 2), whether it is more important to serve students or preserve programmatic goals (item 3), whether you are more of a caregiver or a policy wonk (items 18 and 19), and so on. Although the dichotomies created by the inventory are admittedly strained, they can help you come to terms with your own position on issues.

Most important, review how you scored each item and ask yourself, "Which questions were most challenging; which choices were the hardest?" The items that you found particularly difficult to answer—as well as the choices that you found so clear cut that it seemed almost ridiculous to ask the question—tell you a great deal about your stand on various issues. If a particular choice seemed too easy, you may need to seek out other perspectives on that issue. If a choice was too hard, you may need to think through the various implications of each alternative and decide how you or the college would fare as a result of them.

Knowing what sort of dean you are doesn't mean that there is only one kind of dean who can succeed at all institutions and in all situations. Some deans are better at creating programs, while others are better at building on what has already been established. Some deans are more effective working with students and faculty members, while others do better when they focus on external donors and implementing the goals of the upper administration. Nevertheless, when you have an understanding of the type of dean you are, you will find yourself better able to play to your strengths, compensate for your weaknesses, and balance the numerous conflicting needs of the unit that you serve.

Resources

Beck, J. D. W., & Yeager, N. M. (1994). *The leader's window: Mastering the four styles of leadership to build high-performing teams.* New York, NY: Wiley.

Glanz, J. (2002). *Finding your leadership style: A guide for educators.* Alexandria, VA: Association for Supervision and Curriculum Development.

Heimberg, J., & Gomberg, D. (1997). *Would you rather . . ? Over 200 absolutely absurd dilemmas to ponder.* New York, NY: Plume.

Kippenberger, T. (2002). *Leadership styles.* Minneapolis, MN: Capstone.

Leaming, D. R. (2007). *Academic leadership: A practical guide to chairing the department* (2nd ed.). Bolton, MA: Anker.

Would you rather . . . ? [Board game]. Los Angeles, CA: Zobmondo!! Entertainment (Available at www.zobmondo.com)

References

Fogarty, T. J. (2006, Summer). The good, the bad, and the ugly: Knowing your dean. *The department chair, 17*(1), 10–11.

4

Creating a Vision for the College

As we've seen, there is no one perfect type of dean; chief officers of the college have a wide variety of strengths and weaknesses. Some are better at managing day-to-day details, others are better at large-scale strategic planning, and still others make their greatest contributions in such areas as fundraising, personnel management, and policy development. One way of compensating for the skills a dean lacks—or lacks in sufficient measure—is through team building. A dean's department chairs, assistant and associate deans, and administrative staff can help bring balance to those areas for which, either because of temperament or lack of experience, the dean needs additional support. Another way of compensating for the dean's weaknesses is to seek out additional training or information that will help him or her develop those skills.

Some administrative skills, like efficient budgeting and interviewing candidates, can be learned relatively quickly. Others, such as developing a vision for your unit, may seem impossible if you don't regard yourself as a visionary person. In fact, it is often believed that a sense of vision comes naturally to certain people and that those without this gift cannot be taught it. The first President Bush once spoke dismissively of "the vision thing" when reporters repeatedly sought what he hoped to achieve in his presidency besides serving as a caretaker for the Reagan revolution. In a similar way, even the most managerial dean, the type of person who is more comfortable keeping things running smoothly than pursuing grandiose plans, will be asked from time to time, "What's your vision for the college? Where do you see our programs going? What would you like your legacy to be?" Any dean who cannot advance a compelling answer to these questions is likely to be regarded as lacking in vision. In extreme cases this perception can even cripple a deanship.

So, if you have never thought of yourself as a particularly visionary person, how do you deal with "the vision thing"? How can you develop this seemingly elusive skill? *Can* you develop it? Although certain people appear to have a greater talent for imagining exciting possibilities than others, developing a vision for your college is possible if you are willing to give the matter a little thought. The following steps are a sort of visioning exercise.

Establish a clear sense of the ways in which your college is distinctive now.

Take a blank sheet of paper, and write down as many adjectives or phrases as possible that describe how your college is different. What sets it apart from the other colleges at your institution? What differentiates it from similar colleges at other institutions? What are your core values—the very things that, if they were to change or be removed, your college would cease to be what it is? Keep working at this exercise until you have filled the entire sheet of paper. Then begin ranking all your adjectives and phrases from the most important aspects of your college's identity to the least important. After you have finished ranking these qualities, the top three to five should tell you something fundamental about your college's unique identity. See whether statements similar to the following are anywhere on your list:

- Excellent faculty

- We care about our students

- Small class size

- Student oriented

- Superb curriculum

- Inadequate funding

If you find statements like these on your list, cross them off. Every college in the country believes that it has an excellent faculty, that it cares about students, that it has a high-quality curriculum, and that it doesn't have enough money to do the things it needs to do. (Even those institutions that you don't regard as possessing these attributes believe that they do.) These terms are simply not distinctive enough to produce a vision for the future; continue looking.

Extrapolate from the core strengths you find.

After you've developed your list of truly unique attributes—and every college is unique in certain ways—you are ready to see what you may be able to build from your current strengths. For instance, if the opportunity to engage in undergraduate research is a distinctive feature of your college, what are some logical next steps that could be developed from it? Is every senior given an opportunity for substantive research before graduation? If you've already attained that goal, can these opportunities be extended downward through your program? Or can you guarantee a dedicated research space (an office, lab, or studio) to every student majoring in your college? Do they all work extensively with full-time faculty members as their mentors? Do they present their findings off campus at professional conferences or research symposia? Are they encouraged or required to submit written versions of their research to undergraduate or peer-reviewed journals? In other words, what can you do to build on an existing strength and make your college's programs truly exciting for potential students, potential donors, and senior administrators?

Explore the possibility of a vision based on your institution's strategic plan or mission statement.

Presidents and provosts, like deans, are expected to have visions for their institutions. For this reason, it may be possible to build the vision for your college on one that has already been created for the entire university. The advantages of such an approach are that the institution as a whole is strengthened (because there is greater synergy among the goals of its various units) and that you are far more likely to receive funding for a plan that helps the institution progress than you are for a strategy that carries your unit off into its own orbit. For instance, if "improving international opportunities for our students" is a central element of your institution's strategic plan, how can your college develop a vision of its own to promote this objective? (Provide an opportunity for every major to travel abroad at a reduced cost before graduation? Include an international component in every course taught in the curriculum? Begin an international center dedicated to your college's specific needs? Aggressively seek visiting scholars from other countries to teach in your program? Ensure that all your college's web sites and publications are available in multiple languages?) Similarly, if increasing experiential learning is one of your president's most cherished goals, how can you build a vision for your college around it? (Are internships available in all your majors? Could you incorporate community service-learning into more of your introductory courses? Are there ways of substituting traditional lecture courses with practicums, labs, or simulations? Is there a way of developing a senior capstone requirement that uses an experiential activity to help students build on what they have learned in your program?)

Consider developing a vision for your college through innovative forms of teaching, scholarship, or service.

Ernest Boyer's landmark book *Scholarship Reconsidered* (1990) noted that the usual way in which the professoriate thinks of scholarship (i.e., as research) is only one of several legitimate forms of scholarship that are found in academia. In addition to this Scholarship of Discovery, as Boyer calls traditional research, he also identifies the Scholarship of Integration (which includes such activities as interdisciplinary studies); the Scholarship of Application (through which developments in a discipline are used to solve a practical problem or to produce a tangible benefit); and the Scholarship of Teaching (in which advances are made in a discipline's pedagogy). Your college's vision might be based on one of these alternative forms of scholarship, providing an exciting model for other colleges. In the same way, you might consider developing a vision for your cluster of disciplines that is based on incorporating certain instructional innovations (simulations, podcasts, immersion courses, case studies, internships, etc.) in your curriculum. You could even develop a vision that involves a distinctive program of service to your community or to some segment of it. In other words, although the content of your disciplines may not be much different from that of similar colleges at other institutions, your unit's unique vision might be derived from the manner in which that content is applied to practical situations or shared with those who need it.

Use a focused brainstorming exercise to explore ideas that can be integral to your college's vision.

One well-known, but still effective, technique that you can use in developing possible directions for your college's future growth and advancement is to brainstorm ideas with a particular focus. For instance, you might choose an arbitrary date in the future (10, 25, or 50 years out) and begin jotting down ideas about what your college's best-case scenario would be at that date. What internal steps could you then take that would start your unit moving in that direction? Another focused brainstorming activity is to take your college's or institution's acronym and to list a positive adjective or noun that begins with each letter and that can crystallize the essence of a strategic vision. As rudimentary as this activity may sound, it actually does work. A similar exercise in 2003 provided Mary Baldwin College with the theme of "Mind—Body—Character" that became a key ingredient of a new approach to transformative, holistic education, which was guided by the institution's strategic plan. In a similar way, pairing words to create a striking oxymoron (such as Innovative Tradition, Where We Do the Impossible Daily, Fanciful Practicality) can help reveal the ways in which your college's distinctive nature can guide its future. Even the combination of commonplace, noncontradictory nouns and adjectives can help. Thus, for a time in the 1990s, Georgia Southern University's College of Liberal Arts and Social Sciences used the phrase "The College of the Creative Mind" to emphasize the central importance of both creativity and scholarship to its plans for the future.

Consider a vision in which your college achieves national or even international recognition for creating a particular award, event, or distinction.

One of the quickest ways to form an identity and draw media attention is to establish a highly publicized award (see Chapter 44, "Dealing with the Media"). For instance, if your college has a particular strength in advisement, you might consider an award that honors the individual or program that has made the greatest contribution to student advising. Bringing the recipient to campus, providing an honorarium and lodging, and creating a suitable award are all expenses that can more than pay for themselves in the visibility that they bring. Suddenly, your college has become the college that is known for the quality of its advising, and your vision for the future may be clearer. Any area in which your college already excels—or wishes to excel—can provide the basis for such an award (e.g., medical school placement, promoting leadership among women, developing creativity, serving first-generation college students, publishing student research, etc.). In a similar way, an event that either occurs annually or was critical to your college's history can provide you with a vision for the future. Thus, Westminster College, the site of Winston Churchill's famous "iron curtain speech" of 1946, has long parlayed this event into a vision of serving as an American center for Churchill studies and memorabilia. Whittier College has begun exploring ways in which it can partner with other institutions and serve as a focal point for the study of Richard Nixon, the college's most famous graduate. If your college does not have an alumnus whose name is instantly recognizable and if no historical events occurred on your campus, you can still begin developing a vision by planning a recurring event: A lecture series, annual day of commemoration, or conference could bring individuals from all over the world to your college, and they will take home with them the notion that your programs are particularly noted for that event's theme.

Once you have developed a clear sense of what your vision for the college should be, it will be critically important for you to share this vision with others, to enrich it with their perspectives, and to begin building their support. After all, a vision that does not inspire your faculty members, students, and donors is unlikely to be successful, even if it has received substantial support from the upper administration. As you begin to share your vision and to move your college toward fulfilling it, keep in mind the following general principles:

- *Be consistent:* Speak about your vision for the future as often as possible, and be certain to relate new developments and opportunities to it. At times, you may begin to feel like a broken record, repeating the same thing over and over. At other times, people may even grumble that you seem to have only one idea. These criticisms, although annoying, are actually preferable to the situation where no one can ever guess the dean's values and direction. Deans who appear to have a new vision every week come across as not being committed to anything and only frustrate the people who are trying to fulfill the last great plan.

- *Be flexible:* Being consistent is not, however, the same thing as being rigid. Faculty members in your college, and perhaps even your president and provost, will undoubtedly have suggestions about the precise direction your vision should take and how it might be implemented. Give a respectful ear to every voice; not every suggestion may be worth adopting, but they are all worth hearing. Allowing people to buy into your vision extends your support base and makes it more likely that your vision can be achieved in a timely manner. Although there may well be naysayers who state that instead of doing what you have proposed, the college is better off doing something completely different, you should not let these voices distract you unless you begin seriously to believe that your basic ideas are flawed. In most cases the naysayers are simply fixated on one of their own pet projects that does not benefit the entire college or institution. Be respectful of these voices and incorporate what you can into your planning, but do not allow them to divert you from your vision.

- *Be practical:* A properly conceived vision should be both inspiring and attainable. It should inspire the college to reach just a little further than it thought possible, without draining resources from critical areas or imposing a goal that is completely beyond the realm of possibility. A true vision should excite people to move in a direction that will take some time to achieve. The goal may not be reached even within your tenure as dean. But the vision should not simply be pie in the sky. Always seek a balance between the challenging and the realistic, and strive to preserve an attitude that we can do this if we put our hearts into it.

Deans who serve as visionaries for their colleges are not always born dreamers; many of them find that the most practical way to unite their faculty and manage their college well is to establish an inspiring image of what their shared future can be. Even if you have never felt comfortable with "the vision thing," following the guidelines outlined in this chapter can help move your college toward becoming the institution's most visionary unit.

Resources

Dolence, M. G., Rowley, D. J., & Lujan, H. D. (1997). *Working toward strategic change: A step-by-step guide to the planning process.* San Francisco, CA: Jossey-Bass.

Hill, C. (Ed.). (2004). *Leading lights.* Madison, WI: Magna.

Keller, G. (1983). *Academic strategy: The management revolution in American higher education.* Baltimore, MD: Johns Hopkins University Press.

Keller, G. (2004). *Transforming a college: The story of a little-known college's strategic climb to national distinction.* Baltimore, MD: Johns Hopkins University Press.

Percy, S. L., Zimpher, N. L., & Brukardt, M. J. (Eds.). (2006). *Creating a new kind of university: Institutionalizing community-university engagement.* Bolton, MA: Anker.

Rowley, D. J., Lujan, H. D., & Dolence, M. G. (1997). *Strategic change in colleges and universities: Planning to survive and prosper.* San Francisco, CA: Jossey-Bass.

Watson, D. (2000). *Managing strategy.* Buckingham, UK: Open University Press.

Zimpher, N. L., Percy, S. L., & Brukardt, M. J. (2002). *A time for boldness: A story of institutional change.* Bolton, MA: Anker.

References

Boyer, E. L. (1990). *Scholarship reconsidered: Priorities of the professoriate.* Princeton, NJ: The Carnegie Foundation for the Advancement of Teaching.

5

Building a Shared Vision for the College

In the last chapter we explored how to develop a vision for your college and build support for it among your various constituencies. But are there other ways that you can help your entire faculty, staff, and student body share a common vision? Even better, are they ways in which you can help them develop a common vision, a plan for the future that you can pursue together for the good of your college as a whole?

Deans can play an important role in helping their units work together cooperatively and create a new direction for the college. Even more important, however, working together on a shared vision for the future is an excellent way to instill greater unity of purpose, improve morale, and direct energy that might be wasted in complaining about minor problems to more constructive outlets. By cooperating in the creation and fulfillment of a shared vision, your college might take the lead in helping your institution advance its strategic plan and at the same time bring positive attention, even a degree of prestige, to your unit. The following are a few simple, practical steps that can prepare your college for a collaborative development of a shared vision.

Create an environment in which people are free to discover areas of commonality.

See whether you can identify fundamental principles that a vast majority, if not all, of the faculty members in your college can agree on. What are the elements of your unit's identity that, if they were to change, would destroy or diminish an essential aspect of who you are? These are the nonnegotiables of your college's identity. If you have an annual faculty retreat or a faculty meeting that addresses more than routine business (perhaps it's your college's opening meeting of the year), conduct an exercise in which people explore what your college is as a means of discovering where it needs to go. In a small unit this can be done as a brainstorming exercise, with ideas recorded on a chalkboard, flip chart, overhead projection, or computer projection. In larger units break-out sessions might have groups of 12–20 faculty members discuss this issue and then report their ideas to the entire group. Challenge your unit to think of all the essential elements of its identity. The results may include basic principles, elements of pedagogy or research methods, commitments to certain student-to-faculty ratios, cherished programs (a time-honored lecture series, senior requirements, outreach efforts, etc.), college traditions, distinguished alumni—anything that comes to mind when a majority of people consider, "Who *are* we?"

Help people discover areas of distinction.

The next step then is to ask, "What makes us better than others like us?" Have faculty and staff members compare your unit to others at your institution, as well as to similar colleges and schools at other institutions. If it seems too extreme to ask, "How are we unique?" (because that would imply being truly one of a kind), then at least ask what makes your unit special in some way. When students are thinking about majoring in a discipline represented by your college versus those offered elsewhere in your institution, what would faculty and staff members say to confirm the students' good impression of you? What would current majors in your unit say? If a student was thinking of transferring to a rival program outside your university, how might you make the case that your college really is the better choice? It may be that your curriculum is structured more sensibly than your rivals'; that you have more (or fewer) required courses; that you have a better placement rate into graduate programs or first-choice careers; that you provide students with better contact with senior faculty members even in introductory courses; that you offer opportunities for students to travel more widely (either to attend conferences in their field or to study abroad); or that you are distinctive in a way that others outside your program cannot even imagine.

With your areas of commonality (i.e., your core values) and distinction (i.e., your comparative advantages) clearly outlined, begin exploring practical ways of building on your current reality to move toward an improved future.

Perhaps at the same retreat or faculty meeting, or perhaps at a separate event (a series of lunches with mixed groups of faculty and staff, several focus group sessions, a threaded online discussion, a listserv, etc.), brainstorm with members of your unit for possible answers to this question: Based on who we are and where we are now, where should we go from here? Get as many ideas as you can about possible new directions or emphases for your college. What steps do you need to take just to preserve your current strength and identity? What possible new opportunities may arise for the disciplines in your area over the next few years?

Are there curricular areas or productive lines of research that are not currently being addressed by your peers that your college might pursue? Are there ways of bringing greater visibility to existing programs of distinction that could make your entire unit stronger as you compete for students, resources, and recognition? At this stage in the process, don't spend a lot of time weighing and evaluating different suggestions. The important thing is to allow all your constituents to have a voice, to consider as many ideas as possible, and to see what elements of a potential new vision might emerge from the combined efforts of your faculty and staff.

After listing all the possible elements of a college-wide vision, promote widespread discussion of these ideas to discover obvious connections and to set priorities.

Once several ideas are on the table, it's time to begin sorting through them to see which perspectives have the greatest potential. Discussing a potential new vision for your unit can be an important team-building exercise itself. The process of building consensus for any type of plan encourages individuals to discover issues of shared concern and to understand ways in which their own pet projects may not have widespread support or be in the best interests of the unit as a whole. This part of your long-range planning is probably best done not in a single meeting or retreat but in a series of sessions that extend over several weeks or months. The idea that seems hot one afternoon may not, after all, stand the test of time. Consider beginning the process with four or five mixed sessions of faculty members, students, staff employees, alumni, and other external constituents (e.g., parents of students, consistent donors to your college, or representatives from your college's advisory council). Pay close attention to where there is widespread agreement across various groups and where ideas tend to splinter people into clear factions.

Encourage others to realign, where necessary, your unit's goals and rewards to begin realizing this shared vision.

One of the great truisms of academic administrations is:

> *Colleges and universities tend to get more of anything they reward people for doing.*

For instance, in evaluation structures where publications are counted for the purposes of promotion and salary increases, faculty members tend to produce more individual works, even when those publications are brief or of relatively minor significance. In structures where pages of published scholarship are tallied, faculty members tend to produce longer works, though not necessarily more total works. Being aware of this principle should help you as you pursue your unit's new vision. It will be extremely difficult for any substantive progress to be made if this vision is not adequately reflected in your unit's annual goals and evaluation procedures. Try to tie aspects of the proposal to your institution's strategic plan, and then set annual goals that will move you closer to your objective. Organize a faculty committee, if appropriate, to recommend ways in which your unit's evaluation criteria can be revised to reward progress in achieving the college's new vision. For instance, if the unit's plan is to become a leader in internationalizing its curriculum, you might consider an annual report format in which faculty members can be given clear credit for such efforts as enhancing the global dimensions of existing courses, applying for Fulbright fellowships and other international travel awards, encouraging students to pursue international study opportunities, and making arrangements for visiting faculty members to come to your college from other nations. By tracking and rewarding progress toward fulfilling your unit's new vision, you will help preserve buy-in.

Enlist support for your unit's shared vision from your institution's upper administration as well as from your external constituencies.

One effective way of building momentum toward attaining your goal is to seek support from outside your school or college for the vision that your faculty and staff have developed. Taking advantage of external support is a doubly effective strategy because it brings additional enthusiasm, resources, and excitement and holds you accountable for producing results. Once you go public with your vision, members of your school and college will continually be asked, "How's that new plan coming?" And it will be extremely uncomfortable if you have little progress to report. On the other hand, by tying your unit's vision to, for example, the president's strategic plan or your governing board's new initiatives, you will obtain strong allies who can help you make these dreams a reality. You may become eligible for funding that targets the strategic plan or special initiatives. You may prompt the staff in your advancement office to begin thinking about potential donors who can help you achieve your goals. Similarly, those who are involved with sponsored programs may know of other sources that can help fund your unit's vision. At the very least, you will gain for your school or college the reputation of being a team player because, rather than developing a plan for the future that takes you in a radically different direction from the rest of your institution, you have taken the appropriate steps to correlate your goals with those of the institution as a whole.

Be generous in acknowledging and praising others' contributions.

An important means of securing the continued support of your faculty and staff for making your unit's vision a reality is to help them appreciate how essential they are to the plan's fulfillment. Public acknowledgment of a person's contributions is both a valued reward for all the effort involved in the activity and a powerful motivation for others to work further on achieving the plan's goals. People begin to understand that their efforts in making the vision a reality are not taken for granted and are appreciated in a very public and satisfying way. Others who have not yet given their full support to the unit's new vision will be encouraged to do so when they see that their peers are commended for accomplishments. These public recognitions make it clear that the unit's vision is not just your personal vision for your school or college but something that is widely supported and embraced. Moreover, these public acknowledgments are good ways of getting people to know that progress is being made, that the vision is becoming a reality. A sense that things are changing for the better can help create a positive atmosphere for your unit that will improve morale, promote retention of your most effective faculty members and your most capable students, and strengthen your unit's reputation for excellence. Remember that, as a dean, your success is measured by the success of those who work for you and enroll in your programs even more than by what you achieve on your own.

Take advantage of every opportunity to preserve momentum in attaining your vision.

Frequently, colleges make a lot of initial progress in developing a new plan for the future, only to see these developments quickly stall as new demands are made on people's time. You are more likely to preserve momentum if you take steps to reinforce the plan's importance whenever possible. Regular reference to your college's plan and its progress at college-wide meetings will help confirm the notion that achieving the new vision is an ongoing priority. Other ways in which you can preserve the momentum include:

- Developing a page on your college-wide web site that is devoted exclusively to your unit's vision for the future. Update this site frequently (at least once a week), and be sure that it contains important and exciting developments.

- Working with your college's IT staff to develop a listserv or threaded discussion that is devoted to the plan or vision. Encourage people to post frequent updates on progress, success stories, and other good news about the plan to help preserve the sense of excitement and accomplishment.

- Establishing some type of formal recognition that is directly tied to your college's new vision, perhaps something along the lines of an "Achievement of the Month." This public recognition will give you both a recurring occasion on which to draw attention to progress and repeated opportunities to reward those whose contributions are making your college's vision a reality.

Properly conducted, developing an ambitious but attainable college-wide plan can help build esprit de corps, improve morale, provide a sense of direction for your unit, and help attract positive attention to your college's most important activities. A positive vision diverts attention from the sort of grousing about minor issues that is all too frequent on most campuses and focuses energy on your unit's clear potential for the future. It provides you with an opportunity for constructive delegation, for developing leadership skills in your faculty and staff, for external constituencies to become more active in the life (and financial support) of your college, and for securing additional external funding through grants, sponsored research, and awards from foundations.

Resources

Bensimon, E. M., & Neumann, A. (1994). *Redesigning collegiate leadership: Teams and teamwork in higher education.* Baltimore, MD: Johns Hopkins University Press.

Katzenbach, J. R., & Smith, D. K. (2003). *The wisdom of teams: Creating the high-performance organization.* New York, NY: HarperCollins.

Kouzes, J. M., & Posner, B. Z. (2003). *Jossey-Bass academic administrator's guide to exemplary leadership.* San Francisco, CA: Jossey-Bass.

Lewis, C. P. (1996). *Building a shared vision: A leader's guide to aligning the organization.* University Park, IL: Productivity Press.

London, M. (1995). *Achieving performance excellence in university administration: A team approach to organizational change and employee development.* Westport, CT: Praeger.

6

Launching Initiatives

As part of your effort to help create a new vision for your college, you will probably want to launch one or more initiatives, new ventures that have not been undertaken previously in your college or new directions that affect several of the disciplines in your area. These initiatives might include developing new majors, making large-scale changes to the curriculum's overall focus, creating a new college-wide honor code or college creed, establishing significant new faculty development efforts, proposing additional facilities, forming important policies on matters that have previously gone unaddressed, or making other improvements that could take your college in a significant new direction. Launching initiatives, if done well, can both strengthen your college and boost your own career. On the other hand, launching initiatives that fail or that seem to be adrift for an extended period of time can open you, as well as your entire unit, to ridicule, embarrassment, and financial disaster.

Launching a new initiative can be very attractive. It can bring a sense of excitement and momentum to your college, provide opportunities for new funding, and help solve problems that have been hampering your programs' success. As you consider launching new initiatives, however, there are certain fundamental principles that you will want to keep in mind.

Never seek change merely for the sake of change; only undertake to change areas where there is a genuine problem.

Deans, especially those who are relatively inexperienced in their positions, may feel a need to do *something* to avoid the impression that they're not doing anything. They may wish to embark on a new endeavor, not because it is called for by the circumstances, but merely because they want to make a name for themselves or to build their résumés. Although acting in this manner does not always guarantee disaster, it does make failure more likely and, even under the best conditions, rarely results in the greatest success. Unless you can clearly cite the specific problem you are trying to solve by doing something, you probably do not have a situation that calls for a major new initiative. As an exercise, write a summary, in no more than 25 words, of what critical challenge your unit is facing that cannot be solved without a major new initiative. If you find that you cannot identify the problem clearly and concisely within that word limit, then you probably have not sufficiently thought through the issue to be able to explain it to others. Do you have a problem with student retention that your college's current direction or organization is incapable of addressing? Do your college's assessment efforts repeatedly indicate that your curriculum does not meet your goals for your student learning outcomes, despite the many minor modifications and remedies that you may have adopted in the past? Are faculty members in your college repeatedly denied tenure and promotion at the university level while other colleges at your institution have a significantly better record of success? Has your unit been liable for lawsuits or major grievances because you have not yet adopted policies and procedures to deal with specific situations in a consistent and equitable fashion? In such cases as these, you will find it relatively easy to say, "To solve the problem we face with X, we must consider doing Y." Nevertheless, if you find yourself struggling to identify a clear problem to solve or an imminent disaster to avoid, then you probably need to reconsider whether a major initiative is truly called for. Whatever you do, avoid trying to revolutionize your college just because you believe that all change is good. By seeking changes that are unwarranted, you are likely to learn a painful lesson in how certain innovations can be undesirable and destructive. The law of unintended consequences tends to be most pronounced in situations where the change that was introduced was unnecessary.

Remember that few, if any, institutions are ever ready for as much substantive change as faculty members may say they want.

New deans are frequently surprised by this common organizational reality. Throughout their interviews or their first few meetings with faculty members, they may hear, "We need someone with bold new ideas. People here are hungry for change, and we're all counting on you for some clear leadership about where we need to go. Believe me, change can't happen fast enough for any of us." As a result, new deans often think that they have a mandate to launch important initiatives from the very beginning of their tenure, and they immediately start laying the groundwork for the changes that they believe are both welcome and eagerly anticipated. Soon after beginning this process, however, they discover resistance to their ideas even from (and all too often particularly from) the very individuals who claimed to be so enthusiastic about embracing a bold new plan. The fact of the matter is that colleges, like nearly all organizations, frequently are fascinated with the idea of change but are reluctant to act when it comes to actually doing things differently, even in fairly minor ways. Often individuals who claim that they want to see new initiatives really want other people to change, preferring that their own activities remain largely untouched by the initiative—except for the possibility of greater rewards, lighter workloads, or a higher level of prestige. Deans, therefore, need to gauge the amount of institutional change that their colleges can effectively sustain before those units are likely to become dysfunctional because of excessive anxiety or unmanageable levels of responsibility. Even in cases where a college appears to be openly hostile to new ideas or exceedingly reluctant to think about challenges in new ways, deans do not have to abandon all hope of change or improvement. It simply means that the way in which the initiative is launched may need to be different. More preparation may need to be taken to bring people along and help them understand that the current approach is not sufficient for the college's needs. Rhetoric may have to be revised: Rather than presenting a plan as a new initiative, you may need to promote it as a continuation and improvement of one of the college's traditional strengths. (On the importance of relating new ideas to a unit's history and established strengths, see Chapter 57, "Changing Institutions.") You may need to invest time in conversations with people one on one to discover precisely what their anxieties are and to allay those worries. At the very least, you should be prepared for more resistance to your initiatives than you may have expected—despite how open to change and new ideas the members of your college previously seemed.

Build support for your initiative by helping your constituents understand how the proposal benefits both them and your unit as a whole.

Initiatives that are perceived as being foisted on the college from the top down are likely to be met with resistance. People will view the plan as simply another scheme to make the dean look good, while it creates additional and often pointless work for students and faculty members alike. You can avoid this problem by getting as many people as possible to buy into the initiative and to see it as their own. Identify the opinion leaders in your college: Who are the department chairs, faculty members, and student representatives whose views seem to matter to their peers? Meet with these individuals one-on-one or in small groups to talk about the initiative and how it benefits them or helps them solve a problem. In these preliminary sessions you need not go into every aspect of what you have in mind; doing so may give the impression later that you have been playing favorites by providing a select few with detailed information. Rather, talk about the initiative and your rationale for proposing it in general terms. What concerns do these individuals have? What suggestions can they make to improve the initiative? What ideas do they have for implementing your plan through existing committees in your college? Remember that your goal is not simply to sell the opinion leaders on an initiative that adheres completely to your preconceived plan. As we have already seen, delegation always implies some surrender of control over the final product. These individuals will certainly have perspectives on improving the direction of your initiative that you'll need to make it a success. Then, when you've laid some groundwork by discussing the initiative in general terms with several members of the faculty and student body, it's time to begin going public with your ideas. Present a general overview at an appropriate venue for your college. A suitable group for this type of presentation might be a full faculty meeting. If your college is large enough, a more productive discussion might occur at a gathering of department chairs. Based on the ideas that you've received from the opinion leaders, go into more detail, explaining how the initiative will come about and which groups will begin to implement it. Be receptive at this level to ideas about how the plan might be adapted to make it more successful. Allow people to buy into the initiative by making it their own in ways that do not significantly detract from its overall direction. Frequently, a change in nomenclature or timing may be all that is required to help people see the initiative as truly their own and to work enthusiastically to bring it about.

Structure your timetable for the initiative with numerous intermediate goals that will mark your progress along the way.

One of the mistakes that deans too frequently make is to present the fulfillment of their plan as their primary goal. The problem with this approach is that it's difficult to see tangible results in a project that may only come to fruition several years from now. Initial enthusiasm for the idea may dissipate as other concerns arise and clear progress does not appear to have been made toward the ultimate goal. The way to avoid this problem is to break the entire plan into several intermediate goals. Rather than presenting, for example, the creation and implementation of a new graduate degree as your initiative, you would be wise to set appropriate intermediary goals, such as conducting a needs assessment, completing a literature review and study of best practices for this type of degree, holding focus groups on the design of the needed curriculum, formulating staffing plans, seeking external funds to defray start-up costs, and so on. For each of these goals, people can see real progress in a short amount of time. Even more important, if you decide to abandon the plan for the new degree program, your college will not feel that its entire initiative has failed. You'll be able to say things like, "Remember that all we set out to do was to complete a needs assessment. Well, we did that and discovered that for an institution our size, with the sort of funding we're likely to have for the foreseeable future and the pool of students we'd be drawing from, the new program simply wouldn't be sustainable. And I'm not about to weaken our current strengths by committing us to *any* program for which we cannot provide in accordance with our standards. I'm certainly not going to mortgage our future on a program that we don't think we can maintain over time. Now, the good thing is that the needs assessment did tell us a few things about how we can strengthen our existing programs and better serve our students. So, I'd like us to begin thinking about those." In this way, you haven't tied your initiative's success to some long-term goal. Your intermediate goal has cautioned you against such an ambitious endeavor, and you've been able to transform a potentially disastrous move into a positive experience for your college.

Put as much energy into following through on initiatives as you do on launching them.

It is easy for faculty members to become jaded by repeatedly hearing about bold new plans from administrators, only to see those plans languish unfulfilled soon after the initial enthusiasm for them has cooled. People grow weary of reports that lie on the shelf and impressive-sounding proposals that never really become reality. It can be particularly damaging to morale when new administrators arrive from outside the institution, launch a new initiative, and then leave for another position before there is any hope of their plans becoming reality. For this reason, it is important for deans to ask themselves these questions when they prepare to launch initiatives:

- *What are the realistic possibilities that my college can achieve the initiative I am proposing?* This question does not imply that a college should avoid stretching beyond what it has always done or seeking to overcome difficult challenges. Nevertheless, there is an important distinction between striving for what is difficult to obtain and wasting resources on what is impossible to attain. The dream that you want your college to share with you will only inspire others if you have some reasonable chance of seeing it come true. If your goal is completely unrealistic, then your initiative will end up doing your college and your career a disservice.

- *Is this initiative possible to attain within my likely tenure at this institution?* Again, this question does not imply that you should avoid beginning a project that will come to fruition under your successor. You should, however, avoid initiatives for which you are the one who will reap all the excitement of the initial launch and publicity while those who come after you must deal with the thorny issues of funding, implementation, and sustainability. Never embark on an initiative that you would not wish to see through to its completion if you were to remain at the institution, and remember that most initiatives should be attainable within the span of your current position. (On the matter of how long that tenure might be, see Chapter 56, "Knowing When It's Time to Go.")

- *What is our college's exit strategy for concluding this initiative?* Be sure to watch indicators that tell you when you have fulfilled your goal and can announce that news to your constituents. Be sure to also have plans in mind in case unforeseen problems arise: If projected funding does not materialize or student enrollment declines, how will your plan be modified? Is there a way of abandoning earlier goals if they no longer seem desirable?

In addition to asking yourself these questions, be certain that your initiative is important enough and exciting enough that both you and all the members of your college will want to see it through. You don't want your college to be dismissed as a unit that doesn't finish what it starts, and you certainly don't want to be ridiculed for coming up with new initiatives every week that never go anywhere. It is important for college-wide initiatives to be inspiring but attainable, challenging but not unreasonable. A good, reliable degree of common sense will help you balance your desire for vision and your need for practicality.

As results begin to occur, celebrate your initiative's success frequently and generously.

No matter how much the plan may have been initiated by your efforts, remember that it won't be as successful as it can be until it is widely embraced as the *college's* plan. For this reason, as your initiative begins to come to fruition, you need to acknowledge its success both openly (so that you can receive the maximum positive public relations from your efforts) and widely (so that as many people as possible feel good about their support of the plan). In fact, it is probably wise to play down your own role in beginning this entire effort. Let others praise you, if they will. In fact, if they don't, your ego should never be so fragile that you feel a need to praise yourself.

Acknowledge each individual's efforts publicly, by name, and at sufficient length to allow each person to understand that you really noticed and appreciate what he or she has done. Formal awards that celebrate the contribution made by an individual or a department should be complemented by more impromptu acknowledgments at meetings. You might say things like, "And while we're talking about the curriculum proposal, I'd just like to say getting it all ready with such a short deadline was important work. None of that could've been done without the really impressive efforts of . . ." Particularly in situations where you cannot reward contributions through salary increases and other tangible means, these public acknowledgments can mean the difference between high morale and grudging resistance to all the time demanded by your big plan. Occasionally being able to say to someone, "You know, I realize how hard you've been working to get this proposal ready. Why don't you take off early for the weekend?" allows you to make a member of your unit feel good about his or her efforts while not incurring a great expense. Of course, if that person reports to you through another supervisor, you'll want to be certain that that individual's boss agrees with your offer of extra time off. Sometimes, too, you can reward those who have made important contributions to the initiative through more frequent computer equipment upgrades, flexibility in work schedules, or other creative means that do not significantly affect your college's budget.

Approached with these principles in mind, launching initiatives provides you with an important opportunity for making a difference in the future success of your college while building morale among faculty and staff members and giving all constituents a positive sense of the college's direction. Not every college needs to undergo a new initiative all the time. Some years, it's preferable for units to lie fallow so that people can recover their energy and not feel that things are constantly changing simply for the sake of change. When a bold new direction is needed, however, following the guidelines presented in this chapter will help you turn your college's important new ideas into widely celebrated successes.

Resources

Dew, J. R., & Nearing, M. M. (2004). *Continuous quality improvement in higher education.* Westport, CT: Praeger.

Judson, A. S. (1996). *Making strategy happen: Transforming plans into reality* (2nd ed.). Malden, MA: Blackwell.

Rowley, D. J., & Sherman, H. (2001). *From strategy to change: Implementing the plan in higher education.* San Francisco, CA: Jossey-Bass.

7

Leading Reform

Leading a reform has a great deal in common with launching an initiative. In both cases you are asking the constituents of your college to think in new ways, to exert their creativity, and to tolerate a significant amount of ambiguity while your unit undergoes an important change. But launching an initiative involves creating something *new* for your college (such as an additional academic program or a fresh way of thinking about your mission), and leading a reform involves revising existing procedures or shifting priorities in some way. As a result, reforms can involve an even higher degree of change—and anxiety about change—than an initiative. No matter how unsuccessful or unpopular a particular way of doing something may have been, there will always be at least a small group of people who will be unwilling to give it up. For this reason, deans may often find that getting people to change the way that they're doing things can be a greater challenge than getting them to try something new.

Although launching initiatives is very exciting and brings much energy to the college, leading reform almost always occurs not because it is truly wanted but because it is desperately needed. Either there is an ongoing problem that continues to harm the unit (possibly even threatening its ability to survive for the future), or new circumstances have occurred that make business as usual no longer acceptable. Regardless of the reason for embarking on the reform, you will find the task much easier if you adhere to the following general principles.

Whenever possible, seek a consensus recommendation on the need for reform from an established and respected group.

Because, as we've just seen, even the most desirable change is likely to meet resistance from a small group of vocal individuals, the case for change is easier to make if you have the backing of a well-respected, established group. A college senate, a faculty/staff management group, a committee of department chairs, or some other body that is widely representative and respectful of the best interests of your entire unit can provide great assistance in demonstrating to others that staying the course is no longer an option. If your unit is so politicized that all its internal groups are distrusted, you might consider bringing in some external body for a more objective assessment. Possible external groups include accrediting committees, professional organizations, and representatives from peer or aspirational institutions. Individual consultants can be considered if there are no other options, but consultants are frequently suspected of saying whatever they're being paid to say and of not having an institution's best interests at heart. In a similar way, an ad hoc committee of faculty, students, and staff members might be useful in situations where no existing committee in your college would be appropriate, but a special committee is rarely the most appropriate first choice: Precious time may be wasted as the committee develops procedures for working together, and, like outside consultants, members may be viewed as having been charged with the task of giving you the opinion that you want to hear. If there is an existing curriculum committee or intracollege council that you can rely on for objective and candid advice, it will always be your best option, and its recommendation will carry more weight with your constituents.

Try to identify alternative solutions to the problem before embarking on a plan.

Deans tend to be problem solvers: They are the type of people who, when confronted with a challenge, will want to develop a plan to overcome it as soon as possible. When dealing with major reforms, however, it can be disastrous to move too precipitously, particularly if you proceed without considering all your options. New deans may be especially susceptible to forming opinions about the best way of solving a problem, perhaps because a certain approach was successful for them in a previous position or at another institution. Recently appointed deans may also move too quickly because they don't know all the issues involved in the situation and have only been exposed to a few perspectives or because they are too eager to be seen as acting decisively. Even experienced deans may need to pull back when considering a problem and ask themselves, "Is there more than one way of achieving this goal?" If the dean has an advisory council (particularly a group consisting of experienced academic professionals), it may be worthwhile to explore with the council what possible ways of solving the problem have been attempted previously or elsewhere. Are there clear patterns of best practices? Even if the conclusion is that the reform is needed, this discussion is a useful investment. As the dean begins to explain the plan for reform to faculty members and other constituents, he or she will be able to provide reasons why other alternatives were less desirable or simply not feasible.

Consider exploring all feasible alternatives with focus groups.

Unless the reform you are initiating involves a problem that is extremely time sensitive, it can be useful to discuss several possible ways of solving the problem with mixed focused groups of faculty members, staff representatives, and selected students. This approach will help you avoid embarking on a reform that solves one problem but leads to three or four new ones. Having representatives from various groups can provide insight into the various ways in which a change of policy or procedure will affect them. Would a curricular reform delay the likelihood that students could graduate in a timely manner or have access to the internships they need? Does a schedule revision create problems for other events that cannot be moved? Does a reassignment of responsibilities that creates a more equitable workload in one area lead to unforeseen inequities elsewhere? Are there external constituencies who may have a vested interest (or perhaps merely a *perceived* interest) in this change and should be informed of the plan as it proceeds? Holding a few well-planned focus group discussions can help you avoid problems at an early stage of your reform that may be more difficult to correct at later stages. In addition, giving people a chance to shape and respond to your ideas as the reform is being developed may foster greater buy-in as its implementation gets under way.

If at all possible, create a cost-benefit analysis for the reform you are considering.

Not all problems lend themselves to clear cost-benefit analysis. In some situations, however, performing an analysis can help you make the case that the proposed change is both desirable *and* efficient. Try to determine all the costs involved in the way the situation is being addressed now. Remember that, in addition to actual cash expenditures, there are also costs involved with opportunities that the current approach does not pursue; these are known as "opportunity costs." Inefficient workload assignments also result in higher salary costs because duties that could be handled in-house or with fewer employees must be outsourced or assigned to additional staff members. Consolidating publications and seeking publicity through news stories and other no-cost means can free up funds that you can then redirect elsewhere in your unit. If you identify as many of these opportunities as possible, gather information about savings that can accrue from more efficient procedures, and outline new opportunities to pursue once the reform is implemented, you will be well on your way toward making a compelling case for why your reform benefits the members of your unit and deserves their full support.

Communicate as extensively as possible about plans for reform as they develop.

Although change is always difficult, most people will accept the need for a reform if they are given reasons for why it is needed and if they do not feel blindsided by the plan for change. Too often deans see a need for a reform because they have information that department chairs, faculty members, students, and external constituents do not have. They know the budget for their college as a whole and understand how it is allocated. They hear complaints from students and usually see course evaluations from every department in their college. They meet with parents, potential donors, and other supporters of the college who can bring a valuable external view about how the college and its programs are perceived. With all this information at their disposal, deans frequently understand where the real problems lie, and they may have a good perspective and sufficient management experience to determine the best solution. Nevertheless, if they act in a unilateral fashion—indeed, if they are even *perceived* as acting in a unilateral fashion—they can doom their reform efforts from the very beginning. Even if they work in concert with a small group of advisors, such as department chairs or a committee of faculty representatives, they risk the accusation that their reform plan was generated by a cabal or in a Star Chamber. To avoid this problem, it is essential that the entire reform process be as open and transparent as possible. Speak freely at meetings about what you perceive the college's challenges to be. Explore several of the possible solutions that may be considered. Keep everyone in the college informed about what your process for developing the reform may be, whom to contact if they have questions or suggestions, and at what point a decision is going to be made. You will find that this operating procedure brings you useful suggestions and alternatives to consider as well as prepares the way for the reform plan's acceptance.

Understand that men and women may respond differently to reform and may even approach the process of change differently.

Although all individuals are different and tend to approach problems and solutions in their own ways (see, e.g., Chapter 3, "What Kind of Dean Are You?"), a great deal of research has been conducted into the different ways in which men and women respond to change and lead reform efforts, particularly in western societies (e.g., Brooks & Mackinnon, 2001; Eggins, 1997.) Women are more likely to engage in a process of change by first studying the mechanism by which the reform will occur: who needs to be consulted, what procedures are to be followed as the change is being considered, and how much consensus is possible as the plan is put into effect. Men, on the other hand, are much more likely to focus on the result that is needed and to seek the shortest, most efficient route of getting there: what has to be done, when it needs to be done, and what we can do with the benefits once the change has been made. As deans, we need to be not only aware of our own working style, its strengths, and its limitations, but also sensitive to others' needs as our plan proceeds. Men may become frustrated with a process that seems to be taking too long or that aims at bringing everyone on board. ("Why do we keep talking this to death? Let's just put it to a vote.") Women may become frustrated by a process that seems to be so focused on reaching a goal quickly that it rides roughshod over many people's opinions. ("Why are we so focused on just this one possibility? Can't we talk about this some more and get some other perspectives on the table?") Understanding how others may perceive our own leadership styles will help us explain why we are proceeding in the manner that we are. It may even help us alter our leadership styles to accommodate different people's needs.

Provide incentives for change.

As we've seen, people are frequently reluctant to change because they are comfortable with their current situation or because they are reluctant to learn the new skills, or take on the workload, that the change will require. One of the ways in which we can respond to inertia, hostility to new ideas, or even passive-aggressive resistance to reform is to help individuals see that the change is beneficial not simply to the college and the institution but also to them personally. Although cutting private deals with individuals should be avoided, there are often situations in which incentives can be provided to the unit as a whole (or at least to a significant segment of it) that will encourage more widespread reform support. For instance, in a unit where the limitations of faculty development funding has been an issue and has led to morale problems, you might demonstrate how funding saved by your reform can be used to increase support for faculty research and travel. Similarly, if a large amount of course preparation is harming your faculty's scholarly productivity, your reform might provide less course preparation as an incentive for larger section sizes in certain courses. Whatever problem you are trying to solve, determine the key segments of your college that will need to support it and ask yourself, "How can this reform be modified or presented in such a way that it will help alleviate a serious concern of this group? How can it reward the group for its valuable contributions and remove a difficulty that it is facing?"

Regardless of whether your reform is a large-scale effort that will require several years of planning or a more modest effort that can be completed within a single term, it is important to approach all change carefully, understanding the implications that any alteration from the status quo will have for certain individuals. Be sensitive to their reluctance to tolerate a change that is pursued merely for the sake of change, explain your reasons carefully, and then proceed, doing what is necessary for the benefit of your college and the entire institution.

Resources

Freed, J. E., & Klugman, M. R. (1997). *Quality principles and practices in higher education: Different questions for different times.* Phoenix, AZ: American Council on Education/Oryx Press. (Explores reform initiatives aimed at introducing quality principles and practices into institutions of higher education.)

Shapiro, N. S., & Levine, J. H. (1999). *Creating learning communities: A practical guide to winning support, organizing for change, and implementing programs.* San Francisco, CA: Jossey-Bass. (Although this book focuses on reorganizing institutions of higher education into learning communities, several of its suggestions for leading organizational change are transferable to other types of reform that deans may be considering.)

References

Brooks, A., & Mackinnon, A. (Eds.). (2001). *Gender and the restructured university: Changing management and culture in higher education.* Buckingham, UK: Society for Research into Higher Education & Open University Press.

Eggins, H. (Ed.). (1997). *Women as leaders and managers in higher education.* Buckingham, UK: Society for Research into Higher Education & Open University Press.

8

A Scenario Analysis on the Dean's Role

In this chapter we'll explore the first of our nine scenario analyses. Exercises of this kind are useful tools to help deans develop and critique their skills as administrators, consider other alternatives to difficult problems, and prepare for challenging situations. Each scenario analysis will consist of three complementary parts:

- *A case study:* This will be a fictional, though plausible, situation that depicts one or more challenges similar to those that deans actually face.

- *Considerations:* These will be questions that may cause you to see the case study in a different light or to alter how you would respond to it.

- *Suggestions:* These will be a critique of the case study itself, providing ideas about possible actions to remedy a similar situation or to lessen its severity. Although the case studies by their very nature do not lend themselves to right or wrong answers or to only one solution, this section of the scenario analysis is based on practical and field-tested responses to similar challenges. The suggestions provided in this section should not be regarded as "the answers" but rather as advice that should prompt further consideration about what you would do to find the best possible solution to a difficult problem.

Case Study

You've just been hired as dean of one of the colleges in a rather complex university. You've arrived from outside the institution, so you are still in the process of gathering information. You are climbing a rather steep learning curve, but one point is already clear to you: Throughout the interview process you were told repeatedly, "What we need is a change agent. We want to be sure that the next dean has the vision and the courage to make a real difference." This message was consistent at all levels of the institution, from the president down to every student you met. In your private interviews and public statements, you began to outline a few ideas about what you thought should be done: tightening the curriculum; modernizing facilities; streamlining the number of majors; balancing workload; and reexamining the procedures in place at the college, many of which are so outdated that they are now counterproductive. Your bold vision won you a great deal of support. In fact, it was probably the leading reason why you were offered this job. Moreover, even though you had other offers (some of which were at more prestigious institutions), you accepted this position because you've always seen yourself as a problem solver, an innovator, and a visionary. You were attracted by the opportunity to make a genuine difference in the life of an institution. This feeling is confirmed when, on the day you start your new job, you have a meeting with the university's president, who tells you, "I'm so glad you accepted this position. You were everyone's first choice, and you were *my* first choice. Now, go out there and do whatever you need to do to get that college back into shape."

It's summer, and the university is less busy than it will be in the fall. You spend much of your time going over records, exploring files, and seeing what needs to be done. It becomes very clear to you why everyone was so insistent on the need for a major change. Unlike most colleges at the university, your unit has been operating at a mounting loss for several years. Student attrition is significantly higher than that of comparable colleges. Several of your major programs are being offered to relatively few students. Course rotations seem poorly planned: Some departments are actually competing with themselves through ineffective scheduling; other areas create obstacles for students by offering required courses at overlapping times. For all these reasons, there are signs of poor morale throughout your entire unit: Alumni donations are down, and few students even bother to attend mandatory meetings for majors. Although you knew some of this information before you arrived, when you see the details of the budget and enrollment reports, you realize just how severe the situation has become. As the fall semester draws near, you know that you must act—and act quickly.

Traditionally, the dean holds a retreat for department chairs just before students return each fall. You use this event to begin putting your strategy into effect. You outline the college's problems as you see them. There is a general nodding of heads; some chairs are even shocked by how bad the situation has become. Then you proceed to identify what can be done to remedy it: "This year's retreat is going to be dedicated to planning what we can do to get back on track. As you know, I believe in collegial, consensus-based management. That's why we're here. I need you to work with me to address our college's problems. How can we streamline our programs so that we stop our inefficiencies? Where do we target resources to make improvements, and from where should those resources come? I'm looking for your help and advice on all these issues. I have ideas, but I don't have any magic wand. So I'm counting on you to be as creative as you can in helping me plan a solution."

The retreat proves to be a lot of hard work, but definite progress is made. You are impressed by the cooperative spirit that the chairs bring to their task. By the end of your time together, a general plan has come together. You will restructure the college, reducing it from 14 departments to 9. Three majors will be eliminated; six others will be consolidated or revised. A new, more centralized scheduling procedure will be developed to avoid overlapping required courses and other such inefficiencies. Several positions will be phased out once pending retirements and planned departures occur. Other faculty members will be reassigned from areas with lower enrollments to those with greater needs in similar academic disciplines. Adjunct costs will be decreased through improved scheduling, reducing the number of courses offered, and slightly higher enrollment caps in introductory courses. You are pleased that the plan is precisely what you had hoped the chairs would suggest to you.

After the students return, your college's next important event is a large convocation. Majors and prospective majors are present. Faculty and staff members are required to attend. The president has come to lend support and sits in the front of the auditorium with you. Because you are new to the institution, several of your fellow deans have attended to promote a sense of unity. The convocation is the event at which you will go public with your plan for the college's major reform. You begin with a variation of what you had told the chairs at the retreat: "These are the problems that our college faces, and these are the problems that we must work together to solve." You outline the plan that will be implemented over the coming year. "Many details still need to be worked out, and I need every one of you to contribute your best ideas and advice to help solve the problem. Every existing committee in the college, along with several new ad hoc groups, will take on implementing this plan as their highest priority for this year. But we're a great college and a strong university. Together, I know we can make a difference."

Your presentation is met with applause. At the reception afterward, the mood is a bit somber because people are already thinking of the work that lies ahead. A few people tell you, "Good speech!" or "Thanks for saying what's needed to be said for so long." By the end of the day, you feel exhausted, but you believe that the right groundwork has been laid for what will need to be accomplished over the coming months.

The following day arrives, and suddenly everything seems to fall apart. A headline in the local paper reads, "College at Local University to Downsize Because of Attrition and Budget Problems." Your email inbox is filled with angry messages from every conceivable constituency. People are asking why they were not consulted about these proposed changes, what they can do to stop the changes, and how you can be so insensitive to the college's time-honored traditions. Faculty members seem to panic about the loss of jobs, even though you tried your best to assuage this fear. Students are outraged because they believe their majors will be eliminated. Alumni threaten to withhold their annual giving because "the new dean" is changing everything that they have come to regard as important in "their college." Several of the other deans are upset because you spoke of cutting back on courses, and they rely on sections your college provides to serve their majors. Even the department chairs who helped draft the plan at the retreat are annoyed: They believe that you simply pressured them into adopting a plan that you had in mind all along; they also think that you've blindsided them by revealing your proposal to their employees before they had a chance to discuss it further. After taking several calls from angry parents who tell you, "I don't pay good money to send my child to a college just so that you can eliminate the major we've been counting on," you've been informed that you have another call waiting on line 2. Your secretary says, "The president's been holding for quite some time. Apparently there are grave concerns about something you said at the convocation yesterday. Anyway, I'm putting the call through to you now."

Considerations

1. What might be the nature of your telephone conversation with the university president?

    •   Suppose that the president's "grave concerns" are with the plan itself. "This isn't at all what I had in mind," you are told. "I wanted you to make some big changes by going out and recruiting more students for your programs. I didn't expect you to come in here with a meat cleaver and start hacking away at everything! I'm very disappointed. I'm starting to wonder whether we made the wrong choice in hiring you." How do you respond? Do you reconsider any or all aspects of the plan? Do you resign? Do you try to persuade the president to see the reasons for your proposal? Do you mention the department chairs' role in drafting this proposal at the retreat? Do you point out to the president that your instructions were rather vague and that you took them as a mandate for the radical solution that you have proposed?

    •   Suppose that the president's grave concerns are about the criticism the proposal received at the reception afterward. "I can't stand that sort of attitude," you are told. "Small-mindedness is what got us into this mess in the first place. Look, don't let the complainers wear you down on this issue. I hired you, and I'm behind you all the way. Tough it out." Does the fact that your supervisor supports your plan make you adhere to it even if all your other constituencies resist it? Do you suggest to the president taking a modified approach to the college's problems or extending your timetable?

2. Review the case study, and identify what you might have done differently at each step along the way. Were there mistakes that you made at any point? If you do not think that you have made any outright mistakes, were there ways in which you may have handled the situation differently to achieve a better result?

3. Do you respond any differently if those who contact you by email give you information that you had not known earlier? For instance, do you reconsider your plan if you learn that one of the programs you proposed eliminating . . .

    •   Although small in number of majors, plays a disproportionate role in retaining members of an underrepresented minority group, ethnic group, or other student population that is specially targeted in your university's diversity plan?

    •   Was initiated as a result of a restricted gift from a significant donor? (Does your answer change if the donor is still living and is threatening to remove funding from another major project that is vital to the university unless you cancel your reform?)

    •   Was the subject in which the president's child (or the child of the chair of your governing board) is currently majoring?

    •   Although low in enrollment, turns out to play a central role in the university's vision for the future according to its strategic plan and mission statement?

    •   Was likely to become one of the hot new majors according to a recent study that explored demographics and enrollment trends?

    •   Had the potential to receive a large grant that could, by itself, eliminate your college's deficit?

Suggestions

Based solely on the information contained in the case study, an outside observer may have several concerns about the approach that you have taken so far. Chief among these concerns would be that you:

- Began to act without receiving a sufficiently clear mandate

- Attempted to reform too much too soon

- Did not understand the implications of being new and an authority figure

- Failed to consult with a wide enough cross-section of the college before embarking on a radical plan of action

You began your position aware that there were problems and that you were expected to bring about change. You did not take sufficient steps, however, to understand everyone's perspectives on the nature of the problems and what you might do about them. Your own study of the college's documentation, coupled with the support given to the general ideas that you presented during your interview, led you to conclude that you knew what the issues were, how they should be solved, and whether people would accept your solutions. Remember, though, that the dean must lead from the middle (see Chapter 38, "Leadership from the Middle"). A wiser course of action might have been to follow your initial meeting with the president with several other such meetings once you started to gain a clear sense of what needed to be done. You may then have realized whether you were proposing solutions that your primary supervisor could not support. In the case of those who report to you, discussing the issues in existing committees or with mixed focus groups may have given you a better understanding of what people expected from you.

Second, you were probably far too ambitious in setting out your plan so soon into your tenure as dean. Beginning a major new plan at your very first meeting with your chairs and announcing that plan at your first public meeting is likely to make even a unit that is already committed to change uneasy. In most cases it is far more beneficial for you to take sufficient time to prepare your unit for a necessary change, let people get used to the idea that genuine reform is coming, and allow them to play a role in shaping the change before you begin implementing your ideas.

Finally, you proceeded to launch a major reform without thoroughly consulting those who would need to implement it and live with its results. Despite your statements about adopting a collegial, consensus-building approach, you only spoke to one segment of your unit (the department chairs) before unveiling the plan at convocation, and then you seem to have manipulated the chairs into not really developing their own recommendations but parroting back what you wanted to hear. A warning sign should have been when the chairs recommended to you "precisely what you had hoped the chairs would suggest to you." That result should have been a clear indication that the department chairs were acting not as true advisors but merely as your agents. They did not really develop a plan; they simply wrote out *your* plan. Remember the essential principle that we encountered in Chapter 2 ("Preparing for the Dean's Role"): Delegation always implies a certain loss of control. The report or decision that is delegated to someone else is unlikely to be *exactly* like your own. Any time that a committee or employee gives you a report that contains exactly the conclusions that you wanted or recommends exactly the plan that you had in mind, it is time to scrutinize your own actions. Did you really give people sufficient freedom to apply their own best judgment? Were they truly agreeing with you, or did they feel that they were expected to agree? Finally, as you considered the groups to consult early in the process, bringing your university's public relations staff into the loop may have saved you the embarrassment that you suffered from the newspaper article.

Can This Deanship Be Saved?

Knowing some of the ways in which you *should* have handled the situation differently is valuable; it will help you avoid similar problems in the future. But what do you do now if you find yourself in the situation outlined in the case study? First, you should start engaging in the type of communication that should have occurred before the problem ever arose. Everyone who emails and calls should get a legitimate acknowledgment of their concerns, an expression that you appreciate their willingness to bring these matters to your attention, and a candid explanation of why you made the current proposal. Have a series of discussions with your president and fellow deans to see how you can address their concerns and provide them with the insight they need to understand your position. (Listen to them; don't just be defensive.) Meet with existing committees in your college; charge them with specific aspects of the plan that are germane to their mission; allow them to adopt a reasonable timetable for their work; and give them the freedom to propose, where appropriate, alternative solutions to the problems you outlined. Certainly, you do not have to accept any recommendation that you think is ill advised or merely goes through the motions of making a change. You should, however, be prepared to explain to a committee why its recommendation is unacceptable and what you intend to do as a result. Receiving multiple unacceptable reports from multiple college committees should be a red flag. Your charge to them was unclear, your reform plan is fatally flawed, or there is a clear mismatch between you and the rest of your college, which would indicate that it is time for a wholesale reassessment both of your reform and of your fit at the institution.

9

Students

There are many reasons why students may have contact with a dean. Students may need help in understanding how the college's academic rules and regulations apply to them. They may be unaware of certain procedures that they need to follow. They may be encountering a barrier to academic success that is appropriately addressed at the dean's level. They may be seeking letters of recommendation or verification that they are in good academic standing. They may have exhausted all their preliminary appeals in addressing a concern with a faculty member or in requesting that a grade be reconsidered. They may be pursuing an independent major that is supervised at the dean's level or require assistance in applying to graduate school, an internship, or a study abroad experience. They may need the dean's permission for an incomplete, a late withdrawal from a course, or a grading system change (such as letter grade to pass/fail or vice versa). They may be the recipients of a major award, and the dean would like to congratulate them. They may be having such severe academic difficulties that the dean's office needs to intervene, either to help them get back on track or to have them removed from the institution.

Some dean's offices include formal centers of academic advisement, tutoring support, and other forms of assistance that students may require from time to time. At some institutions, too, various records are stored in the dean's office, and students who need information from their files may need to submit a request to the dean. So even if your position does not require extensive interaction with students, there are certain issues that every dean needs to consider to maintain the highest level of student success.

Are students "customers" of the college?

One question that colleges most frequently debate about students is this: Are our students customers, and if so, how does that affect our relationship with them (see, e.g., Schwartzman, 1995)? There are several aspects of a student's relationship with colleges or universities that bear similarity to the relationship that a customer has with a business. For instance, students pay fees to colleges, receive services from them, and are entitled to certain expectations. Moreover, in specific aspects of students' experience on campus, they literally are customers—

for example, when they purchase items in the bookstore, lease space in a residence hall, or acquire a meal plan.

Nevertheless, in the academic sphere, the relationship between a student and a university is significantly different from that between a customer and a provider of goods or services. Sometimes students (or their parents) will not understand the difference. They will take this attitude: "I'm paying the tuition. Why can't you offer courses at the times I want, give me all the courses I desire, and offer me a grade that reflects my effort and aspirations rather than my performance?" What is misunderstood in this scenario is that a student's relationship with a college is much less like a customer's relationship to a provider of goods or services and much more like a client's relationship with a doctor, lawyer, architect, or personal trainer. That is to say, the student-university relationship is more of a professional relationship.

The following analogy may serve to clarify this distinction. In a customer relationship the purchaser pays a fee and has the right to expect whatever he or she has paid for. It's an even exchange. For instance, a customer in a restaurant is entitled to purchase as much as he or she can afford, within very broad limits. For example, a restaurant may not serve a customer who is inebriated, disturbing other customers, or acting in a manner that is detrimental to the restaurant's business. Even if the patron's requests are utterly irrational—wishing to be served every single entrée on the menu or only dishes that begin with the letter *p*—the restaurant, if it cares to remain in business, will most likely serve that person. But something quite different occurs in a professional relationship. In these cases the client pays a fee and has the right to expect that his or her needs—not his or her desires—will be taken seriously, subject to the professional's training and sound judgment. Thus, in a doctor's office, a patient may request a certain medication, but the physician is not obliged to provide it. What the doctor is obliged to do is to consider the patient's needs in terms of a proper diagnosis and the doctor's own ethical code. "Well, rather than simply prescribing that for you," the physician might say, "let me run a few tests, and I'll use the results to plan the best course of treatment for your needs."

In much the same way, students may often tell professors, advisors, and other academic professionals what they want, but it is the duty of the academic professional to determine what a student actually needs. Prerequisites, general education requirements, graduation requirements, and other aspects of a well-constructed academic program are so designed to reflect educators' sound professional judgment. Part of what a student "pays for" in college is the exercise of that judgment, just as would be the case if the student were consulting any other type of professional. The dean is thus in a very good position to clarify this matter for those students who impose unrealistic demands on the faculty because they misunderstand where their customer rights end and their student obligations begin.

How may students serve as an important source of information for deans?

Students are well situated in the overall organization of the college or university to provide insight into certain important matters about which the dean needs to know. For example, students will know whether a faculty member is regularly late for class, cancels classes or labs frequently, and fails to distribute a syllabus on the first day of a course. Students will know whether the instructor speaks distinctly enough to be heard everywhere in the classroom. They will know whether classes always consist of one activity—lecture, discussion, experiment, and so on—or are likely to be more varied. They will know whether the professor is accessible outside class. The dean should, however, expect a certain degree of exaggeration to the effect that "I looked for Professor Smith just now, and she's never in her office." Students will often resort to this excuse when they are up against a deadline, have checked once or twice at someone's office door, and could not find the person they were looking for. Students can also provide more subjective information, such as whether they enjoyed a particular course, are likely to recommend that course to a friend, or would probably enroll for another course from the same instructor.

Unfortunately, many systems of course evaluation ignore one or more of these issues and replace them with other questions that a student is simply not in a good position to answer. Too many ratings instruments ask questions about whether the professor has:

- Remained current in his or her field (a judgment far better left to the instructor's peers)

- Been sensitive to the student's needs (a question that is too easy to misconstrue and that, at best, calls for students to mind-read)

- Motivated the students to do their best work (an expectation that, in most cases, reflects more on the student than the faculty member)

Course evaluations, by and large, ask too many questions of every kind for students to respond to them thoughtfully.

For this reason, deans should supplement the admittedly imperfect information that they gain from student ratings of instruction with genuine insights from students. The time spent walking with a student to another office on campus can provide a valuable opportunity to discuss the positive aspects of the student's experience at the institution. Even in cases when students have gone to the dean's office to make a complaint, they can be asked questions that help them view the situation in its larger context and provide the dean with information based on actual situations, not passions or exaggerations. By posing such questions as "Do you have your course syllabus with you? Could I see it for a moment?" the dean can begin to direct the conversation into a more constructive and useful direction. You can see whether the faculty member has a policy outlined on the matter of the complaint (missing classes, turning in work late, being available outside class, etc.). You can discuss whether the syllabus was followed or changed frequently. You can review the faculty member's description of the course's primary focus to determine whether the student's perspective is unrealistic. In every case, however, you will not want to make any decisions based on this single discussion or complaint. You will always want to check the student's allegations with the faculty member and with that faculty member's chair. In extremely serious matters you may even wish to interview a few other students from the course to determine whether others corroborate the allegations.

Which student allegations are so serious that you *must* act immediately?

If your institution does not have a uniform student complaint or grievance procedure, you should work in concert with the upper administration and campus attorneys to develop one as soon as possible. In some cases your institution's regional accrediting body requires you to have such a policy. In all cases this policy will provide you with some valuable guidance about when you must act on a student complaint and when you are free to use your own judgment about responding. Allegations of sexual harassment—and, more generally, allegations of infringement on an individual's rights that are protected by your institution's policy of nondiscrimination—require immediate action on your part. Your college's equal opportunity officer, affirmative action officer, ombudsperson, or some other official will almost certainly need to be notified. Legal counsel should also be brought into the matter early in the process so that you will avoid making a mistake that could have serious implications later. Such mistakes might include not responding quickly or aggressively enough, not respecting the rights of all parties in the allegation, or divulging information in an improper manner. Serious allegations are never matters that you should attempt to address or investigate on your own. Always follow existing policies carefully, include all appropriate parties in the reporting process, and maintain accurate but highly confidential notes.

Should students be included on committees?

Deans should be open to the idea of revising appropriate committee structures to allow for student representation, as long as the committee is not dealing with matters that are either highly confidential or outside a student's area of direct concern. Approving curricula, making promotion and tenure decisions, investigating professional misconduct, and the like are best left to faculty peers and supervisors. On the other hand, calendar committees, event planning groups, hiring committees, strategic planning bodies, and a wide variety of other groups essential to running the college could well benefit from constructive student involvement. These groups tend to be genuine learning opportunities for the students themselves and can help the college avoid implementing a new policy or procedure that results in unanticipated student resistance. In addition to your regular committee structure, therefore, you might consider creating several groups that operate as cross-functional teams—that is, committees of faculty, staff, students, administrators, and other constituents who meet to address specific issues. Cross-functional teams help institutions avoid horizontal tunnel vision—the narrow perspective that can occur when department chairs discuss major issues only with other department chairs, deans only with other deans, students only with other students, and so on.

How can deans partner better with student affairs to improve students' overall educational experience?

Keeling (2004) discusses an important new concept for the way in which colleges and universities should operate. Rather than isolating a student's experience into such artificial compartments as academic affairs, student affairs, housing, and other campus offices, colleges and universities need to think of a student's time at the institution in the way that students themselves do: a single, unified experience. Keeling defines learning "as a comprehensive, holistic, transformative activity that integrates *academic learning* and *student development,* processes that have often been considered separate, or even independent of each other" (p. 4). A student's development of knowledge does not occur only in the classroom. A student's leadership skills do not develop only in cocurricular activities. A student's self-image does not develop only in extracurricular activities. All aspects of a student's collegiate experience can be improved through carefully and intentionally integrating the goals that deans and faculty members have with the goals that student affairs professionals have.

Breaking down the artificial barriers that many institutions create through nomenclature can be valuable in providing students with the rich, life-improving experience that we want college to be for them. If this philosophy has not yet been adopted by your entire institution, it is even more important for you to begin your own efforts in this regard.

Resources

Bok, D. (2006). *Our underachieving colleges: A candid look at how much students learn and why they should be learning more.* Princeton, NJ: Princeton University Press.

Braskamp, L. A., Trautvetter, L. C., & Ward, K. (2006). *Putting students first: How colleges develop students purposefully.* Bolton, MA: Anker.

McDaniel, T. R. (2002). Academic standards vs. customer service. In T. R. McDaniel, *Dean's dialogue* (pp. 5–8). Madison, WI: Magna.

Nathan, R. (2005). *My freshman year: What a professor learned by becoming a student.* Ithaca, NY: Cornell University Press.

Nealon, J. L. (2006). *College and university responsiveness to students-as-customers: The reorganization of service delivery in the enrollment service arena.* Ann Arbor, MI: ProQuest/UMI.

References

Keeling, R. P. (Ed.). (2004). *Learning reconsidered 1: A campus-wide focus on the student experience.* Washington, DC: American College Personnel Association & National Association of Student Personnel Administrators.

Schwartzman, R. (1995, Winter). Are students customers? The metaphoric mismatch between management and education. *Education, 116*(2), 215–222.

10

Parents

There was a time not long ago when deans would have had little, if any, contact with the parents of current or prospective students. Perhaps over the course of a new student orientation or family weekend, the dean might make a short presentation to parents or mingle briefly at a social event. The presentation itself was likely to focus on the institution's prestige and history, and it may have included some sober warnings about the intellectual rigor of the program that the parents' child was attempting. "Look to the family on your right. Now look to the family on your left," one dean was noted as saying on such an occasion back in the 1960s. "One in three families won't be here at this time next year." Many deans recall hearing similar pronouncements early in their careers. What was then regarded as a realistic assessment of the college's high academic standard would today probably be challenged by a parent who asks, "So why aren't you doing more to increase your retention rate?"

The days of limited decanal contact with parents are gone, probably forever and almost certainly to the improvement of the overall student experience. Nowadays parents expect to play a vital role in their children's collegiate experience. Many more parents than in previous generations are themselves college graduates, and these parents tend to have preconceived notions of what their children's campus experience should be. The ease of communication—because of cell phones, email, instant messaging, and other forms of technology—means that many parents are in daily contact with their children at college. The rise of what Cline and Fay (1990) have dubbed "helicopter parents" (parents who are always in the background, hovering over their children) has impacted the way in which colleges and universities all over the country do business. Moreover, the phenomenon of the highly involved collegiate parent is growing. Even graduate program deans report that it is now not uncommon to receive a call or visit from a parent who is dissatisfied with the way in which his or her child has been treated, with the grade that a professor has awarded, or with the availability of certain courses. Although in many situations parents can be strong allies and help deans secure resources, attract potential students, and gain exposure, parents can also occupy a disproportionate amount of deans' time, cause a great deal of aggravation over extremely minor issues, and require deans to develop a special set of communication skills. What, then, are the various issues that deans should be aware of in dealing with students' parents? In general, deans should try to see matters from a parent's perspective to avoid miscommunications and exacerbating already tense situations. By doing so, deans will learn that parents—even those who are themselves college educated—may not know things about higher education that we as professionals take for granted.

Parents don't always know what a dean does.

As we saw at the beginning of this book, the very nature of what an academic dean does can vary widely from institution to institution. Even beyond this general rule, however, some individuals outside academia tend to be confused by the title of *dean.* Some parents mistake the dean for the president or chancellor, thinking that he or she runs the entire institution. Others are bewildered by the sheer variety of deans that universities sometimes have (dean of this college, dean of that college, dean of students, dean of admissions, dean of multicultural affairs, dean of advising, etc.). It is not surprising, therefore, that parents may not always know which issues are appropriate to bring before an individual dean. Thus, they may call an academic dean when their child is having a quarrel with a roommate. They may contact the dean of students when their child is having difficulty in a course. They may write to the dean of admissions on *any* issue because that dean may have been the first administrator whom they encountered at the institution and the only one they feel they know.

Parental confusion can increase because they may think of the dean of an institution as the person who handles all problems and complaints. Their understanding of the dean's function may be more of that of an ombudsperson than someone who is responsible for a certain set of academic programs. As we saw in Chapter 2 ("Preparing for the Dean's Role"), parents are not always going to consult the institution's organizational chart when their child is having a problem; they're going to shout, "Get me the dean!" And in many cases, that call is going to be put through to you. Parents rarely, if ever, shout, "Get me the provost!" or "Get me the registrar!" So performing triage on parental calls is simply one of the challenges that goes with being a dean.

Even parents who have a legitimate academic issue to discuss may not understand the role that deans play as faculty supervisors. Like the students whom we discussed in the last chapter, they may see you only as a faculty member's boss, the person who will intervene to change a grade that is lower than they would like, waive a departmental requirement that is inconvenient for their child, or permit their child to participate in commencement exercises without having completed the minimum requirements. Just as you may need to explain to a student the difference between a customer relationship and a professional relationship, so may you need to discuss it with parents. You may need to explain why academic requirements are what they are, what rights academic freedom guarantees to professors, and why certain decisions are delegated by you to individual academic disciplines. It may well be that your institution's policies are different from what they were when that parent was a student. It may be, too, that your college's policies are different from those of other institutions with which the parent is familiar. "Look," you may be told, "I know it's possible to do this at Prestigious University, and obviously, you don't know what you're doing." As difficult as these exchanges become, you should explain—with firmness but with civility—why you will not grant an exception and whether the parent has any further avenues of appeal.

Parents don't always understand the limits of their rights to information and involvement in the lives of college-age students.

Parents of college students are frequently used to being involved in every aspect of their children's educational, social, and extracurricular lives. As a result, they may expect this to continue in college. They try to assert certain rights simply because they are paying for tuition, and they may expect you to give them information that is inappropriate (and, at times, simply *illegal*) to provide.

For this reason, every dean must become familiar with three essential web sites:

- www4.law.cornell.edu/uscode/20/1232g.html, which contains the full text of U.S. Code 1232g, 34 CFR Part 99, commonly known as the Family Educational Rights and Privacy Act (FERPA)

- www.ed.gov/policy/gen/guid/fpco/ferpa/leg-history.html, which outlines the history of FERPA

- www.ed.gov/policy/gen/guid/fpco/ferpa/index.html, which is the government's official FERPA site and contains updates made to or changes in the law

FERPA legislation dates back to 1974 when it was signed into law by President Ford and quickly amended by Senator James Buckley of New York and Senator Claiborne Pell of Rhode Island. The law intended to limit access to confidential educational records to parents—and parents only. FERPA rights revert to the students themselves, however, when they turn 18 or enter a postsecondary educational institution. Although FERPA does give certain rights to parents who claim a child as a dependent on their federal income taxes, these rights are not automatic and often require parents to file a request every time they want to access their child's educational record. Most colleges and universities, too, have developed forms by which students may waive their FERPA rights, but not all students sign such a form. Parents may sometimes ask, "If there was a form on which my child could waive FERPA rights and have me notified of what's going on, why didn't you tell me about it?" From the institution's perspective, completing these forms involves surrendering a legal right, and few institutions want to be perceived as encouraging individuals to surrender their rights.

When contacted by a parent whose request may require the release of FERPA-protected educational records (including a question like "I just need to know . . . is my kid going to class/flunking out/turning in assignments/likely to graduate this spring?"), you should never provide information without thoroughly understanding how your institution handles FERPA requests, whether the student has submitted a waiver that allows the parent to receive the requested information, and whether your institution allows you to disclose protected educational record information orally (as opposed to disclosure in writing only). Even in cases where a waiver *has* been signed and all institutional policies allow you to speak with the parent, it is probably preferable for you to suggest meeting with the student, the parent, and any faculty members whose courses are relevant to the matter in question. Having everyone gather together in a single place is far preferable to a long exchange of telephone calls or emails in which any number of statements may be misunderstood or misreported. When the faculty members themselves are present, the student will be less likely to exaggerate his or her own record of attendance or completion of required course assignments. When the student is present, he or she will know precisely what has been disclosed to the parent and will have the right either to reaffirm his or her FERPA rights or to waive them in accordance with the parent's wishes. Moreover, with the parent present, you will know what has and has not been revealed in case the parent should raise the issue again later.

Parents don't always know the best ways of helping their children succeed in college.

Parents naturally want the best for their children. They want their son or daughter to succeed academically, to be happy, and to graduate with sound career prospects in sight. Frequently, however, they do not know the best way to go about achieving these aims. Sometimes the parents have not been to college themselves and assume that colleges work in the same way that elementary and high schools do. At other times, parents who have gone to college attended a very different type of institution or at a time when colleges were organized in less complex ways than universities currently are. At the very least, most parents have experienced college only as students themselves and thus may not have a good understanding of how colleges and universities are structured. They may not understand the differences between such offices as business affairs and financial aid because both deal with money, and they may not know which course-related questions should be directed to your office and which to the registrar because both you and the registrar deal with grades.

As a means of clarifying many of these issues, it can be extremely useful to establish a parents council. The purpose of this council is to help parents get the information they need and channel their natural inclination to help their children in the most constructive directions. To be effective, a parents council should not be too large; councils larger than 30 people tend to get unwieldy and are almost impossible to assemble at a single convenient time. Moreover, a parents council for your college should consist of parents of students at *all* program levels. Nevertheless, if you are the dean of a professional college, it is likely that the parents would largely be drawn from families of juniors and seniors, with perhaps only a few parents representing students who anticipate declaring a major in one of your disciplines. If you are the dean of arts and sciences, you may wish to draw members from those with children completing general education courses (who perhaps rotate off the council if their child declares a major in another college) and those with children who intend to graduate with one of your majors.

Parents councils can be useful. First, like any advisory body, they can give you advance notice of issues that might otherwise blindside you. Second, they can be powerful advocates in helping you make the case for additional faculty lines or facility improvements because their own children will benefit when these requests are granted. Third, they can intervene with other parents who may not understand how the college works or who may have encountered a difficulty with one of their children. Having someone who is able to say, "I experienced that very same problem with my child, but here's why it ended up working out for the best" can make a case to another parent that you, even if you are a parent, may not be able to make due to your position. Fourth, a parents council can be invaluable in helping you recruit additional students, make contact with potential donors, raise funds for various projects, or secure goods-in-kind contributions to benefit your programs. Even though parents may already be paying a high tuition for their children's education, they are often willing to contribute to programs that have special meaning to them. A parents council scholarship for study abroad or a parents college distinguished visiting author can capture parents' imagination because parents can see the direct effect these opportunities will have on their children's education. As long as parents are approached early in their children's academic career and solicited for the kinds of projects that matter to them, they can be a great (and often overlooked) source of external funding. Finally, parents councils can be good training programs for your college's other boards. You will have an opportunity to see who has creative ideas and the stamina to see them through, who has excellent management skills, and who may be well intentioned but is ultimately ineffective.

With the increasing involvement of parents in their children's education, few deans are likely to be in positions where they have no contact whatsoever with parents of current or prospective students. The more deans try to anticipate what issues students' parents are likely to have and the more they start viewing issues through the lens of "How would I see this if my child were a student in this program?" the more effective they will be in assisting this important segment of their external constituency.

Resources

Barkin, C. (1999). *When your kid goes to college: A parent's survival guide.* New York, NY: Avon. (Presents the challenges of dealing with administrators from a parent's point of view, actually urging parents to think matters through carefully before even considering contacting the dean.)

Coburn, K. L., & Treeger, M. L. (2003). *Letting go: A parents' guide to understanding the college years* (4th ed.). New York, NY: HarperCollins. (Contains useful information about the advice that many parents are given concerning when to contact the dean, such as when there is a suspicion that the student may be involved in a religious cult. Does not provide clear distinctions between academic deans and student life deans, possibly inadvertently directing parents to the wrong office.)

Maynigo, T. (2003). *A girl's guide to college: Making the most of the best four years of your life.* Boulder, CO: Blue Mountain Arts. (Another source of possible confusion for parents over the academic dean's role. On p. 37, for instance, students are informed to move out of their residence hall rooms if they feel threatened or if a relationship with a roommate has become truly dysfunctional: "If you complain enough [and get your parents involved], your college dean will make the arrangements for you. But use this only as a last resort.")

McEwan, E. K. (2004). *How to deal with parents who are angry, troubled, afraid, or just plain crazy* (2nd ed.). Thousand Oaks, CA: Corwin Press. (Although dealing with the pre-college environment, this book presents much useful advice on how best to handle upset parents.)

University of North Texas. (2005). *FERPA training.* Retrieved July 5, 2007, from www.unt.edu/ferpa/ (A web site on what administrators and parents need to know about the Family Educational Rights and Privacy Act.)

Whitaker, T., & Fiore, D. J. (2001). *Dealing with difficult parents: And with parents in difficult situations.* Larchmont, NY: Eye on Education. (This book focuses on the pre-college environment but contains much information that is valuable at the college level as well.)

Woodacre, M. E. B., & Bane, S. (2006). *I'll miss you too: An off-to-college guide for parents and students.* Naperville, IL: Sourcebooks. (Provides deans with valuable insight into the challenges parents face as their children leave home for college.)

References

Cline, F., & Fay, J. (1990). *Parenting with love and logic: Teaching children responsibility.* Colorado Springs, CO: Piñon Press.

11

Faculty

Most academic deans find that the vast majority of their work involves the college faculty, either directly or indirectly. As deans, we work with departments to create job descriptions to hire new faculty members. We interview candidates for full-time teaching or research positions. We evaluate faculty members ourselves or oversee the evaluation process. We sign off on tenure and promotion applications, often playing a critical role in that process. We participate in post-tenure reviews. On rare occasions we may need to terminate or not renew the contract of a faculty member who is not performing as well as anticipated. We almost certainly were once faculty members ourselves and may still see ourselves primarily as members of our institution's corps of instruction and research, perhaps teaching a course or publishing our own scholarship whenever we can.

Because of the centrality of the faculty to deans' work, it is vital for every administrator to have a clear philosophy of their relationship to faculty's concerns, issues, and interests. In the midst of an otherwise laudable effort to redesign our institutions into student-centered learning environments, are we acting in ways that cause the faculty, our most cherished resource, to feel unappreciated? How do we improve morale and reward truly outstanding effort without being perceived as weak, taken advantage of, or succumbing to the whims of prima donnas (who, let it be said, appear on the faculties of nearly every institution)? Is there, in other words, a way to support faculty, to be a faculty-friendly dean, while still keeping the institution's overall needs firmly in view? Achieving this balance can be difficult, but it is more likely attainable if the following principles are observed.

Understand that an essential part of your role as dean involves both faculty development and developing a faculty.

Nearly every college or university has some form of a faculty development program. Unfortunately, many of these programs are quite rudimentary, funding travel to conferences and perhaps offering a series of workshops, often on the topic of technology in the classroom. In some cases a center for excellence in teaching may exist to help faculty explore the most effective instructional methods in various types of environments. Research foundations may assist faculty members with scholarly projects that cannot be funded by the institution's regular resources. Some institutions, too, may sponsor highly developed first-year faculty experience programs (see Buller, 2006, pp. 263–270) or teaching circles, scholarship networks, and service alliances (see Buller, 2006, pp. 255–262) that promote colleague-based support for faculty members' various duties. Nevertheless, there still is much more that deans can do to provide truly comprehensive faculty development systems, and the rewards are well worth the effort. A well-constructed faculty development system improves morale, illustrates that the college's central administration has its priorities straight, and adheres to the following essential principle:

> *Genuine faculty development provides training, support, and improvement of every aspect of a faculty member's professional responsibilities.*

In other words, faculty development efforts that focus simply on teaching, scholarship, service, advisement, or any other single aspect of a faculty member's duties are too limited in their focus to be highly effective. They can send the wrong message about what a college considers to be important (e.g., funding advanced research at a "teaching first" institution) and can mislead faculty members about the activities that the institution will reward during the tenure and promotion process.

In preparing your college's faculty development efforts, begin by asking yourself the following question: What are the central activities at which my faculty needs to excel, and how can I assist my faculty in performing those activities? For instance, if your faculty evaluation system assigns different weights to teaching, scholarship, and service for the purposes of promotion and tenure, do your faculty development efforts address those responsibilities in roughly the same proportion? Do you train faculty members to be most effective as members or chairs of a committee? Do you guide advisors in your programs' requirements and in the role that they should play in mentoring students? Do you assist faculty members not only in attending conferences and defraying publication expenses when necessary but also in learning about how to contact publishers effectively, how to prepare an abstract for consideration, and how to organize their résumés for the greatest impact when applying for research fellowships? Do you work with your office of sponsored programs in exposing faculty members to external funding sources in their area and in teaching them how to write and submit a successful grant proposal? Do you discuss instruction not only in general terms about how to teach well at the college level but also about how to take full advantage of the resources, teaching techniques, and approaches to active learning that have a demonstrated record of success in the disciplines in your college? Do you assist faculty members with the resources available to them when they suspect that students are facing severe health or psychological problems? Are faculty development efforts offered in a variety of formats and at different times so that even adjunct faculty members can take full advantage of them?

If you did not answer yes to each of these questions, then you still have abundant opportunities to expand your college's faculty development program and meet a broader range of needs. Of course, there is no reason why you need to offer all these services yourself. Partnering with appropriate offices on your campus (e.g., a teaching excellence center, a sponsored programs office, or a human resources center), deans of other colleges, or the college's upper administration can help with the extensive work involved in a truly comprehensive faculty development program. If your college is large enough, assigning a faculty member or associate dean to serve as director of faculty development can also be of value in achieving this goal quickly.

Of equal importance to faculty development, however, is the matter of developing a faculty. In other words, faculty development efforts tend to focus on the needs of individual faculty members, but developing a faculty involves finding ways of helping your faculty work better as a team. If faculty development focuses largely on people and their individual needs, then developing a faculty involves studying your corps of instructors, balancing the various abilities that they have and the contributions that they are in a position to make. Developing a faculty begins even before someone is hired. Too often when we set up searches, we focus merely on the area of academic specialty that we want in our programs, forgetting about the other factors that can make a faculty member successful as a member of the college. For instance, Smith, Wolf, and Busenberg (1996) and Turner (2002) provide excellent advice on how faculty searches can be designed to increase the likelihood of achieving your college's diversity goals. In addition, there may be other nonacademic areas of expertise (such as grant writing, serving as liaison with accreditation bodies, fundraising, mediation, and long-range planning) that your college needs for its ongoing success. If your institution's mission emphasizes excellence in instruction, ask yourself whether your job descriptions and search announcements make it clear that teaching is the most important thing that you do. Even more important, ask yourself whether the interview process gives you adequate exposure to each candidate's teaching abilities in realistic settings. If the advisement load for a position is likely to be heavy, do you ask prospective candidates to address their prior success in this area? If the faculty member will be working with relatively few colleagues in his or her field of specialty, or is expected to cooperate with members of other departments in an interdisciplinary program, is this expectation featured prominently in all the search materials? As a general principle, you should approach each search by asking yourself what academic field prospective candidates should represent and what qualities they should have, what value-added components would be most important to your program, and what nonacademic contributions each new faculty member will be expected to make.

Discuss with your faculty how strategic hiring may help the college meet its overall objectives.

Faculty members frequently have a difficult time comprehending why the college may wish to view vacant faculty lines not as curricular areas that need to be filled but as opportunities to meet your college's larger objectives. For this reason, deans should begin the hiring process with a series of candid discussions with faculty members about why a "whole" college approach to staffing is preferable and ultimately benefits everyone. For instance, if the college lacks diversity in gender, race, or ethnicity, it is probably not appropriate to declare that "rather than searching for a faculty member in such-and-such a discipline, this year we're going to seek an excellently qualified faculty member in whatever area can best diversify our ranks." On the other hand, if you begin your discussion with the faculty by talking about your current lack of diversity, the reasons why this is pedagogically disadvantageous for your students, and your willingness to consider any number of solutions that will adequately address this problem (provided, of course, that you really *are* open to more than one possible solution), you may discover that your faculty can be extremely creative and flexible in proposing ways of fixing the problem.

Similarly, if the college's overall needs lie in some other area—improved advisement, greater grant activity, a more complete international perspective throughout the curriculum, better cooperation with other colleges, or whatever goals you have—it is best to be open about your desire to address this need from the very beginning of the search. "Look," you might say, "we know we've got a huge challenge coming up with our accreditation review next year, and none of us has the sort of expertise we're going to need to be successful with that process. Maybe the most important thing as we begin this search is not the precise academic specialty someone represents but all the other value-added components that our college is going to need: success in writing accreditation self-studies, excellent teaching in our general education courses, and the willingness to advise students from a broad range of disciplines. I think that, if we're creative enough, we can develop a job description that reflects what we really need rather than define our positions too narrowly in terms of academic specialty. After all, we're not going to find someone who has the capabilities we're looking for if we're not up front about what we really want."

One of the most critical areas of developing a faculty is in identifying those candidates who are likely to be good colleagues. Nevertheless, "success in supporting an atmosphere of collegiality" is rarely seen in search announcements. As a result, committees tend not to emphasize collegiality when screening candidates, in the questions they ask references, and in the hypothetical situations they discuss with the candidates themselves. The result, all too often, is a hire who fills a desirable academic niche but whose uncooperative behavior is ultimately destructive. Given the opportunity, most faculty members are willing to be flexible about a candidate's academic field provided that he or she is likely to contribute to overall morale and make the college a more productive place for faculty members to work and students to learn. Strategically hiring individuals who have demonstrated their willingness to work as members of a team, to refrain from harping on pet issues or perceived injustices, and to promote both civility and the free exchange of ideas can contribute immeasurably to a college's overall growth and success (see Buller, 2006, pp. 50–55). Remember that even one uncollegial faculty member in a unit can greatly increase everyone's dissatisfaction with the institution and, in extreme cases, send productivity plummeting.

Enhance morale by developing faculty-friendly policies and eliminating unnecessary obstacles to faculty success.

In addition to including collegiality as a job-related criterion in faculty searches, deans can also help improve morale in their colleges by reconsidering policies and procedures that sometimes stand in the way of faculty success. We frequently lose highly desirable faculty members to other institutions not because faculty members are offered more money elsewhere but because their lives are complicated by matters for which we could provide assistance, if only we thought to do so. Among the policy changes that you might discuss with your upper administration are the following:

- *A tenure stop-clock policy:* Six- or seven-year probationary periods for untenured faculty members were originally created to protect faculty. Such a policy prevented institutions from keeping faculty members untenured for long periods of time and then suddenly dismissing them so that they could be replaced with lower-paid junior faculty members. For this reason, an "up or out" tenure policy really is in faculty members' best interests. Nevertheless, the inflexibility of tenure policies can create unnecessary problems. For example, instructors who have young children or who must care for a parent may have difficulty meeting the challenges of their day-to-day lives while at the same time meeting the institution's expectations for teaching, scholarship, and service.

- *A spousal placement policy:* Academics frequently are members of two-career families. There are numerous cases of faculty members who have had to forgo full-time academic appointments because their spouses were offered attractive positions elsewhere. "Trailing spouses" can have a significant effect on the family's happiness, likelihood of remaining in the region, and quality of life. For this reason, institutions may wish to develop policies for the appropriate career placement of faculty members. Some institutions create full-time positions for spouses to the extent that budgets allow. Other institutions give spouses access to placement services that work aggressively to locate appropriate full-time positions for them.

- *A residential assistance plan:* In some areas of the country, there is a wide discrepancy between faculty salaries and the cost of affordable housing. Residence assistance plans consist of several approaches to address this problem, including subsidized housing in university-owned homes, low-cost mortgages, assistance with down payments, programs where institutions and owners share the equity in a home, reduced rent, incentives to purchase homes in economically depressed areas, and interest-free second mortgages.

Seek to promote equity in departmental workloads at the same time that you permit a desirable amount of departmental flexibility.

Faculty members' workloads vary by discipline. Although there may be an institution-wide standard of the number of credits faculty teaches, these standards are usually based on a typical 50-minute period of lecture and discussion. The problem is that relatively few disciplines are really typical anymore. In addition to the extremely common deviations from regular lecture/discussion courses—such as laboratory sections, private studio instruction, thesis supervision, student teacher supervision, internship supervision, and the like—the changing nature of higher education continually offers new challenges. How, for instance, do we count a course load if the same lecture/discussion section simultaneously involves students at other sites through distance learning and podcasts *and* students who are enrolled online? As technology continues to evolve, such questions will only increase. Although disciplinary accrediting bodies frequently provide guidance in establishing equivalences between, say, private music instruction and standard lecture sections, it is all but impossible to develop a table of equivalencies for every new technology. For most deans, the result is either inequity from failing to recognize the added workload created by new technologies ("It doesn't matter how many different delivery mechanisms are involved in this course: You're getting credit for only one section.") or inequity from making numerous exceptions. For this reason, you are far better off being proactive by establishing a committee that helps you resolve questions of load. Workload is simply one of those matters where equity may not be the same as absolute equality. At some level a degree of professional judgment will be needed.

One overall principle to keep in mind when working with faculty members is that:

> *In the end, candor is always preferable to secrecy.*

In the long run it is far better for your college for people to disagree with you than to distrust you. As academics, we are all used to disagreement. We respect diversity of opinions, and regardless of our personal perspectives, we tend to be convinced that, in a free exchange of ideas, the most reasonable will win out in the end. Once you sacrifice trust, however, you will never gain it back. You will find that even your best intentions are treated with suspicion, and you will have made your job much more difficult than would have been the case if you had been open and honest with your faculty from the beginning.

Resources

Alstete, J. W. (2000). *Post-tenure faculty development: Building a system for faculty improvement and appreciation.* San Francisco, CA: Jossey-Bass.

Buller, J. L. (2007, Winter). Mentoring challenges: Tailoring advice to the individual. *The Department Chair, 17*(3), 22–25.

Cambridge, B. L. (Ed.). (2001). *Electronic portfolios: Emerging practices in student, faculty, and institutional learning.* Sterling, VA: Stylus.

Heath, M. S. (2004). *Electronic portfolios: A guide to professional development and assessment.* Worthington, OH: Linworth.

Kelly, T. (2006). *A case study of a college faculty's use of technology, professional development and perceptions of organizational support.* Ann Arbor, MI: ProQuest/UMI.

Kramer, G. L. (Ed.). (2003). *Faculty advising examined: Enhancing the potential of college faculty as advisors.* Bolton, MA: Anker.

Middaugh, M. F. (2001). *Understanding faculty productivity: Standards and benchmarks for colleges and universities.* San Francisco, CA: Jossey-Bass.

Murray, J. P. (1995). *Successful faculty development and evaluation: The complete teaching portfolio* (ASHE-ERIC Higher Education Report No. 8) Washington, DC: The George Washington University, Graduate School of Education and Human Development.

Poskanzer, S. G. (2002). *Higher education law: The faculty.* Baltimore, MD: Johns Hopkins University Press.

Quinn, S. S. (2006, July). A descriptive case study of the organization-based self-esteem, institutional belongingness, and career development opportunities of adjunct faculty at a small northeastern college. *Journal of Social Change, 1*(1), 46–71.

Saroyan, A., & Amundsen, C. (Eds.). (2004). *Rethinking teaching in higher education: From a course design workshop to a faculty development framework.* Sterling, VA: Stylus.

Sorcinelli, M. D., Austin, A. E., Eddy, P. L., & Beach, A. L. (2006). *Creating the future of faculty development: Learning from the past, understanding the present.* Bolton, MA: Anker.

References

Buller, J. L. (2006). *The essential department chair: A practical guide to college administration.* Bolton, MA: Anker.

Smith, D. G., Wolf, L. E., & Busenberg, B. E. (1996). *Achieving faculty diversity: Debunking the myths.* Washington, DC: Association of American Colleges and Universities.

Turner, C. S. V. (2002). *Diversifying the faculty: A guidebook for search committees.* Washington, DC: Association of American Colleges and Universities.

12

Challenging Employees

In the best of all possible worlds, every college employee would be productive, dedicated, efficient, and a joy to work with. Unfortunately, most deans have to contend with at least one individual (sometimes many more) who either cannot or will not work cooperatively and effectively. This chapter explores principles that may remedy the problems caused by challenging employees. When do you attempt to change an employee's behavior? When do you conclude that changing that behavior is no longer possible and the individual should be terminated? Are there strategies to use when termination is not an option?

Evaluate the situation and determine, as specifically as you can, the difficulties that the problem is causing.

Frequently, we are annoyed by problems caused by a faculty or staff member in what we might describe as a general or undirected manner. We think, "So-and-so is ruining morale because he is so negative" or "Those two people just need to get along better; their constant tension is affecting our whole area." But these very general impressions do not help you solve the problem. You need to determine for yourself—and ultimately for the employee who is responsible for the problem—precisely what behavior is causing the difficulty, in which settings it tends to occur, and why it prevents your unit from functioning effectively. To achieve this goal, begin by asking yourself, "Why do I need that particular behavior to change? And precisely *what* needs to change?"

As you consider the problem, try to distinguish relatively minor behaviors—mere pet peeves that get on people's nerves but that don't really have a detrimental effect on work—from truly disruptive behavior. For instance, if people are reluctant to speak their minds in an open meeting because another faculty or staff member often resorts to bullying tactics, ridiculing people for their ideas or insulting them, then you have a clear idea of where to begin solving your problem: You need to address the chill that has been imposed on the free exchange of ideas that your college, like any other, needs to do its work effectively. If excessive gossiping is ruining morale or causing important work to go undone, then you have identified a clear negative effect in your area that can be traced to a specific behavior. On the other hand, if a person's individual mannerisms are simply annoying or an employee's style of dress, while appropriately professional, is out of style rather than in poor taste, you need to ask yourself whether the situation is important enough to require intervention. Each of us has idiosyncrasies and personal traits that can become minor annoyances to others. Nevertheless, each of us is also entitled to a certain degree of personal freedom, and, even in the workplace, that freedom needs to be respected.

Categorize the problem in terms of the response that is likely to be required.

Problems vary in severity and thus require different levels of response. A difficult employee may not always need to be terminated: Replacing employees can be an expensive, time-consuming process. There may also be several ways in which the employee is contributing to your college's work in positive ways that will be lost if you end that person's employment. Moreover, terminations can be traumatic even for the faculty and staff members who are left behind, regardless of how much they may have wanted the person causing the problem to be fired. For all these reasons, helping the employee redirect his or her negative behavior into more constructive outlets is often preferable.

Your second step, therefore, after carefully evaluating the nature of the problem is to categorize it into one of the four following likely levels of response:

- This problem is likely to be solved through intervention.

- This problem is unlikely to be solved, but its negative effects can be managed.

- This problem is unlikely to be solved or managed, but its negative effects can be isolated.

- This problem is unlikely to be solved, managed, or isolated.

Each of these four situations will require a different course of action. A problem that is likely to be solved through proper intervention may be handled by such activities as mentoring the employee, reassigning various responsibilities, changing office or desk locations, or providing clear guidance in performance evaluations. These are the situations in which the individual either is unaware that certain behavior is causing serious problems for the college or lacks the skills needed to change the behavior. The assumption is that, with proper instruction or minor changes (e.g., relocating someone's desk so that the person doesn't delay other people by engaging them in conversation every time he or she goes to the copy room), the problem will be solved and the work environment will improve.

Although it is preferable to solve problems, the realities of interpersonal relationships suggest that many issues cannot be completely remedied. Frequently, however, these problems can be either managed or isolated. What is the difference between managing and isolating a problem? A problem is managed if steps are taken to reduce its severity, even though the issue itself does not go away completely. A problem is isolated if its severity cannot be reduced but steps are taken to control its effects. For instance, suppose that there is a particularly severe personality conflict in your area. Despite repeated discussions and mediation, you have been unable to solve the problem and have concluded that both individuals are equally at fault. Managing the problem might include meeting with each person separately and then together to establish ground rules for conduct. You might also reorganize committee assignments or other responsibilities to minimize contact between the two individuals. You might establish some inducements for the two parties so that their hostilities no longer interfere with the college's business. You haven't really solved their problem, but you have managed to control it for the college's benefit.

Isolating a problem is, on the other hand, a more extreme solution. It is the approach that might be taken if, for instance, you have a tenured faculty member whose utter lack of collegiality is affecting the job satisfaction of valued junior faculty members but whose behavior is still not extreme enough to warrant revoking his or her tenure. If you've tried solving the problem and failed, and then tried managing the problem and failed, one last resort might be to separate the problem from the people who are affected by it—or, at least, to separate the person who is causing the problem from others in the college. For example, the uncollegial faculty member might be "excused" from certain committee work, not as a reward for his or her poor behavior, but simply as a practical response to improve your unit's operation.

See whether you can determine the problem's underlying cause.

If you've concluded that the personnel problem you're addressing can be either solved or managed, your next step is to consider the problem's root causes. Sometimes individuals cause troubles in meetings because they're simply unaware of how others perceive their negativity and abruptness; they believe that they're just telling it like it is and have no idea that their colleagues see them, and not the issues that they bring up, as the real problem. Other employees are excessively focused on their own little area and do not understand how aspects of the college must fit into the larger picture. Some people are overly bound to rules, believing that, if you don't adhere to every policy, chaos will result. Still others have a need for attention or to feel in control of their lives. And other employees find it difficult to let go of past injustices or even perceived injustices, continually dredging up matters that their colleagues have long since ceased to care about or to find relevant to their situations today.

By identifying the underlying causes of the person's difficulty with others, you will develop a much more constructive course of action than if you simply conclude that the person has poor interpersonal skills or is habitually rude. Providing college-wide workshops on constructive ways of working in groups, developing plans, and making suggestions can help set a positive tone for your unit. Individuals who are particularly in need of this advice might even be required to attend the workshops as part of their annual performance reviews. You will then have an opportunity to refer to these workshops' content whenever you need to redirect an inappropriate behavior. "Well, as we've been discussing in our sessions on positive group dynamics," you might say, "how we should really address that concern is . . ." Resources by Lencioni (2002, 2005) can be particularly effective as starting points for your own sessions on how to work together more effectively as a college.

For individuals whose behavioral problems appear to stem from sources other than a lack of knowledge about how to contribute constructively, a different tack will be necessary. You may need to enlist the help of others in your college to ensure that the negative behavior is not being inadvertently reinforced. For example, if certain members of the college always seem to confront a particular faculty member after an outburst (thus increasing the duration of the outburst), you might discuss with those faculty members more effective ways of handling these situations: They can change the focus of the discussion to a different topic, respond in a manner that's less likely to push the other individual's buttons, or simply ignore the situation rather than feeding its intensity. You can even use other department members to redirect negative behavior in a more passive way, by saying such things as, "From the looks that I'm getting, many of you are not interested in addressing this issue yet again. Is that correct? Shall we move on to something else?"

Include a clear action plan with a timeline and expectations when conducting performance reviews.

Attempting to improve problematic behavior through general advice (such as "You need to work on your people skills" or "You have to stop wasting so much time") is rarely productive. Your expectations for the employee's behavior are likely to be quite different from the employee's own understanding of what you are demanding because your advice has been so vague. For this reason, it is important for you to provide—or to cooperate with the employee's direct supervisor in providing—

both an action plan that states your expectations in clear, behavior-specific language and a timeline for when these expectations are to be met. Examples of how to phrase these expectations in a performance review include:

- Effective immediately, you are to be present for work each day when the office opens at 8:00 a.m. and to leave no earlier than when the office closes at 5:00 p.m.

- You are to prepare no fewer than three proposals for external funding by June 13. At least one of these proposals must be submitted to the National Science Foundation, the National Endowment for the Humanities, or the National Endowment for the Arts.

- By the end of the workday on Friday, May 30, you are to have removed from your office computer all items not permitted by the "Policy on Appropriate Use of Electronic Resources," a copy of which is enclosed with this letter.

- During the spring semester you must participate in at least four workshops sponsored by the Center for Effectiveness in Teaching and document how you will improve your quality of instruction based on those sessions.

- Effective immediately, you will not engage in any written or verbal communication whatsoever with Professor Smith.

These expectations should then be followed by the action you will probably take if the required activity does not occur. Among the statements you might include are:

- Failure to do so will result in an official reprimand being placed in your personnel file.

- Failure to do so will result in your forfeiture of any cost-of-living or merit increase for the coming fiscal year.

- Failure to do so will result in your reclassification and reassignment.

- Failure to do so will result in your immediate termination.

When possible, provide the employee with an opportunity to make a more positive contribution to the college.

It is true that challenging employees, in many cases, cannot be "fixed" and that their negative behaviors are too deeply ingrained to be altered. Nevertheless, in other cases the threat of sanctions combined with your redirection of the employee's behavior will produce a significant change in how the employee approaches his or her responsibilities. In these cases it is beneficial to find some appropriate venue for the individual to make a more positive contribution to your college. Colleagues thus begin to see the employee in a different light—no longer the troublemaker or problem, but a constructive and valued member of the community. Even more important, employees who are offered these opportunities often see themselves in a different light and begin the process of carving out a new identity. Heading up the college's effort for a charitable campaign, serving on a committee designed to bring in external speakers, or editing an important document as part of a reaccreditation effort all provide the employee with positive means of working on the college's behalf. These assignments also demonstrate that the employee has not lost your trust and confidence. Now that the problem is solved or at least managed, you are putting aside past differences and working together on a new basis.

Assign the employee a peer mentor.

At times, your very status as dean hinders your ability to mentor an employee effectively. Regardless of how you view your role, the employees themselves may see you as the boss and fear that any discussion they have with you may be detrimental to their future work at the institution. In these cases assigning a trusted colleague of the employee as a peer mentor may be effective in helping redirect inappropriate or undesirable behavior. A peer is able to say things that you simply cannot say (e.g., "I want you to consider for a moment how your behavior is affecting me and others who work with you") and to provide advice in a non-threatening manner. If you offer to respect the confidential discussions the mentor has with the employee, keep your promise. The peer mentor may learn personal details of the employee's life or problems that that person would feel uncomfortable sharing with you. In all respects the peer mentor's role should be formative and constructive, complementing the summative and evaluative role that, as the employee's ultimate supervisor, you will need to take at some time. (On the difference between formative and summative evaluation, see Chapter 30, "Faculty Evaluations.")

Seek ways to reward progress and positive behavior.

Anyone who has served as a supervisor eventually learns that positive reinforcement ("carrots") have more value in the long term than negative reinforcement ("sticks"). Threats of sanction may at first be necessary to get an employee's attention and to underscore the situation's severity. They may also produce an initial dramatic change of behavior. Ultimately, however, it is more effective to support positive behavior than to focus solely on threats. Sincere praise for a job well done, restoring certain privileges that were removed as the result of a sanction, and other means of rewarding the employee's constructive efforts can help make a temporary change permanent.

Not every type of employee problem is, of course, a matter that you can or should handle on your own. For example, in dealing with the very complex challenge of a faculty or staff member who appears to have a substance abuse problem, see the excellent account that appears in Leaming (2007, pp. 352–354). Many institutions have formal processes for counseling referrals and assisting a faculty or staff member who has substance abuse problems, psychological problems, or other disabilities that may be covered under the Americans with Disabilities Act. You will want to take special care and follow your institutional guidelines scrupulously in such situations.

Resources

Cheldelin, S. I., & Lucas, A. F. (2003). *Jossey-Bass academic administrator's guide to conflict resolution.* San Francisco, CA: Jossey-Bass.

Coffman, J. R. (2005). *Work and peace in academe: Leveraging time, money, and intellectual energy through managing conflict.* Bolton, MA: Anker.

Higgerson, M. L., & Joyce, T. A. (2007). *Effective leadership communication: A guide for department chairs and deans for managing difficult situations and people.* Bolton, MA: Anker.

Lieberman, D. J. (2005). *How to change anybody: Proven techniques to reshape anyone's attitude, behavior, feelings, or beliefs.* New York, NY: St. Martin's Press.

Lloyd, K. (1999). *Jerks at work: How to deal with people problems and problem people.* Franklin Lakes, NJ: Career Press.

Masters, M. F., & Albright, R. R. (2002). *The complete guide to conflict resolution in the workplace.* New York, NY: AMACOM.

Scott, G. G. (2004). *A survival guide for working with humans: Dealing with whiners, backstabbers, know-it-alls, and other difficult people.* New York, NY: AMACOM.

Topchik, G. S. (2001). *Managing workplace negativity.* New York, NY: AMACOM.

References

Leaming, D. R. (2007). *Academic leadership: A practical guide to chairing the department* (2nd ed.). Bolton, MA: Anker.

Lencioni, P. (2002). *The five dysfunctions of a team: A leadership fable.* San Francisco, CA: Jossey-Bass.

Lencioni, P. (2005). *Overcoming the five dysfunctions of a team: A field guide for leaders, managers, and facilitators.* San Francisco, CA: Jossey-Bass.

13

Department Chairs

Like the dean's own position, the role played by department chairs can vary considerably from institution to institution. Particularly at small schools, the department chair may simply be a member of the faculty who serves as a clearinghouse for routine administrative matters such as course schedules, textbook requests, and budget requisitions, without having supervisory authority over other members of the department or receiving release time or even a stipend. At more complex institutions, the department chair may be hired from the outside specifically to serve as a chair. In these cases the department chair is frequently seen as a first-level administrator who may not be expected to directly contribute to the department's mission in the areas of teaching or scholarship. In addition to these two scenarios, there are almost endless varieties of department chair responsibilities in between. Nevertheless, whatever the job description at your institution, it is likely that, as dean, you will have significant interaction with department chairs. Good relationships between the dean and chairs can determine whether a deanship succeeds or is fraught with seemingly endless problems. So how can you promote the best possible relationship between your office and your department chairs? How can you help your chairs succeed (thus encouraging them, in turn, to help *you* succeed)?

Provide the appropriate amount of administrative training to new and continuing department chairs.

Chairs frequently rise to their positions because they have demonstrated some level of administrative acumen, have the confidence of faculty members in their departments (at least, at first), and have shown their willingness to balance their scholarly pursuits with the challenges of administration. All too frequently, however, institutions provide little or no specific training for chairs—or for any other kind of administrator, for that matter. Although nearly every university has established a center dedicated to improving instruction and the scholarship of teaching, and although other programs exist to help those wishing to pursue research or service projects, very little is generally available for those who perform administrative tasks. Most chairs' only real financial training occurs when they have been put in charge of a budget. Guidance in resolving complex personnel issues is often given on a case-by-case basis when a problem actually arises. The only instruction offered on how to interview a candidate properly is what the chair may have learned from his or her own experience with other searches. Colleges and universities need to offer better administrative training. As a dean, you are in an excellent position to begin making these improvements.

Of course, the quickest way to begin training for your department chairs is to tie into national or regional programs. The American Council on Education (ACE) has long been a leader in this type of development (see www.acenet.edu for details). In addition to sponsoring programs itself, ACE also provides an extensive resource center of materials and information that deans will find useful in helping train their chairs more effectively. Moreover, several professional organizations offer training seminars or workshops in their disciplines. Discipline-specific administrative training includes the American Mathematical Society's one-day workshop for department chairs (www.ams.org), the American Association of Physics Teachers' Department Chairs Conference (www.aapt.org), and the Technical Symposium on Computer Science Education's Workshop for Department Chairs (www.cs.rit.edu).

To complement these external resources—or if you prefer a more highly focused program for department chairs that addresses your own institutional needs—you might consider offering a series of administrative training workshops that you develop yourself. Many outstanding models for such a program already exist. Yen (2007) discusses an innovative leadership workshop series developed by the University of Washington's ADVANCE Center for Institutional Change and offers guidance to department chairs on such issues as:

- Dual-career hires

- Faculty development opportunities

- Dealing with difficult people

- Offering feedback and delivering bad news

- Family leave and tenure-clock extensions

- Nominating faculty members for awards and recognition

- Building consensus among faculty

- Making job offers

Other topics that department chairs are likely to find useful in a training program include:

- Planning and implementing budgets

- Communicating effectively

- The chair's role in assessment

- Legal issues

- Departmental outreach

- Responding to an emergency or campus crisis

- Strategic and tactical planning

- Developing departmental mission and vision statements

Rather than simply lecturing in the workshops, try to include pedagogically effective techniques such as role-playing, case studies, what-ifs, and scenario analysis. Just as students tend to benefit more from active and interactive methods than from passive learning, so will participants in your administrative development series. By offering practical hands-on experience for your chairs, you'll help them better see the principles you are outlining and their day-to-day professional activities.

One way of structuring your own series for department chairs is to organize it around one of the many books or articles that deal with the responsibilities of academic administrators. Such works as Barron (2003); Bennett and Figuli (1990); Buller (2006a, 2006b); Chu (2006); and Hecht, Higgerson, Gmelch, and Tucker (1999) will provide you with all the topics and discussion points you need for your own set of workshops. Alternatively, you might begin with your institution's job description for department chairs and build a series that addresses each of the primary responsibilities contained in that document. Of course, if your institution does not already have a clear job description for department chairs, you should take this opportunity to work with your fellow deans to create such a document.

In addition to your regular meetings with department chairs, include a few sessions that are devoted to exploring specific topics in depth.

Although you will want to have regular meetings with your department chairs in which you discuss all the items that need to be considered for your college to operate efficiently, you may also want to consider holding focused meetings or mini-retreats once or twice a term. These focused meetings allow you to take a single topic and explore it in greater depth than you would have the luxury to pursue in a normal meeting. Focused sessions might be devoted to legal issues and the changes in higher education law that are relevant to department chairs. In another meeting you might explore assessment with your chairs, allowing them to learn from one another about innovative techniques for assessing the attainment of learning outcomes and to provide you with an informal progress report so that you know the college's assessment efforts are well under way. Another meeting might be devoted to enrollment trends, where you explore likely student demographics for the future, how these enrollment patterns may affect each of your disciplines, and specific courses with histories of over- or underenrollment. Another session might be devoted to the university budget accompanied by a presentation by a financial officer from your unit or from the institution. The presentation can focus on the big picture itself or on your unit's specific contribution to it. Each college will have its own unique needs for focused meetings, but you will find occasional sessions of this sort far more productive than a customary meeting devoted to miscellaneous items.

Use full retreats wisely—and sparingly.

As we have seen, focused department chair meetings can almost serve as mini-retreats in which you explore specific issues for an extended period of time. As an added advantage, these focused sessions decrease the need for full-day or multiday retreats that, while extremely valuable on occasion, are all too frequently ill conceived, unnecessary, overused, and resented. Many deans schedule retreats for department chairs (sometimes extending the event to the entire faculty) annually, even when there is no compelling reason for carving a day or two out of everyone's busy schedule. The assumption is that the retreat will foster team building, provide an opportunity to accomplish a good deal of concentrated work, and reward participants for their past efforts by offering them meals and, in most cases, a chance to work in an attractive setting off campus. The problem is that even the most luxurious of retreats rapidly lose their effectiveness when they are overused. Without a solid reason for taking people away from their regular schedules, department chairs begin resenting the time devoted to the retreat that could have been spent in other (and, in their minds, more productive) pursuits. Moreover, in all too many cases, retreats are scheduled at awkward times, such as just before courses begin in the fall or between terms, when the workload for chairs can be particularly heavy. Because the dean is the person who has mandated the retreat and because chairs report to the dean, they may not feel comfortable expressing their feelings that the time and money spent on this activity could have been better directed elsewhere, but they often feel that way all the same.

These problems do not mean that you should *never* conduct a retreat with your chairs, merely that you need to be certain that it is the best possible way of fulfilling a task. You will need a substantive agenda, and planning for the coming year is rarely a sufficient reason for scheduling a retreat. When a new strategic plan is being prepared, an institutional accreditation review is about to get under way, or a capital campaign is about to be launched, you will probably have sufficient business for a full retreat (see Liteman, Campbell, & Liteman, 2006). Nevertheless, if you find yourself scheduling retreats every year or have difficulty filling all the time that you have set aside, you may need to reconsider whether formal retreats are the best possible means of achieving the goals you have for your chairs.

Develop your department chairs to serve as an internal advisory council.

It is important for you as dean to have a well-rounded view of how your college is perceived, what its needs are, and what its future potential may be. Different constituents are likely to see these issues in different ways. As we saw in Chapter 9 ("Students"), including broad representation on cross-functional teams can be extremely valuable in helping you make wise decisions and attain the student body's support. As we shall see in Chapter 17 ("Friends of the College"), an external advisory council, if properly organized, can help promote your college in the community, alleviate town-gown conflicts, and move you more easily from "friend-raising" to fundraising. It is also important, however, for you to have an internal advisory council, and your committee of chairs could easily fill this need.

An internal advisory council can be valuable as a sounding board for new initiatives and can help you avoid policy decisions that are either poorly conceived or difficult to implement. Nevertheless, many department chairs are not used to functioning as advisory bodies. Because chairs report to you, they may be reluctant to offer you their candid recommendations, the very sort of advice you need the most. At the opposite extreme, some groups of chairs, when canvassed for their opinions, may immediately assume that they are now the decision-making body for all the college's policy matters, posing objections when they have not approved or been consulted on matters that you do not regard as being within their purview.

For your committee of chairs to function as a true advisory council, you'll need to mentor them in how such bodies should function. One of the key principles that you should keep in mind with any advisory group is:

> *Never ask an advisory body for advice unless you truly wish to be advised.*

In other words, an advisory council should never be abused. Don't try to get the group to feed you a recommendation for a plan or policy that you've already decided to adopt. At best, the members will sense that they have been duped and become increasingly cynical about their role. At worst, they may become adamant about a plan or policy that is quite different from the one that you prefer, and your task in advancing your own ideas will be more difficult. If you already know what you're going to do, simply announce your decision, defend it, and try to enlist your council's support. In matters where you truly need advice, however, your chairs can be invaluable. They bring to the table a great deal of experience. They understand how certain decisions will go over with their students, faculty, and staff members. They can help you evaluate decisions from a different perspective.

Explain to your council members that their task is to give you their best professional judgments on matters that you bring to their attention. Although the decision about whether to implement the advice will always remain yours, you are committed to listening to their advice. If you decide to pursue a different path, you will keep them apprised of your decision, explain the reasons that led you to this choice, and value them all the more because they helped you see a different point of view. Explain the difference between the bodies to whom you have delegated various decision-making responsibilities (such as a curriculum committee, which may or may not be the same as your committee of chairs) and those to which you turn for advice. Discuss the difference between talking a matter through and talking it to death: Although you want to allow enough time to consider all the different perspectives on an issue, there will come a time when it is appropriate to move on and to refrain from constantly reconsidering past issues.

Department chairs are among the most important constituents you have in performing your job effectively. It is essential for deans to develop chairs properly, discuss issues with them candidly, and respect their expertise appropriately. If you were once a chair yourself, always keep in mind the special demands of the position. Don't try to continue chairing your own academic discipline—that's no longer your job—but provide the sort of mentoring, guidance, and support that chairs need to fulfill this critical administrative role.

Resources

Dean X. (2006, Fall). Working with an academic affairs council. *The Department Chair, 17*(2), 9–11, 13.

Higgerson, M. L. (1996). *Communication skills for department chairs.* Bolton, MA: Anker.

Lucas, A. F., & Associates. (2000). *Leading academic change: Essential roles for department chairs.* San Francisco, CA: Jossey-Bass.

McDaniel, T. R. (2002). Dean-department chair relationships. In T. R. McDaniel, *Dean's dialogue* (pp. 25–26). Madison, WI: Magna.

Seagren, A. T., Cresswell, J. W., & Wheeler, D. W. (1993). *The department chair: New roles, responsibilities and challenges* (ASHE-ERIC Higher Education Report Vol. 22, No. 1). Washington, DC: The George Washington University, Graduate School of Education and Human Development.

Walvoord, B. E., Carey, A. K., Smith, H. L., Soled, S. W., Way, P. K., & Zorn, D. (2000). *Academic departments: How they work, how they change.* San Francisco, CA: Jossey-Bass.

References

Barron, D. (2003, September 26). Learning to be a department head. *The Chronicle of Higher Education,* p. C5.

Bennett, J. B., & Figuli, D. J. (1990). *Enhancing departmental leadership: The roles of the chairperson.* New York, NY: American Council on Education/Macmillan.

Buller, J. L. (2006a, Spring). Advice for future department chairs. *The Department Chair, 16*(4), 1–3.

Buller, J. L. (2006b). *The essential department chair: A practical guide to college administration.* Bolton, MA: Anker.

Chu, D. (2006). *The department chair primer: Leading and managing academic departments.* Bolton, MA: Anker.

Hecht, I. W. D., Higgerson, M. L., Gmelch, W. H., & Tucker, A. (1999). *The department chair as academic leader.* Phoenix, AZ: American Council on Education/Oryx Press.

Liteman, M., Campbell, S., & Liteman, J. (2006). *Retreats that work: Everything you need to know about planning and leading great offsites* (Expanded ed.). San Francisco, CA: Pfeiffer.

Yen, J. W. (2007, Winter). Proactive leadership development for department chairs and emerging faculty leaders. *The Department Chair, 17*(3), 12–14, 16.

14

Staff

Deans' offices have staffs that vary from the extremely large and complex to the virtually nonexistent. The latter scenario is not an exaggeration. In a very small college, the dean may be assigned, at best, only a secretary or administrative assistant to help with the routine details of day-to-day business. This situation contrasts sharply to what can occur in a large university where the dean may be aided by multiple assistant and associate deans, communication officers, budget officers, directors (dealing with a broad range of administrative functions, including advising, faculty development, research, alumni relations, etc.), web masters, event planners, and possibly other administrators as well. Despite these differences, deans face challenges in managing any staff, regardless of size. For instance, the most important factor in making sure that your staff functions effectively is determining that all the essential duties of your office are appropriately covered and that you've balanced your need for various skills and ways of approaching situations. The dean's office, when it is functioning smoothly, should operate as an efficient system: Every member of the system should maintain his or her own unique individuality and area of specialty, but together, the office should function as a supportive team, complementing one another's deficiencies and recognizing one another's strengths.

As a way of determining how well your own office has progressed toward achieving this ideal, spend some time examining your staff from the following perspectives. If you already have a staff fully in place, this exercise will help you determine where additional training, reassignments of responsibilities, or (in the most extreme of situations) replacement of individual staff members may be necessary. If you have one or more staff openings, this exercise will help you develop a clearer picture of the person or persons to seek in the hiring or appointment process.

Make a list of all the critical activities that your office must perform.

Take a blank sheet of paper, and on the left side, identify all the functions, duties, and responsibilities that are associated with your office. Be as comprehensive as you can, even if your final product requires several more sheets of paper. As you conduct this exercise, ask yourself the following questions:

- Is your office responsible for overseeing student advising?

- Docs it propose and allocate budgets?

- Does it interact with parents?

- Does someone in your office sign off on curricular proposals?

- Are hiring decisions made at this level? (If so, don't forget about all stages of the search process that someone in your office may supervise: requesting positions, approving job descriptions, placing advertisements, collecting dossiers, screening candidates, scheduling interviews, selecting a finalist, making an offer, notifying unsuccessful applicants, processing paperwork for the new employee, and so on.)

- Does your office run a faculty development program?

- Do you approve travel requests?

- Do you evaluate faculty members or other employees, such as department chairs?

- What role does your office play in the promotion and tenure process?

- If faculty members have complaints or concerns, are they likely to come to your office?

- Are salary increases established there?

- Is your office involved in termination decisions or contract nonrenewals?

- Do you have to deal with the media, plan events, or finalize publications?

As you create your list of responsibilities, don't overlook seemingly minor functions of your staff. Does your office have visitors that need to be greeted? Does it receive phone calls? Does it file documents? Does it shred confidential materials? Does it prepare items for the mail or for routing to other campus offices? What are the other critical functions that someone in your office needs to do?

Once you've established a comprehensive list of the functions, duties, and responsibilities that involve your office, on the right side of the paper list by name and title all your staff members. Then draw a line from each item on the left side of the page to one or more of the names on the right side. Don't draw a line to yourself if you have ultimate responsibility for a particular duty but do not actively engage in it. Do, however, draw multiple lines if several staff members are all actively involved in one of the responsibilities you have indicated. Continue through the list until you have connected each duty with at least one staff member. If you find that you have an area of responsibility that does not clearly fall to one or more staff members, then that is a first red flag. Either you have an unmet staffing need (which means that you will require additional employees to meet your office's basic responsibilities), or you have not placed anyone clearly in charge of that important responsibility. The latter situation should be a cause for concern. After all, one of the most important essential principles that every dean eventually learns is:

> *A responsibility that no one owns is a responsibility that*
> *no one is likely to perform.*

After you have matched all your office's areas of responsibility to different staff members (noting any area of responsibility that does not appear to belong to anyone), your next step will be to examine your diagram from another perspective. Are there any responsibilities that are connected to *too many* staff members? In other words, are there duties that are so spread out among the individuals in your office that it's unclear which staff member feels responsible for that function when a need arises? Certainly, it is a valuable thing to cross-train staff members in different duties. For example, if only one individual has been trained in how to advise students, there can be a real problem when someone suddenly needs a time-sensitive approval to override an enrollment limit. Should the only advisor in your office be out sick or on vacation, the student either will not be served or will be poorly served. Nevertheless, you will also have a problem if no one in your office can identify the logical first point of contact for students with advising problems. In fact, for certain areas of responsibility, having too many people in charge is nearly as bad as having no one in charge. So review your duty assignments to determine whether there is clearly one person who is known by everyone in your office to head up that task.

Finally, look at your list of responsibilities and staff members to ensure that it makes sense. Could the duties be better reallocated so that one individual handles most issues that deal with students, another those that tend to involve faculty members? Are responsibilities inefficiently broken up so that one person initiates a process but then must interrupt someone else for a routine signature or approval? Are functions assigned in such a way that people who come to your office tend to get the runaround, going to one person for this, another person for that, and a third person (who will end up being at lunch or in a meeting) for yet another aspect of their request? Look at your office's duties and the staff members assigned to them to make sure that the workload is equitable and that you can clearly explain each person's primary assignment in a few words. If you find that you cannot introduce a staff member in an easily comprehensible manner (such as "Our associate dean primarily deals with faculty matters, everything from setting up searches and promotion and tenure to requests for emeritus status"), then you probably do not have a sufficiently clear set of duties assigned to each individual.

Make a list of all the skills that your office needs.

In addition to your office's areas of responsibility, you will also need to outline the various types of training that people need to perform those duties. Prepare this list in the same way that you did the last one: Outline on the left side of a piece of paper the various types of skills that your office needs, and then record the staff members by name and position down the right side. Among the various skill sets that you should consider are those related to:

- *Technology:* What level of technological skill must some staff member have? Your answer to this question will differ depending on your institution and the way in which your unit is configured. In some offices it is important for a dean's staff member to be fairly sophisticated in knowing how to analyze and repair networking problems, getting new hardware up and running, and being able to interact at an advanced technical level with members of the IT staff. For other deans, that high level of technical skill need only be found in an institution-wide computer center; all that someone in the dean's office must know is a few specific software applications. In other words, first you should try to determine the level of technological expertise that your office needs and then write out as specifically as possible the individual technological skills and programs that someone on your staff needs to master. Don't forget that, aside from directly computer-related applications, there may be certain features of distance learning, information retrieval, audio-visual resources (including web sites, podcasts, and presentation software), and other aspects of technology in the broad sense that must be addressed at your level.

- *Mastery of details:* Deans' offices tend to be inundated with details. Contracts must be issued accurately. Deadlines must be kept. Information that is shared with the public must be free of grammatical and typographic errors. Documents must be easily understood. Names must be remembered.

As you think of the various tasks for which your office is responsible, try to determine in which areas accuracy is most crucial. Alternatively, consider where the biggest problems or greatest embarrassment would occur if your office failed to keep track of all the details. By asking the question in this way, you will start to identify the type of skills you need to keep your college operating efficiently.

- *Budgeting:* All deans' offices tend to be involved with budgeting on some level. In smaller or less complex colleges, the skills needed for effective budgeting may require little more than basic bookkeeping or maintaining a spreadsheet. More complex units may require a much more highly developed knowledge of accounting practice. Try to determine the individual budgeting skills that your office requires to do its work. What are the skills that you rely on when making a budget proposal for future years, defending that proposal, implementing higher administration's budget decisions, dealing with cutbacks, and planning for new programs, positions, or facilities?

- *Project flow:* Consider the various events and projects that your office oversees. What are the skills needed to ensure that those initiatives proceed in a timely fashion? Do you need someone with actual experience in event planning, or is knowledge of your institution's calendar system sufficient for your purposes? What systems do you have in place—or what systems *should* you have in place—to ensure that critical deadlines are kept and that adequate preparation goes into reports and proposals before they are due? Keep in mind not only lecture series and other major events that may be unique to your college but also annual processes at your institution, such as promotion and tenure considerations, contract issuance, budget proposals, performance reviews, and other responsibilities that must be completed in a timely manner. What are the skills that you need to make sure no deadline is missed?

- *Vision:* The type of vision your college requires will be different from that of other units. At some institutions a college will need to reinvent itself completely, to develop bold new strategies that take it into a wholly different direction from that previously pursued (see Chapter 4, "Creating a Vision for the College," and Chapter 5, "Building a Shared Vision for the College"). Other units may need little more in the way of vision than continually improving the curriculum, identifying innovative sources of funding to maintain established excellence, and reinterpreting the college's ongoing mission as student needs change. Review candidly the types of visions that best suit your own college, and then see whether you can determine the precise skills required to pursue that vision. Are you in need of someone who can think about your mission in radically new ways, an entrepreneur who can address unmet needs in your region, a problem solver who can find practical new solutions to your college's vexing problems, or someone with more fundamental skills?

- *Serving as an effective liaison with other units:* What sort of interactions does your office have with other offices on campus? What sort of requests must be submitted for review elsewhere? What sort of information needs to be retrieved from outside your unit? Do you have cooperative programs with other colleges? Do you supply seats to other units or receive seats from other units in classes that function as service courses? Do you share faculty members with other units or offer released time to faculty members to teach outside your unit (perhaps in an honors program, graduate school, or institution-wide core curriculum)? Once you have outlined all the ways in which you may interact with offices outside your own, consider the skill sets those interactions require. Is it simply a matter of completing some paperwork, or does it require the ability to negotiate and the authority to make a decision? Is some degree of institutional memory necessary because of problems that were encountered in the past or procedures that have not been written down? Does your institution operate on the basis of "it's not what you know; it's whom you know," with the result that being well connected is an important skill set?

As you did earlier, connect each item on the left side of your list with the names and positions that appear on the right side. In this exercise, however, you will analyze the results differently. It is relatively unimportant if you discover in this exercise that many people share the same skill set. For instance, if three or more of your staff members are all excellent proofreaders, have advanced training in preparing spreadsheets, and are very effective in serving as liaisons to other colleges, you really don't have a problem. What you're looking for are skill sets that you need but are completely missing from your current staff or that do not run very deep. (Perhaps the only staff member with any institutional memory is due to retire within two years.) Items on the left side of the list that are not connected to anyone indicate that additional training or cross-training may be needed. If many items fall into that category, you may have a far deeper problem: You do not have the right people in the right jobs, have not adequately met your staff's needs for training, or are severely understaffed at some level. In any of these cases, review the skills that are missing and ask yourself, "Which positions on my staff *should* have these skills?" You may answer with a position (e.g., a dedicated budget analyst or event planner) or type of training that you do not yet have.

Be particularly careful when you are attributing the skills related to vision to your staff's various members. As deans, we frequently expect developing an overall vision to be our job, and so we are reluctant to recognize these skills in anyone else. Remember, however, that your goal in this exercise is not to present an image of how you would *like* to be perceived but rather to evaluate candidly what your actual needs are. It may well be that another staff member is more effective than you are in generating new ideas, seeing alternative ways of solving problems, and identifying innovative funding sources. If this is the case, be certain to reflect that fact as you perform this exercise. After all, if that staff member should resign, the skills you lose will be an important consideration as you search to assemble an effective administrative team.

Make a list of all the personality types that would best serve your office.

Just as there are responsibilities and skills that should be found in every dean's staff, so are there various personality types. As we search for future staff members, we tend to be attracted to people whose personality is in some ways similar to our own, but too much uniformity can hinder the smooth operation of an office. If every staff member is overly serious, for example, the dean's staff will begin to be perceived as a group of people with whom others may *need* to work but with whom they probably don't *want* to work. At the other extreme, if every member of the dean's staff is a jokester, the office may end up being dismissed as superficial, incapable of dealing earnestly with important matters, or simply annoying. So, in a third iteration of your matching exercise, try to determine who among your staff fills the various personality types that most offices need, asking yourself these questions:

- Who is your wise counselor, the person to whom others go when they have a problem?

- Who is your inspirational speaker, the person who can get others excited about what they're doing even when they're feeling down?

- Who is the consistently thoughtful person, the staff member who keeps track of birthdays or takes the lead in planning social events for your office?

- Who is the office nudge, the perfectionist who keeps bringing up even minor flaws in a project or a document until everything is just right?

- Who is absolutely objective, the person who can look at an idea and determine not just whether it's good for us but whether it's just plain good, will work, and is important?

- Who is the office advocate, the person who will stick up for the underdog and make sure that no one's rights are violated?

As you consider these and other personality types, look for patterns that are overrepresented in your staff or an attitude that is missing entirely. If there have been instances where your unit's effectiveness has diminished not because people lacked skill but because they lacked that particular personal attribute, reconsider how you interview candidates for staff positions in the future. Are you asking the sort of questions and creating the sort of situations that allow candidates to tell you what you really need to know?

As you reflect on your work with your staff, keep in mind these important principles:

- Staff members of a dean's office frequently have maximum responsibility with minimum authority. They are asked to get things done and to get people involved with important tasks, but they rarely have the needed supervisory authority. As a result, staff members can cajole, charm, barter, and wheedle others, but they can rarely order others to do anything. You can help your staff members by providing them the gravitas that is derived from your own position, intervening on their behalf if required, and understanding that their approach may at times need to be less direct than your own.

- Few members of a dean's staff have academic degrees directly related to their job responsibilities. If your institution does not provide adequate in-house training for administrators, work with your staff members to find conferences, seminars, and workshops that can expose them to best practices in academic administration and keep them informed about issues directly related to their roles in your office.

- Few young people look themselves in the mirror and say, "When I grow up, I want to be an assistant dean." Except for clerical help and certain budgetary offices, most members of the dean's staff see their position as a stepping-stone to doing something else. Do not resent them for thinking this way. (Perhaps you were a member of a dean's staff once yourself.) Rather, understand that a certain amount of turnover in your staff is desirable: Every resignation is an opportunity for you to balance your team according to your shifting needs for different areas of responsibility, additional skill sets, and the appropriate mix of personality types. You will be more helpful to your staff and receive better support from them as a result if you actively assist them in meeting their career objectives than if you appear to begrudge them their dreams.

Resources

Bright, D. F., & Richards, M. P. (2001). *The academic deanship: Individual careers and institutional roles.* San Francisco, CA: Jossey-Bass.

Krahenbuhl, G. S. (2004). *Building the academic deanship: Strategies for success.* Westport, CT: Praeger.

15

Other Deans

Unless you're the sole academic dean at a small institution, one of the most complex, challenging, and potentially rewarding constituencies you will have is your fellow deans. Your relationship with the other deans at your school may vary according to your institution, the personalities of the individuals involved, and your own past history with these administrators. At some universities fellow deans view one another largely as competitors; the budget, they think, is a zero-sum game, and so any gain in one area must mean that someone else has lost. There is perennial conflict over how "important" one college is relative to another, and the deans continually jockey for position with the provost and president. At other universities interactions are far more collegial, and the deans see one another as members of the same administrative team, working on behalf of the university as a whole. And, of course, the possibilities along this spectrum of friendly to hostile relationships between deans are infinite. But how *should* you interact with the other deans at your institution? And if the relationship you have with them is already strained, how might it be improved?

It is natural for deans to view each other as competitors for certain resources. New facilities are relatively rare commodities. If one college is granted priority in a major building project, it may be years before other deans' new facilities will ever be approved. Similarly, faculty lines are limited resources, and every new position that is granted to one college may mean one fewer faculty member who could be teaching and doing research in another. Seats in courses are in limited supply, and another dean who is stingy about providing you with space in a desperately needed service course can be a real detriment to your program's success. Nevertheless, your fellow deans face many of the same problems that you encounter year after year. Policies and initiatives developed by the upper administration can either ease or complicate other deans' work in precisely the same way that they help or hinder you. In other words, few other people at your university can truly understand the complexity of the issues you are called on to address and feel your pain when budgets are tight, enrollment is down, or faculty members seem to be particularly annoyed (or annoying).

Because of the interests that you share with other deans, the following are some general guidelines to follow in establishing or maintaining excellent relationships with them.

Propose occasional meetings in which the deans get together by themselves.

It's not uncommon for institutions to have a deans council or some similar body. In the majority of cases, however, these bodies meet under the supervision of the provost or with some other representatives of higher administration. The result is that those who attend these meetings sometimes feel pressure, consciously or unconsciously, to affirm their status, to show off for their superiors, or to establish their prominence for subordinates. One way to create a better working relationship with your fellow deans may be to propose periodic meetings in which *only* the deans gather to discuss items of current concern, to inform one another of issues that may involve students and faculty members in other colleges, and to get to know one another better in a more relaxed, less formal setting. Meetings such as these can give you an opportunity to discuss each college's different missions and approaches in a constructive, nonthreatening manner. For instance, if one of the other deans has intimated that the enrollment caps in your courses have prevented students in his or her programs from getting the courses that they need, you can explore this issue together without concern that either of you may simply be playing to the provost or your subordinates. You yourself can explain the reason for the enrollment caps. Perhaps there are only a certain number of lab stations available or the amount of writing required in the course restricts the number of students that each instructor may effectively teach. In a more informal setting, you can explore such possibilities as reserving a certain number of seats in a course for students from outside your college, joining forces with the other college in making a united budget request for additional faculty lines in this area or for renovations to your facilities, or modifying course requirements that may ease the current registration bottlenecks.

Other problems that result from not fully understanding one another's needs may also be addressed in these informal meetings. You can explore why your college's workload may be different from that of other units, why more stringent entrance requirements are effective or undesirable in certain programs, and why certain disciplines may require a student-to-faculty ratio that is not typical of the institution as a whole. Most important, however, by meeting with your fellow deans as colleagues rather than as competitors, you establish a new working relationship with them that can carry over into your other meetings. You'll have an opportunity to ask questions that will minimize the likelihood of being blindsided by the individual who has previously taken delight in discussing, in a very public setting, the one disastrous registration problem in your area that involved his or her student. Indeed, in many cases, your fellow deans may be more reluctant to embarrass you publicly with such bad news because of the improved relationship.

Explore issues that you and your fellow deans have in common.

Either in these informal meetings or in individual conversations, it can be extremely useful for you to explore areas of common interest or shared opportunities. Searching for common ground helps improve your relationships, sends a positive message to the upper administration, makes better use of scarce resources, and may lead to innovative programs that will help you better serve your students. Some of the issues that you will have in common with your fellow deans include:

- *Faculty and administrative development:* Particularly if your college is not large, it may be extremely difficult for you to offer all the faculty development opportunities that you may like. This challenge is even greater when you are trying to provide administrative development; for instance, it is difficult to justify an entire series of sessions for new department chairs when you have only a handful of new chairs each year. Partnering with another dean in these efforts creates good ties between your colleges and helps ensure that your workshops and discussions will draw the critical mass of participants that they need.

- *Externally funded grants:* Foundations and government agencies like to see partnerships between administrative units when they consider grant applications. Such collaboration demonstrates that the need for the grant transcends the interest of a single department or college. They also realize that any funding they provide will have a larger effect at your institution and will be more likely to result in a program that continues once the initial grant has been expended. Working cooperatively with another dean thus demonstrates, to the funding agency as well as to your internal constituents, that you are open to making connections between disciplines, free from the silo mentality that causes people to view things only from their perspective, and a good team player when it comes to sharing responsibility and credit.

- *Internally funded grants:* If you have access to your own internal funds for research, scholarship, or creative activities, you may want to explore with a fellow dean the possibility of pooling resources and offering grants to faculty members who collaborate on projects. With such funds, you may be able to support proposals that have a much larger impact than those you were able to support using only your own resources. For instance, a college of arts and sciences could offer a joint grant with the college of education for faculty members interested in developing innovative ways of incorporating access to primary sources of information into elementary or secondary school education. A college of engineering and a college of science could offer grants for projects that extend the university's efforts in the area of biotechnology. Your grants' individual focus will depend on the nature of your college and the history of your institution, but they can help bring about new partnerships between faculty members that may not have occurred without the collaboration that began with your telephone call to a fellow dean.

• *Special events:* Every college has several lectures, exhibits, recitals, concerts, or other events that are open to the public. All too often, the people who attend these events are the usual suspects, the obvious individuals who have a particular interest in the specific topic. We would all like our events to be more widely attended, particularly by individuals from outside our own colleges. One way to achieve this goal is to issue personal invitations to other deans, making it clear that they are being individually invited to attend the event. A handwritten note, a phone call, or an office visit is far more effective that a general flier or a mass email. Face-to-face, you can explain why you think that that particular person would enjoy or be enriched by the event. Be sure, of course, to reciprocate. Go out of your way to attend events sponsored by other colleges, too. This practice can help immeasurably with improving the relationship between colleges.

In situations where there is a serious or chronic impasse with a fellow dean, have a private, closed-door meeting as a way of clearing the air and seeking a new beginning.

If, after all your efforts to reach out and build constructive relationships with another dean prove to be ineffective, it might be time for a candid heart-to-heart talk with the individual involved in an impasse. Offer to meet for lunch or at an off-campus location. A conversation of this type is best not held in either dean's office, which is one person's turf and where the other person is an outsider. Begin the discussion candidly by saying something like, "I keep noticing that there's a sense of antagonism or competition between us that I think is hindering our ability to work together. Have you noticed that, too? Why do you think that perception may exist?" After raising this question, be sure actually to listen to and consider the answer that you're given. Don't be defensive. Don't try to explain or justify your actions immediately. Through this conversation, you want to get the other dean's perspective. Perhaps there's some policy in your college that has been detrimental to the success of the other dean's programs. Perhaps you have been acting inadvertently as though you have little respect for the other college, its students, or its programs. Perhaps there is a matter of history that predates your arrival at the institution. Give the other dean plenty of time to discuss the issues that seem to him or her to be at the root of the problem.

Once you know what the basic issue is, explore ways of solving it. Ask the other dean, "What would you like to see happen?" You don't necessarily have to agree to that particular course of action—it may not even be within your power to do so—but at least you will better appreciate the other college's position. In certain cases you may be surprised to find that the solution requested by the other dean is so minor that it seems incredible there has been friction over something so small. In other cases you will find that there really are philosophical differences between the two colleges that simply cannot be bridged and that the best you can do is agree to disagree. Most frequently of all, however, you will need to explore some compromise that will help the other dean address the problem that he or she is facing without undue detriment to your own programs. Whatever you learn in this conversation, be sure to follow the three principles of diplomacy outlined in McDaniel (2002):

- *Identify real interests and needs.* Sometimes people talk about surface issues and conflicts for rhetorical purposes rather than because they actually believe what they are saying. Do you or the other dean fall into this trap?

- *Develop patience.* "Patient deans do not force unwise, ephemeral solutions but do nurture the processes of dialogue, debate, and decision-making" (p. 34).

- *Be flexible.* Remain true to your actual needs and core values, but remember that there may be more than one way to achieve your goals.

By following these simple principles of diplomacy, you may well find yourself asking the other dean at the end of the conversation, "Why did we wait so long to discuss this?"

Too frequently, colleges and their deans operate independently, losing sight of the common cause they share with other units at their institution. If communication between deans has not already begun at your institution, you may be the very person who is in the best position to help change that unhealthy situation.

References

McDaniel, T. R. (2002). The art of diplomacy. In T. R. McDaniel, *Dean's dialogue* (pp. 33–35). Madison, WI: Magna.

16

Upper Administrators

The relationship that deans have with the upper administration is likely to depend on the institution's traditions, the way in which the administrative hierarchy is structured, and most important, the personalities of the upper administrators themselves. Just as deans come in all varieties and with many different types of management philosophies, so do the individuals to whom they report. Some presidents and provosts are micromanagers: They want to know about every detail of your college, express their opinions about every decision, and control the way in which your college functions, even on the most insignificant and routine level. Other members of the upper administration fall to the other extreme. They may appear to be overly laissez-faire, focusing on the governing board and fundraising, not on your day-to-day activities. This second type of administrator may seem uninterested in hearing about even severe problems in your unit; as long as there are few complaints, such administrators may give you absolute freedom in how you do your job. The contact you have with your upper administration may also be quite different from your peers at other institutions. You may meet with your supervisor regularly (weekly and, in some cases, daily meetings are not uncommon) or only on an as-needed basis. If you are new to your position or if the upper administration is new, it may take some time for you to develop a working relationship that suits both parties' needs. As you strive to build an optimal working relationship with your upper administration, here are a few guidelines that you may wish to consider.

Keep upper administrators in the loop to the extent that *they* believe is necessary, even if that would not be your own preference were the positions reversed.

No one likes to be blindsided, just as no one likes to feel as though they're drowning in a sea of useless information. Where are you along this spectrum of how much you must know and what you're comfortable letting others handle? Where are each of your reports on the same spectrum? It is probably better to begin by providing too much information rather than too little; you can always scale back the amount of detail that your president or provost thinks is necessary. You'll know—and if you don't, you can always ask—if you report too much. As you consider what to share with the upper administration, be sure to include not only updates on situations that are already in progress but also advance notice of issues or complaints that may become important in the future. This approach is important both because it helps prevent your supervisor from being caught off guard in a situation about which you could easily have provided some assistance and because it offers the upper administration a more complete understanding of an issue's context. Like any of us, presidents and provosts may misunderstand a problem's genuine complexity when they hear only one side of it, particularly if it's a matter that has been dropped on them in a public meeting or as they walk down the hallway. Not realizing that there are multiple dimensions to the problem, they may commit to pursue a specific course of action—perhaps they are just *perceived* as committing to a course of action—that they would not have chosen had they been previously informed of the other sides of the story.

At the same time that you want upper administrators to be fully informed about important developments and challenges in your area, you do not want them to feel overburdened by too much information. As we have seen, every administrator's tolerance for detail is different, and as your upper administration changes, you may find that what one president considers a comfortable level of information is considered excessive reporting by another president. By providing upper administrators with more explanation than they may want or find useful, you could be perceived as someone who is in over your head, unable to make appropriate decisions without constant checking and rechecking. Particularly if you are, or your supervisor is, new to the position, you may need to ask candidly, "Is this the level of detail that you'd like in my reports? Am I giving you all the information that you need? Would you rather just know what's going on in broad strokes?" Don't be surprised or offended if you are told that you have been under- or overreporting what is going on in your area. As a good middle manager, you should be able to respect and adapt to your supervisor's needs.

Develop the three Cs of interacting with the upper administration.

You will have more effective interactions with your president and provost if you develop a relationship with them in which each of you feels comfortable speaking *candidly, collegially,* and *confidentially:*

- *Candor:* Just as much as you rely on the upper administration for support, advice, and timely information, so do these administrators rely on you for your unique perspective and sound advice. If they are about to embark on a new direction that you believe is ill advised or likely to be poorly received by one or more of your constituencies, it is your obligation to point out these potential problems. A dean who functions simply as the upper administration's yes-man may find that meetings with the president and provost are quite pleasant in the short term, but he or she ultimately does a disservice to the institution and fails to perform an essential duty of the job. It is your professional obligation to give your best possible advice to your upper administration, regardless of whether this means supporting a decision (if it is the best plan even though it may not be popular in your unit) or offering an alternative perspective. Your role is to be neither the perpetual gadfly nor the administration's toady, but rather a sage counselor who provides your supervisors with the information and insight they need to do *their* jobs effectively.

- *Collegiality:* Disagreement in a professional setting rarely, if ever, needs to be made in an unpleasant or threatening manner. Collegial disagreement means pointing out to your supervisors why your perspective on a matter differs from theirs (perhaps a policy that will be seen in one light by the governing board will be viewed quite differently by your college's faculty or students, or a new initiative will have repercussions that are more immediately noticeable at your level than elsewhere) and exploring with them alternative approaches. You would expect a faculty member or department chair who disagrees with one of your decisions to focus on the issue itself and not attack you as a person, and you should adopt this method of handling differences in your own interactions at the university level. You want to make it clear that it is the initiative, policy change, or direction with which you disagree strongly, not the administrators themselves, who may well have approached this issue with great thought and care.

- *Confidentiality:* Discussing matters candidly and collegially behind closed doors with a supervisor is not the same thing as concealing important information from your faculty, acting deceptively, or operating in an underhanded manner. Rather, it means that you and the upper administration have developed a relationship in which your support for each other is so strong that you can constructively air your differences in private while working for the institution's common good in public. There will inevitably be issues when you have done your best to dissuade your supervisor from adopting a particular course of action but your recommendation is overruled. If this is a matter of such dire consequence that you feel your entire working relationship with the upper administration has been compromised, then you will need to do some serious soul-searching about whether you can continue in your position (see Chapter 56, "Knowing When It's Time to Go"). These extremely serious situations should be, however, extremely rare.

You should question your own objectivity if you feel yourself reaching this point more than a *very* few times in your entire career. It is simply not worth going to the wall over most policy decisions. You may even find that an initiative you had originally questioned or regarded as ill advised turned out to be the best possible course of action after all. For this reason, leaving differences of opinion behind when you emerge from a private meeting is, in the vast majority of cases, the most productive approach. Support what you can in the way you feel you can support it. You need not lie. You should not call an initiative "wonderful" if you think it is flawed. Nevertheless, you can say such things as, "The president has outlined several important benefits that may arise from this plan" or "I think we need to assess this proposal in terms of its effect on the institution as a whole." The important thing is not to undermine your supervisor's idea simply because you disagreed with it. There are times when being a team member means working supportively on behalf of a proposal that you yourself have privately not endorsed.

Seek to understand the full range of your supervisor's priorities.

Many conflicts arise between deans and the upper administration because both parties assume that they have the same priorities. Although this assumption is undoubtedly true at certain levels (no one, for instance, objects to the goal of "improving the institution's level of academic excellence"), you should not assume that you know all your supervisor's primary concerns unless you have discussed them openly. If your institution has a solid strategic plan, particularly one that was authored or revised by the current upper administration, that document can be an excellent guide to many of these priorities. You will still want to make certain, however, that your unit's interpretation of the institution's strategic goals is in line with upper administrators' interpretation of them. Never assume that, simply because you and the upper administration are using similar language, you have precisely the same objectives in mind. To you, "strengthening the academic program" may involve expanding the number of majors and reducing your overall student-to-faculty ratio. To your president, it may mean offering fewer majors to create a more focused curriculum and redirecting funds to the largest and most popular majors. Until you have a clear conversation about how you intend to implement the institution's strategic goals, you'll never know whether your priorities are in line with your president's.

Of course, *understanding* your president's priorities does not necessarily mean the same thing as *agreeing* with them. You'll still have an opportunity—using the candid, collegial, and confidential approach discussed earlier—to clarify where you think the upper administration should reconsider its priorities. Nevertheless, you will never get to this point unless you make a concerted effort to find out precisely what the president's ultimate goals really are and which of those goals may be nonnegotiable. At the very least, you will emerge from these conversations with a much clearer understanding of where you and your college stand in relation to the upper administration's vision for the future.

Try to find ways in which your college's own priorities can be better integrated into the upper administration's objectives.

Once you understand what your supervisor's priorities are, you have an opportunity to reevaluate your college's own mission and objectives within the framework of those overarching goals. For instance, suppose you are dean of a liberal arts college, and your president has told you that "economic development for the region" will be his or her administration's single highest priority. This knowledge will give you the opportunity to:

- Position the way in which the disciplines of your college develop strong communication skills, critical thinking skills, and leadership development within the framework that your upper administration has identified as important

- Begin a conversation in which you clarify the ways that cultural development and academic development need to go hand-in-hand to achieve true economic development

- Highlight your graduates' success in contributing to the economic development of your region either directly after their graduation or via placement in highly desirable graduate programs

- Summarize the rates at which graduates from your college tend to remain in, or return to, the region after their positive experience in your programs

In a similar way, if you are dean of the graduate school and your president has indicated that undergraduate education will be his or her administration's highest priority, you can demonstrate how the presence of graduate students as teaching assistants enhances the institution's undergraduate program; how the availability of graduate assistants for research has helped retain the very faculty members who are most critical to your undergraduate program's success; and how your graduate programs' prestige has played a significant role in recruiting students to all levels of the institution. Nearly every presidential priority can relate in some manner to what a college does; your challenge as dean is to help interpret those presidential goals into objectives that your college can help achieve.

Respect the boundary of authority between you and the upper administration.

All too frequently, deans make decisions or take actions that are really within the president's or provost's province. Directly contacting a governing board member, soliciting donors for gifts (particularly without clearance from the development office), and speaking with the media on the institution's behalf (particularly without the involvement of the public relations office) can all be regarded by presidents as infringements on their areas of authority. You should never initiate these contacts without discussing it with the upper administration in advance and receiving their express approval. Nevertheless, the real challenge occurs when it is the donor, media representative, or governing board member who contacts *you.* Even in these cases you need to keep the upper administration fully informed. Deans who have not done so have found themselves in a bind, at times even terminated, for appearing to overstep their bounds. For this reason, any interaction with external constituencies that may be regarded as the president's or provost's prerogative should be cleared with one of them before proceeding. If you are the one who is being contacted, ask whether you can call back at a more convenient time. Then immediately notify the appropriate offices on your campus. If it is acceptable for you to return the call, at least you have taken the initiative to keep other offices in the loop. If there is some reason why you shouldn't return the call, ask that the request be handled at the appropriate level (perhaps by the president directly, perhaps by someone from another office that deals most directly with these constituents) and that you be informed of the outcome.

It is not possible to develop a strategy for dealing with every possible type of upper administrator. Most presidents and provosts will be good partners with you, generally interested in your area, and eager to help you succeed. Others, because of their own blind spots or preconceived notions about how your college should function, will seem to impede you every step of the way. Though you may not be able to fix these situations, your own flexibility and understanding will go a long way toward helping you manage them more effectively. Most important of all, be sure that you model the same candid, collegial, and confidential approach with your own department chairs and faculty members that you expect from your supervisors. Good administration can be contagious, and your president and provost may be guided by your own example.

Resources

Futterman, S. (2004). *When you work for a bully: Assessing your options and taking action.* Montvale, NJ: Croce.

Lencioni, P. (2002). *The five dysfunctions of a team: A leadership fable.* San Francisco, CA: Jossey-Bass.

Lencioni, P. (2005). *Overcoming the five dysfunctions of a team: A field guide for leaders, managers, and facilitators.* San Francisco, CA: Jossey-Bass.

McDaniel, T. R. (2002). President-faculty relations: A dean's dilemma? In T. R. McDaniel, *Dean's dialogue* (pp. 1–3). Madison, WI: Magna.

17

Friends of the College

The term *friends of the college* encompasses many different groups of external constituents, all of whom have a vital interest in supporting your programs and seeing them flourish. This group of supporters may include alumni, parents of alumni, community members who have an interest in your college's disciplines, donors, potential donors, community leaders, and other individuals who are likely to contribute to and benefit from the college's work. If skillfully handled, relationships with external supporters can help you achieve objectives that would be impossible to attain otherwise. If poorly conducted, these relationships can actually lose you friends of the college, destroy your reputation in the community, and create problems that could easily have been avoided. How then should you go about creating the best possible relationship with your external constituents?

Use external advisory councils wisely.

In the 1990s, many colleges began forming external advisory councils. Pioneered by colleges of business administration, where advisory councils of successful representatives from various professions often served as mentors to students and provided insight into the business world's evolving needs, advisory councils soon became common in all types of academic units. A significant number of these advisory councils were highly successful enterprises and proved invaluable to the colleges that established them. Many more such endeavors languished, however; they had difficulty taking root and ultimately were disbanded. What accounted for the difference? One factor that should be considered is that too many colleges set up their external advisory groups unaware of the following important principle:

> *An advisory council will only flourish if it has a clear purpose, a sense of direction, and most important, a genuine opportunity to provide meaningful advice.*

In other words, the creation of many advisory councils resulted from little more thought than "Lots of other colleges have successful advisory councils; we need to have one, too." The problem with this approach is that the people whom you will want to serve on your council will be individuals whose time is extremely valuable. These are precisely the people who are most likely to become disillusioned with the process if they think that their time is being wasted. As a result, before forming any sort of external advisory council, you need to ask yourself:

- Will I have enough substantive business for this group to perform every time it meets?

- Is it likely that there will be a significant amount of substantive business for the foreseeable future?

- Is it truly advice that I'm seeking from my external constituents or something else?

Unless your answer to each of these questions is an emphatic yes, you probably should find other opportunities for friends of the college to contribute to your efforts. For instance, if you have an issue on which you need advice and support now but not likely in the future, you are probably better off creating a short-lived planning group that will address the topic at hand, perform its task or solve its problem, and then simply dissolve. If you have several issues about which you want advice but don't foresee the ongoing utility of a council, you should consider establishing an ad hoc advisory body that will consult with you for a semester or an academic year and then graciously disband. If you are not actually seeking advice but want other types of participation from the community— financial contributions, volunteered labor, guest speakers, and the like—then you might consider forming a group with a different focus and mission. Remember the rule presented Chapter 13 ("Department Chairs"): Never ask an advisory body for advice unless you truly wish to be advised. As true as this rule is for internal advisory bodies, it is doubly or triply true for groups of external constituents.

Colleges use the term *advisory council* far too loosely, applying it to groups that are really in no position to provide useful advice or offer well-informed opinions. The problem is that, if you appear to ask for advice from a group of highly respected professionals, they will see it as their duty to provide it—and they'll be annoyed with you if you do not take it and take it quickly. For this reason, you may even want to reconsider the name *advisory council*. Perhaps the group that you need to form is better designated as a leadership council, fundraising board, external relations board, board of executives, visiting committee, dean's circle, executive council, campaign committee, board of counselors, development committee, or simply "friends of the college." Alumni might be organized as an "affinity group," a designation that can be particularly useful if your institution's alumni office does not want graduates splintered into numerous competing alumni bodies. However you organize your external constituents, the important principles to keep in mind are:

- Be honest with them about the group's purpose.

- Respect members' time.

- Be generous in expressing your gratitude for any type of contribution (whether it's time, talent, or treasure) that a group member makes.

Consider travel opportunities as a means of establishing or strengthening your connections with friends of the college.

Most faculty members already know that, if you really want to get to know students well and as individuals, you can do one of two things: perform with them in a play or travel with them on an extended trip outside the country. Seeing people daily for several weeks, having meals with them, enjoying the luxury of prolonged conversations, facing challenges together, and all the other experiences resulting from enforced togetherness can be a highly rewarding bonding experience. What is true for students is at least as true for getting to know friends of the college. Sponsoring a 10- or 14-day trip to some exotic locale can open your college to an important source of unrestricted contributions. It is not uncommon for colleges to add a premium of $500 or more to the cost of travel packages as a required contribution to the college's annual fund. With the average travel group size of about 30 participants, the added funding may not be massive, but it is still a significant amount.

In addition to this initial contribution, however, travel programs with friends of the college pay off in the extended access they give you to these potential donors. Your external constituents will get to know you personally, and you will have an opportunity to learn about issues that are important to them. Photographs that you take while on the trip will provide an opportunity to follow up with your travel companions. ("I was just going through our travel photos, and I found an excellent picture of you. Here's a copy that I hope will serve as a memento of our fantastic trip. I'd also like to give you a call sometime to talk about . . .") Some trips even conclude with a final dinner at which donors may be asked to make multiyear commitments or to increase their giving for the coming year. Even in cases where that approach might be too aggressive or where not all participants are likely to be donors, the trip will at least help increase the ties that people have to both you and your college.

An opportunity to travel for an extended period with the dean may appeal to community leaders and other supporters of your program. Another lure for friends of the college might be a travel opportunity in which they can mingle with current students, reliving for a short time the intellectual and cultural experiences of their youth. In particular, mixed travel groups of alumni and current students can be extremely popular. Current students frequently find mentors among the institution's previous graduates. Alumni often have an interest in what another generation of college students is experiencing in a program that they know well and love.

Although travel experiences outside the country tend to have the most allure for donors and other influential friends of the college, they are not the only program that you might consider. Domestic trips, possibly including a popular faculty member who has expertise in a certain region of the country or with historical events that occurred at your destination, can also create an opportunity for you to meet at length with friends of the college. A series of theatrical or operatic performances in New York (combined with presentations made by members of an arts faculty) or a visit to the space center in Florida or Texas (featuring special lectures by members of a science faculty) can also be exciting experiences for the college's supporters. Short-term events—day trips to athletic competitions, cultural events, performances, or festivals—are also possible. Although they do not offer you extended time to get to know people as long trips do, they can allow you to test the waters. If a short trip works well, you can follow up with a longer private meeting with the potential donor or possibly even consider a longer trip for your college.

Explore ways of providing special premiums to valued friends of the college.

One effective means of strengthening the ties with external constituents is providing them with special premiums or perquisites that demonstrate how much you value their support. All colleges are likely to have some sort of gift or promotional item that both advertises the college and is highly desirable. The college's logo can be placed on such items as leather bookmarks, wine glasses, lapel pins, portfolios, notepads, and other items. Even more creative are packages of services for donors who have made significant or long-standing contributions to the college or one of its programs. Examples of such premiums include:

- *The golden ticket:* guaranteed seating at certain performances, lectures, and other cultural events, perhaps combined with reserved parking, dinner, or other perquisites

- *Friends-only lecture series:* opportunities to meet in smaller, more personal settings with distinguished lecturers when they come to campus or with outstanding members of your own faculty

- *Dessert with the dean:* periodic opportunities to meet with you in a casual setting where you can provide information on upcoming initiatives, allowing friends of the college to be in the know before the general public

- *Academic privileges:* access to special collections in the library, opportunities to sit in on certain classes (on a space-available basis), the use of the institution's electronic databases, and a special parking permit

- *Electronic "perks":* providing password-protected access on your web site to special materials, lecture transcripts, advance news items, and other information of interest

There is, of course, no single way to serve all your college's external supporters. Be certain to listen to what they perceive their needs to be, just as you are open to the ways in which they wish to serve your college. If properly treated, external supporters can be extremely powerful allies in advancing your programs' mission. If *superbly* treated, friends of the college can become some of your college's most loyal donors.

18

Donors and Potential Donors

In addition to supervising their college's academic programs, deans frequently are expected to devote time meeting with donors and potential donors and seeking sources of external funds. This expectation has radically altered the dean's position over the past few decades. For instance, it has long been standard practice for presidents to be active in fundraising; after all, more and more chief executive officers, particularly at private colleges, reach their positions after serving in development offices or centers of institutional advancement rather than, as was almost universally the case before the 1970s, through work in academic affairs. Moreover, even presidents who rise to their positions by other routes are expected to receive significant training in development. Deans, however, almost never have a strong background in development. It is expected that a dean have a distinguished academic record and rise to his or her position by demonstrating leadership as department chair, faculty senate chair, associate dean, or some similar role. Once in place, however, most deans are expected to engage in development activities almost immediately. The need to become an expert in fundraising quickly can pose a genuine challenge, particularly with deans' full schedules. So how can you be effective at an activity for which you've received no formal training and little preparation? Where can a dean go to find out how to be more effective in advancement? The following guidelines are intended to serve as a primer on the most essential information deans need to know in dealing with donors and potential donors.

In fundraising, never go it alone. Always involve members of your institution's development staff in planning and conducting your visits with donors or potential donors.

Deans who are new to fundraising frequently assume that they will receive more credit and possibly have more success if they make direct contact with probable donors whom they already know, develop their own proposals, and bring a signed agreement back to campus. This approach is likely to be a recipe for disaster. By acting independently, deans deprive themselves of the development office's expertise, risk complicating relations with a donor who may already be under solicitation for another (possibly much larger) gift by the institution, and create unnecessary difficulties for themselves when it's time to finalize a complex gift agreement.

Development professionals have at their disposal a vast amount of invaluable information. From public records, development officers can ascertain a potential donor's gift-giving capabilities and tailor a proposal that matches the institution's larger needs to those capabilities. They may also know a donor's past giving history, thus indicating his or her philanthropic interests and the likelihood that the current request will be successful. They will certainly know the individual's history of giving to the institution's annual fund, a useful predictor of his or her readiness to consider a larger request. For instance, one general rule of thumb is that individuals who have contributed $250 or more to the annual fund each year for 12 or more years are quite likely to respond favorably to a major gift request of $10,000 or more, as long as the request is in an area of their interest. Because of development officers' experience in dealing with many donors or potential donors, they can also provide guidance in how specific individuals should be approached. They often can determine which potential donors should be approached directly, which should be handled more circumspectly, and when the proper moment has arrived for the "ask"—that is, the specific request for a gift.

Moreover, unless you work closely with your development office, you have no idea of which donors may be in the process of being recruited by your institution for other, larger gifts. As a result, you may be very proud of the $100,000 gift to your college's scholarship fund, and the donor will now feel that he or she has made a sufficient contribution to your institution, even though the president had been anticipating a capital campaign pledge from this donor of more than $1 million. For this reason, proceeding blindly into the world of advancement holds great potential for alienating your institution's upper administration, as well as your fellow deans because you may be perceived as having taken advantage of someone else's prospect. Only your institution's development office will be aware of the university's big-picture fundraising goals. Development staff can guide you toward more appropriate prospects and away from those who have already been cultivated elsewhere in the institution.

Finally, you should be aware that the work involved in handling a gift is far from concluded when the ask is made and the gift is offered. There are legal implications in receiving, recording, and allocating contributions. Unless you yourself have been trained as an attorney, these are not details for which you will want to be responsible. The campus's development office will be experienced in the language necessary for executing valid gift agreements, in the timing when a gift may be booked, and in the restrictions on when the funds will be available to your program. At the very least, that office will prevent you from making promises that you will not be able to fulfill. Even more important, the advancement office staff will protect you from taking actions that could place both you and the institution at legal risk.

Remember that development involves far more than simply asking for money.

Development professionals frequently distinguish "friend-raising" from fundraising. Friend-raising involves creating close relationships with individuals, making them think positively about your college, and instilling in them a desire to help you succeed. People rarely give contributions to causes they care nothing about. Your first task, therefore, is not to ask for donations but to get people excited about your mission and to increase their regard for your college and its programs. Much of the work that you will do is actually cultivating prospects who may contribute to your college at a later date. Nevertheless, you will also enhance your unit's reputation, which will benefit your programs in nonfinancial ways. You never know when an individual who looks favorably on your college will encourage an excellent student to enroll there, introduce you to another individual who *will* become a donor, or help you publicize an important event. Fundraisers frequently say that there are three primary ways in which people can contribute to causes—by donating their time, talent, or treasure—and that *all* these forms have great value. Through your friend-raising activities, you will encounter many people whose resources or other commitments do not allow them to donate treasure to your college, but whose generous gifts of time and talent are even more meaningful to you in the long run.

It should not surprise you, therefore, if you need to be patient when you meet with prospective donors. Several visits may be necessary for them to get acquainted, or feel comfortable, with you. Even more visits may be necessary before they fully understand your funding priorities and how they can make a difference to these priorities directly or indirectly. It is rarely the case that you will meet with a prospective donor for the first time, outline a proposal, and walk away with a check or even a general commitment. Donor relations can involve protracted discussions before you get to the point of outlining a proposal. After all, one of the most widely cited essential principles of fundraising is:

> *Ask for money, and you will get advice. Ask for advice,*
> *and you will get money.*

Donors, like everyone else, want to feel that they are in charge of situations where they are making a substantial contribution. No one likes to feel that they have been taken advantage of or used. As a result, many times when you ask for a gift, the prospective donor will end up taking charge of the situation and advising you how to raise the money elsewhere or how to focus your proposal more effectively. Conversely, when you ask for ways in which your proposal might be strengthened or improved, people are often impressed by your willingness to hear their ideas. If they are interested enough in seeing those ideas come to fruition, they may even provide you with the resources to turn your dreams into reality.

Prepare for every donor visit carefully. Do your homework so that you know about the donor and possible variations that could be made to your proposal before you actually make your request.

The individuals you are likely to solicit for donations are busy people for whom time, as well as money, is important. If this were not the case, they likely would not have accumulated the resources they have. As a result, you never want to go unprepared into a meeting with a potential donor. Your institution's development office, as noted earlier, can assist you with information about the individual's capacity for giving, past record of contributions, and social or philanthropic interests. In addition, you will also want to know as much as possible about the person's background, concerns, and style of interaction (e.g., whether you will be expected to get down to business immediately, or whether there will be a prolonged period, perhaps even several meetings, at which you're simply getting acquainted). For instance, it is important to know whether there are any topics that are off limits for the potential donor. Finally, you will want to know the general strategy for the meeting itself. You will be expected, of course, to do some talking as well as some listening, but how much of each tends to suit this particular donor? If you are perceived as not talking enough, certain donors may assume that you are not as interested as you should be in the proposal you're discussing. On the other hand, if you are perceived as talking too much, certain donors may assume that you are not really interested in them. Once again, your development officer may be able to guide you in reaching the appropriate balance.

In the same way that you want to be prepared about the donor and his or her interests, you want to be fully prepared to discuss the proposal or project: That is the central goal of the meeting. Many donors, particularly those with careers in business or public service, have a great deal of experience evaluating proposals, business models, and strategic plans for their soundness and feasibility. Your proposal should be so sufficiently thought through that you could answer even very detailed questions about how the plan might be implemented. At the same time, the plan should allow for flexibility so that the donor can play an important role in refining it. The buy-in that results from helping shape a project can induce donors to contribute to it.

One important way to begin preparing your thoughts on a proposal is by developing a case statement. A *case statement* is a concise summary of your college's mission, whom it serves, and its specific need in terms of the proposed project. A good case statement should also address the college's potential to fulfill its mission more effectively, better serve its constituents, and satisfy your established need through completing the current project. Case statements should not be lengthy; a reader should be able to digest them quickly and easily. Each case statement should represent a clear plan that will be important to the reader, inspire that person to become part of the solution to the problem you have outlined, and supply a sufficient amount of evidence that the proposed project is both realistic and significant. Case statements are sometimes divided into three parts that make it easy for potential donors to grasp and absorb a complex idea quickly:

- *Concept:* two or three sentences outlining the proposal (the description of the concept should be brief, but it should immediately engage the reader)

- *Need:* information about your unit that clearly summarizes why it is necessary to achieve the goal you have proposed (the statement of need should make the problem you are trying to solve clear to the reader)

- *Opportunity:* a description of how the reader can make a positive difference by satisfying this need

Your case statement should be specific enough that the reader can visualize the project but general enough that the donor can easily modify it further in line with his or her own philanthropic interests.

Remember that many donors will be more willing to contribute to a project if you can demonstrate widespread support for it.

By presenting evidence of broad-based support for your project, you will underscore to donors how important it is to meet this need. There are several effective ways to demonstrate widespread support for your project:

- *Levels of contribution within your college:* Donors will not want to contribute to a project if they think that the people most closely connected to it do not care as deeply about it as they do. You can demonstrate your own unit's support for the project by citing levels or rates of contribution within your own college. There are various ways in which you can describe contribution levels, so you should feel free to cite whichever figures help make the case. For instance, if relatively few individuals have contributed but one or two of the gifts were rather large, you should cite the *total dollars raised.* ("We only launched this project a month ago, and already faculty members have contributed more than $5,000 to bring it about.") Conversely, if the total amount raised is rather small but many faculty members have contributed $5 or $10 each, you should cite the *total amount of participation.* ("We only launched this project a month ago, and already more than half of the faculty have made contributions to help bring it about.") In a similar way, if your cash-in-hand happens to be the most impressive figure available to you, you would emphasize the *total dollars raised.* But if you have received promises of significant amounts that are still outstanding, you can make your case far stronger by citing *total dollars pledged.* Moreover, if faculty contribution levels are not impressive, there are other ways of describing broad-based support. You could cite, for instance, staff or student contribution levels; support from your parents council (see Chapter 10, "Parents") or community advisory council (see Chapter 17, "Friends of the College"); or matching funds pledged by the upper administration. ("This project has received such strong support from the administration that they've pledge to match dollar-for-dollar every contribution we raise for it. I think that demonstrates just how seriously we take this issue. It's also an important way to make your own contribution go further.")

- *People closely connected to or benefiting from the project:* Nothing can make a need seem as compelling as seeing the human face behind it. For instance, if the proposed project concerns increased support for scholarship, visit the donor with one or two articulate students who either have already benefited from similar programs or could stand to benefit from this project. Immediately, the proposal will cease being an abstract idea and become a matter of real people who have real needs. Other projects might be better served by having faculty members, previous donors, or friends of the college accompany you on your visit to the prospective donor. Faculty members can discuss the impact of projects in their areas with a passion and a vision that many donors will find compelling. Previous contributors can help form a bond with the prospective donor; because they will not be benefiting directly from the gift, their motives are not suspect, and they can invite the prospective donor to "join me in helping make this vision a reality." In a similar way, friends of the college can provide a broader community perspective, demonstrate ways in which the college helps people other than its own students, and illustrate the project's breadth of support in the region.

- *People who support the project from outside your college:* Departmental and college structures matter to us as academic professionals. These organizational details, however, usually matter very little to donors. They care about the project and making a difference in someone's life. For this reason, don't let your institution's organizational chart blind you to opportunities for demonstrating a potential gift's broad support. Another dean who can argue that the institution as a whole will benefit from the project or faculty members from other disciplines who may benefit from a new, university-wide collaboration can help make the case that your idea is both widely supported and significant to many disciplines. Just be sure to reciprocate the support that other deans or their faculties lend to your development efforts.

Don't forget: When the gift is received, your work has just begun.

Many deans mistakenly assume that the development process ends as soon as the gift has been booked. All too often this assumption strains donor relations and sours a once promising relationship. Donors expect follow-through in return for their financial support. Not only should they be kept in the loop about absolutely everything connected to the project itself, but they should also be made to feel like members of the college community. Be certain that they are invited to college events; extend these invitations, whenever possible, in the form of handwritten notes or personal telephone calls. Let donors hear about publications and grants for which the faculty has been responsible, honors bestowed on students, and other ongoing projects in the college. Too many donors have felt that they were actively visited, courted, and consulted during the solicitation phase, only to be ignored once the gift was made. The most frequent complaint that donors make is this: "The only time I hear from them is when they want something." Stewardship of a gift involves both properly using it and displaying the appropriate respect, gratitude, and interest in the donor who gave it in the first place.

Try to do a small amount of stewardship every day. Make a call to a donor just to find out what's new and to give a brief update on the college. Have your assistant pre-address envelopes for thank-you notes that you can fill out while waiting for a meeting to begin, sitting at the airport or on a plane, or taking a brief break from the other concerns of your day. If you travel on business, take along the telephone numbers of donors in the area where you'll be visiting; give them a brief call to say, "I just happened to be in the area, and I wanted to touch base with you."

Resources

Buchanan, P. M. (Ed.). (2000). *Handbook of institutional advancement* (3rd ed.). Washington, DC: Council for Advancement and Support of Education.

Elliott, D. (Ed.). (1995). *The ethics of asking: Dilemmas in higher education fund raising.* Baltimore, MD: Johns Hopkins University Press.

Greenfield, J. M. (2002). *Fundraising fundamentals: A guide to annual giving for professionals and volunteers* (2nd ed.). New York, NY: Wiley.

Hall, M. R. (1993). *The dean's role in fund raising.* Baltimore, MD: Johns Hopkins University Press.

Kuniholm, R. (1995). *The complete book of model fund-raising letters.* Paramus, NJ: Prentice Hall.

Panas, J. (2002). *Asking: A 59-minute guide to everything board members, volunteers, and staff must know to secure the gift.* Medfield, MA: Emerson & Church.

Rhodes, F. H. T. (Ed.). (1997). *Successful fund raising for higher education: The advancement of learning.* Phoenix, AZ: American Council on Education/Oryx Press.

Tromble, W. W. (1998). *Excellence in advancement: Applications for higher education and non-profit organizations.* Gaithersburg, MD: Aspen.

Worth, M. J. (1993). *Educational fund raising: Principles and practice.* Westport, CT: Oryx Press.

Worth, M. J. (Ed.). (2002). *New strategies for educational fund raising.* Westport, CT: Praeger.

19

Boards, Trustees, and Legislators

As we saw in Chapter 16 ("Upper Administrators"), it is not always appropriate or wise for deans to work directly with members of their institution's governing board, trustees, or legislators. Many presidents view interactions with these groups as their personal prerogative, and deans who lose sight of this fact tend to do so at their own peril. Nevertheless, there are several situations in which deans may *need* to deal with these important constituencies.

First, institutions frequently rely on numerous types of boards, and the president may not have time to deal effectively with all of them. For instance, in addition to the institution's governing board (usually called a board of trustees, regents, governors, or visitors), the university may also have a foundation board; a community advisory board; some type of secondary board (sometimes providing preparation for individuals who are being considered for the institution's governing board); and other boards that have a more restricted focus (a media advisory board, community relations board, planned giving board, etc.). At some institutions the president traditionally serves as the primary liaison to the governing board, with other administrators assigned to supervise interactions with the other boards.

Second, there may be times when special situations in your college—a new program or scholarship opportunity for students, a conference or scholarly initiative in your area, or (in the worst possible case) a serious problem involving your students or faculty members—in which you are asked to meet with a board or group of legislators. Third, depending on your president's and provost's management style, they may encourage your close involvement with these external constituencies because they want to keep such constituencies fully informed about developments occurring throughout the institution.

If you find yourself in a position where you need to have contact with your governing board, a trustee, a regent, or a legislator, how can you do so effectively? How can you best help the person or group with whom you are dealing while at the same time advancing your own unit's best interests? There are several key principles for deans to keep in mind in these situations.

Remember that many external constituents care deeply about higher education but they may have a very limited understanding of how higher education actually functions.

Relatively few board members or legislators are professionals in higher education. As a result, they may not be familiar with even fairly basic aspects of how higher education institutions are structured and operate. Board members may have only the most rudimentary idea of what a dean actually does and of how disciplines are organized into administrative units at many colleges and universities. This lack of knowledge does not make them ineffective in their positions or prove that they don't care about issues of vital concern to those of us who work in academia. If the roles were reversed and any of us were asked to serve on an advisory board to the state legislature or a business operated by a particular trustee, we would find ourselves in an analogous situation. We would want to do a good job. We would take our responsibilities seriously. But we would also find our knowledge of the legislature's or corporation's day-to-day business rather limited.

For this reason, it may be necessary to inform or remind board members and legislators of things that you and your colleagues may take for granted. You can say things like, "Well, as the college's dean, as I'm sure you're aware, I have ultimate responsibility for the academic programs of the disciplines in my area. Other aspects of collegiate life—such as housing, financial aid, student organizations, and so on—report to other directors. My main concern is with hiring and developing an excellent faculty, keeping our curriculum focused and up to date, and ensuring that we can meet our educational objectives within our budget. In fact, that's why I'm here today . . ." Alternatively, you might say, "Now, as dean of the university's liberal arts program, I'm responsible for a significant portion of the university's general education program (the required courses that every student has to take), service courses (the supplemental courses that we offer to majors outside our college), and undergraduate majors in 11 disciplines: American studies, art, classics (ancient Greek and Latin language, civilization, and literature), communication, English, foreign languages, history, international studies, Latin American studies, philosophy, and women's studies." By doing so, you've given people context for your conversation, and you have helped them avoid incorrect assumptions. You've neither insulted them by assuming that they don't know what you're telling them nor risked a miscommunication by assuming that they understand everything. You've achieved a collegial and informative balance.

Remember that external constituents may apply models from their own experience or field of expertise to your institution, even when those models do not apply to higher education.

As we saw earlier in Chapter 9 ("Students") and Chapter 10 ("Parents"), many people who are not involved with higher education daily may assume that colleges and universities function exactly like other institutions in society. They may be familiar with how corporations are structured or with the configuration of places of worship, community service organizations, the state legislature, or a host of other institutions. As a result, they may misinterpret your relationship to your "employees" and your "customers," not fully comprehend such concepts as academic freedom, and otherwise make assumptions about how your unit works that are simply not appropriate for a college or university. (On the complexities of the concept of academic freedom, see Chapter 52, "The Unionized Environment.") Because even many academics misunderstand such concepts as tenure—assuming that it guarantees job security rather than the right to being informed of the cause for termination and have access to due process before being terminated—it is not surprising that many board members and legislators may similarly fail to grasp the true complexity and value of the academic protection provided through tenure. You may find yourself, therefore, challenged not only to defend your own program but to explain the values of higher education in general. That can be a rather daunting task, particularly when you assumed the conversation would be focused on a single aspect of one of your programs.

When these situations arise, it is important neither to appear defensive nor to treat the board member or legislator as though that person were obtuse for not understanding the basics of how higher education works. As we saw earlier, any of us, if asked to help an institution or organization vastly different from our own, might draw incorrect conclusions because we assume that other entities function as ours does. You have, once again, an opportunity to seize the teachable moment, provide a better understanding of how higher education institutions actually work, and explain your unit's needs all at the same time. For instance, if the legislator or board member shifts the conversation from its primary topic to "the problems we keep facing because of tenure," you might explain the benefits of the tenure system in terms of advantages that matter most to the other person. Too many deans immediately retreat to familiar arguments like "the need to protect academic freedom" that may have little direct relevance to the world of the legislature or board. "Certainly, one of the things we have to keep in mind," you might say, "is that we both have a genuine interest in attracting and retaining the best possible faculty members who can most ably meet the needs of students at our institution [or 'in our state']. The tenure system is one of the things that help us attract the best and brightest. If an outstanding faculty member has an opportunity to work in my college and at another college, but we are not able to offer the possibility of tenure, then we're at a competitive disadvantage. The quality of education here is going to suffer, and I don't think that's something either of us wants. In fact, I think there are several ways in which we can *improve* the educational opportunities available to our students, and that's what I'd like to talk about today . . ."

In a similar way, if you perceive that the board member or legislator is assuming certain things about your unit or program that are simply not relevant to higher education institutions, you have an opportunity to provide some insight into how colleges and universities actually function. "It's true," you might say, "that I serve as a faculty member's 'boss' or 'supervisor.' But I think it's important to remember the long tradition of shared governance in American colleges and universities. On one of your own legislative committees [or 'non-profit boards'], the chair functions more as a 'first among equals' than as a traditional corporate manager; that's similar to a dean's role in our unit. I do evaluate faculty members and set their salaries; that's true. And in extreme cases I may even have to terminate someone. But much of what I do, just as much of what you do, is accomplished through persuasion and mutual respect, not through direct commands. I hire the best possible faculty members I can find, and then I give them the freedom they need to do their job effectively—within certain guidelines, of course, but they do have a great deal of freedom. So a better way of accomplishing your goal, I think, might be . . ." In this way, you've related how you interact with faculty members to the speaker's own frame of reference, helping that person understand both the similarities and the differences between your two professional worlds.

Remember that many external constituents may not fully realize the diversity of options available in American higher education and why those options exist.

We sometimes speak of students "going to college" as though they were all sharing a single experience. To the contrary, higher education is becoming increasingly diverse in terms of both the experiences students are offered and the ways students will be changed through that experience. What students encounter in the undergraduate program of a large public research university will differ distinctly from what they encounter at a small private liberal arts college, seminary, conservatory, online university, community college, pre-professional school, for-profit institution, or any of a wealth of other opportunities that students have to choose from today. Even more important, the product of that experience—*what* students will learn, *how* their lives will be improved by the curricular, cocurricular, and extracurricular elements of their college years—will be different as well. The skills developed in a 300-seat lecture hall with multiple-choice examinations are not identical to the skills developed in a 12-member seminar with weekly reaction papers, at least one extensive research paper, and required oral debates and critiques of one another's arguments. In a similar way, the insights gained by a student who has access to state-of-the-art scientific equipment and teachers who are leading researchers in their field are not the same as that gained from simply reading a textbook.

This vast diversity of higher education is an undeniable benefit to students and society as a whole. Not every student learns best in environments where they are continually put on the spot and challenged by highly articulate peers, just as not every student is prepared for the challenges and responsibilities of independent scientific research. The breadth of options available to students benefits society, too, because it helps prepare a citizenry with broader skills to respond to the problems that arise and will continue to arise in the future. Nevertheless, it is clear that many board members and legislators don't understand such educational diversity or its benefits. For instance, they may talk about how much more cost effective online courses are, unaware that your college specializes in art and design where studio space, peer critique, and access to physical galleries are central to your curriculum. Similarly, they may question your program's high cost per credit hour, even though your college's curriculum relies on advanced technology that must be upgraded extensively every year or two.

In these situations, you, once again, have the opportunity to explain your college's mission in terms that the board or legislature will most readily appreciate. As deans, we realize that our college's goal is never as simplistic as "getting students to graduate" or "increasing knowledge." We are also trying to develop skills in critical and creative thinking, oral and written communication, creativity, innovation or entrepreneurship, leadership, teamwork, civic engagement, responsibility, independent research, and self-understanding. We are attempting to add to our community's intellectual, economic, social, and cultural capital. We are preparing students to make a living and to lead a life worth living. All these issues are matters about which governing boards and legislatures care deeply. It is up to us as deans to help them understand that these goals are as essential to our mission as generating student credit hours and helping students graduate in a timely manner. At times, in fact, pursuing such goals may even be the most important part of our jobs.

Be sure to listen at the same time that you explain your needs or position.

So far in this discussion, we have been focusing on matters that board members and legislators may not understand. Certainly, there will be many aspects of your college, its programs, and its needs that you will have to clarify or explain to your external constituents. But remember that these meetings give you an important opportunity to *listen* as well as to explain. Just as meeting with a potential donor involves perhaps 80% listening to their goals and aspirations and about 20% explaining how your proposal can help meet those goals and aspirations, so should a meeting with any external constituent give you an opportunity to learn more. By listening to the board member or legislator, you will better understand what that person's priorities are. You will then be in a better position to understand how your college's programs can address those priorities. Even if, by listening, you learn that the individual with whom you're conversing has a highly distorted understanding of your college or higher education as a whole, you will be able to dispel those misconceptions—but you have to first ascertain what they are. You may also learn important information that helps you do your job better—either because you now have a deeper understanding of how the governing board or legislature works or because you see more clearly how external constituencies perceive your unit. For all these reasons, you will want to do a great deal of attentive listening whenever you have an opportunity to interact with a board member or state legislator.

Keep the upper administration fully informed about what occurs in your conversations with board members or state legislators.

Even if your president has given you carte blanche in meeting with your institution's external constituents, you will want to keep the upper administration advised about what transpired. At the very least, the person with whom you were speaking may meet with your president or provost and assume that that person is fully informed about the conversation you've had; you don't want your upper administration to be blindsided by a situation that you could have easily avoided by sending a short memo or email. In more extreme situations your president may even need to follow up on (or alter!) some of his or her actions based on your conversation with the board member or legislator. A quick document titled "Summary of My Conversation with Karen Schwartz on February 18" can be extremely useful in keeping your upper administration informed about your contact with external constituents, creating a paper trail for further action or follow-through, and avoiding any future misunderstandings when the details of a meeting are not remembered accurately.

The most important thing for every dean to understand before meeting with a regent, trustee, or legislator is how that individual's own governing council functions and makes its decisions. No dean should go into any of these meetings unprepared. Fortunately, there is material available on governing boards and state legislatures for those who may have little, if any, knowledge about their structure or operation. If you are dealing with a legislature, the best place to begin is your institution's own historical account of its origins and developments. Nearly every state institution has a written history that details the legislature's initial role in establishing the university and subsequent issues that have guided the institution's development. These sources can then be supplemented by reviewing your state legislature's web site (to familiarize yourself with the names of key players and important committees) and such works as those written by Budig (2002) and Kuh and Whitt (1988).

If you are dealing with a board of regents, trustees, or visitors, the best place to begin is the web site of the Association of Governing Boards of Universities and Colleges (www.agb.org), supplemented by such works as Ewell (2006) and Houle (1997).

Resources

Duryea, E. D. (2000). *The academic corporation: A history of college and university governing boards.* New York, NY: Falmer.

Guston, D. H., & Keniston, K. (Eds.). (1994). *The fragile contract: University science and the federal government.* Cambridge, MA: MIT Press.

Morill, R. L. (2002). *Strategic leadership in academic affairs: Clarifying the board's responsibilities.* Washington, DC: Association of Governing Boards of Universities and Colleges.

Weerts, D. J. (2002). *State governments and research universities: A framework for a renewed partnership.* New York, NY: RoutledgeFalmer.

References

Budig, G. A. (2002). *A game of uncommon skill: Leading the modern college and university.* Westport, CT: Oryx Press.

Ewell, P. (2006). *Making the grade: How boards can ensure academic quality.* Washington, DC: Association of Governing Boards of Universities and Colleges.

Houle, C. O. (1997). *Governing boards: Their nature and nurture.* San Francisco, CA: Jossey-Bass.

Kuh, G. D., & Whitt, E. J. (1988). *The invisible tapestry: Culture in American colleges and universities.* San Francisco, CA: Jossey-Bass.

20

A Scenario Analysis on the Dean's Constituents

Note: For a discussion of how scenario analyses are structured and suggestions on how to use this exercise most productively, see Chapter 8, "A Scenario Analysis on the Dean's Role."

Case Study

Each year your college sponsors a major series in which one faculty member presents several public lectures before an audience that includes current students, alumni, supporters of the college, parents of current students, media representatives, and even a few members of the governing body to which your president reports. This year's series will commemorate an important anniversary in the institution's history, so attendance is expected to be even larger than usual. Due to your development efforts, these lectures are now a specially budgeted item, and because this year's series will be so important, you have made arrangements with several additional external donors to provide supplemental funding. For this reason, a commemorative volume of the faculty member's lectures will be published for the first time, and a gala banquet will follow the first night of lectures. You have handwritten invitations to many of the college's most generous donors, and you are hoping that several of them may be sufficiently impressed by the event that they will increase their contributions, possibly even endowing a second such series.

The evening of the first lecture arrives. So many people are in attendance that, at the last minute, you have to move the lecture to your institution's largest auditorium. Even with that late change, however, the audience is in a particularly festive mood as the ceremony gets under way. The faculty member who will be speaking was selected by a college-wide committee, and because you are not personally acquainted with much of the speaker's work, you had your introductory remarks prepared by a staff member. Nevertheless, you have practiced your introduction carefully and feel extremely comfortable reciting the speaker's many accomplishments. You note that the faculty member who will be speaking is a relatively new member of your campus community but has already developed a reputation as a distinguished scholar, a highly popular teacher, and a dedicated member of your community. Your introduction is glowing, and the speaker comes to the stage with thunderous applause.

The first few minutes of the presentation go quite smoothly. Suddenly, however, you are rather startled to hear the faculty member utter a rather coarse obscenity. It is clear from the context that the speaker had planned to use this language, and so far as you can tell, it was included in the speaker's written notes from which the publication will be made. The remark makes you uncomfortable because the audience includes children, members of the press, your institution's president, parents of students, and several important members of the community, not to mention your college's largest donors, several of whom you know to be quite socially conservative. You assume, however, that the faculty member's language was a single statement intended for shock value, and it is certainly clear that the coarseness of the remark has focused attention completely on the speaker. Several minutes go by, and the speaker utters the same obscenity again. Then again. Before the presentation is over, you estimate that the speaker has used what you believe most members of the audience would regard as a highly offensive term more than 20 times. It is with great trepidation that you exit the auditorium with the rest of the crowd and proceed to the gala banquet.

The audience's reaction is immediate. As you had feared, many people think that the speaker's choice of words was completely inappropriate for the occasion, offensive, and not justifiable under any circumstances. Other audience members, however, come to the speaker's defense; they call the ideas that were presented "innovative and challenging," arguing that the speaker was perfectly justified in using whatever language seemed most effective in stirring the audience from its complacency and causing people to grapple with such difficult material. You are constantly asked what you think of the presentation and why, if you knew the speaker was likely to use such obscene and offensive language, you had so lavishly praised the speaker in your introduction. You have barely had time to think about what you might do or how you might react to the evening's turn of events when you reach your table. There you discover your president on one side of you, your college's largest donor on the other side, both of whom want to have a word with you about "your" speaker's choice of language this evening.

Considerations

1. Does the type of constituent who responds negatively to the faculty member's presentation affect how you respond to this situation?

    *   Suppose that both your president and your big donor strongly support the speaker, whereas a small but vocal group of students and their parents

were offended by the speaker's remarks. Do these factors change how you respond?

- On the other hand, suppose that students and their parents were excited by the speaker's "use of contemporary language to draw attention to an ongoing social problem," whereas your president and donor are shocked and angered by what the speaker said. Do you react differently?

2. Imagine that the important donor is extremely angry because of the speaker's conduct. You are told that, unless you either terminate or severely reprimand the speaker, your college will never again receive a gift from this particular donor. How do you respond?

- Is your response any different if the donor is the very person who endowed the lecture series?

- Is your response any different if your college has been named in honor of this donor?

3. Does the type of obscenity affect your response in any way? For instance, do you respond any differently if the repeated vulgarity were a . . .

- Sexual term?

- Scatological term?

- Term offensive to a particular racial or ethnic group?

- Term offensive to members of a particular sexual orientation?

4. Suppose that the obscenity used by the speaker was offensive to a particular racial or ethnic group or to members of a particular sexual orientation. Would your response be any different if the speaker . . .

- Were a member of the very racial/ethnic group or sexual orientation that would be most likely offended by the term?

- Made it clear that he or she was not endorsing the term but used it as an example of "the very sort of stereotyping we are all fighting"?

- Suggested that "if we keep repeating these words ourselves, then they cease to be effective as weapons against us. By constant repetition, even the most disgusting words lose their power"?

- Proposed that the term be adopted in an academic context for a new cutting-edge field of scholarly studies that would henceforth be called [offensive term] studies?

5. Would your response be any different if you and most of your colleagues were not offended by the term but it caused a strong reaction with a very vocal religious minority?

   - Suppose that this religious minority staged violent protests in the past when similar situations had occurred at other institutions. Does this change your response?

   - Suppose instead that most people you know regard the religious minority in question as a cult. Do you react any differently?

   - Does your institution's designation as a public or private college/university affect how you might respond?

6. How do you react based on the fact that members of the media were present at the lecture?

   - Do you try to be proactive and contact them immediately, even before you know how they will react?

   - Do you wait until stories about the event appear in the media and respond to them case by case?

7. Considering that there are additional lectures remaining in the series, do you take any action in advance of those lectures?

   - Do you ask the faculty member to make changes to future lectures?

   - If so, do you give a direct order that changes be made? (What would the consequences for the faculty member be if your order is not followed?)

   - If so, do you try to persuade the faculty member that changes should be made?

   - If not, do you at least talk to the faculty member about the incident before the next lecture? What is the purpose of the conversation?

8. How concerned are you by the presence of students in the audience? If you are concerned, is it because you are worried that the students . . .

- May transfer out of your college because they were offended by the speaker's remarks?

- Did not receive a good educational experience because of the speaker's remarks?

- May be more reluctant to attend such presentations in the future?

9. Suppose that several days after the presentation, you receive a letter from a parent who was very angry about the speaker's language. The parent demands that you take immediate and serious action against the faculty member who spoke at the lecture series.

    - How do you respond to the parent?

    - What form of communication do you use in responding—a phone call, letter, email, or personal visit (if the parent happens to live in the immediate vicinity)?

10. Would your reaction be different if, after the night of the first speech, you heard from only a single concerned individual than if you had received numerous angry letters and calls about the incident?

11. Because the offensive term appears to have been part of the speaker's written notes, do you excise it before the commemorative volume is published?

12. Is your response any different if the faculty member were untenured rather than tenured? If so, is your response directed more toward assisting the faculty member, protecting the institution, or some other goal?

Suggestions

Give yourself time to sort through your own reaction to the presentation. If the speaker's language upset you, did you react this way because you were embarrassed that you might be considered responsible for the speaker's remarks or because you found the remarks truly offensive and inappropriate? Had you known in advance what the speaker was going to say, what would you have done? Maintaining good relationships with your many constituents is difficult enough without the unexpected disasters that happen along the way. Those disasters are certain to occur, however, and one of the best tests for you as a dean will be in handling them capably, decisively, and with good grace.

Specifically, situations involving proprieties in public speech are among the most complex that a dean may face. Certainly, the right of free speech is protected by the U.S. Constitution. In addition, the legal system has ruled continuously that one's right to free speech is limited by certain time, place, and manner restrictions. That is to say, the context in which remarks are made *always* has a bearing on whether the remarks themselves are deemed to be appropriate or justified. In this situation the very context of where you work will have some influence on your response. If you are a dean, for instance, of a small, conservative, church-related institution, your response may well differ from what it would be if you were dean of a large, diverse, state-supported institution. Similarly, the type of obscenity uttered by the speaker may well guide your response. If the speaker simply used vulgarities that seemed out of place in the very formal and public setting of the lecture series, you have an issue resulting from a lapse of professional judgment. If, on the other hand, the speech involved an outright insult to any group of individuals protected by your institution's equal opportunity or diversity statement, then both you and the speaker may have a much more serious legal problem to deal with. Failure to act in such a situation could leave you liable to charges of fostering a hostile environment for the protected class. Your college, as the official sponsor of the lecture series, may need to disassociate itself more clearly from the speaker's remarks than would have been the case with a simple lapse of judgment.

As you consider your response to the situation, one factor to consider is the degree to which the speaker's remarks seemed gratuitous and unnecessary as opposed to having genuine pedagogical or scholarly merit. In other words, was the term in some way *essential* to the speaker's point, or was it adopted merely for its shock value or as a result of the speaker's carelessness? If the term was particularly relevant to the speaker's thesis, then its use, while unfortunate in light of the difficulty that it creates for you with your external constituents, may well be justified and needs to be defended. One of higher education's goals must always be to inform people and help them see the world in new ways; higher education is not about making people comfortable. As we all tell our students from time to time, there are situations in which being offended is the best thing you can do for your education; it reminds us that we have left our comfort zone and are being forced to reflect on our most cherished convictions. If you find, however, that the speaker's use of the term was gratuitous, unnecessary, and irrelevant to the point being made, then your reaction is likely to be different. It's difficult to justify an individual's language in a public setting if it alienates a significant portion of the audience for no pedagogical or scholarly reason. Then how do you best deal with the situation?

In one sense, according to the scenario outlined in the case study, much of the damage has already been done by the time you become aware of the issue. Moreover, it is not clear what steps you could have taken to avoid the situation before it occurred. You can, of course, demand to see a copy of each lecturer's remarks in advance of every public presentation and schedule rehearsals for any time a faculty or staff member is going to address your external constituencies. If you do so, you will both put a chill on the free exchange of ideas in your unit and increase your workload by an unsustainable amount. Yet, even if you take those steps, you will not be guaranteed against every form of public embarrassment. Moreover, you are likely to lose more than you gain, being dismissed as a micromanager or control freak. The current case study, in other words, is more an exercise in damage control than it is in risk avoidance.

Because there are other lectures remaining in the series, the best course of action is probably to schedule a meeting with the faculty member as soon as possible and discuss the situation candidly. How that conversation develops will depend largely on the seriousness of what the faculty member said. If the incident involved a violation of the institution's equal protection code, it may be necessary to have one of the campus attorneys explain to the faculty member why the term used is unacceptable and could leave the speaker open to a grievance or even a legal challenge. With other speeches remaining in the series, the speaker could be encouraged to open the next presentation with an apology or retraction to alleviate the damage. If the speaker proves recalcitrant and refuses to take any action, the institution may need to decide how it will respond on its own. Options might include canceling the remaining lectures in the series, issuing a statement to the press, or offering a disclaimer before the speaker begins the next presentation. The disclaimer or statement to the press might make it clear that, although the institution supports a free exchange of ideas, the speaker's views and terminology do not necessarily reflect those of every member of the campus community and certainly should not be regarded as an official statement made on behalf of the institution.

In situations involving a lack of judgment rather than a serious breach of policy, your conversation with the faculty member might take several different directions. You might explore why the faculty member chose the language that he or she did. You could outline why it created difficulties for the college in light of the constituents who were present. If the individual resorts to invoking the right of free speech, you might respond by saying, "That's all well and good. But what I'm talking about is not restricting your right of free speech. What I'm talking about is whether you were effective as an instructor. There are situations in which the *way* we say something undermines our message, and I'm afraid that's what happened last night. For instance, you wouldn't expect a nonprofessional audience to understand the technical terms of your discipline; you'd have to explain them or use more conventional words to be understood. Similarly, when you've got an audience like the one we had last night, you can't expect people to listen to what you have to say if you use language that makes them not want to hear your message. So let's talk a bit about how you might be more effective in your future lectures with tailoring *what* you have to say to *whom* you are saying it . . ."

Resources

Downs, D. A. (2004). *Restoring free speech and liberty on campus.* New York, NY: Cambridge University Press.

Golding, M. P. (2000). *Free speech on campus.* Lanham, MD: Rowman & Littlefield.

O'Neil, R. M. (1997). *Free speech in the college community.* Bloomington, IN: Indiana University Press.

Wolfson, N. (1999). *Hate speech, sex speech, free speech.* Westport, CT: Praeger.

21

Searching for and Building a Strong Administrative Team

In Chapter 14 ("Staff"), we saw how important it was for the dean's staff to develop a proper sense of balance. For instance, we saw that, in addition to covering all the central functions, duties, and responsibilities of the dean's office, it is equally important for you to understand the skills and personality types that will help keep the college running smoothly. But once you have identified what you need, how do you find people who can help you meet that need? Or once your staff is fully in place, how do you go about building them into an effective team, not just a group of individuals who happen to work together? Administrators frequently speak of seeking *synergy*, creating a staff that's greater than the sum of its parts. So how do you go about achieving such a desirable but difficult goal?

One of the most commonly cited examples of a successful approach to searching for and building a strong staff is found at Southwest Airlines, the idiosyncratic company begun in 1971 by Rollin King and Herb Kelleher. Freiberg and Freiberg (1996) summarize the counterintuitive approach to employee development that has made Southwest Airlines both a highly sought-after employer with extremely low staff turnover and a surprising financial success in an industry where others have failed. Many of the Freibergs' conclusions about what made Southwest Airlines prosper are transferable to an academic setting. Although we are more concerned with producing educated students and sound scholarship than ending the year with a profit, the following are important team-building principles that academic deans can learn from Southwest Airlines.

Hire on the basis of the qualities that you *can't* teach someone; then teach them everything else.

A common mistake in academic hiring is structuring searches in such a way that people are hired for all the wrong reasons. For instance, because there is a particular database or student information system in use at our institutions, we may immediately start screening out any candidate who is not completely familiar with that specific application. Or an academic specialization may be underrepresented in one of our programs, so we discard applications that don't devote a great deal of attention addressing that specialty in the cover letter. Or we are asked for our recommendations on the finalists for the dean's position in another college, and we base our decision on one candidate's years of experience and number of scholarly publications, without considering that another candidate may be a better fit for the unit. The problem is that each of these situations involved examining the applicants' strengths from one perspective, what we might call each person's "surface credentials," the details that can be quantified or recorded on a résumé. Unfortunately, we too often realize after an appointment has been made that success in a position involves far more complex factors than these surface credentials alone. In fact, the items that one lists on a standard employment application often have surprisingly little relevance in determining whether a person succeeds at a job.

Employees do well in a particular position not only because they have the basic training needed to perform their assigned tasks but also because they have certain skills, attributes, and characteristics that make for a good fit with that environment. As we've all experienced at least once in our careers, a person who is quite effective in one type of institution or department may be utterly disastrous in a different one. In our haste to find someone with the perfect surface credentials, we may overlook the intangible factors that can make the person a valuable asset to our unit. Certainly, accreditation agencies do require faculty members to have an appropriate amount of graduate coursework in the discipline that they are teaching. Nevertheless, even in these situations, search committees are often far more scrupulous than the accreditation bodies themselves in giving priority only to individuals who have advanced training in the most precisely defined subspecialty suggested by a position description. As long as you make a compelling case that an individual's advanced preparation was appropriate to the courses the faculty member will be teaching, most accrediting bodies will understand that no one can be expected to have numerous graduate courses in *every* aspect of what he or she is assigned to teach, particularly when that instruction occurs at the undergraduate level. Moreover, when we overlook potential staff members because they don't have advanced training in a particular computer application, we may be overlooking the fact that they have obvious experience in plenty of *other* applications and so are likely to adapt to new software with great ease. As a result, we often hire someone who meets our surface qualifications but who cannot function well as a member of a team, does not demonstrate a high level of productivity, or cannot easily master other important pieces of software.

The lesson to be learned from all these situations is that searching for and building a strong administrative team involves more than just paying attention to the job responsibilities. This is why, in Chapter 14 ("Staff"), we analyzed your staff in terms of their skills and attributes in addition to their specific functions. It is also why Southwest Airlines inverts the traditional hiring process and searches for people demonstrating certain characteristics—in their case, a sense of humor, a willingness to take calculated risks, and an independent spirit—rather than those all-too-misleading surface qualifications. As Southwest's board chairman and cofounder Herb Kelleher once said to prospective employees, "We'll train you on whatever it is you have to do, but the one thing Southwest cannot change in people is inherent attitudes" (Freiberg & Freiberg, 1996, p. 68). The company's philosophy statement also summarizes this important principle: "It's difficult to change someone's attitude, so hire for attitude and train for skill" (Freiberg & Freiberg, 1996, p. 68). As you build your own administrative team, consider looking at prospective staff members in much the same way. Perhaps your next associate dean does not need to begin the position already knowing the precise curricular requirements of all your departments, the hiring procedures established by your institution's governing board, and the payroll tracking system through which your office interacts with the human resources staff. Perhaps having excellent people skills, a willingness to learn, a good service ethic, and a self-starter attitude are far more important qualities. Everything else can be learned.

As you examine your administrative team, therefore, think of it not as a collection of job responsibilities but as a web of personal attributes. What are those intangible qualities that your team members need to be effective themselves and to make your entire office effective? What qualities is it necessary for *everyone* on your staff to have? What qualities is it necessary for *someone* on your staff to have? Which of these essential qualities is currently missing in your staff or not as strong as they should be? Thinking about what you will need in your team as a whole or as a system, not as mere boxes on an organizational chart, is your first step in building a strong and successful administrative team.

Make the students come second.

The next step in building a strong administrative team is to inculcate a philosophy that, in a surprisingly large number of areas, your institution's students are your office's *second* highest priority. Admittedly, this approach runs so contrary to the philosophy we hear at nearly every conference and from nearly every professional group that it requires substantial explanation. "We exist solely for the students," we are told over and over. "We are a student-centered institution. We always place their interests first." To be sure, that is a perfectly good philosophy for your institution as a whole to have, and it is admirable to see faculty members do everything they can to benefit their students' best interest (see, e.g.,

Braskamp, Trautvetter, & Ward, 2006). The problem is that when everyone is focusing exclusively on the needs (and often also the desires) of the students, no one is looking out for what's in the best interests of your faculty and staff. That's your job. If you and your administrative staff give everyone at the institution the impression that the students are the only people who matter, you are likely to see significant problems in faculty and staff morale, high turnover rates, and an actual decline in service to the students. As counterintuitive as it may seem, your office can actually serve students better by putting their interests second and the interests of your chairs, faculty members, and staff first. By increasing professional satisfaction among those who work at your institution, you'll end up educating your students better.

Keep in mind that a philosophy that students come second doesn't mean that students don't matter. In fact, by putting your faculty and staff first, you're creating the best possible environment for students to be served. Faculty and staff members will feel that they are truly valued for their contributions, not merely seen as unappreciated laborers whose interests are always insignificant when compared to those of students. By looking out for your college's most valuable assets— *literally* the most valuable, because personnel costs probably account for approximately 95% of your total budget—you set your faculty and staff free to look out for students' needs. In such a situation everyone feels valued and everyone wins. That result too often does not occur at institutions driven by an it's-all-about-the-students mentality. By putting the faculty and staff first, your office is modeling how a college or university should work. In other words, your focus on the faculty and staff *demonstrates* the way in which the faculty and staff should focus on the students, who in turn should focus on their studies.

Moreover, the students-come-first philosophy actually backfires at many institutions. As everyone in higher education knows, there will periodically be some students who have an exaggerated sense of entitlement—students who believe that paying tuition (or even having their parents pay tuition) gives them the right to be rude to faculty and staff members, have "inconvenient" policies waived for them, and appeal each negative decision to the next level. By underscoring that only the students are important, administrations may actually exacerbate this situation, creating a poor learning environment for the students who are guilty of this rude behavior and for the rest of the student body as well. By demonstrating to your faculty and staff that you expect them to be courteous to students and focused on students' needs but that you will back them up when students have clearly overstepped boundaries, you end up serving both your college and its students far better.

As Southwest Airlines' statement of philosophy puts it, "Employees are number one. The way you treat your employees is the way they will treat your customers" (Freiberg & Freiberg, 1996, p. 151). In an academic setting we might say that the way a dean treats the faculty and staff helps determine the way that the faculty and staff will treat the students. Moreover, Southwest Airlines has demonstrated that it is willing to pursue this philosophy at the risk of offending a few customers:

> While [Southwest Airlines' board chairman Herb] Kelleher gives his customers a great deal and a great time, he's clear that the people of Southwest come first—even if it means dismissing customers! Are customers always right? "No they are *not*," Kelleher snaps. "And I think that's one of the biggest betrayals of your people you can possibly commit. The customer is frequently wrong. We don't carry those sorts of customers. We write them and say, 'Fly somebody else. Don't abuse our people.'" (Peters, 1994, p. 165)

Students, too, are frequently wrong, and in extreme situations it may be up to the dean to suggest that they find another college.

Stand for something.

Every good college or university has a mission statement. Your unit—and probably every department within your unit—also has its own mission statement. These can be extremely valuable documents. But now ask yourself, "If I had to write a mission statement for myself and my administrative team, what would it be? Do we actually stand for something, or do we just work together for the sake of working together?" In the case of Southwest, the airline's central values, such as a bias for action rather than a blind adherence to the rules, a respect for the individual, and a commitment to "Positively Outrageous Service," are reinforced through numerous corporate publications, videos, and training sessions. "The company instills in every employee the idea that happy, satisfied customers who return again and again create job security" (Freiberg & Freiberg, 1996, p. 149). In *Joy at Work*, Dennis Bakke (2005) writes, "Purpose matters. . . . People want to be part of something greater than themselves. They want to do something that makes a positive difference in the world" (p. 149). Having a sense of purpose, a sense that being a member of your office matters—a conviction that all of you on the administrative team are on a mission to do something important—can be a vital factor in developing positive staff morale.

So, ask yourself what your office does—or *can do*—better than anyone else. Perhaps your goal is accessibility, a dedication to serving anyone with the help they need, without an appointment, whenever they need it. Perhaps you see your role as facilitating communication, both listening to the concerns of everyone in your unit and making certain that as soon as you learn something, you tell the rest of the team. It could be that you see your strengths as supporting scholarship, a willingness to be flexible with workload and aggressive in seeking external funding for truly innovative projects. You may have a mission based on student-faculty collaboration, working to reduce enrollment caps in key classes and encouraging faculty support of undergraduate research. Perhaps the unique quality of your office is a more intangible value—something like creativity, leadership, teamwork, entrepreneurship, or vision—that you are trying to instill in every single course, program, and degree offered by your unit. Only you and members of your administrative team can decide the most appropriate elements of your creed. The important thing to keep in mind, however, is that you need to have a sense of purpose, you need sincerely to believe in that purpose, and your unit's overall theme needs to be distinctive enough to give it a clear and recognizable identity.

Never underestimate the power of celebration.

As academic administrators, we believe that higher education is important and serious business. Moreover, a great deal of our work requires us to do important and serious things, such as solving difficult problems, handling crises, making major decisions, initiating policies, developing visions for the future, and coping with the sheer quantity of issues that are brought to our attention day in and day out. As a result, it can be easy in an environment that is preoccupied with what is important and serious to give short shrift to the many wonderful successes occurring all around us. Students are being accepted into graduate school, law school, or medical school. Articles and books are being published. Awards are being won. New insights are being formed. The mission of the institution is being fulfilled. Lives are being changed. *Our efforts as educators are paying off.* So why is it that we so rarely celebrate these successes?

Nearly every institution has an awards ceremony once a term or once a year in which major academic achievements are touted. Nearly every institution has some sort of internal newsletter or web site in which people are praised for publications, awards, and other achievements. But this type of recognition is not enough. A college should engage in frequent, abundant, and spontaneous celebrations of all the terrific things that are happening in it. Colleges should celebrate when enrollment is up and when a history of enrollment decline appears to have tapered off. They should celebrate whenever a grant is received, but they should also celebrate the effort required for a grant application to make it out the door. They should celebrate all the routine employee milestones (birthdays, years of service, promotions, etc.), but they should also celebrate the sheer good fortune their employees have in working together. They should celebrate the adoption of a new platform for administrative computing and bid farewell to the cumbersome technology that's been holding the college back for so many years. Celebrations should be frequent, and they should be joyous. When you can't think of any other reason to celebrate, invent your own occasion and then celebrate the start of a new tradition.

Why are celebrations so important? Celebrations build esprit de corps because they remind us why we entered higher education in the first place. They remind people that we value them enough to set aside time just to show them our appreciation. By providing a temporary diversion, they help us become more efficient at our work when we return to it. They dispel the notion that the dean's office is just the rest of the college's complaint department by providing people with access to you when they *don't* have a problem or criticism. Most important, celebrations with members of your administrative team help reinforce a positive working environment. To cite one final example from Southwest Airlines' history:

> Southwest's formal and informal celebrations are opportunities for relationship building. Terry "Moose" Millard, a pilot and alumnus of Southwest's Culture Committee, explains: "If you want your company operating at maximum efficiency, you have to have trust. In order to have trust, you must have some kind of relationship. So all the things we celebrate give us opportunities to establish and strengthen our relationships." (Freiberg & Freiberg, 1996, p. 178)

Building a strong administrative team results from searching either internally or externally for the right kind of *people* (not just the right set of qualifications), making the success of the people who work with you your highest priority, uniting them in a common purpose, and rewarding them for all the good that they do. At most institutions, it can be difficult to bring about this type of change overnight, particularly when less effective habits may already be ingrained and when you were not the one who hired every member of the current staff. Nevertheless, even incremental changes in attitude can produce profound benefits in the long run. The important thing is not to be overwhelmed by the enormity of improving everything, but to be excited by the possibility of improving something.

References

Bakke, D. W. (2005). *Joy at work: A revolutionary approach to fun on the job.* Seattle, WA: PVG.

Braskamp, L. A., Trautvetter, L. C., & Ward, K. (2006). *Putting students first: How colleges develop students purposefully.* Bolton, MA: Anker.

Freiberg, K., & Freiberg, J. (1996). *NUTS! Southwest Airlines' crazy recipe for business and personal success.* New York, NY: Broadway Books.

Peters, T. (1994). *The pursuit of wow! Every person's guide to topsy-turvy times.* New York, NY: Vintage.

22

Interviewing a Candidate

You will eventually reach the point in your effort to build a strong administrative team where you are able, or perhaps even need, to interview candidates for a staff position. Perhaps you have the opportunity to appoint a new assistant or associate dean, college budget officer, or director of faculty development. Perhaps you use *staff* in a slightly broader sense and include in this term department chairs and any other person who meets with you regularly and reports directly to you. Perhaps you even regard your administrative team in the most global way possible, incorporating into this category every faculty member, as well as anyone else who works for the college. At some point in your deanship, you are likely to have an opportunity to interview candidates in all these areas. So how do you go about conducting these interviews effectively? What sorts of questions will most likely reveal to you what you need to know? What, besides the content of the candidates' answers, should you look for when interviewing? The following are some basic principles that will help make your interviews more productive, revealing, and likely to provide you with the insights that you really need.

Open your interview with the candidate by making a few general comments, and then begin the actual question-and-answer session by making a fairly broad inquiry.

Interviews are stressful. No matter how experienced a person may be, it is difficult for anyone to have each word evaluated, to have every move scrutinized, and to be judged. You can't eliminate this stress entirely, but you can help create a situation in which anxiety does not prevent candidates from making their best effort. To get the interview started effectively, begin with a few general remarks. For instance, if the person is an internal candidate, you might mention how glad you are that he or she has pursued this opportunity, say that you hope the entire process will be a positive experience for him or her, and note that you're looking forward to getting to know the person a little better during this interview. If the candidate is from the outside, welcome the person to the area, ask whether his or her trip went smoothly, and mention one or two reasons why the institution is such a great place to work. Inquire whether the schedule seems adequate or whether there are other meetings that the candidate would like to arrange. If your interview is not the first item on the candidate's schedule, you can also ask how the person's day has been going so far and what most interested, or surprised, the candidate about what he or she has learned from the day's other meetings. Then proceed to ask a general question that the candidate can take in any number of directions, something like "What about this position particularly interests you?" or "What in your experience has best prepared you for this position?" Although you may learn something important from your opening question, its real purpose is to create a more relaxed atmosphere so that the rest of the interview will be more productive.

Then proceed to questions that you really need to have answered.

Many deans waste precious time in interviews by asking obvious and routine questions. They might ask a potential administrator, "What's your management style?" or a future staff member, "What's your work ethic?" They might ask a candidate for a faculty position to describe his or her current research. They might ask any type of candidate such questions as:

- What is your greatest strength (or biggest weakness)?

- What are your career goals for the next 5 or 10 years?

- How would you describe yourself?

Nothing is particularly wrong with such questions, but they are such common questions that any candidate who has given thought to the interview will know the answer that you are expecting. ("My management style is collegial and consensus based." "My work ethic is to 'go the extra mile.'" "My current research is likely to result in several prestigious publications and to have an extremely positive effect on the quality of my teaching." "My greatest weakness is that I'm sometimes just too dedicated to my work; I'm my own worst critic." And so on.) For another thing, these questions don't really get to the heart of what you need to know. After all, you are interested in whether this person (who is obviously well qualified, otherwise he or she would have been screened out before even getting to the interview) is the best possible candidate for *this* job in *this* unit. Questions that are more tailored to the position's requirements will thus help you understand whether this candidate is a good fit. "One of the challenges of the position you've applied for," you may explain, "is that the person needs to be able to do very detailed work accurately and with an extremely quick turnaround time. Some years we may have only 24 hours between when we get information about our salary increase pool and when we have to report salary recommendations to human resources. And my personal conviction is that you just can't afford to make a mistake when you're dealing with someone's livelihood, even if you're working under a lot of pressure. So give me some good, specific examples of how you've had to process huge amounts of information very quickly, confidentially, and accurately. How have you handled that kind of pressure?"

Good interviewing techniques are the result of two things: doing your homework properly and using the limited time available in the interview to discover the sort of things that you can only learn face-to-face. For instance, by the time of the interview you should already be quite familiar with the candidate's curriculum vitae. There is thus no reason to waste the short time you have with a candidate asking about his or her educational background, current position, publications, or field of research. On the other hand, follow-up questions in those areas, probing deeper than what you can possibly learn from the résumé alone, can tell you something important about the candidate. For example, you might say, "I notice that several years ago you wrote quite a number of articles and gave a large number of presentations about the election of 1912. Is this still an active area of your research, or have you moved on to new interests?" By asking candidates to describe their single most important contribution to scholarship or the accomplishment of which they are the most proud, you will gain some insight into what they regard as their priorities. This information will help you evaluate whether each candidate's priorities are at all similar to those needed to be successful in the position.

It is relatively uninformative to ask a candidate a blunt yes-or-no question or a question that has an obvious "right" answer. For instance, a question such as "Are you willing to become involved in committee work?" or "Can you work well with tight deadlines?" is answerable in only one way. Every candidate knows the answer you're looking for. A much more constructive way of discovering whether the candidate is a good fit for you is to ask, "In addition to the duties outlined in the job description, what sort of service to the college would you see yourself providing?" or "Can you give me two or three good examples of your ability to work effectively with tight deadlines or under pressure?" In the first instance you can tell whether candidates bring up the possibility of committee work by themselves. In the second case you'll be able to tell from their examples whether the sort of intensity they've encountered in their working environments has prepared them for the situations they would encounter in the new position. In cases where you really have no alternative to a direct yes-or-no question, you might eliminate the question entirely and state the matter in the form of a job responsibility: "This position requires absolute confidentiality about all the information contained in the student records you'd be working with. So, if you are offered this position and you decide to accept it, I'm going to take that as your willingness to carry out these tasks with the utmost confidentiality."

Another type of question that can be extremely useful is one involving a hypothetic situation. In this sort of question, the candidate is asked to address a problem or issue similar to what would be encountered in the position and to develop an appropriate solution. Questions involving hypothetical situations are thus rather similar to the fictional case studies that appear in this book's scenario analyses. They should, however, be much briefer and allow the candidate a variety of ways in which to respond. A hypothetical question in which you are probing for the one right answer, a so-called litmus test, is really unfair because candidates are almost certainly unaware of the background issues that, for your institution, make the single acceptable answer "correct." A more productive way of asking a question about a hypothetical situation might be phrased along these lines: "Suppose that one of your coworkers habitually comes in a bit late, takes longer at lunch than is allowed, and leaves a bit early at the end of the day. You're not the person's supervisor, and in fact, the person's supervisor isn't in a position to know that this is going on. Your coworker's behavior isn't causing a *huge* problem, but it has meant that you've repeatedly had to take time away from your own work to cover for him or her. What do you do?" In a faculty interview you might pose a question like this: "Suppose you've just revised one of your courses, changing textbooks and adopting several new teaching techniques that your colleagues have told you are very effective. The first exam comes along, and almost every student in the class fails. What's your next step?" Each of these questions allows the candidate to reply in several different ways. There are many different right answers in each situation (and there are several different wrong answers as well). You'll learn about the candidates' abilities to think on their feet, to respond in a way that suits their own personalities and interpersonal styles, and to give you a fairly realistic depiction of how they might respond in an actual situation.

As candidates answer your interview questions, you'll want to consider the following issues at the same time that you are evaluating the content of each person's responses:

- *Are the answers of appropriate length?* Does the candidate take sufficient time to answer each question thoroughly and thoughtfully without going off on tangents or into too much depth? An excessively brief answer may indicate that the candidate sees complex issues as too cut and dried, or it may suggest that the candidate is not really interested in the position. An overly long answer may suggest that the candidate cannot focus on an issue's essential points; it may also suggest that the individual is verbose in general, which could create a problem for coworkers.

- *Are the answers too rehearsed?* In preparing for the interview, every candidate tries to imagine what questions people will ask. By the time a candidate has been interviewed several times, he or she is likely to have an extremely good idea of the precise questions that are going to be asked. For this reason, if his or her answers feel overly scripted, probe more deeply with follow-up questions and hypothetical situations. After all, it is not the candidate's fault that he or she is well prepared for the interview. It can be *your* fault, however, if you don't assist the candidate in moving beyond these automatic responses to answers that are more revealing about his or her fit for the position.

- *Do the answers seem out of character with the candidate's experience?* Is the candidate describing situations that he or she likely did not encounter in previous positions? The graduate assistant who speaks of completely revising a department's curriculum, the administrative assistant who claims responsibility for a series of large grants, and the assistant to the dean who states that he or she controlled a multimillion-dollar budget all call for scrutiny. None of these individuals may be misrepresenting his or her level of involvement in an activity, but the replies should be questioned closely. Ask particularly probing follow-up questions. Check details with the candidate's references. See whether you can determine why the candidate was given what appears to be an inappropriate level of responsibility.

- *Are the answers overly general and lacking in specific examples?* A good interview answer addresses the precise question that was asked and then, when appropriate, gives an example of how the candidate has actually applied the principle in question. For instance, in response to a question about a candidate's work ethic, the person might respond, "I think it's important to do whatever it takes to get a job done right. For instance, in my current position, we were in a situation where the entire undergraduate catalog had to be revised in 48 hours because of a set of new state-mandated curricular requirements. This was a particularly difficult challenge because I'm working in a unionized environment with strict rules about overtime and uncompensated labor. So here's what we had to do . . ." Without clear and compelling examples, the candidate's answer is not particularly informative. Every candidate claims to be hard working, creative, and a people person. It's only through the quality of the examples used to illustrate these virtues that you'll learn what you really need to know.

Avoid asking questions that may lead you, even inadvertently, into inappropriate areas.

As a dean, you are already aware of how inappropriate it is to ask candidates most questions about their age, gender, ethnicity or national origin, religion, or disabilities. The reason why these questions are inadvisable is that it is illegal to hire based on these factors. By asking inappropriate questions, you give a strong impression that you are going to disadvantage protected classes when you make your decision. Even so, it is important to clarify that only *most* questions in these areas are inappropriate. For instance, although you shouldn't ask about a candidate's personal impairments, you may ask the person how he or she will perform the specific responsibilities outlined in the job description. Although it would be inappropriate to ask about national origins, you are actually *required* to determine whether a candidate is legally authorized to work in this country. Most areas that require caution are fairly clear in an actual interview. The real challenge often arises in more informal settings, when you're out to lunch with a candidate or at a cocktail reception. In such situations it's all too easy to ask questions that may accidentally lead you into unacceptable areas. For instance, the following are some examples of inappropriate questions that can result from someone's attempt to be sociable and find out more about a candidate as a person:

- *Questions about marital status:* How shall I address you—as Mrs. or Miss? Do you have a family? Will your wife be accompanying you when you visit? What are the ages of your children? What will your husband do if you relocate to this area?

- *Questions about clubs, organizations, and religious affiliations:* We have quite a number of wonderful civic and religious groups here in town—would you be interested in hearing about any of them?

- *Questions about national origin:* What a fascinating name—what nationality is that?

- *Questions about age:* These are very impressive credentials for someone your age—how old were you when you started teaching? Why would you want to move so far away from home when you'll be retiring in a couple of years?

Before you actually meet with candidates, review the areas of inquiry that you're going to pursue. The following are some suggestions of the most appropriate and productive questions to ask candidates during an interview.

Administrative staff candidates

- What do you regard as the biggest challenge facing college and university administrations today?

- Describe a particularly challenging problem that you solved.

- What was the most unpopular decision that you have had to make in your career? How did you go about making that decision? What made it so unpopular?

- What do you regard as the single most important asset for a higher education administrator today?

- In which professional organizations do you think administrators in our area should maintain active memberships? Which professional organizations do you believe have the most productive and informative meetings?

Faculty position candidates

- How would you go about promoting active learning and a high level of engagement among your students?

- What do you regard as the proper balance between scholarship, teaching, and service for a faculty member?

- What are some examples of your creativity and innovation as a teacher?

- What is the biggest challenge facing college professors today?

- How do you go about promoting collegiality in an academic setting?

- Over the course of your teaching, which three students were the most memorable for you? Why?

Any type of candidate

- What's the most interesting book you've read in the past six months?

- What makes you unique as an individual?

- What part of your current responsibilities gives you the most pleasure?

- What part of your current responsibilities annoys you the most, exasperates you, or is a pet peeve of yours?

- What has been your most significant accomplishment in your present position?

- What achievement would you like to look back on after your first year here?

- Describe a mistake that you made in your professional life.

- Describe a problem that you have solved in your professional life.

- (Give each candidate a list of the position's essential functions.) Let's go through this list. How would you accomplish each of these tasks?

- If you could develop your knowledge or skills in any one area, what would it be?

- If you were to leave your current position, what quality or aspect of your work would others at your institution miss the most?

Interviewing candidates will always remain an imperfect science. No matter how well we hone our interviewing skills, there will always be people who will make a wonderful impression at the interview but whose work or interpersonal skills will end up being unsatisfactory. Despite these challenges, interviewing faculty and administrative staff members is one of our most critical duties as deans. Few choices determine the quality of our working environment as the people we choose to join us. For this reason, every dean needs to be certain that the time spent interviewing a candidate is productive, informative, and effectively organized.

Resources

Fear, R. A., & Chiron, R. J. (2002). *The evaluation interview: How to probe deeply, get candid answers, and predict the performance of job candidates.* New York, NY: McGraw-Hill.

Formo, D. M., & Reed, C. (1999). *Job search in academe: Strategic rhetorics for faculty job candidates.* Sterling, VA: Stylus.

Koral, A. M. (1994). *Conducting the lawful employment interview: How to avoid charges of discrimination when interviewing job candidates.* Hoboken, NJ: Wiley.

23

Closing the Deal

One of the most critical moments in building a strong administrative team comes when you have already decided on the candidate for a position and now must make the offer and close the deal. Although much of what we'll explore in this chapter concerns discussions you may have with potential associate deans, program directors, and other members of your immediate staff, the basic concept also applies to other hiring situations. The type of start-up funds required by a senior researcher will be significantly greater than the initial equipment allocation and office arrangement that you may offer your next assistant dean, but the basic approach to how you negotiate the entire package will be fundamentally the same.

Many deans feel uneasy when a search or selection process moves into its final stage. Up until that point, the dean and the college have been in charge; they have been the ones who have had the right to choose or refuse any particular candidate. Once the dean tells an applicant, however, "You're the candidate recommended by the search committee," the dynamics of the relationship change significantly. It is now the candidate who is in control, being lured by the college and dean. As a result, there are several guidelines to keep in mind when you must close the deal with limited resources. That is the reality for most deans during most searches at most institutions.

Keep in mind that interviews always work both ways.

The time to begin closing the deal with a chosen candidate is not when the search committee has made its final recommendation; it's while the initial interview is still under way. One of the most common mistakes that deans make is in assuming that interviews work in only one direction: that the college is sizing up the candidate, not the other way around. Nevertheless, you must remember that the applicant is also in the process of making an important decision, asking himself or herself, "Is this an environment in which I can see myself?" If you or someone in your unit comes across as disdainful, dismissive, or discourteous during the interview process, closing the deal will be harder later on. You will need to overcome the candidate's sense that working on your administrative staff or in your college will be filled with tension and personal conflict. As a result, questions that are designed to trick a candidate, statements that convey the impression that the candidate needs you more than you need the candidate, and an interview atmosphere that makes an applicant feel uncomfortable will work strongly against you during the negotiating phase. Although many deans might say, "But I just wanted to put the applicants through their paces" or "This is a high-pressure environment; I needed to see whether they could take the heat," such an approach will frequently backfire. What you will convey is not that the college is a fast-paced, challenging place in which to work but rather that the candidate's prospective colleagues are hostile and unwelcoming. You may also convey the impression that the institution is so inept that it cannot even conduct an interview very well.

For this reason, take time to sell the opportunity to each candidate even before you select your finalist. Present the college's mission and this particular position's unique opportunities in a manner that makes the candidate *want* to accept the job. If you convey that the work environment will be stimulating, sufficiently challenging but not impossibly so, and fun, the applicant will be eager to accept the position even before an offer is made. Remember, too, the advice given in Chapter 21 ("Searching for and Building a Strong Administrative Team"): People want to feel that what they do *matters*. The more candidates come away from their interviews feeling that the work they will do is important, that the college as a whole or the administrative staff in particular stands for something, and that, by accepting this position, they will have an opportunity to make a real difference in people's lives, the more readily they will want to accept the position when it is offered. Your negotiation will be, in other words, practically completed before you begin your formal proposal.

Carefully prepare your offer before you make it.

Frequently, we complete searches under time constraints. It has taken so long to develop the position description (see Chapter 32, "Position Requests and Descriptions"), post the advertisement, screen the applications, interview the candidates, and select the finalist that we rush to make the offer, believing that we must act quickly to get the candidate before he or she gets away. Although time frequently *is* of the essence in closing the deal, you never want to call a candidate until you know precisely what the offer's parameters will be. In other words, develop a clear understanding, in advance, of what is negotiable and nonnegotiable. Although you will rarely make the best possible offer at first, you must be aware of your institution's limits on the following issues:

- *Salary:* Although you are likely to offer a specific salary for the position, will you consider a higher salary if the individual counters your proposal? If so, what are your absolute limits? Are there issues of equity with current employees that would need to be addressed if you agreed to a higher salary? Reflect on the issue of the candidate's salary in the broadest possible sense. What sort of morale problems are likely to result if you offered a higher salary than one or more current employees receive? Should you (and does your system *permit* you to) discuss this matter candidly with current employees even before you extend the offer? If a candidate counters with a request that is only slightly above your upper limit, how will you respond? In light of how expensive searches are, are you better off agreeing to the higher request—thus avoiding the possibility of having to run the search again and, at the same time, securing a new employee who is, at least initially, eager to work for that salary—or incurring the expense of a new search, possibly one that yields a less desirable candidate? In other words, balance how much you desire to close the deal with this particular candidate and the other issues (budget, employee morale, etc.) that may result from the salary offer that would be required to do so.

- *Start-up funds:* As we saw earlier, start-up funds can extend from the extremely large (equipping an entirely new lab for a senior researcher) to the relatively modest (reallocating some existing computer equipment to a new administrative assistant). Regardless of the size of the start-up funding required, be sure you know your limitations before you call the candidate. Ask yourself this question: What sort of initial investment will be required so that this employee will be able to work as effectively as possible from his or her starting date? If you are unable to meet the candidate's specific request for start-up funding, are there any creative ways in which you can achieve the same goal? For instance, are there research funds available at your institution for which you can promise to lend your support in securing? Is it possible to reallocate your pool of continuing funding in such a way that you offer a slightly lower salary but include a nontaxable annual research or equipment fund from which this employee can draw? Can you partner with your institution's other units to provide the employee with access to equipment or space that is currently underutilized? Keep particularly good notes on any discussions you have with a candidate about start-up funding. Have the individual sign a memorandum of understanding that clearly outlines what you will provide and how you will provide it. More misunderstandings arise with new employees about start-up funding than about any other aspect of remuneration packages. For this reason, you want to be absolutely explicit about what you will provide, when you will provide it, and what expenditures must count against the start-up funds.

- *Moving expenses:* If the candidate you wish to hire is relocating from another area, does your institution allow you to pay for moving expenses? If so, know your precise limits—what you can and cannot offer—before contacting him or her. In addition to the costs associated with moving furniture, can you cover packing and unpacking? Can you reimburse the person for meals and mileage expenses? Can you cover the cost of transporting office equipment and laboratory items in addition to household furnishings? If you cannot cover moving expenses, can you compensate the candidate in any other way? Can you increase the salary offer slightly so that, for instance, moving expenses are covered within the individual's first three years? Can you hire the candidate as a consultant, bringing the person in for a few days before the official contract start date and paying a stipend large enough to defray part of his or her moving expenses? If no other alternative is possible, can the institution or its foundation loan the individual the cost of the move to be repaid over an extended period via payroll deduction? If the institution is private, are there vehicles and employees who can be used to assist with the move? Frequently, you can find ways of addressing the candidate's need even if your institution's policy prohibits reimbursing moving expenses.

- *Special benefits:* At times, what a candidate is most interested in when receiving a job offer is not a matter of money itself but some less tangible factor that will make his or her life better. Institutionally subsidized day care centers, flexible working hours, the ability to continue one's education, assistance with spousal employment, workload adjustments, opportunities for advancement, and help in securing affordable housing are all special benefits that may matter more to a candidate than salary alone. If negotiations come to an impasse because of your inability to meet a candidate's expected salary, and if you truly want to employ this candidate, find out what you can about the person's needs. Remember that certain questions that would have been inappropriate during the interview phase of the hiring process are now permissible. For instance, because you have already extended the offer, you cannot be accused of discriminating against a person on the basis of marital or family status. You may now ask whether the candidate has other persons in his or her life who would be affected by this career opportunity. What could you do to help them? Candidates who are concerned about relocating children, for example, may be more attracted to a position if they can visit the school their children would attend. In such cases a second visit for the candidate, accompanied by the entire family, may accomplish what a salary offer over the telephone cannot.

Don't hesitate to ask a candidate, "What would it take for you to accept this position?"

In closing the deal with a prospective employee, we sometimes fail to meet the person's needs or expectations simply because we never bothered to ask what they are. If a candidate balks at a salary offer, asking "What would it take to make you say yes?" can help keep a negotiation alive. You may discover that the $5,000 difference in salary expectation that the candidate assumed was insurmountable can actually be met or at least addressed in part. You may discover that, although you cannot achieve the candidate's salary expectations, you can offer other inducements that are even more important in the end. Sometimes it is a good policy to ask finalists what it would take for them to accept the position before you even extend the specifics of your offer. Certain candidates will have expectations that are so much higher than anything you can conceivably offer that you need to be aware of them before you even begin to close the deal. Other candidates will have expectations so modest that you know you will be able to exceed them. In any case you won't know what it is that a candidate is looking for unless you ask.

One way of keeping negotiations alive if all else fails is to request that, before the candidate gives you a final answer, he or she have an extended conversation with a member of your benefits staff. Human resources personnel who are trained in benefits can give a much more comprehensive picture of your institution's remuneration package than you or some printed materials are likely to be able to provide. A representative from the benefits office who can say something like, "But remember that your contribution to this benefit is paid for with pretax dollars. So that is essentially like saying that your salary is 10% higher" can be your best advocate in negotiations. The benefits officer will also be able to ask freely about the candidate's individual situation and describe how your institution's retirement plan, health plan, disability plan, and other benefits extend the salary dollars that you have offered. Following this discussion, when you speak again with the candidate, you may find that the individual is more willing to consider your offer because he or she now has a more comprehensive understanding of it.

Plan how you will notify unsuccessful applicants.

Telling applicants that they have not been selected for a position means conveying bad news, and there is no perfect way to make bad news palatable. Deans sometimes wonder whether there is a best possible way (by telephone, mail, email) to notify unsuccessful applicants. The fact is that your preferred method of telling candidates that they were not selected for a position depends very much on both the situation itself and your individual style.

Certainly, external applicants who were screened out before the interview stage should be notified in writing, either by regular mail or email. And any notification that is made to a candidate orally, whether in person or on the telephone, should be followed up by an official notification sent by regular mail. But when is it appropriate to deliver this bad news in person or over the telephone? Some deans believe that it is more humane to call every candidate who was interviewed but who was not offered the position. If doing so is extremely important to you, then you may wish to adopt this practice, but you should remember that you are probably doing it more to satisfy your own need to be direct than to meet the candidate's need for a personal communication. Receiving a negative result by mail allows a candidate to be disappointed in private, rather than having to be cordial over the telephone at a time when he or she may be extremely disappointed, upset, or even angry. A telephone call sometimes makes candidates feel that they must be polite and thank you for calling when all they really want to do is to cope with their disappointment privately. For this reason, written notification to unsuccessful candidates is almost always preferable. These notifications should be considerate. They should thank the candidates for their time. You may say, if it is true, that the decision was difficult and that you felt fortunate to have had such a strong pool of candidates. Some deans like to include information about the successful finalist. This is rarely a good practice. Unsuccessful candidates are unlikely to rejoice with you about the admirable qualities of the individual who was hired. Your upbeat paragraph about the successful applicant is likely to come across as rubbing the rejected candidate's nose in it and should thus be omitted. In the worst cases this information can even prompt a legal challenge if a candidate feels that his or her own credentials were equal or superior to those of the person who was hired.

The one time in which a personal conversation with an unsuccessful candidate is almost always desirable is in the case of internal applicants. These are individuals whom you will continue to see regularly after the search's conclusion. They are already members of the institutional family, and they deserve to hear the bad news directly from you. A telephone call or, in many cases, a brief but cordial personal visit is really called for in these situations. What you are doing is not only conveying a result, after all, but also continuing to strengthen institutional morale for the future.

Closing the deal is thus, in many ways, the most challenging part of a search. Your dynamics with the applicant have changed: It is now clear that you want to hire him or her. Nevertheless, whether or not you see yourself as an effective negotiator, your best preparation is to have sold the individual on the position in advance, to know your limits in terms of salary and benefits, and to be creative in meeting the candidate's needs.

Resources

Kinni, T. B. (2002). *Making the job offer that no one can refuse: Recruiting employees holistically.* Louisville, KY: BrownHerron.

Rosenberg, D. (2000). *A manager's guide to hiring the best person for every job.* Hoboken, NJ: Wiley.

Rosse, J. G., & Levin, R. A. (2003). *Jossey-Bass academic administrator's guide to hiring.* San Francisco, CA: Jossey-Bass.

24

A Scenario Analysis on the Dean's Staff

Note: For a discussion of how scenario analyses are structured and suggestions on how to use this exercise most productively, see Chapter 8, "A Scenario Analysis on the Dean's Role."

Case Study

You are conducting a search for a new associate dean. Of your three finalists, two are external candidates and one is an internal candidate, a program director in one of your departments. Following institutional policy, you interviewed the internal candidate first. (Your institution adopted this policy because it avoids giving internal candidates the unfair advantage that might occur if they happen to learn some of the questions that were asked or issues that were raised in earlier interviews.) As far as you can tell, the first two interviews went smoothly. You are about to interview the third and final candidate when you start to learn about problems in the search.

You notice that the candidate, who had seemed quite excited about the position in earlier meetings, now seems distracted and uninterested. The candidate answers your questions perfunctorily, without much enthusiasm. You don't say anything for the first few minutes of the interview, wondering whether the candidate is merely tired from two long days of questioning. Finally, however, the candidate's apparent lack of interest in the interview becomes so noticeable that you feel you must say *something.* "Is there anything wrong?" you ask. "Yesterday you seemed so eager for this position. Today you seem—perhaps—not to care all that much. Or am I just misreading the situation?" The candidate hesitates a moment or two and then launches into a long speech.

"Well, it's just that I'm not sure you're really serious about me as a candidate. And I'm not certain I'd want this job even if you did offer it. You see, yesterday one of your department chairs—I'm not sure which one it was; I've met so many people during the past couple of days that I can't remember anyone's name anymore—pulled me aside for a private conversation in the chair's office and told me a bunch of things that, frankly, made me uncomfortable.

"The chair told me, 'You've got to understand a couple of things about this search. The odds are against you right now. We've got an internal candidate, and if I had to vote right now, I think knowing a great deal about this institution and already being familiar with its policies would carry a lot of weight with me. I think most of the chairs want the internal candidate to get the job, and that's probably where all of us are headed at the moment. But I'm not *completely* convinced that the internal applicant is our best candidate, so I wanted to have a chance to ask you a few things off the record. I can talk to the other chairs, and I think I could change a few minds. But before I do that, there are three things that I want to see happen in this search. First, I want an associate dean who's going to be our advocate—by which I mean the *chairs'* advocate—in the dean's office. Right now, we don't always feel that our voices are heard by the dean, who seems to view that office's role mostly as a conduit for whatever the president wants. Second, I've got a faculty member going up for tenure next year, and I think there's going to be a big battle over that case. I want my associate dean to make sure that my department gets what it wants because we can't afford to lose this position. Third—and this is the most important thing—I need to know that the associate dean's going to be my front line of defense when it comes to student issues.

"'Here's the problem,' the chair continued. 'I'm up to my neck in my own research, not to mention teaching my classes and serving as chair. Now, we're pretty lax at this institution, and so I'm constantly interrupted by all these students who are coming in and out of our departmental office with petty complaints about this course or that course, not being able to get the schedules they want because we don't offer enough sections of certain classes—all that kind of nonsense. I've heard the dean say plenty of times how we on the staff come first and the students come second, but so far that's just been lip service. I need my associate dean to step up to the plate, handle all this student traffic for us, and let us get our work done. OK, so those are my three conditions. And I'm not going to support anyone who doesn't agree to them. What I need to know is this: Where are you in all this? Do you agree to do what needs to be done?'"

The candidate pauses for a second and then continues. "I really didn't know what to say. I mean, I thought I wanted this job, so I said more or less, 'Yes, I can do all that' in general terms. But then I started to think, 'Do I have any chance of getting this job when they've got an internal candidate whom most people seem to like? And do I really *want* this job if that chair is any indication of the sort of people I'd have to work with? I mean, I don't know much about you and your style yet, but what the chair said about your office being just a conduit for the upper administration concerned me. I'm not even sure that this associate dean position is right for me if it involves intervening on behalf of the chairs and handling student problems, doing a lot of faculty work with tenure, promotion, and everything else."

Having heard the candidate's remarks, how do you handle the interview, the search, and your relationship with your staff from this point forward?

Considerations

1. Has the chair's conduct so compromised the process that you feel it is necessary to cancel the search and start over?

    •   Do you make the decision about how to proceed on your own or only after consulting someone else? If you feel that consultation is desirable, whom do you call—your immediate superior, the human resources office, one of your peers here or at another institution, or the department chairs?

    •   If you decide to continue the search, what strategies do you follow to make sure that the process is not affected by the chair's remarks?

    •   If you decide to cancel the search and start over, on what grounds do you make this decision?

2. Do you try to determine which chair was involved in this conversation? If so, how?

    •   Do you try to gain more information from the current candidate? For instance, do you try to determine more precisely where the conversation occurred as a way of figuring out which chair was involved? Do you gather all the chairs together for one more meeting with the candidate and then have the candidate discreetly identify the chair to you?

    •   Do you try to determine whether other candidates had similar conversations with one of your department chairs? Because you have easy access to the internal candidate, do you begin by calling that person?

    •   If you prefer not to find out which chair was involved, why? What strategy do you follow instead of investigating the chair's identity? For instance, do you gather all your chairs together and talk about appropriate search procedures?

3. Suppose you learn which chair was involved in this conversation, confront this person, and are told, "Whoa! That wasn't the way it happened *at all.* Sure, I had a casual conversation in the hallway and my office, but it was the candidate who asked *me* about my biggest frustrations. I said, 'Well, three

things basically. I don't think that we as chairs meet often enough with the dean and the dean's staff, so it's hard sometimes to get our needs heard in a timely manner. I don't think that other disciplines really understand how research is done in my field, so I'm concerned about a tenure case that is coming up next year. And we're so short-staffed in my office that I find myself inundated with student issues that I believe really should be handled elsewhere.' I wasn't saying all that behind your back; you've heard me raise these issues plenty of times. Now, I'll admit that I did say I hoped having a new associate dean would help with some of these concerns, but they weren't presented as *conditions* for my support. You know me better than that."

- Does this new information change your perspective?

- On what basis would you decide whether the chair's depiction of the conversation was more accurate than the candidate's?

4. The candidate quoted a chair as saying that, in your view, the staff comes first and the students come second in a manner completely different from how you meant it (see Chapter 21, "Searching for and Building a Strong Administrative Team"). How do you go about clarifying your true intentions to the candidate? To your chairs? Do you begin to feel that a phrase like "the students come second" is simply too easily misunderstood?

5. If you identify the chair and learn that the candidate's account was correct in most details, how do you proceed? Do you attempt to reeducate the chair? Is this situation serious enough that you require the chair to step down?

   - Is your response any different if the chair's term were to end within the next three months?

   - Is your response any different if the chair were to retire within a year or two?

6. Do you feel that this situation is not very serious and can be addressed with a fairly modest solution, such as excluding department chairs from the final vote on the candidates so that the chair who acted inappropriately has no effect on the search's outcome?

7. How do you deal with a secondary issue that was raised by this problem: the perception of you and your role as dean that at least one of your current department chairs has developed?

Suggestions

Any situation in which a search is compromised should be regarded as serious. This is not a problem that is likely to be handled most effectively with modest solutions. You risk having wasted a significant amount of time and resources on a process that may not result in hiring the best candidate for the position. Even worse, the institution may be liable to a lawsuit from a candidate who believes that the search was not fair and open, particularly if the internal candidate ends up being hired. This is a situation in which you are probably well advised to be proactive. Don't assume that the problem will simply resolve itself once one of the candidates has accepted the position.

There are several things you could have done to reduce the likelihood of this scenario in the first place. To begin with, you should never assume that, simply because people have been involved in a large number of previous searches, they understand proper procedures. Workshops on effective searching and proper search etiquette should occur every year, and any individual who will play a role in a search (as a member of a committee, as an interviewer, or as someone a candidate is likely to meet) should be required to attend. If such a workshop had been conducted before the current scenario, the chair would already have known why the information that was shared with the candidate threatened the search and left the institution liable to a potential legal challenge.

Nevertheless, because this case study presents you with a fait accompli, there are several courses of action to consider. First, explain to the candidate that the chair's actions in no way reflect either your own thoughts or the way in which searches are conducted at your institution. Tell the candidate that you're very concerned about the situation; underscore the fact that the search is an open process in which no candidate—either external or internal—has an advantage over any other candidate; and promise that you will take this situation seriously. Ask the candidate whether he or she would prefer that you keep in confidence what you were told about the chair's conversation or whether you may mention the candidate's name when you inquire about the incident. If your institution has a formal procedure for irregularities in searches, you will want to contact the individual in charge of that process, describe what has occurred, and follow your internal process to the letter.

Second, you would be well advised to follow up on this situation and to determine as accurately as you can what really occurred. Perhaps this is best handled by a quick call to *both* of the other candidates, presented as a brief update on the progress of the search. It is usually not desirable to have this type of conversation with the internal candidate only; any situation that may give the impression that the internal candidate has been granted privileges should be avoided. If you have a follow-up call with one of the candidates, call the others as well; don't just meet the internal candidate in the hallway or in his or her office because that person is local. Make it clear from the very beginning of the call that the search is not yet over; otherwise, the person may assume that the call will be a job offer and become disappointed when it moves in a different direction. Say something like, "The search committee hasn't had its final meeting, and we're still not at the point of making a decision. I'm just calling the finalists to find out whether they have any additional questions." That type of opening gives the candidate a chance to raise a concern with you if he or she had a similar conversation with the chair. If the candidate does not offer any information, you might continue by saying, "I just want to be sure, too, that everyone on our staff was as courteous and professional as possible. Did anything occur during your interview that ever made you feel uncomfortable, or did anyone say anything that you felt was not professional?" By not asking a leading question, you are giving each candidate an opportunity to present his or her own version of the conversation. If the candidate responds by saying, "No, not at all. Everyone there was terrific. I can't think of a thing that was inappropriate," you probably should pursue the matter no further with that individual. You've learned that that particular candidate saw no problem with the search process, and anything more you say on the issue is likely to cause a problem unnecessarily.

Third, your best course of action is probably to speak one on one with each of your chairs to learn which of them may have spoken to the candidate inappropriately or at least *given the impression* of having spoken inappropriately. Holding these conversations individually will avoid having a chair become defensive in front of his or her peers if inappropriate statements were actually made. Moreover, one of the other chairs may have heard about the incident already and be willing to provide you with information in confidence. At the very least, you will be sending a clear message to the chairs that you have high standards for how searches should be conducted and that you take it very seriously when someone alleges that these high standards have not been met.

Certainly, situations will arise in your deanship where people whom you supervise do foolish or inappropriate things despite being trained to do otherwise. Your best response in such situations is to determine the seriousness of the problem, to intervene quickly to solve it to the extent possible, and then to take steps to reduce the likelihood that such a problem will recur. If you discover that, indeed, the candidate's account was reasonably accurate, you'll need to determine whether the search should continue based on how much damage the chair's statements have done. For instance, if a candidate withdraws from the search or even seriously *considers* withdrawing because of the chair's inappropriate comments, the situation may be serious enough to cancel the search and to reprimand the chair. If the candidate's account of the conversation proves to be accurate, an appropriate sanction will have to be imposed on the chair. This sanction could range from a letter of reprimand (if the chair's comments had relatively little effect on the search) to dismissal as chair (in more serious situations). Although this situation is not a problem that you yourself have caused, it is one by which your deanship is likely to be judged.

25

Setting Budgetary Priorities

The dean's role in budgeting falls largely into three main areas:

- *Budgetary planning:* This involves developing requests for additional funding, reallocating current resources, and tying college-level spending to the institution's overall strategic goals.

- *Budgetary supervision:* This involves tracking spending over time to ensure that the college and all its departments or programs remain within their budgetary limits throughout the fiscal period.

- *Budgetary modification:* This involves reconsidering budgeted amounts midyear as a result of changing situations.

In the next three chapters, we'll examine the dean's most important considerations in each of these three areas, beginning with budgetary planning.

Budgetary planning concerns estimating anticipated income and expenditures that are likely to occur within a specific predetermined period, usually a *fiscal year*. A fiscal year consists of any contiguous 12-month period over which an institution plans and tracks the use of its funds. Although fiscal years are calendar years at some institutions, most institutions have found that some other 12-month division—frequently July 1 through the following June 30—better suits their academic calendars, state legislative cycles, and student enrollment patterns. It is traditional to denote a fiscal year by using the abbreviation FY, followed by two or four digits that specify the calendar year in which the fiscal year ends. For example, most institutions use the designation FY20 or FY2020 to indicate a fiscal year that begins sometime in the calendar year 2019 and concludes on a predetermined date in 2020.

Nearly every state institution and many private institutions require that budgets be closed out at the end of each fiscal year. In other words, funds and deficits usually cannot be carried over from one fiscal year to the next. In these systems, on the last day of the fiscal year, all unexpended monies must be spent and all unreconciled deficits must be covered. This practice leads to the possibility of year-end funds, which can become an important factor in your budgetary responsibilities. Systems that do allow unexpended funds to transfer from one fiscal year to the next (a category of funding known as "carry forward") are likely to have stringent rules about what types of funding may be transferred, what sort of accounts may be involved, and the maximum amount a unit can carry forward. Your upper administration or budget office knows whether you can carry forward. In situations where transferring positive balances from one fiscal year to the next is possible, accumulating carry-forward funds can be a significant element of your planning. For instance, carry-forward balances are particularly useful for:

- Extremely costly equipment purchases that cannot be accommodated within the equipment budget of any single fiscal year

- Furnishing new facilities, particularly when, as frequently occurs, construction costs are more than the initial estimates and the project can only be completed by using funds originally set aside for furnishing the facility

- Unanticipated situations, such as matches for grants, repairs after natural disasters, and opportunities that, although unplanned, are in the unit's best interests to pursue

Carry-forward accounts are extremely valuable, but they are also risky. In years of fiscal exigency, they are almost always the first account designated to meet a sudden institutional shortfall. It is not uncommon, therefore, for colleges to bank carry-forward amounts for a large expense in the future only to have the account raided during a particularly bad budgetary year. For this reason, if your institution or system is one that permits carry-forward balances, you need to be fully aware of both the benefits and the risks that this type of account can pose.

As you begin to develop your unit's budgetary plan, you need to create it within the framework of your unit's overall budgeting philosophy. Although there are many different ways of describing institutional approaches to the budget, all of them fall largely into two main categories: zero-base budgeting and historical budgeting. *Zero-base budgeting* occurs when an institution resets its budgetary sources and allocations each time a new budget is created. Previous years' income and expenditures do not matter; the entire budget is designed each year from scratch or, as the name of this approach implies, from a zero base. *Historical budgeting,* the most common type of budgeting at colleges and universities, relies on the institution's past record of income and expenditures to help plan for the future.

The advantages of zero-base budgeting are that it is extremely flexible, helps free institutions from budgeting patterns that no longer make sense, and causes every single revenue and spending goal to be developed with a clear and defensible rationale. The disadvantages are that it is extremely time intensive;

can exacerbate divisiveness because it forces each unit to compete every year against the others for a share of limited resources; and frequently does not result in budgets that are significantly different from an easier, more historically based approach. The advantages of historical budgeting are that it is quicker to implement, gives institutions an initial plan that they can adjust according to their needs, and has been tested by the experience of previous years. The disadvantages of this system result from the philosophy of basing each year's budget (at least initially) on the previous year's income and expenditures. Thus, it can be extremely difficult for institutions to change poor but well-entrenched practices; it can also be relatively easy to overlook poor financial plans because every category of income and expenditures need not be justified each time the budget is set.

Regardless of whether institutions use zero-base or historical budgeting, almost all budget planning processes tend to be hierarchical. That is to say, departments submit budget proposals to colleges, colleges to the university, and the university to the university system. Even at small institutions, private colleges, and autonomous state institutions, the budget planning process follows *some* sort of hierarchical structure: Plans and proposals move from smaller units to larger units (bottom to top); budgetary decisions are passed from larger units to smaller units (top to bottom). Most colleges have established formats for budget requests. In other words, there is a standardized design that you will use in requesting new funding or reallocating current funding, justifying your request, and tying that request to the institution's strategic plan. In other colleges, particularly at small institutions, budget proposals are developed in a more informal manner. The dean might contact chairs and program directors, saying, "Get me a list of your most critical needs for the coming year by March 1." The dean will then collect these statements, prioritize them, and decide which of them to include in his or her own budgetary proposal to the higher administration.

At some institutions a formal budget hearing is an important part of the planning process, once proposals have been received from all units. In a *budget hearing*, each unit is given an opportunity to elaborate on and justify its requests for the coming fiscal year, each unit's requests are discussed, and the relative merits of the competing proposals are debated before the budget is set. A budget hearing process can be useful because it allows the upper administration to see the big picture of the institution's anticipated needs. Such an approach allows deans to comment on increases in another academic unit that are really in the best interest of their own college and the institution as a whole. For instance, a dean of business administration who has known that students who majored in one of his or her disciplines were delayed in their program because of insufficient seats in English Composition or Calculus I may prefer that additional faculty lines be added to the colleges that provide these courses. Similarly, several deans may support a request for an additional staff member in advising or counseling because needs in those areas are impacting their own academic programs. At institutions where formal budget hearings are not conducted, a designated committee, the president's cabinet, or even, at times, the chief financial officer alone will collate the various units' individual requests and establish an overall budget (see Chapter 29, "Budget Proposals"). This type of approach can result in setting a budget more quickly, but greater efficiency can come at the expense of the consensus building that usually occurs during a formal budget hearing process.

As you establish your budgetary plan and proposal each year, ask yourself these questions to make the best use of your institutions limited resources.

On what basis am I setting my budgetary priorities?

The temptation for most deans is to create a budgetary plan or request as a reaction to specific problems. For example, during the current academic year, there may have been problems resulting from higher-than-expected enrollments in particular courses. Students and their parents may have been angry because the demand for particular sections far exceeded the supply of seats. A dean may want to address this problem with a new faculty line to demonstrate that the problem is being taken seriously and to avoid similar complaints in the future. But this year's enrollment pattern may not be indicative of the college's continuing needs. Demographic patterns may suggest that a current overall increase in institutional enrollment is likely to be followed by several years of steep decline. The current high enrollment may be the result of a temporary fad rather than a more lasting trend. Economic situations in other countries, international crises, and even shifting fashions in popular culture and entertainment may result in enrollment spikes for certain courses that are not sustainable in the long run. For example, immediately following the Watergate scandal and the publication of Woodward and Bernstein's *All the President's Men* (1994), deans experienced a sudden but temporary increase in enrollments for introductory journalism courses. A similar fad arose for archaeology courses in the wake of the film *Raiders of the Lost Ark* (1981) and its sequels, for Japanese language instruction during the surge in the Japanese economy between 1985 and 1991, and for Arabic language instruction following the 9/11 attacks.

Although it can be extremely difficult for a dean to distinguish between a temporary fad and a long-standing trend, it is always important to consider what may be the root causes of a change in enrollment patterns. Shifts that occur because of demographic changes are likely to continue, and shifts that occur because of new employment opportunities may cause you to seek more permanent staffing for courses. On the other hand, shifts that result from news events, trends in popular culture, or the initiatives of individual political administrations are unlikely to be sustained. You are far better off meeting these needs not by seeking or reallocating tenure-track lines but through temporary employment, grant-funded positions, visiting scholars, or short-term changes in your course rotation. These approaches make it easier to adjust your schedule once the fad is over than would be the case if you hired new tenure-track faculty members.

Another very ineffective way of setting budgetary priorities is by "greasing squeaky wheels." Every college has certain constituents who voice the loudest and most frequent complaints about some perceived need. Deans may be tempted to address the issues raised by these squeaky wheels simply to placate them. Moreover, because these individuals mention their specific needs so often and so forcefully, deans may actually begin to see these needs as having a higher priority than they may merit. It is important when setting budgetary priorities to view each request not in terms of how stridently it was made but in terms of its overall benefit to the college or the department making the request. Ask yourself, "If this complaint were not one that I heard so frequently from this one individual, how would I evaluate it on its own merits? In terms of absolute, lasting benefits to the college or department, does this request outrank the other items in my budget proposal?" Try, to the greatest extent possible, to separate a request's value from the individual who is making it. Consider the likely possible benefits that would result if the demand were met and the likely possible problems that would result if it went unaddressed. Which seems most compelling?

Perhaps the best way to evaluate priorities objectively is to tie all your requests to either your institution's or your individual unit's strategic plan. Keep in mind the following essential principle:

> *At institutions with well-designed strategic plans, the budget is guided by the plan; at institutions without well-designed strategic plans, the budget is the plan.*

In other words, budgets are always manifestations of institutional priorities. If your institution and your college have taken the strategic planning process seriously, you already have a clear framework in place for ranking your college's budgetary needs. The individuals who make decisions at your college or university are unlikely to take seriously a request that is not supported by planning and data. Moreover, why would you advocate on behalf of a need that does not help your institution pursue its stated objectives and fulfill its mission? Unexpected situations may arise—unanticipated opportunities to take advantage of, unforeseen emergencies to address—but these situations should be rare and sufficiently compelling that everyone will understand why an exception is required. If you find that you are regularly giving high priority to items not easily tied to your strategic plan or mission statement, you probably need to reevaluate how you plan your budget.

Have I given due attention to revenue as well as expenditures in planning my budget?

Budget planning must take into account not only where resources will be spent but also how those resources will be acquired. Frequently, an increase in institutional funding is not the sole way in which your college can achieve an important goal. Consider, for instance, these questions:

- Is a particular budgetary item a suitable goal for a development project?

- Can a fee be established that will fund the item that you need?

- By charging admission for a particularly popular college event, can you accumulate a pool of funds that can be directed toward some of your college's most pressing needs?

- Are there foundations that can be approached for seed money for a project?

- Can you look at your existing funds to determine whether resources could be redirected from a low-priority item to this new higher priority?

Deans should examine their budgets each year and see what might occur if they were to redirect 5% of their operating budgets from low-priority items to clearly established new priorities. (This exercise is particularly useful for focused meetings or mini retreats for department chairs.) Although most deans initially approach this exercise as a hypothetical experiment, they frequently discover that there are ways of achieving important goals by reallocating current resources.

Budget plans that take into account both resources and expenditures tend to be more compelling for upper administrators. They demonstrate that you have grappled with the difficult challenge of finding ways to pay for new initiatives and that you are aware of the importance of tying spending levels to your highest priorities. Deans who view the budgeting process as an opportunity to present new wish lists to the upper administration are less likely to have even their most pressing needs taken as seriously as they would like. They make the mistake of paying attention only to what they *want,* not to what they already *have* and how they may use it more efficiently.

Have I clearly examined the budgetary implications of my one-year expenditures and my continuous expenditures?

As every administrator knows, not all spending is alike. Purchasing an extra piece of equipment affects a single year's budget. On the other hand, a new faculty line, a permanent increase in scholarship aid, or the start of a distinguished lecture series requires ongoing support. In your budgetary planning you need to treat each of these categories differently. One-year expenditures may be addressed through year-end funding; one-time gifts; annual fund contributions; temporary salary savings (e.g., one-year salary savings resulting from hiring a leave replacement who earns less than the faculty member on leave); or budgetary transfers that are effective for only the current academic year. Continuous expenditures may be addressed through permanent budgetary increases; endowments; long-term salary savings (e.g., hiring a new faculty member who earns less than a retiring faculty member); and budgetary transfers that endure beyond the current fiscal year. Try to be creative in moving funds from one type of continuous expenditure to another. For example, if a highly paid senior faculty member is leaving the institution and you have consistently found your unit short of faculty travel funding, propose to your upper administration that this problem be addressed in part through using the resulting salary savings creatively. A faculty member who currently earns $83,000 plus 23% in fringe benefits results in a continuous expenditure of $102,090. If an entry-level replacement is hired for $50,000 plus 23% in fringe benefits, the remaining continuous pool of $40,590 could be redirected to faculty travel. Although some systems have rules against transferring funds from personnel lines into nonpersonnel services accounts, it is worth investigating whether some of your college's priorities can be addressed not by increasing your entire budget but by reallocating current resources from one type of expenditure to another.

The fundamental principles in budgetary planning, therefore, are these:

- Be sure that your budgetary priorities reflect your unit's overall priorities.

- Remember that your unit's needs can be met in ways other than an increase in overall funding.

- Where possible, partner with other units in seeking innovative ways to meet one another's needs. These collaborative endeavors can then better serve the institution as a whole.

Resources

Barr, M. J. (2002). *Jossey-Bass academic administrator's guide to budgets and financial management.* San Francisco, CA: Jossey-Bass.

References

Bernstein, C., & Woodward, B. (1994). *All the president's men* (2nd ed.). New York, NY: Touchstone.

Spielberg, S. (Director). (1981). *Raiders of the lost ark* [Motion picture]. United States: Paramount Pictures

26

Supervising a Budget

Once a budget proposal has been developed (see Chapter 25, "Setting Budgetary Priorities") and your college has received its allocation for the fiscal year, one of the dean's most important duties is monitoring expenditures to ensure that the unit remains within its budgetary limits for the year. You may have your own budget officer who oversees accounts for you. You may delegate this duty to an assistant or associate dean. Or you yourself may monitor all the unit's budgets.

Regardless of the system you use, remember that budgeting requires proactive monitoring and supervision, not simply keeping an eye on details. Anyone who has ever told a child, "Watch your little brother" only to be told later, "But I *did* watch him. I watched the whole time he climbed up on the counter and the whole time he fell off" has encountered the difference between active and passive supervision. Overseeing a budget requires the most active form of monitoring, the kind where you check on every unusual detail and intervene before, rather than after, the shortfall occurs. At most institutions budgetary information is provided to deans electronically and updated continually. At some institutions printed statements are still distributed every week or every month, listing income, transfers, and expenditures by category.

Supervising budgets within your college involves tracking transactions according to the department, program, object code, or category in which they have occurred. Institutional systems for tracking transactions can often be extraordinarily complex, depending on the nature of the college or university, its organizational structure, and how it follows the practices required by its board of accounting standards. (These boards are the Governmental Accounting Standards Board for public institutions and the Financial Accounting Standards Board for private institutions.) In most cases the object codes used by institutions will be nine or more digits long, with each digit or group of digits providing such information as the specific campus on which the transaction took place (in multicampus systems); the source of funding (education and general, foundation, sponsored programs, etc.); the unit responsible for the transaction (college, division, department, program, etc.); and the precise nature of the income, transfer, or expenditure, which can include full-time salaries, part-time salaries, casual labor, benefits, postage, local telephone charges, toll telephone charges, subscriptions, memberships, equipment over a certain amount, equipment under a certain amount, travel, food, lodging, office supplies, and so on.

Because institutions almost always allow at least some types of transfer between these various funds, your general approach should be—unless otherwise instructed by your business office—to tie each transaction as closely as possible to its *actual* object code, not simply to any account that happens to have sufficient remaining funding. For instance, in a year when a particular department has already depleted its small equipment account, you may be tempted to allow an additional item of equipment to be purchased through its postage account or supplies and expenses account. Nevertheless, it is almost always desirable—and, at many institutions, it is required—for that purchase to be funded from the proper account, even though that account is depleted, and that you then submit a one-year transfer from another account to cover that expense. This procedure makes reconciling and auditing accounts much easier and provides a far more realistic picture of the unit's needs when each budget year is reviewed. If you notice that funds must be transferred from operating supplies to small equipment in the same department over several consecutive years, you may decide to realign these accounts permanently. On the other hand, if you are chronically short of funds in one account and must repeatedly cover those expenditures from remaining funds from several other accounts, you may need to request that the institution increase the underfunded account (see Chapter 25, "Setting Budgetary Priorities").

Transfers between certain accounts may not be possible at your institution. As we saw in the last chapter, there may be restrictions on transfers between personnel services accounts (i.e., accounts used to pay for salaries and benefits) and operating supplies accounts that limit whether you can transfer unexpended salary funding to such accounts as travel, photocopying, and equipment. Other institutions may have restrictions on whether institutional funds (i.e., the type of accounts usually known as "education and general funds") may be used for such purchases as student travel, entertainment, food or alcoholic beverages, and the like. Your institution's business office or chief financial officer can give you an overview of your system's restrictions. When restrictions on transfers or expenditures do exist, be sure to ask about *permissible* ways to achieve your ultimate goal. Restrictions on institutional funds may not apply, for instance, to funds overseen by a college's foundation; it is possible that the foundation may be willing to cover the cost itself or to swap a cost with you, paying for some permissible item or activity while you absorb one of its equivalent expenses. In other cases it may not be possible to transfer the *funds,* but it is perfectly permissible to transfer the *cost.* It may be a long time before you discover all the intricacies of your institution's budgetary procedures. The basic point is not to assume that there is only one way of accomplishing a budgetary goal. If you are informed that a certain type of purchase or transfer is not allowed, be flexible in your response. Say something like, "Well, this is essentially what I need to do. What ways can you explore with me that would allow me to accomplish the same goal within our existing operating procedure?"

No matter how much budgetary information your institution provides, most deans find it useful to maintain their own shadow budget in the form of an electronic spreadsheet. Items are occasionally coded incorrectly at other levels of an institution, and shadow budgets can help you detect discrepancies when you are charged for something that should have been charged to a different unit or when you are not credited with the proper funding. It is often the case, too, that official institutional budget reports lag behind the actual activity; preserving records in a shadow budget prevents you from accidentally spending the same money more than once, resulting in an end-of-year deficit. You can think of your shadow budget as something similar to your checkbook record: Reconciling this record with your bank statement helps you spot errors and avoid overdrawing your account. It also assists you in identifying funds that you have already allocated for a particular purpose, although you haven't technically spent them yet.

On both your shadow budget and official budget, one figure that you will wish to track is the percentage of each account expended versus the percentage of the fiscal year expended. If your institution does not calculate this ratio for you, it is extremely easy to set up a spreadsheet formula that does so. For instance:

(Amount Expended ÷ Original Amount) x 100 =
The percentage of that account expended to date

(Day Within Fiscal Year ÷ 365) x 100 =
The percentage of the fiscal year that has passed to date

After you have tracked this information for several years, you will learn your departments' particular budgetary patterns and rhythms and the red flags you need to watch for. Thus, an account that is 98% expended with only 35% of the academic year gone may or may not be an area of concern. This apparent discrepancy could result from an equipment account that supports only one or two purchases each year or from an account used for funding supplies or services needed at the start of the academic year but rarely again afterward. On the other hand, a photocopying account that is depleted too rapidly may leave that department vulnerable when final exams must be copied at the end of the semester. Your own familiarity with the needs of your area's disciplines, coupled with a healthy dose of common sense, will guide you in determining which percentages are problematic and which are not. (And you may need to explain your departments' spending patterns to budget officers outside your college.)

One other budgetary item that you may wish to track is your unit's cost vis-à-vis other colleges at your institution and similar colleges at other institutions. How much does it cost to produce, for instance, one student credit hour of instruction in a particular discipline at your institution compared with similar programs at other institutions? Frequently, your business office can calculate these figures. If your business office cannot do so, you can determine a crude cost approximation by adding a particular department's expenditures in salaries, benefits, and all categories of operating expenses (being sure to include travel funding and other accounts that may not be controlled within the department itself) and then dividing that figure by the number of student credit hours that the discipline produced during the same fiscal period. The reason why the resulting figure is crude is that it does not account for overhead and other institutional expenses, such as the expense required to operate essential offices on campus. For instance, an academic department is not billed for a share of the salaries paid to the institution's president, provost, dean, librarians, support staff members, custodial workers, registrar, and so on. Nevertheless, the department could not function without these individuals. Despite this methodological limitation, you will get a good general sense of how expensive each program is to maintain, provided that you calculate rates for other departments in precisely the same way. If you discover that it costs significantly less to produce a student credit hour in one department than it does in other departments at your institution or in similar disciplines at other institutions, you may be able to use this information to argue for your program's efficiency and sustainability. If you find that a particular program's costs are much higher, you can be proactive in identifying actions that you can take internally to help reduce those costs. In either case this type of very basic cost accounting can only benefit your institution. You might even begin using it to determine the cost-benefit ratio of making certain equipment purchases.

What should you do when a department appears to be expending its budget too quickly?

You should not immediately conclude that a department that is expending its budget quickly is doing anything wrong. As we saw earlier, certain spending patterns do not correlate well to the passage of the fiscal year; they make perfect sense when understood within their own rhythms. At times, too, a particular department or program will have an unusual budgetary year because of an emergency, a sudden increase in enrollment, the needs of a new or visiting faculty member, or some other unusual occurrence. It is possible that what appears to be an excessive expenditure at the moment will be covered by student fees paid into an *agency account* or *custodial account*. These accounts are so named because the institution is merely acting as the agent or custodian for funds that are paid into them—through such revenue sources as student fees or ticket sales—and expended as needed. For instance, an account into which students pay laboratory fees that are used to purchase chemicals and glassware for lab sessions is an agency or custodial account. As long as the individual responsible for this department or program is fully aware of how this account works and has incorporated it into his or her own budgetary planning, the situation is probably being addressed appropriately and requires no intervention on your part.

If you are unable to find your own compelling explanation for a department's or program's spending pattern, meet with the appropriate chair to review income and expenditure patterns from the start of the fiscal year. The chair may well be aware of special circumstances that help explain the financial situation that you have observed. If the chair is unable to offer any compelling reason for the excessive expenditures, you can begin to work together to explore strategies that will help the department or program end the year without a deficit. In certain cases it may be possible to transfer funds to this unit from resources that you know will not be expended elsewhere. (One-year salary savings for a sabbatical or leave replacement are common options, as are carry-forward accounts.) In other cases expenditures may be reduced for the rest of the year to avoid a deficit. Nonessential purchases may be deferred or made only in the event that year-end funding is available. (On year-end funding and carry-forward accounts, see Chapter 25, "Setting Budgetary Priorities.") Copying expenses may be reduced by providing course materials to students electronically rather than in hard copy. Mail and telephone charges may be trimmed by encouraging Internet communication rather than regular mail or toll calls. In certain cases merely making a department chair aware of the severity of a budgetary issue will prompt him or her to explore creative solutions.

What should you do when a department consistently overruns its budget?

Frequent budgetary overruns by a department or program could be indications that the unit is insufficiently funded, that the unit is not a good steward of its resources, or that some other factor is complicating the unit's budgetary history. To determine which of these possible causes is most significant, you will need to acquire more information than you are likely to find in the budget and ledger listings alone. The information that you will need is:

- *Synchronic:* How do this unit's revenue and expenditure patterns compare to similar units during the same fiscal years? Compare the unit with similar departments or programs at your institution, if at all possible. Try to think not necessarily in terms of the number of faculty members or the number of majors served but in terms of the unit's overall mission, reliance on equipment or travel to fulfill that mission, and other factors that would have a direct budgetary impact. In addition to these intra-institutional comparisons, see whether you can locate several departments or programs in comparable academic areas at peer institutions. Then examine each major area of the units' budgets (supplies, copying, postage, adjunct and overload hiring, etc.) divided by such factors as the number of student credit hours produced by each unit per fiscal year, the number of majors graduating from the unit as a rolling five-year average, the number of full-time or full-time-equivalent faculty members in the unit, and the like. Examined in this way, does this unit have atypical budgetary areas? Where does the difference appear to be: in insufficient funding or in excessive spending?

- *Diachronic:* Next examine the unit's budgetary patterns over time. If at all possible, examine these patterns over at least the past five years. Has the overrun been consistent in size relative to the unit's entire budget over time, or did it increase? If you discover that the size of the overrun is actually decreasing, the unit may be addressing the problem in an appropriate manner; all that the unit may need is your help and support. Is there a specific turning point at which the unit suddenly passed from balanced budgets into deficits? If so, what factors changed in the department or program at that time? Was the chair new? Did the department receive a new faculty line without an increase in its nonpersonal services budgets? Did enrollment start to rise? By pinpointing the time frame in which the unit's fiscal situation changed, you can begin to isolate the factors that may have accounted for the difference.

What should you do if your entire unit appears likely to run a deficit for the current fiscal year?

Just as you monitor your departments' and programs' expenditures to ensure that your entire college or school remains on budget, so does your upper administration monitor your unit's enrollment and spending patters to ensure that the institution as a whole remains within its budget for the fiscal year. Although you will want to be proactive in assisting your individual units to remain within their budgets, there will inevitably be years in which your college or school itself may be unable to adhere to its spending limits. Reasons for a budgetary shortfall may include enrollment declines, budget cuts imposed by the legislature or governing board, emergencies, rising costs that affect your unit disproportionately, one-time situations (such as the need to furnish a new facility), and similar factors. Whenever a situation of this sort is likely to occur, you should inform the upper administration as quickly as possible so that plans can be made and your supervisor will not be blindsided. In sharing information of this sort, you need to do your homework so that you can address each of the following areas:

- *The likely size of the anticipated shortfall:* Estimate to the best of your ability the probable scope of the deficit. Be as specific as you can. After all, if you say, "It looks as if we're going to be short in our equipment fund this year," you don't want your president to assume that you are speaking of a few thousand dollars when the actual shortfall is many times that amount.

- *The likely cause of the anticipated shortfall:* Try to determine, before your meeting with the upper administration, what seems to be leading to a deficit this year. If it is a factor that can be controlled or compensated for at your level, you will be asked for your plan to deal with it. Even if it is a factor beyond your control, you will still be expected to help deal with the situation's impact.

- *Some possible plans for dealing with the anticipated shortfall:* No administrator likes to be handed problems by people who have given no thought to a solution. Come to your meeting ready to propose possible solutions to the deficit. In doing so, be sure to give attention to what you intend to do within your unit, not simply to what other units or the upper administration can do for you. In fact, to the extent possible, come to this meeting ready to cover the shortfall by reallocating your college's resources.

Deans are unnecessarily intimated by the prospect of supervising a budget, especially when they are new to the position. Good budget management is, however, not much different from any other type of management. Pay attention to the individual expenditure patterns created by the needs of your disciplines. Ask questions whenever something strikes you as unusual or different from the practices you are observing elsewhere. Never sign authorizations unless you understand what you are signing. If you need suggestions on how to trim budgets and reallocate resources, see the next chapter, "Implementing Budget Cuts."

27

Implementing Budget Cuts

If you serve as dean long enough, you'll almost certainly experience a year in which your institution faces a severe financial challenge. At private institutions budget crises tend to occur when enrollment fails to meet projections or when the return on the institution's endowment is so low that it cannot sufficiently augment shortfalls. At public institutions budget cuts tend to occur for those same reasons and also when the state experiences a financial downturn and the legislature must reduce allocations to state agencies. In the best situation involving a budget cut, you will have plenty of warning so that you can make plans and deal with your reductions in a deliberate, careful, and well-considered manner. All too often, however, budget cuts occur unexpectedly. For instance, a state appropriation may be cut midyear. Enrollments that looked solid in May can prove to be surprisingly soft as classes begin in August. A sudden stock market plunge could make it impossible for an institution to receive its anticipated annual draw from the endowment. How you handle these situations will prove to be one of the clearest tests of your deanship. Good deans help colleges fulfill their missions during times of economic strength. Excellent deans help colleges fulfill their missions during times of severe budget cuts. The following are among the most important principles to keep in mind when implementing budget cuts.

Develop contingency plans each year.

Eventually, a budget cut will affect your unit. As a result, good budgetary planning involves preparing for those cuts before they are ever required. In Chapter 25 ("Setting Budgetary Priorities"), we discussed some of the steps to follow in creating a budgetary plan. In Chapter 29 ("Budget Proposals"), we'll explore ways of formulating those plans into documents that will help explain your needs and their rationale to your upper administration. Part of every good budget planning process—whether strategic (i.e., tied to long-range goals, more than one year in the future) or tactical (i.e., tied to more immediate goals, particularly those of the current or next fiscal year)—should be developing contingency plans that outline what you would do in the event of a budget reduction. For instance, suppose that you are severely understaffed but a budget cut imposes a hiring freeze before any of your available positions are filled. Suppose that travel budgets are eliminated but you have several junior faculty members who need to present their research to submit successful tenure applications. Suppose that you receive a mandate to reduce the number of sections you offer (and thereby reduce what you spend in personal services) by 5%. How would you handle each of these situations? More important, how would you handle these situations *while still fulfilling your college's mission?*

As part of your regular budget planning process, you should always develop contingency plans that explore how you would respond to several scenarios, including the following, if a crisis unexpectedly arose:

• *Across-the-board cuts:* How would you implement a 5% budget cut if you were given the liberty to reduce your existing budget in any way you wished as long as you met the 5% target? How would you handle the same situation if a 10% budget cut were mandated? Most academic units find that approximately 95% of their budgets are dedicated to salaries and benefits. Nevertheless, it is the rare college that can implement even a 5% budget cut without affecting salaries or reducing the number of sections taught by temporary faculty members, such as part-time or adjunct employees. After all, course materials still have to be photocopied. Telephones still have to be connected. Mail still needs to be sent. For this reason, study carefully both operating budgets and staffing patterns as you consider how you would implement a potential budget cut. Develop a plan that you could actually put into effect, not merely one that meets the reduction goal on paper.

• *Specified cuts:* How would you reorganize to fulfill your college's objectives if specific areas of its budget were reduced or eliminated? For instance, how would you respond to restrictions in travel, supplies, equipment, maintenance, part-time faculty, or overloads? If one of these areas were greatly reduced or eliminated, could you transfer funds from other areas to help cover the shortfall? Could you make cuts in other areas so that the mandated reduction or elimination was less severe?

Anticipating how you would handle cuts in particular areas is important because that is the way deans often receive budget reductions. State legislators or upper administrations may target a particular area of the budget, perhaps without regard to how that one area affects your unit's overall mission. By forming contingency plans, therefore, you may be able to transform a specified cut into a more general (and hence, for your planning purposes, more flexible) across-the-board cut by shifting funds from different areas to cover the reduction.

Let your strategic plan guide your budget cuts.

If you originally set your budgetary priorities properly by aligning them with your institutional and collegiate strategic plans (see Chapter 25, "Setting Budgetary Priorities"), now is not the time to abandon strategic thinking. Moreover, if you *didn't* originally establish your budgetary priorities as part of an overall strategic process, it is now imperative that you think strategically as you plan your cuts. After all, a strategic plan outlines both where your institution or college intends to go and how it intends to get there. If you do not incorporate this plan while identifying cuts, you may stall your momentum toward achieving goals that are far more important than the current fiscal year. Make no mistake: For most institutions, dire financial times, like prosperous financial times, come and go. The challenges that appear so pressing now will be a distant memory within just a few years. Don't abandon your most important initiatives simply because you've hit a bump in the road.

As you consider the cuts you will make, therefore, examine each of them in the following light: To what extent does this particular cut threaten the vision outlined in your strategic plan? For instance, if your institution's vision statement says, "Within 10 years, this institution will be one of the top five research universities in the region," this goal provides you with an essential tool for planning your budget cuts. If you have to make a choice between increasing course enrollments and cutting equipment funding for scholarships, you will not hesitate to expand the size of current courses. On the other hand, if your strategic plan says, "Within 10 years, this institution will be recognized throughout the region as a premier 'teaching first' institution with high retention rates and improved measures of student engagement," your decision will be quite different. If your strategic plan does not provide adequate guidance—if it is, for instance, so generic that it promises to do all things for all people—the fault lies not with the principle of tying budgetary decisions to the strategic plan but with the quality of the strategic plan itself.

Examine all the implications of every cut.

Deans need to approach budget cuts as they might approach a game of chess: studying the implication of each decision several moves hence. Although it is obvious that every budgetary cut will have consequences, you don't want a cut to have *unanticipated* consequences. For example, suppose that you are dean of a college with 80 faculty members. At your institution travel budgets are allocated to the college, not the individual department, and your annual faculty travel budget is $100,000. By January of the current academic year, just over

$80,000 remains on this budget line. Because of a midyear budgetary crisis, you are asked to return to the central administration $75,000 of your budget. "This seems to be a slow year for travel," you conclude, "so I'll take the cut from there. After all, we have to copy exams and provide supplies for our classrooms and labs. No one *has* to travel." You transfer the funds back to your president and inform your chairs of what you have done. There is an immediate outcry. The reason so much money remains in the travel budget, the chairs tell you, is that most conferences in their disciplines are held in the spring. Faculty members have already submitted abstracts for numerous conferences, made commitments to attend, and assumed financial obligations that cannot be reimbursed. Even worse, several faculty members *need* to attend these conferences because this last bit of professional development may be just enough to ensure their tenure or promotion. Also, several chairs are outraged that your unilateral decision has privileged those few faculty members whose conferences happened to be in the fall. What had once seemed such an obvious decision is now beginning to look like a very poor choice.

This situation occurred because you failed to anticipate the implications of the budget cut. Midyear cuts are particularly challenging because they don't allow sufficient time for planning and adjusting goals in light of a new financial situation. Nevertheless, the crisis could have been avoided if you had better understood the unit's spending rhythms. If you had been aware that springtime travel commitments are usually made in the fall, you might have sought other options, such as requiring funding to be secured before travel commitments are made. Perhaps a less wholesale reduction in the travel budget, complemented by reducing the number of sections taught by faculty members and making modest cuts in supplies and equipment budgets, would have allowed you to meet your target less destructively. Moreover, remember that your chairs can serve you well as an advisory body (see Chapter 13, "Department Chairs"). A focused meeting in which you establish a $75,000 reduction as the goal and explore with your chairs strategies for attaining that goal will almost certainly produce a more carefully considered plan than you could develop on your own.

Be as open and transparent about the situation as possible.

All the considerations outlined in this chapter lead to the most important principle in implementing budget cuts: Be as candid as possible as soon as possible and with as many people as possible. Budget reductions are difficult for everyone. Students complain about sections of courses becoming larger or more difficult to get into. Faculty members are frustrated by the loss of funding for research, travel, or instructional materials. Parents can't understand why they're paying so much money when their children can't even get the classes they need. Donors and potential donors become skittish because they are afraid their contributions will be wasted. As difficult as all these situations are, however, there is one principle that you must always keep in mind:

> *When you aren't candid in giving bad news in a bad situation, people will always imagine that the truth is even worse than whatever you would have told them.*

In other words, by not sharing disturbing news about the need for a budget cut as soon as possible, rumor and innuendo will fill the void that should have been filled by your effective leadership. Given the facts, the vast majority of our constituents are reasonable individuals who can both handle bad news and think constructively about possible solutions. Attempting to fix the problem by yourself or with a small group of trusted advisors only exacerbates the situation. It makes your constituents distrust your leadership and resist solutions that you may develop. It is far better to inform people about the extent of the problem as soon as possible, demonstrate that you are taking the situation seriously, and enlist them in resolving the matter.

In its essence, budget reduction does not involve any separate strategy than that used in planning an expansion. You must be guided by your strategic plan, your vision for your unit, and your good common sense. Avoid draining any particular line item simply because it is a convenient target: You are not a lion, and budget items are not herds of wildebeests; the slowest moving victim should not automatically become your prey. Your approach to budget cuts should be one that allows your unit to advance toward its strategic goals at the same time that it tightens its belt in less-than-critical areas. Above all, be forthright in presenting what needs to be done and in encouraging sound, constructive ideas for achieving that objective.

Resources

Dickeson, R. C. (1999). *Prioritizing academic programs and services: Reallocating resources to achieve strategic balance.* San Francisco, CA: Jossey Bass.

Eckel, P. D. (2003). *Changing course: Making the hard decisions to eliminate academic programs.* Westport, CT: Praeger.

Schuster, J. H., Smith, D. G., Corak, K. A., & Yamada, M. M. (1994). *Strategic governance: How to make big decisions better.* Phoenix, AZ: American Council on Education/Oryx Press.

Wolverton, M., Gmelch, W. H., Montez, J., & Nies, C. T. (2001). *The changing nature of the academic deanship* (ASHE-ERIC Higher Education Report Vol. 28, No. 1). San Francisco, CA: Jossey-Bass.

28

A Scenario Analysis on the Dean's Budget

Note: For a discussion of how scenario analyses are structured and suggestions on how to use this exercise most productively, see Chapter 8, "A Scenario Analysis on the Dean's Role." For additional case studies involving budgetary challenges and dilemmas, see Buller (2006, pp. 154–158).

Case Study

Imagine that it's time for you to start preparing your budget proposal for the coming fiscal year. Your institution follows a practice of historical budgeting rather than zero-base budgeting, so unless you propose a change or the upper administration mandates an overall cut, next year's budget for your unit will be identical to the current year's budget. (On historical vs. zero-base budgeting, see Chapter 25, "Setting Budgetary Priorities.") You do not expect that the upper administration will impose a budget cut. In fact, because enrollment has been increasing, it is likely that you will request and receive the first significant *increase* to your budget in many years.

As you organize your thoughts for the budget proposal, you identify the following unmet needs (listed in no particular order), which could form the basis of your request:

1. The department that offers your largest major is desperately in need of a new full-time faculty line. You've already increased the section size in as many courses as you possibly can and adjusted the course rotation to its maximum efficiency. Without a new full-time faculty line, this large program will see reductions in quality that could soon hurt enrollment as well as the department's national reputation.

2. Salaries in your college lag behind those of other colleges at your university as well as those of similar colleges at other universities. In part, this problem has been caused by rapid growth in the disciplines that you supervise, forcing you to devote a portion of your raise pool each year to new faculty and staff positions rather than to salary increases. The situation has now

become critical: Last year several of your best faculty members left the institution because they found better paying jobs elsewhere.

3. The disciplines in your college are highly dependent on technology. The institution's technology funding has been insufficient to upgrade this equipment as often as your college really requires to stay competitive. You are in desperate need of a large, permanent increase to your college's own technology fund to address this issue.

4. Travel funding in your college has remained flat for many years. At the present time, it is woefully insufficient. This year you were able to fund only $600 per faculty member in travel for scholarship. Because of rising costs for airfare, hotels, and conference registration, the actual need per faculty member in your area is approximately three times your current budgeted amount. Several faculty members whom you believe made important contributions and deserved tenure were denied it; the reason cited was "insufficient presentation of scholarship at national meetings." You are convinced that your meager travel budget is at least partly responsible for your faculty members' inability to attend national meetings.

5. There has long been discussion of adding a new emphasis in one of your college's departments. To achieve this goal, however, you will need to begin phasing in several new faculty positions and one new staff position. If you don't begin pursuing this initiative soon, your college is likely to fall behind its peer and aspirational institutions, which have already established this area of emphasis.

6. Students in one of your disciplines are failing a required introductory-level sequence at an alarming rate. You've conducted a study and discovered that successful programs in this discipline maintain a well-staffed tutorial center. Because the discipline is declining in majors, you've concluded that its long-term success can only be achieved if it creates one of these intensive, well-staffed, discipline-specific tutorial centers.

7. A department in your college has requested an additional full-time faculty member. Without this new position, the department chair states, it is unlikely that the discipline will be successful in its bid for reaccreditation.

8. Your institution has recently allowed colleges to have their own development officers—as long as the college can fund the position from its own

budget. To achieve this goal, your college would require a budget increase. Nevertheless, you believe that having your own development officer might bring into your college many times what it would pay out each year in salary and benefits to staff such a position.

9. The dean from another college has told you repeatedly that students majoring in that college's disciplines are delayed in their programs because your college's service courses quickly reach maximum enrollment. You have raised enrollment caps as far as you believe to be appropriate, and you can only provide the relief that the other college requires by hiring an additional full-time faculty member.

10. A recent needs assessment indicated that students in your college would be much more successful in finding employment or being accepted into graduate school if they had experience presenting and defending their original research at an undergraduate research conference. No appropriate conference takes place anywhere near your school. To achieve this goal for your college, you'd have to fund a conference yourself each year.

11. Aside from your meager travel budget, your college has never had its own faculty development program. You have no resources to conduct workshops and other forms of training on effective classroom techniques, promoting active learning, increasing student engagement and academic success, grant writing, submitting research proposals, and the like. Because the institution itself has no plans to provide such training, you believe that your college's faculty will be best served if you can start your own program. You can't do that, however, without increased funding.

12. Because you are short-staffed in several academic areas, you know that the most cost-effective way of providing additional sections of courses would be a permanent increase in your adjunct budget. Adjunct faculty members are hired at your institution on a per-term basis, so this solution provides you with the most flexibility in meeting your students' course demands. Because adjunct faculty members do not receive benefits, you have calculated that you could add more than 20 adjunct-taught sections for approximately the same cost as a full-time, tenure-track faculty member.

13. Your own office has been insufficiently staffed for many years. Because you have no one assigned to monitor the budget, deal with student requests for course overrides and policy exceptions, and provide administrative support

to faculty searches, you have had to handle most of these responsibilities yourself. This situation has limited the time that you are able to spend on grant development, donor visits, and foundation calls—all of which could significantly improve your college's financial situation. You believe that another assistant dean, assigned many of the duties that you find burdensome, would quickly pay for itself and produce additional revenue that could help fund your college's other pressing needs.

How do you go about determining which of these needs are among your unit's highest priorities?

Considerations

1. How might your budgetary priorities change if your institution's strategic plan contained the following statement. (As you do this exercise, assume that *only one* of the statements may be found in the strategic plan at a time. Reconsider your priorities in light of each statement in turn.) "Within 10 years, this institution will be nationally recognized as . . ."

    *   "Having placed the needs of its students *first* in every decision that it makes."

    *   "One of the top five research-oriented institutions in its region."

    *   "Providing the highest quality of instruction because it is wholly dedicated to its students' academic success."

    *   "A model for efficiency in all the services it provides, fully respectful of the sacrifices students make to pay tuition, donors make to contribute support, and state taxpayers make to defray costs."

    *   "Having attained discipline-specific accreditation in every possible program."

    *   "A leader in both its retention and graduation rates."

    *   "On the cutting edge in all its disciplines."

    *   "Having placed a priority on the needs of *all* its constituents: students, their parents, community supporters, faculty members, staff members, and alumni."

2. Suppose that your institution's strategic plan included a goal that you believed was philosophically wrong or ill considered. For instance, what if your institution's strategic plan gave high priority to:

    *   Granting students access to classes by increasing the number of adjuncts hired, thus increasing the total number of sections offered? Nevertheless, you believe that the quality of education provided to the students suffers through an already excessive reliance on adjuncts, and you fear how accrediting bodies will regard this trend. How do you handle budget item 12 now that the strategic plan and your personal outlook are in conflict?

    *   Expanding existing academic programs into innovative, at times even experimental, new areas? You believe, however, that the institution's actual funding has barely been sufficient to maintain *current* programs, much less expand into risky new areas. How do you handle budget item 5 now that the strategic plan and your personal outlook are in conflict?

3. Two of the possible items for your budget, 8 and 13, concern positions that you believe will more than pay for themselves, probably even generating enough additional income to fund other priorities on your list.

    *   How do you make the case (both to the upper administration and to members of your own college) that it may be preferable to secure funding for an item that is not itself a high priority but that could increase funding for several items that *are* high priorities?

    *   Suppose that you are preparing your budget request in a highly politicized environment. The dean who preceded you frequently requested additions to the dean's office staff and operating budget; departmental needs went unaddressed. This practice has made your faculty highly cynical of any request from the dean's office that does not immediately serve the needs of academic programs. You are new to your deanship and have not yet established a track record of trust. You believe that adding a college development officer and associate dean will truly serve the faculty's needs better in the long term. Nevertheless, you also know that most members of the faculty will be skeptical, perhaps even hostile, to such a proposal. Do you make this proposal anyway?

4. Suppose that item 1 was, according to both your strategic plan and your personal conviction, your highest priority. Nevertheless, funding this position

would be so expensive that you believe this request may be ignored if you give it precedence in your budget proposal. Items 4, 10, and 11 are, respectively, your second, third, and fourth priorities. You think that all three of them could be funded for less than the position outlined in item 1. You have reason to believe, however, that your upper administration will ignore these requests unless you argue that they are your top priority. Is it ever legitimate to resort to realpolitik and structure your priorities according to what is more *likely* to be funded than according to your actual convictions? Assume that all these items are needed but that the position discussed in item 1 is simply needed *more* than the other items.

Suggestions

The way in which you evaluate these funding priorities will reveal a great deal about your own decision-making processes. You will probably have a very obvious preference in situations where you have an established mandate from your institution's strategic plan that corresponds well with your own beliefs and convictions. But what about those messy situations when the plan tells you one thing but your gut tells you another? You do not want to ignore your strategic plan's guidance too frequently. If you find yourself year after year setting budgetary priorities that deviate from it, then something is decidedly wrong. The plan itself is poorly designed (and you need to have a serious discussion with the upper administration about why it should be changed); your personal priorities are distorting your ability to see what is in the best interests of your institution as a whole; or you are not the right person for your current position. You need to conduct a candid, objective analysis of why your priorities seem to differ so frequently from your institution's. Once you have clearly decided where this disconnect originates, you'll have a better understanding of how you should respond.

Nevertheless, if you truly believe that it is better for your unit to pursue a different priority than those established by strategic goals—and you have come to this conclusion only once or twice during your tenure—then go ahead and make the strongest case you can for your position. Remember the following essential principle:

> *One of the most important duties that any dean has is being the official exception maker. If it were not occasionally necessary to make exceptions to existing policies, plans, or procedures, colleges would simply develop rulebooks; they wouldn't need deans.*

In other words, effective deans realize that strategic plans are important road maps for an institution's future but that they are only plans. They cannot cover every contingency that will arise after they are created. Just as only a foolish pilgrim completely ignores his or her road map (and will unlikely reach the appointed destination), so does a foolish dean completely ignore the institution's strategic plan. Nevertheless, a pilgrim is also foolish if he or she thoughtlessly adheres to the map despite changing circumstances, such as a washed-out route, the opportunity for a productive side trip, or the completion of a new bridge that can shorten the journey. You should be willing to advocate for that rare departure from your institutional strategic plan as long as you can defend its importance to others.

On further suggestions for the actual formatting, structure, and phrasing of your college's budget request, see the next chapter, "Budget Proposals."

References

Buller, J. L. (2006). Five case studies in budgeting. In J. L. Buller, *The essential department chair: A practical guide to college administration* (pp. 154–158). Bolton, MA: Anker.

29

Budget Proposals

In Chapter 25 ("Setting Budgetary Priorities"), we explored some fundamental strategies for ranking your unit's various budgetary needs. But once you have set your priorities, how do you go about making the best possible case for the items that you need the most? How do you create budget proposals that are both compelling and most likely to result in the funding your unit needs to flourish?

By this point in your administrative career, you are probably well aware of the following essential budgetary principle, although it is frequently unknown to faculty members and to a surprising number of department chairs:

> *A statement of need alone is never a sufficient argument that a need must be addressed. This is particularly true when there are insufficient resources to meet all of an institution's competing needs. At colleges and universities, there are always insufficient resources.*

Stephen Crane once expressed this essential principle on a more metaphysical scale: "A man said to the universe: 'Sir, I exist!' 'However,' replied the universe. 'The fact has not created in me a sense of obligation.'" Replace "the universe" in this maxim with "the university," and you have encountered one of the harsh truths of higher education budgeting. For this reason, a good budget proposal should not merely argue (even if it argues quite persuasively) that a need exists; a good budget proposal should take notice of the reader's requirements and goals, relating each request to them. With this general framework in mind, ask yourself the following questions as you begin to prepare your next budget proposal.

Who is my audience for this proposal?

Every budget proposal has a target audience who will be reading, evaluating, and deciding on the proposal's recommendations. In many cases there will even be multiple audiences for the proposal as it winds its way through a committee structure, is modified at the vice presidential level, and then is possibly modified again at the presidential level. It is important to keep these audiences in mind as you draft your document because these individuals may not share your knowledge, values, and outlook as they make their decisions about what you are requesting. Any one of these three areas may cause you to phrase your budget proposal differently:

- *Knowledge:* Are there particular terms, acronyms, or concepts that you take for granted in your college but that may be unclear to those outside your unit? In terms of equipment requests, be sure to specify in nontechnical terms the reasons why the item is essential to your academic programs or your faculty's scholarly activity. Do not state merely the need for the item but the benefit to the institution as a whole that will result from its acquisition. Why is an outright purchase preferable to renting equipment or entering into an agreement with another institution that would allow the occasional use of this equipment? With regard to position requests, how is the prospective hire's field vital to your institution's overall mission and plan?

- *Values:* You may be basing a budget proposal on values that are completely different from your audiences'. For instance, you may be trying to decrease your student-to-faculty ratio because you believe that small classes are better pedagogically, but you may be making this request to individuals for whom productivity and maximizing student credit hour production are more important. In such a case, consider providing statistics indicating that increasing section size beyond a certain point produces diminishing or even negative returns because of the impact it has on student retention. In the long run, you could argue, decreasing the student-to-faculty ratio actually produces a higher sustainable student-credit-hour production in your area. You won't realize that you need to make this argument, however, if you don't consider the intended audience's values.

- *Outlook:* We all have individual vantage points. Making a case for increasing faculty lines to reduce course load and increase scholarly productivity may not be the most useful approach if your audience consists primarily of representatives from student life, the business office, and the registrar's office. Take time in structuring a budget proposal to consider the possible outlooks of the people evaluating your proposal. If many of these individuals tend to see the world from a student services perspective, then a proposal that is based on a more faculty-oriented approach may be doomed to fail. If your audience tends to view the world from a data-oriented perspective, then be sure to include results that are easily quantified.

What are the audience's primary concerns?

Once you have established the knowledge base, values, and outlook of your proposal's primary audiences, you are ready to ask these questions: What are my readers' primary concerns? What do they need most, care deeply about, or wish to see happen? For instance, you will obviously always want to tie your budget proposal to your institution's strategic plan. Nevertheless, if your institution is in the initial stages of fulfilling a new strategic plan—particularly if that plan has been the pet project of an incoming president—you will want to especially link your budgetary requests to upper administration's goals. Your proposal's audience will be concerned with making clear and demonstrable progress on the plan; whatever you can do to help connect your budgetary goals to that progress will best serve the interests of the disciplines you supervise.

The following are a list of common concerns by decision-making constituencies at many colleges and universities. Identify those items that are primary concerns of the people who will be evaluating budget proposals at your institution, and explore how to present your area's needs as ways of addressing those concerns:

- Retaining a higher percentage of students; improving graduation rates

- Increasing research productivity (among students, faculty, or both)

- Enhancing the institution's profile and academic reputation (regionally, nationally, or internationally)

- Internationalizing the curriculum

- Improving graduates' placement rates in first-choice careers or graduate and professional schools

- Raising minimum admissions standards

- Attaining a higher ranking in one or more of the annual surveys of American colleges and universities

Once you identify the primary concerns of the audiences who will be reading and evaluating your proposal, you will be in a good position to reread your draft through their eyes. Have you tied your requests to their priorities? If not, your budget proposal is unlikely to be effective. You'll be arguing on one set of fundamental assumptions, and those who make the budgetary decisions will have a completely different set of assumptions. It's time to rework your draft.

How can this proposal be structured to address those concerns?

If you find that your budgetary requests do not correspond well with the review committee's priorities and concerns, you should not necessarily conclude that your budget proposal is doomed or that the committee won't understand your needs. It is always possible, of course, that your priorities are indeed idiosyncratic, of interest only to your unit, and not reflective of the best interests of the whole institution. You should come to that conclusion, however, only after some serious and candid reflection on your entire proposal—for instance, if you were an outside reader with no direct association with your college, how important would you regard these requests?—and on the recommendation of a trusted confidant. It's more likely that although the items on your proposal are necessary and important, you have not tied them sufficiently to the budget committee's concerns and priorities. Making this adjustment is your next step.

Writing an effective budget proposal is a lot like writing a successful grant proposal. The granting agency has concerns or a philanthropic focus to which you might tailor the rhetoric of your grant proposal. It's the rare situation that someone in your college will want to secure external funding for a project and immediately locate a foundation that is interested in funding that precise idea. Grant applications always involve a process of refining the idea for a project so that it better meets the funding agency's interests. So it is with budget proposals. The only difference is that now the granting agency consists of individuals from your own institution.

As you review your institutional strategic plan and any tactical goals that have been established for the coming year, look for possible linkages between what your unit needs and what the institution is trying to accomplish. At the very least, most strategic plans devote a section to enhancing the quality of academic programs; you will want to be certain that the vast majority of your budget requests are clearly tied to that goal. Even beyond that general goal, however, find ways to speak the budget review committee's language, demonstrating that granting a request that helps you actually helps committee members and the institution as a whole. You may well find that the arguments you need to justify a budgetary priority internally ("This item will help us reduce the pressure on workload that we've been so concerned about") are quite different from those that you use to justify the item outside your college ("This item will help us improve our retention and increase our chances to receive discipline-specific accreditation in several of our areas"). Spinning arguments in this way is not being disingenuous. Budgetary priorities always fulfill a multitude of needs. Your task is simply to identify the needs that will be most compelling to each audience and then to highlight those needs as you develop your request.

How can you strengthen the case for your proposal?

As we have seen, submitting a budget proposal is a lot like applying for a grant. This observation is true in another way as well. Just as many granting agencies will look more favorably on proposals that provide at least some matching funds for the project, so is your budget proposal likely to be strengthened if you can find ways to demonstrate your own commitment to its priorities. For example:

- Are there funds that you can transfer from low-priority areas to the budget proposal's high-priority areas? You could explain, for instance, "Now that I've outlined all the reasons why creating this new position at the senior level rather than at the entry level helps us advance our institutional strategic plan, I'd like to demonstrate how important this position is to us. Within our own college, we've identified $40,000 of funding to shift from our adjunct budget—thus also helping achieve the strategic goal of reducing our institutional reliance on part-time faculty members—and salary savings to this new position. In other words, if we can receive funding for an *entry-level* position from the institution, we ourselves will make up the difference to elevate the position to *senior rank*."

- Are there other types of contributions that your area can make that would result in a stronger proposal? For instance, if proposal readers are concerned about productivity, can you tie a slight increase in the enrollment caps in certain courses to the funding of your budget request? If the concerns are about promoting undergraduate research, can you reassign another faculty member to take charge of this endeavor once the position that you are requesting is funded?

- Are there ways in which you can leverage this request to obtain other items of great concern to proposal readers? For instance, can you argue legitimately that, if your request is granted, you'll be in a better position to secure external funding for the institution's other priorities? Are there ways in which the position or item will pay for itself over time? Could this particular budgetary priority account in any way for increased revenue to your department through providing fee-based services to other entities, increasing enrollment in your area, or justifying a fee for use?

Ineffective budget proposals frequently result from assumptions that, simply because an item appears compelling to *us,* it will be compelling to *everyone.* A budget request is, in the end, a rhetorical document: You are trying to persuade someone to do something. For this reason, you need to apply the basic rules that you learned in Rhetoric 101 to every budget proposal:

- Know your audience.

- Know what motivates your audience.

- Relate what you want to occur to that motivation.

30

Faculty Evaluations

All deans are involved in evaluating their units' faculty members. Frequently, evaluations tend to begin in a department or with a faculty review committee before reaching the dean for approval, modification, or elaboration. At very small institutions, however, the dean may be completely responsible for faculty evaluations, devoting a significant portion of the administrative year to this task (see Chapter 54, "The Dean as Chief Academic Officer"). Some institutions have rigidly prescribed formats, specifying how written evaluations must be structured; other institutions allow faculty evaluations to be organized in any manner that the dean deems most appropriate. Nevertheless, despite these differences, there are several ideas that every dean needs to keep in mind when reviewing faculty performance.

Link the quality of one's performance to clearly articulated roles and responsibilities.

Every institution outlines in writing the responsibilities that its faculty members are expected to fulfill. Such documents may be as general as a brief statement in a faculty handbook that says, "Faculty members are expected to devote full time to teaching, scholarship, and service." They may be highly detailed sections of a collective bargaining agreement that assign specific percentages of a faculty member's time to various categories of responsibility (see Chapter 52, "The Unionized Environment"). Or they may fall somewhere in between. Whatever is the case at your institution, the most important aspect of every faculty evaluation is that the criteria on which the faculty member is evaluated must match the responsibilities that he or she has been assigned. Nothing is less useful for improving both faculty performance and employee morale than an evaluation system that faults someone for failing to perform a task that he or she did not even understand to be part of the job.

To the extent that your institution allows, therefore, you should structure your evaluation to follow your unit's assigned faculty duties. In most cases this structure will include at least three statements clearly labeled "teaching," "scholarship," and "service," perhaps even followed by some indication of each category's weight, such as "teaching (50% of performance)," "scholarship (40% of performance)," and "service (10% of performance)." Headings like these clearly indicate to the reader the basis on which the evaluative statements are made. Even more important, they reiterate for the reviewer the proper and appropriate grounds for evaluation, reducing the likelihood that statements irrelevant to the faculty member's professional responsibilities will be included in that section of the performance review. Stating each category's weight also clarifies for both the reviewer and the faculty member the relative importance that should be assigned to the statements made in that area. For example, with the weighting outlined in the example, a conclusion that "definite improvement *must* be made in this area" carries far more significance to the individual being reviewed if it occurs in the section on teaching (which constitutes 50% of the faculty member's responsibility) than in the section on service (which accounts for only 10%).

Be sure that the performance review includes truly evaluative language.

One of the worst problems that can occur in a faculty evaluation is when the reviewer simply lists accomplishments without evaluating them. All too often, a review will include a sentence such as "During the past academic year, you completed two research papers that were submitted for editorial review and had one additional article appear in print." The difficulty with such a statement is that it does not indicate whether that particular amount of scholarly activity *exceeds* your college's expectations for a faculty member at that rank and in that discipline, *meets* those expectations, or *falls short* of them. When items are listed and not truly evaluated, the faculty member may receive a completely different impression than what the reviewer intended. The faculty member may read the summary of activity as acceptance of what he or she has done, even as praise, whereas the reviewer may have intended the list to indicate how little had been accomplished during the past year. Moreover, simply listing teaching assignments, publications, or committee responsibilities gives the reader no indication of whether those responsibilities were carried out well. A faculty member may have had a heavy teaching load but accomplished little in the way of student success. He or she may have published several articles, but they appeared in inferior journals. The faculty may have been a member of many committees but attended relatively few meetings and contributed little when present. Without clearly evaluative statements, neither the faculty member nor any other reader of the letter (e.g., a member of a future committee on promotions) will have any way of knowing what you intended.

There are various ways in which you can include clearly evaluative statements in a faculty evaluation. For instance, you can use:

- *A Likert scale or some other type of numerical rating:* A Likert scale (commonly mispronounced as "LIKE-ert," but more correctly pronounced "LICK-ert") is a numerical ranking, usually consisting of five discrete categories. For instance, on faculty evaluations, this type of rating might take a form such as "On a scale of 1 (low) to 5 (high), I would rate your achievement in scholarly activity for the past year as . . ."

- *A verbal Likert scale:* This type of evaluative ranking is essentially the same as the numerical Likert scale, but it substitutes descriptive adjectives for numbers. Common categories used on faculty evaluations as part of a verbal Likert scale include "excellent," "very good," "good," "satisfactory," and "unsatisfactory."

- *A graded Likert scale:* Because academics tend to be comfortable with letter grading, some institutions prefer to use an A–F scale in faculty evaluations. The advantage of such a system is that it allows for more specific gradations (B+, C-, and so on). The disadvantage of such a system is that the type of grade inflation expected by many students can carry over to this evaluation system; faculty members may thus find even a B evaluation, which should imply "above average," to be cause for an appeal because no grade less than an A is acceptable to them.

- *A statement of meeting expectations:* In many ways, this approach is similar to the verbal Likert scale, but it replaces simple adjectives with a statement about the unit's expectations. These statements may include "Clearly exceeded the institution's expectations for a faculty member at your rank and in your discipline," "Exceeded expectations," "Met or exceeded expectations," "Met expectations," and "Failed to meet expectations." If you are using this type of phrasing, it is important that there be some document (frequently part of a faculty handbook or policy manual) that sets forth what the institution's and unit's expectations *are* in each evaluation category.

Whichever system of evaluative language you use, be sure to adhere to the following essential principle in writing your letter of appraisal:

> *Be able to summarize your overall conclusion in fewer than 20 words. If you cannot express your point with this degree of clarity and brevity, the faculty member is likely to misunderstand you. In fact, once you have reduced your conclusion to a single sentence, consider including that sentence—in bold face type—at either the beginning or the end of your evaluation.*

Make sure that both you and your readers know the difference between formative and summative performance reviews.

Formative evaluations are those intended to mentor or improve a faculty member's performance. *Summative evaluations* are those concerned with making a decision—for instance, the amount of a salary increase, whether a promotion should be granted, or the terms under which a contract should be renewed—that is based on the faculty member's past performance. In the classroom every professor is aware of the difference between formative and summative evaluations. Formative evaluations are the questions we pose in the middle of a class, using the students' responses to gauge whether they are mastering the material and how we should proceed with our lesson; if we are not satisfied with their answers, we restructure our plans and try to help the students understand better. Summative evaluations, in the classroom setting, are our final exams; if we are not satisfied with the students' answers, they fail the course.

In a similar way, faculty evaluations may be either formative or summative. The problem is that we frequently blur these two functions of an evaluation. Even when we don't blur these functions, a later reader of our comments may do so. For instance, we may write a year-end performance appraisal that gives someone constructive advice about how he or she needs to improve in some area, but then we may also use our conclusion as the basis for recommending a lower-than-average salary increase. Correspondingly, we may provide a faculty member with a performance appraisal that contains a lot of useful advice, but a promotion committee might regard that letter as a negative evaluation. For this reason, it is always important to distinguish clearly between constructive suggestions and evaluative conclusions in the written materials that you prepare. In the best systems, formative documents are entirely different in design and structure from summative documents. Formative documents should be clearly labeled for what they are—helpful advice from a mentor or supervisor—rather than disguised as performance appraisals; they can be relatively free form and personal, as opposed to the more prescribed format of summative documents.

Nevertheless, when it is not possible to create wholly separate documents, it is still advisable to distinguish advice from judgment as clearly as possible. This may be done through statements such as "Over the next several years, you may wish to begin revising your course syllabi to clarify more precisely when in the term students are expected to have completed the initial drafts of their research papers. I do not, however, regard this as a serious criticism, and it in no way detracts from my overall evaluation that you have met or exceeded the college's expectations in quality of instruction during the past year."

As a long-term goal, encourage your college or institution to develop evaluation categories that allow for true gradation.

Nearly everyone is familiar with the "Lake Woebegone effect." At the end of each story about the fictional Minnesota setting of Lake Woebegon on *A Prairie Home Companion,* Garrison Keillor describes the town as "where the women are strong, the men are good looking, and all of the children are above average." Faculty members, too, frequently regard themselves as all above average. In some ways, such a conclusion is understandable: If our hiring practices are sound, we seek to hire only the best candidates available; if our tenure and promotion practices are sound, we seek to reward and retain only the best of the best. Nevertheless, systems in which nearly everyone receives a rating of "excellent" in all evaluation categories hurt faculty members in the long run. These systems provide no opportunity to acknowledge the truly exceptional year when someone's important new book comes out, a major new grant is received, or a national award for excellence in teaching is won. Moreover, promotion committees and governing boards tend to dismiss evaluation processes that do not allow for some measure of genuine gradation between degrees of excellence. For this reason, if your institution's or unit's evaluation criteria are not sufficiently stringent to allow for truly meaningful levels of distinction, they need to be revised. At most institutions a dean's attempt to achieve this goal will be met with resistance and much cynicism. Nevertheless, it is an important long-term goal to pursue. Working collaboratively with a faculty committee (particularly a group that includes the faculty's opinion leaders), being completely transparent about your plans and progress, and meeting frequently to explain the need for such a change in your evaluative processes greatly benefit your faculty over time.

As an additional long-term goal, seek to create consistent departmental standards for faculty review while at the same time allowing for some degree of flexibility.

One of the challenges faced by deans is promoting equity while understanding that absolute equality is not possible and, in many cases, not desirable. A degree of flexibility and disciplinary uniqueness is often essential in departmental standards for faculty review, particularly under the category of scholarship. The forms that appropriate levels of scholarship may assume are different for different fields. Books of research and refereed articles in competitive scholarly journals are, of course, highly desirable in most fields, but they may not be the best indicators of scholarship in fields where performance, creativity, or application are the preferred modes of contribution. The question that then arises is this: How does, for instance, a faculty recital compare to a scholarly article in meeting your institutional scholarship standards? If a program is accredited by a disciplinary accrediting organization, that organization may be able to provide guidelines, benchmarks, and examples of best practices at other institutions for calculating equivalencies for different forms of scholarship. Where such examples do not exist, however, you may wish to appoint an ad hoc committee to work out general equivalencies for various forms of scholarship that you can then discuss with the faculty as a whole. Informing new faculty members of the standards they are expected to achieve is extremely important as they plan their work and commitments in the years leading up to a promotion or tenure review.

Whatever system you devise, it is important that it remains flexible enough to incorporate new forms of scholarship. For instance, when online journals and other web-based forms of communication became prevalent, many institutions had to revise their standards of scholarship, which exclusively addressed printed journals and published research. It is impossible to know what future directions scholarship may take because of new technology. A set of guidelines that can be continually updated will help you preserve uniformly high standards across disciplines while still permitting individual departments the flexibility that they need to reflect their unique missions. These guidelines can perhaps be complemented by a review committee that decides on such matters as appropriate venues for research, scholarship, and creative activity, should questions arise.

Consider using qualitative as well as quantitative dimensions to major performance reviews.

Too frequently in evaluating faculty members, we simply *count* things: the average scores on student course evaluations, the number of pages in peer-reviewed journals, the number of committees on which a faculty member has served. The problem is that this numerical approach does not always provide us with the best possible information. The most popular professor may not be the best instructor. The most prolific author may not be the best scholar. The most frequently elected committee member may not be performing service that really matters. For all these reasons, deans should seriously consider complementing quantitative methods with qualitative methods when reviewing faculty members.

What are qualitative evaluation methods? These are forms of evaluation that help deans and committees make more effective judgments about the quality of a faculty member's work in addition to its sheer quantity. One of the most common qualitative forms of evaluation used for faculty members is the portfolio, which allows the dean to look longitudinally at how a faculty member has developed in various areas and which allows the faculty members themselves to report information in its proper context. In a portfolio, for instance, a faculty member can contrast a current course syllabus from one that he or she used five years ago, explaining the precise pedagogical improvements that led to the changes illustrated. Rather than burdening committees with binder after binder of published material, portfolios can require a faculty member to include and defend his or her five best contributions to scholarship (or three best contributions to scholarship since the last promotion), explaining why certain publications made a real difference to the discipline or helped explore significant new territory. A faculty member's philosophy of service can be followed with a list of 5 to 10 service projects or committees in which that philosophy can clearly be seen.

Seldin (2004) and Seldin and Higgerson (2002) offer excellent advice and examples on developing portfolios for qualitatively evaluating faculty achievements. In addition, just as students at many colleges and universities are developing e-portfolios as a way of being more intentional in setting learning goals and assessing their progress in achieving those goals, e-portfolios can be invaluable aids to faculty members in documenting their progress toward tenure, promotion, and other major points of evaluation.

Many deans find the faculty evaluation process to be among the activities they enjoy the least. Negative evaluations frequently lead to unpleasant encounters with the faculty member who objects to the judgment the dean has made. Positive evaluations occasionally draw the complaint that they are "not positive enough." Despite these potential problems, it is vitally important for all deans to master the techniques of thorough and fair faculty evaluation. Your commitment to the quality of education and research at your institution depends to a great extent on your approach to evaluating the faculty members in your unit. Assess each faculty member the way you would want someone to do if your own child were in that professor's courses or if someone about whom you cared were to be affected by that professor's research. Never make an evaluative statement you cannot back up, but never refrain from being truly evaluative in your appraisal.

Resources

Arreola, R. A. (2007). *Developing a comprehensive faculty evaluation system: A guide to designing, building, and operating large-scale faculty evaluation systems* (3rd ed.). Bolton, MA: Anker.

Buller, J. L. (2006). How to write first-rate faculty evaluations. In J. L. Buller, *The essential department chair: A practical guide to college administration* (pp. 86–93). Bolton, MA: Anker.

Falcone, P. (1999). *101 sample write-ups to document employee performance problems: A guide to progressive discipline and termination.* New York, NY: AMACOM.

Furtwengler, D. (2000). *10 minute guide to performance appraisals.* Indianapolis, IN: Macmillan.

Max, D., & Bacal, R. (2003). *Perfect phrases for performance reviews: Hundreds of ready-to-use phrases that describe your employees' performance.* New York, NY: McGraw-Hill.

Neal, J. E., Jr. (2001). *The #1 guide to performance appraisals: Doing it right!* Perrysburg, OH: Neal.

Swan, W. S. (1991). *How to do a superior performance appraisal.* New York, NY: Wiley.

References

Seldin, P. (2004). *The teaching portfolio: A practical guide to improved performance and promotion/tenure decisions* (3rd ed.). Bolton, MA: Anker.

Seldin, P., & Higgerson, M. L. (2002). *The administrative portfolio: A practical guide to improved administrative performance and personnel decisions.* Bolton, MA: Anker.

31

Chair Evaluations

Many of the principles that we explored in Chapter 30 ("Faculty Evaluations") also apply to the evaluations that you write for your department chairs. These principles include:

- Base your evaluation on your unit's statement of the responsibilities assigned to department chairs.

- Include clearly evaluative language, not mere lists of achievements.

- Summarize the overall point of your evaluation in fewer than 20 words.

- Distinguish formative advice from summative assessment.

- Use a clear and meaningful gradation of achievement in your evaluations. Don't simply label each chair as "excellent" in every evaluation category.

- To the extent possible, allow for qualitative as well as quantitative assessment of chairs. In other words, don't merely *count* accomplishments; *appraise* their quality.

In addition, Krahenbuhl (2004) lists five important principles for administrative evaluations, basing his recommendations on those that were originally developed for evaluating deans by the Council of Colleges of Arts and Sciences. Krahenbuhl's five principles are equally relevant when you are evaluating your department chairs and include the following advice:

> There should be clarity and consistency on all aspects of the administrative evaluation. . . . An institution's policies on the review of academic administrators should be congruent with the following principles:
>
> 1. The scope and mechanics of all evaluations of administrative performance should be known, codified, and exist as an aspect of institutional policy.

2. Those individuals asked to provide input should be well informed about the requirements of the position and the job-related accomplishments (or lack thereof).

3. Reviews should occur on a known, regular cycle. . . .

4. The collection, statistical treatment, and conclusions drawn from evaluative data should be handled with the same rigor and objectivity that would be viewed as sound practice in research.

5. Successful administrative evaluations feature an appropriate balance between (a) the right of the [department's] members to have input that is appropriately confidential and access to summary results that are disseminated in a timely way, and (b) the right of the [chair] being evaluated to receive appropriate summary data and to enjoy the same level of privacy normally associated with other related personnel actions in the institution. (pp. 226–227)

The first of these principles reinforces the point we discussed earlier about tying evaluations to statements of job responsibilities. The other four principles are, however, extremely important additions. For instance, with regard to the second principle, too frequently we ask faculty members, students, and other university constituents to evaluate an individual's performance as a department chair without clearly explaining the position's requirements and responsibilities. As a result, the insights we receive from these constituents may not be particularly useful in assessing the person's work as an administrator. In addition, with regard to the fourth principle, data about the performance of department chairs is too frequently collected and analyzed in a manner that would not be acceptable in our own academic research. For example, we might distribute surveys that compel the respondent to reply on a Likert scale (see Chapter 30, "Faculty Evaluations") but then attempt to summarize the data by calculating means rather than medians. (Remember that means can distort the "average" of discrete data, such as that provided on a Likert scale, and are really better suited to continuous data, when a respondent is free to provide any value between 1 and 5, such as 2.487. Moreover, means give undue importance to outliers—that is, unusually high or unusually low answers—particularly in small datasets.) Or we may overanalyze the data, attempting to draw distinctions based on hundredths of a point that are meaningless in terms of the sample size.

In addition to Krahenbuhl's very important observations about administrative evaluation, there are several other guidelines that deans will want to keep in mind as they write their performance appraisals of department chairs.

Use the evaluation process to establish future goals, not merely to review past achievements.

Evaluation is most effective when it combines appraisal of past work, clear advice on ways in which to improve, and goal setting for the future. Too frequently, we focus on the past when we are conducting an evaluation. It is a natural mistake to make because evaluation processes are all geared toward critiquing prior performance. Nevertheless, an evaluation process that leaves a department chair with only a sense of what he or she has done wrong (or conversely, with blanket praise that provides no indication of how to build on such successes) does not offer the best possible sort of administrative development. If you have never used evaluation sessions to set future goals as well as to critique past achievements, begin by developing some strategies for the future based on current challenges and accomplishments. For instance, a positive achievement can lead to goal setting through language such as the following:

- Your outreach efforts have been excellent. In addition to the highly successful departmental lecture series, you have used presentations by visiting scholars and other public events to bring a great deal of positive attention to your department and to the institution as a whole.

    - For this reason, I would like you, during the coming year, to increase public awareness of the departmental lecture series even further by working cooperatively with the university advancement office on a plan for maximum media exposure and targeted invitations to prospective donors.

    - As part of our ongoing series of administrative training workshops, you should also make a presentation to other chairs that explores ways of increasing outreach in their areas. Your expertise in this regard will help the college expand its outreach efforts.

In a similar way, criticism can also be used as a springboard for developing future goals, such as in the following example:

- The paperwork that leaves your office is too frequently late or poorly completed. Typographic errors are common and tend to create a poor public image for your department. To improve your performance in this area, your goals for the coming year are:

- Have all memoranda and significant email messages proofread for spelling and grammar before sending them.

- Put all deadlines on your calendar. Set aside time in advance of the deadline to complete routine reports and recommendations.

- Delegate those tasks that cause your efforts to lose focus. Give faculty members a chance to accomplish some of the tasks you would normally handle. For instance, send a faculty member to an occasional meeting in your place, or put that person in charge of a large project. Monitor progress closely and provide appropriate guidance.

Once goal setting has become a regular part of your evaluation process, you will have in place an even more constructive approach to administrative development. You'll be able to monitor progress in achieving a *previous* evaluation's goals at the same time that you establish future goals. In this way, you'll have two good standards by which to evaluate your chairs:

- The college's written statement of the chair's job responsibilities

- A focused list of goals designed for each chair's unique situation that appears in the prior year's evaluation

Whenever possible, conduct oral interviews with faculty members to obtain a more comprehensive view than you could receive from written (often anonymous) evaluations alone.

An institution's written evaluation forms or online response surveys are extremely useful. They give you a great deal of information that can be summarized quickly. Sections that contain numerical rankings can be efficiently processed into median scores, providing a useful measure for interdepartmental comparison. Many times the evaluation forms or surveys that faculty members complete for their chairs may be submitted anonymously, prompting greater candor from faculty members who may fear (rightly or wrongly) that they will suffer retribution for their criticisms. As useful as standardized evaluation forms may be, however, they frequently do not tell as complete a story as you would learn from conducting brief one-on-one interviews with each department member. Just as certain faculty members will be reluctant to be candid with you unless they have the anonymity of a written response, others will not be candid if they have to put their comments in writing. As a result, these interviews will offer a more complete picture of a department's operation, morale, and plans for the future than you would ever have gleaned from a stack of printed evaluations.

In the course of your conversations with faculty members, you'll be able to ask follow-up questions about items that concern you or that you do not immediately understand. Particularly if you do not know the individual department members well, you'll gain insights into their personalities that can lend a broader context to the written evaluations. Moreover, if you've seen a certain pattern already in people's written comments, you can explore the background for these remarks and ascertain just how widespread that sentiment may be. You can say such things as, "On the written evaluations, several people seemed to indicate that the department chair [fill in the blank]. . . . What's your opinion on this issue?" or "Do you know why people may feel this way?" As you conduct these interviews, one particularly useful plan is to meet the faculty members in their offices, not yours. You learn more about the department that way, and it is a more efficient use of your time because it reduces the likelihood that someone will forget his or her appointment or arrive late. Most important, it allows you to end an unproductive or excessively long conversation gracefully. After all, it is far easier to leave someone *else's* office than to get that person to leave yours. Remember not to talk too loudly, though, in offices with thin walls.

Be specific in both your positive remarks and your criticism.

Most deans are able to be quite specific when making criticisms. They know the problems that poor performance has caused, and they probably have at least a few ideas on how to fix the situation. Few of us are equally specific, however, when it comes to praising department chairs for a good performance. We say things like, "You're doing well," "You conduct efficient meetings," or "Your reports are always submitted on time." Statements like these lack enough emotional resonance to be much of a reward for succeeding in a hard job. For this reason, take your time to be specific when praising a department chair. Allow the person to bask in the glow of a job well done. Examples of good, specific compliments for department chairs include such language as the following:

- You are a terrific leader for everyone in your area. You have a clear vision of where you want your department to go, and you inspire people to carry out that vision. I have never known you to micromanage your faculty members on any issue. They sense—and I believe that they sense correctly—that you treat them as true equals. Faculty members in your department recognize that they have an appropriate amount of freedom in their own areas of influence.

You respect the strengths of individuals by allowing them to *be* individuals.

- Your faculty members admire you for your knowledge of how this institution and our college operate. You are credited with knowing who gets things done and with having access to such individuals. Your faculty members realize that you are well respected outside your department. I concur with that impression, and I have come to respect your expertise as well.

- You are regarded as extremely receptive to your faculty members' ideas. They feel free to voice their needs, state their concerns, and disagree with you when necessary. They know that your office is always open to them. Many faculty members describe you as easy to talk to and supportive of their professional goals.

- Faculty members have great confidence in you as their advocate. Regardless of whether they share your vision of the department's future, all faculty members know that you will always act in what you regard as their best interests, as well as students' best interests.

Similarly, when it is necessary to provide criticism, don't just say, "You do such-and-such poorly" or "Your performance in such-and-such area needs to improve." Take time to explain what the problem is, why it is a problem, and how it might be addressed more productively in the future. A few examples of this approach include:

- Members of your department frequently feel that they do not have a clear sense of where their area is going or what your vision is for the future. This lack of clarity is of particular concern to me because of your area's upcoming accreditation review. Without a shared sense of purpose and mission, I am concerned that we may have a more difficult case to make for reaccreditation. For this reason, I'd like you to take some time at your department's next meeting to explain in some detail your vision for the discipline's future.

- Junior faculty members in your department feel that they do not receive from you the mentoring they need. They are uncertain of your expectations and of the department's criteria for their annual evaluations. They would like you to explain to them both the overall curriculum design and their own job responsibilities. As a result, I'd like you to consider a series of developmental sessions specifically aimed at junior faculty members. In these workshops, make your expectations clear. Be absolutely sure that all department members understand both their duties and the departmental curriculum. If you sense even the slightest confusion, encourage specific questions.

In situations where you must provide serious criticism, also offer serious—and concrete—guidance on what the department chair needs to do differently.

We have already seen that it is important to follow criticism with advice on how to improve. It is even more important, when offering *serious* criticism (i.e., criticism that could lead to a formal reprimand, removal as chair, or dismissal from the institution), to be as specific as possible about both the unsatisfactory behavior and the corrective measures you expect to see in the future. Conclude this section of your evaluation with a summary of the specific action that you may take if the situation does not improve. The following is an example of how to write a section of an evaluation that contains serious criticism, advice on how the department chair should improve, and a warning about possible actions if this improvement does not occur:

- You have displayed frequent fits of temper in the past. The single most common adjective used to describe you on your faculty's written evaluations was "mercurial." These displays of anger hamper your managerial effectiveness. Your energies have been diverted from important academic business because you have had to deal with several formal grievances. At least one junior faculty member has left the institution, partly because of the tension that exists in your department. To improve your performance in this area, I am encouraging you to take the following steps:

  - When you find yourself tempted to reply to someone in anger, delay responding for as long as possible. Say something like, "Ask my secretary to set up an appointment so that we can discuss this in greater detail later this week. I want to get some information together." Give yourself a chance to cool down.

  - Don't immediately send an email if there is any chance that you have written it in anger. Delay a day or two, and see whether your attitude toward the matter changes or softens. On highly sensitive issues, consider handwriting a memo that your staff has to retype for you rather than resorting to email.

  - Remember that your opinions and attitude profoundly affect others in the department, especially untenured junior faculty members. Try to make the most out of challenging or difficult situations by focusing on the positive aspects rather than finding fault with others over relatively minor issues.

- I will be conducting a follow-up evaluation one year (or, in very problematic situations, six months) from today. If I continue to receive what I regard as substantive complaints from your faculty about unwarranted displays of anger and the level of your interpersonal skills, I will require you to step down as chair before the conclusion of your current term. Moreover, if I learn of a particularly egregious example of anger displayed to *any* of the college's constituents before that date, I will require you to step down as chair immediately.

Evaluating department chairs should be an integral part of your comprehensive development plan for administrators in your area. Properly conducted, these evaluations forge a stronger administrative team, improve leadership skills, and reward individuals for exceeding your expectations. Poorly conducted, evaluations waste your time and the chair's time, lead to endless appeals, and increase the faculty's distrust of the administration. Evaluate your chairs as a model to how you would wish to be evaluated by upper administrators and how they should evaluate your faculty. The time spent in doing an evaluation properly will more than repay you in effective departmental leadership.

References

Krahenbuhl, G. S. (2004). *Building the academic deanship: Strategies for success.* Westport, CT: Praeger.

32

Position Requests and Descriptions

Institutions use the term *position requests* or *position descriptions* to refer to several different types of documents. For instance, at your college or university, you might use these terms when speaking of one or more of the following:

- A section of a budget proposal (see Chapter 29, "Budget Proposals") that justifies the creation of a new faculty or staff position

- An application submitted (usually to the institution's chief academic officer) to retain a position recently vacated or to add a new position made possible through a funding increase

- A document, usually kept in the human resources office, that outlines the primary job responsibilities associated with a position and the workload percentage that should be devoted to each of those responsibilities

- A detailed description of the duties associated with a position, usually mailed to all applicants, given to those applicants who are interviewed, or provided to the successful candidate at the time of hiring

- A more abbreviated discussion of a position that is used for advertising purposes

Although these different uses can be confusing, there are certain key principles that deans should keep in mind when developing *any* of these documents.

Begin developing your position request or description by brainstorming all the desirable qualifications, skills, and attributes you hope to find in the person you will eventually hire.

As we saw in Chapter 14 ("Staff") and Chapter 21 ("Searching for and Building a Strong Administrative Team"), we too often think about current and prospective employees in excessively narrow terms. We focus on their surface credentials rather than on all the aspects of a person's work that we really need and that can help the person succeed at our institution. For faculty members, for instance, we tend to define positions simply in terms of the person's academic specialty, overlooking such factors as collegiality, positive energy, a sense of humor, and flexibility—which may ultimately be of even greater importance. At times, too, we focus so much on what a potential faculty member knows that we lose sight of how well the person can convey that information to others, instill in them a passion for the discipline, and promote such desirable activities as critical thinking, independent learning, and creative thought. In staff positions, too, we can become so focused on specific position duties that we ignore the attributes that may help a person be a good fit for the institution.

In a similar way, many units may hope to increase their gender or ethnic diversity by filling a new position, but they fail to take steps that will actually diversify the applicant pool (see Chapter 53, "Promoting Diversity"). They assume that, if they place a standard position description in publications with a strong minority readership and if those advertisements include the phrase "Women and minorities are encouraged to apply," then they will receive a diverse set of applications. Unfortunately, this outcome rarely happens because, when the position request and description were being developed, too much attention was paid to precisely those qualifications and areas of specializations in which women and minority group members are not commonly represented. In other words, if diversity is truly a goal, then perhaps it is worth broadening the job description's disciplinary focus to include those areas where diverse candidates are likely to be found. In a similar way, it may expand your pool of acceptable candidates to modify statements in the advertisement like "Ph.D. required at time of application" to more inclusive statements such as "Doctorate required by time of appointment," which allows candidates pursing Ed.D.s, Psy.D.s and other types of doctorates to apply, as well as individuals who are near the point of completing their degrees but who have not yet defended their dissertations. An even broader statement like "ABD required for rank of instructor; doctorate required for rank of assistant professor" allows you to include in the applicant pool a superior candidate who has not yet completed his or her degree while emphasizing your institution's commitment to employing faculty members with terminal degrees.

Of course, if it is a strategic initiative of your institution to increase the percentage of faculty members who hold terminal degrees, you will need to weigh the competing priorities of diversifying the applicant pool (even if this means considering candidates who have not yet completed their degrees) and of hiring only candidates with doctorates or the equivalent (even if this means potentially excluding from consideration candidates who could add to your institution's success in other ways). In any case, it is important to have a candid discussion of how these priorities stack up relative to one another *before* the position request and description are finalized.

You will also likely improve your recruitment of minority candidates if you replace cold and unwelcoming formulas like "Women and minorities are encouraged to apply" with more inviting phrases, such as "In keeping with its policy of promoting diversity, our institution actively encourages applications from women, minorities, and individuals of every sexual orientation." Also, by giving priority to applicants who have worked in a multicultural environment, had experience with diversity issues, or engaged in the scholarship of teaching your discipline to students from a broad range of cultural backgrounds, you will send a message that your college is committed to a highly diversified faculty. These and other suggestions on how to write position descriptions that will attract more minority candidates may be found in Turner (2002) and Smith, Wolf, and Busenberg (1996).

This same approach can be applied to any area in which your institution or college has a special strategic interest. Thus, in cases where service or advising is important, note this priority in the advertisement itself. Although such statements may dissuade a few individuals from applying for your position, in the long run these people are unlikely to be the ones who can succeed in your environment anyway. In other words, the essential principle that you should follow in constructing position descriptions and advertisements is the following:

> *You may not always get the type of person for whom you advertise. On the other hand, you are certain not to hire that type of person if you fail to mention the most important qualifications in your position description or announcement.*

From your long list of desirable qualifications, skills, and attributes, develop a shorter and more focused ranking of the most important elements that you are searching for.

Once you have brainstormed all the desirable qualifications, skills, and attributes you hope to find in the person you hire, you are likely to be left with a long and unwieldy list. After all, no one could possibly possess *all* those qualities, and you are likely to be tempted to conclude the entire litany by adding "and can walk on water." Nevertheless, reaching this point is an important stage in developing the position request or description that best suits your needs. It is time now to start going through your laundry list of what you *hope* to find and begin identifying those qualities that you most *need* to find. If you were serious about identifying on your list not only surface credentials and specialty areas but also important personal attributes and qualities, it may surprise you to find that the items that rise to the top of your priority order differ from the information that you've usually included in job descriptions. It may well be that collegiality, diversity, a willingness to work on interdisciplinary projects, and effective instruction now seem far more important than a precise subspecialty in this or that field. In any case, the top five or six items on your priority list should provide you with the core of your position request, description, or advertisement.

Start drafting the position request or description by including the features that you are looking for in applicants and the information that applicants need to know about the institution, unit, or position to succeed if hired.

In Chapter 23 ("Closing the Deal"), we saw that selling a candidate on your institution begins before you make the offer. A person's treatment throughout the interview process can play an important role in a candidate's decision to take a position, even if you are unable to meet his or her every expectation in terms of salary, start-up costs, moving expenses, and so on. That said, however, recruiting a highly desirable faculty member begins at the very moment a position request or description is drafted. You may be fortunate enough to work at an institution that everyone has heard of and that immediately receives respect and admiration through its prestigious name. Most deans are not that lucky, however. They are trying to recruit highly talented individuals with excellent teaching skills, a strong commitment to collegiality, and a host of other desirable attributes even though salaries are modest, the challenges are great, and the opportunities for advancement are relatively few. In these situations it is often a position's intangible benefits—a beautiful campus or location, the opportunity to work closely with interesting students, the chance to make a difference in someone's life—that attract and retain members of the faculty and staff. What are your intangibles? What tends to keep employees at your institution even when they could earn higher salaries elsewhere? By including such information in your position description or advertisement, you are more likely to attract individuals who will succeed in your environment and be happy as a member of your community.

Moreover, most applicants have imprecise notions about what it would be like to hold the position you are advertising. Is the job primarily a teaching position, primarily a research position, or some mix of the two? If it is primarily a teaching position, what is the course load? How many courses taught by the faculty member are likely to be at the introductory level? How many are likely to be at an advanced or graduate level? Will there be opportunities for the individual to develop new courses? Will there be opportunities for, or expectations of, doing interdisciplinary work? If the position is primarily research, what are the expectations for research? Will start-up funds be available? Will the faculty member be expected to secure external funding (and if so, will the office of research and sponsored programs support those efforts)? If the position requires a mixture of instruction and scholarship, in what proportions are the two activities likely to occur? Will the person hired be expected to involve students in his or her research, or are the teaching duties and scholarship duties usually unrelated? What are the position's scholarship opportunities and requirements?

You can also undermine a description's effectiveness by being too vague about your institution's expectations. If the position announcement states that you are seeking an assistant professor, would you also accept applications from individuals whose rank is already higher than that? If you state, "Minimum of one year experience preferred," how will you use this preference in selecting candidates? What *sort* of experience will you consider? Does it have to be experience in a faculty position at a college or university? And what does it mean that you "prefer" this type of experience: Does it mean that any experienced candidate will be given an edge over any inexperienced candidate or that you are reserving the right to give precedence to experienced candidates, all other factors being equal?

As you draft your position request or description, you should carefully consider the qualifications and experience that are absolutely essential. For instance, a requirement such as "Minimum of three years of teaching experience at a regionally accredited four-year college or university" is clear, but it also means that you will not consider any candidate who does not meet that criterion, no matter how desirable the candidate may be in other ways. Above all, you will want to avoid meaningless phrases like "Some teaching experience preferred." This requirement is so general that, even if a candidate has taught only a Sunday school class for 10 minutes, the criterion has technically been met. It is far better to have hard-and-fast requirements for the qualifications that you really need and to forgo taking up advertisement space with statements that only appear to express preferences.

For search advertisements, request materials that you truly need to make an informed decision during the first screening. Do not require any item that you will not need until later in the search process or can obtain in another manner.

Here's an example of a statement that is often seen in nationally posted position announcements and advertisements: "In addition to a letter of application and current curriculum vitae, submit three letters of reference, official transcripts of all college work, and samples of publications." The problem with this statement is that it requires materials that are of relatively little help in initially screening candidates and may discourage the most desirable candidates from even applying. Why? Consider these points:

- *Letters of reference:* These are likely to tell you substantially less than you could learn by asking for a list of three to five references and their mailing addresses, telephone numbers, and email addresses. To begin with, anyone can locate three individuals who are willing to write reasonably positive, upbeat letters on his or her behalf. What you really want is the opportunity to ask follow-up questions, to describe your precise position and inquire whether the candidate is a good fit, and to ask the one question that you really need to know (and will almost never learn from reference letters): Do you know anything about this candidate that, if I were aware of it, might make me hesitant to offer him or her the job? Furthermore, many desirable candidates will not apply for your position precisely because you have asked for letters of reference as part of the initial application. No one likes bothering their references to prepare letters for positions until they know that there is a very good chance that they will be considered seriously as a candidate. Moreover, the more distinguished a candidate's references are, the more reluctant a candidate will be to trouble those references with a request for a letter early in the search. By requiring letters of references, you are actually discouraging candidates with the best references from applying! Finally, some candidates will not want current employers and colleagues to know that they are considering new positions; these highly experienced candidates are likely to rule out applying for any position that requests letters of recommendation early on.

- *Official transcripts:* There are almost no searches in which a college needs to request official transcripts as part of an application. To be sure, accrediting agencies do require institutions to obtain official transcripts—transcripts marked with an official seal and mailed directly from the registrar of the issuing institution to the institution requesting them, without ever being in the candidate's possession—*once an individual is hired.* For this reason, submitting official transcripts is often required for initial employment contracts. But candidates should rarely need to face the burden and expense of submitting official transcripts at the time of application. Again, many highly desirable candidates will simply choose not to apply for your position rather than supply the transcripts. So, if you feel that it is absolutely necessary to review an applicant's coursework and grades to prepare your short list of semifinalists, be sure to request *unofficial* transcripts or photocopies of transcripts.

• *Scholarship:* Evaluating applicants' scholarship is certainly an important part of every academic search process. But ask yourself whether it is truly necessary to review the publications of every single person who applies for your position. In most cases it is more effective to request these materials only from a select group of applicants after the initial screening. Mailing books and offprints is expensive for candidates. Returning these items at the end of a search, should a candidate request them (and the vast majority of candidates will), is expensive and time consuming for your college. Furthermore, depending on the position, you are likely to receive between 60 and 200 applications. Is it worth your committee's time to examine all the scholarly products submitted (in fact, are committee members really going to examine them with any care?), and is it worth the space to store these items, even temporarily? In most cases, no. Screen applicants on the information that they provide in their cover letters and résumés; request actual samples of publications later in the search, or ask that they be brought to the interview.

In contrast, many search committees fail to request those items that they really need: statements of a candidate's philosophy of teaching, administration, scholarship, or service; a sample syllabus or final examination; a brief description of the best student project ever submitted to the candidate; suggestions about the one book every student (or faculty member) in the discipline should read; or the outline of a faculty development plan for teaching, scholarship, and creative activity over the next five years.

Certain decisions about position descriptions can be made only in the context of particular institutions and particular positions. For instance, do you ever refer to salary in a job advertisement, and if so, do you provide a range or merely say something more general like, "Salary commensurate with experience"? In this case, there can be no hard-and-fast rule. (Your institution may, however, have such guidelines.) If you provide a salary range, you will lose certain candidates who believe that the range offered is inadequate for their current needs. But that may be preferable to bringing a candidate to campus only to discover that the individual is out of your price range. On the other hand, your position may offer certain intangible benefits—a beautiful physical setting, extensive cultural opportunities, a safe and congenial community, and so on—that candidates will need to experience to appreciate them fully. In any case, you should never state that a salary range is commensurate with experience if the remuneration is already largely fixed. In a similar way, many institutions make the mistake of terming their salaries as "highly competitive" and their benefits packages as "excellent" when neither of these is actually the case.

A properly written position request or description should flow logically from your overall administrative philosophy. It should demonstrate clearly the type of person who can best succeed in your unit and at your institution, not simply include a list of desirable credentials. Remember that the quality of experience students will receive, the reputation for research that your institution develops, and the job satisfaction of many people at your institution—possibly even you—are dependent on finding the right *person,* not just the right set of credentials, for this position. A position description that is hastily or ineffectively written can fail to attract the sort of person you really need. Even worse, it can cause others to draw unfavorable conclusions about your unit or institution. Always take the time to make certain that position requests and descriptions are done *right* before they ever leave your office.

References

Smith, D. G., Wolf, L. E., & Busenberg, B. E. (1996). *Achieving faculty diversity: Debunking the myths.* Washington, DC: Association of American Colleges and Universities.

Turner, C. S. V. (2002). *Diversifying the faculty: A guidebook for search committees.* Washington, DC: Association of American Colleges and Universities.

33

Program Reviews

Formal program reviews are an important ingredient in any institution's commitment to accountability. In current practice colleges and universities are held accountable—that is, demonstrate that they are doing what they say they're doing—through three complementary processes:

- *Evaluation:* This is the means by which we determine whether *individual* employees, students, courses, and the like are meeting institutional standards. The grades professors assign students in courses, the performance appraisals given to faculty or staff members, and the summaries of student ratings calculated for individual courses are all examples of evaluation.

- *Assessment:* This is a way of determining whether *groups,* not individuals, are attaining the objectives or outcomes set for them. Examples include outcome assessment of an institution's performance in its major programs, general education program, degree programs (the B.A., B.S., M.B.A., etc.), and student life office.

- *Program review:* This combines indicators of quality (such as evaluation and assessment) with indicators of two other important components: viability or sustainability (such as student-credit-hour production, trends in declared majors, demands for graduates in the marketplace, etc.) and centrality to institutional mission.

Viewed in this way, it is clear that program review is different from both evaluation and assessment because it moves beyond determining a program's quality to considering whether that program can be maintained at its current quality (or improved) in the future and whether the program is a good fit for the institution. For instance, a well-conducted program review may indicate that a particular program has achieved a high level of excellence and is extremely important to the institution's mission but that it cannot be sustained at its current level. Perhaps the program is no longer viable because of a consistent decline in majors or an insufficient demand for graduates in the field. Alternatively, program review may alert you to a program that is highly successful by all external measures and extremely popular with students but that is developing in a manner that isolates it from the institution's primary goals. (For a more detailed discussion of the differences between evaluation, assessment, and program review, see Buller, 2006, pp. 113–115.)

Program review does not, in itself, tell you precisely what course of action you should take for any particular program. Deans frequently need to make this point repeatedly. Faculty members tend to be extremely worried (at times with good cause) that failing to achieve high scores in each category on a program review may mean that their major will be eliminated or their academic department dissolved. There are, however, numerous courses of action that an administration can take in such situations. For example, a program that rates low in quality and sustainability but high in centrality to mission could receive additional funding to solve the problems identified through program review. On the other hand, a program that rates high in quality and viability but low in centrality to mission might be slightly reconfigured to tie its focus more closely to the institution's priorities.

The dean's role in helping programs collect the right information

Many program review processes are not as effective as they could be in helping institutions strengthen weak programs and capitalize on strong programs. The primary reason for this lack of effectiveness is that administrators examine too narrow a set of indicators concerning the program's quality, growth, and relevance to the institution. For instance, some systems track student-credit-hour production and average student evaluation scores for each program, assuming that these numbers will reveal something significant about the quality and success of each program. In fact, without a clear context for this information, those two statistics can be highly misleading. As a result, one of the most important roles that a dean can play in making program review benefit the institution is to assist both the higher administration and the department chairs to think more creatively about what factors they should consider. These factors should include:

- *Quantitative indicators:* These are data that are countable or measurable in some consistent, reproducible manner. In other words, quantitative indicators may be raw numbers, percentiles, rankings, averages, or similar information. For most institutions, the clearest quantitative indicators tend to be ratios because ratios place a raw figure into at least a partial context. For instance, a raw figure such as "Over the past five years, an average of 27 program graduates were admitted each year to their first-choice post-baccalaureate program" may be interesting, but it is ultimately meaningless for review purposes. Is 27 a high figure or a low figure? Presented in isolation, the statistic gives the reader no way of judging. Presented as a ratio, however, the figure begins to take on meaning and to be incorporated into a larger context: "Over the past five years, an average of 27 out of 33 (81.8%) graduates of our degree program were admitted annually to their first-choice post-baccalaureate program; our overall institutional placement rate is only 53.1%, and the rate of similar programs within our institutional peer group is 65.5%." In a comparable way, some institutions may request raw numbers of student credit hours generated per term or per academic year, but this information only becomes useful when it is calculated in terms of some other relevant factor, such as the number of full-time equivalent faculty members who produced those credit hours and how this relates to other colleges at the institution and at peer or aspirational institutions.

• *Qualitative indicators:* These include sources of information that, although not specifically measurable in and of themselves, are helpful in providing a more comprehensive picture of a program. Because qualitative indicators tend not to result in specific scores, they almost always require more interpretation than quantitative indicators. Nevertheless, this information can demonstrate aspects of a department's success, viability, or unique mission in a manner that proves to be far more compelling than numbers alone. Perhaps the most commonly used type of qualitative indicator for program review purposes is the portfolio. For instance, student portfolios provide a valuable impression of the level of work achieved by students and their rate of growth as they go through a program. In much the same way, faculty portfolios of teaching, scholarship, service, and administrative contributions can provide a much more balanced view of the faculty than student evaluation scores or the number of refereed articles published. Seldin (2004) is a good place to begin for information on assembling this type of qualitative evaluation, followed by Murray (2000). Moreover, Seldin and Higgerson (2002) explore other types of professional portfolios, and the portfolio approach may be used to document faculty's professional contributions in such areas as scholarship and service as well.

• *Indicators of quality:* As their name implies, indicators of quality suggest to an observer how good a program is or the level of success that the program has had in achieving its goals. Indicators of quality may be either quantitative or qualitative and may draw on data dealing with students (such as five-year graduation rates, placement rates for graduates, alumni portfolios of scholarship in the discipline, and so on); faculty (percentage holding a terminal degree, number of refereed publications per full-time equivalent faculty member each year, teaching and administrative portfolios, and the like); support staff; access to information resources; and other elements that contribute to an academic program's overall quality.

- *Indicators of viability:* These demonstrate whether a program is likely to be sustainable in the future. Quantitative indicators of viability include enrollment trends; estimates of probable demand for graduates in the discipline over the next 5 to 10 years; additional sources of program revenue, such as grants and sponsored programs; and ratios of tuition generated by the program to expenditures made in such areas as salaries, benefits, and operating expenses. Qualitative indicators of viability might include a discussion of those factors that are likely to affect demand for graduates within the foreseeable future, a listing of honors or achievements attained by alumni, a statement of the advantages accruing to a program from your institution's location or the uniqueness of its curriculum, and so on. One quantitative indicator of viability that disciplines occasionally overlook is the correlation between enrollment in one or more of the department's courses and retention at the institution. Frequently, courses that have a clear mentoring or experiential component—for instance, studio art, lab science, honors programs, community service-learning opportunities, internships, or applied music courses—produce students who are more likely to persist because they develop a closer bond with a faculty member or supervisor. By differentiating between the retention rates of students who have enrolled in your department's courses and the retention rate of the institution as a whole, you can provide a perspective on viability that your college or university may find particularly compelling.

- *Indicators of centrality to mission:* These indicators suggest the degree to which a particular program is essential to the school's fundamental purpose, strategic plan, and vision for the future. For instance, at a research university, the ratio of books and articles, grants received, patents obtained, or academic recognitions won per full-time equivalent faculty member suggests the vital role that your department plays in advancing the institution's mission. At a liberal arts college, the connection you can make between your discipline and the traditional liberal arts goals of developing critical thinking, improved communication, and aesthetic appreciation is likely to assume greater significance. Church-affiliated schools, professional schools, community colleges, comprehensive institutions, and schools adhering to the model of the "New American College" are each likely to have distinctive missions and goals for the future to which you will need to relate your mission as a discipline. In every case, however, it is likely to be *outcomes*— what students and, under certain conditions, faculty members produce—

that will be important, not such inputs as faculty credentials, incoming students' SAT/ACT scores, or the number of volumes relating to your discipline in your institution's library.

The dean's role in making recommendations based on program review

After each program has collected its data, presented its best case, and submitted its review document, you will almost always be asked to make a recommendation based on its report. Although your recommendation will necessarily vary according to your institutional procedure, the following are four common categories for decanal-level decisions resulting from a program review process:

- *Enhance:* Additional resources (above normal annual increases) should be directed to the program.

- *Maintain:* Current resources (plus normal annual increases) should be continued for the program.

- *Decrease:* The resources directed to the program should be reduced and redirected elsewhere.

- *Eliminate:* The program should be phased out.

You will notice that all four of these categories are tied to budgeting matters. Why? Because program review processes that simply examine disciplines to see how they're doing end up being of relatively little value to the institution despite all the time and effort they involve. Program review should be conducted with the intention of making the institution better and more successful in fulfilling its mission and strategic plan, not of simply conducting an exercise to get it out of the way. For this reason, decisions will be made based on the program review's conclusions, and the most concrete decisions will be those that involve funding.

These decisions can be extremely difficult for deans. You will be making decisions that involve people's livelihoods and the continuation of programs that matter to the faculty members and students involved. How do you go about making your decisions? The following are a few key principles to keep in mind:

- *Begin by examining the program's centrality to the institution's mission:* Too often this review category is treated as an afterthought, but it is really one of the most important factors to examine. How central is this program to what your institution stands for and what it is trying to achieve? Answering this single question may significantly change your recommendation. A program that ranks low in both quality and viability might be a candidate for funding enhancement if it is highly central to your institutional mission and merits improvement. At the other extreme, a program that ranks low in both quality and viability may be a clear candidate for elimination if it is peripheral to your institutional mission.

- *Then proceed by examining relative priorities:* Deans are tempted to want all their programs to be enhanced. If additional funding were coming in from the outside, why not strengthen all the weak programs and highlight all the strong programs? But funding at most institutions is a zero-sum game: For budgets to be increased in one area, they must be reduced in another. How then does this program rank in your own college's priorities? If enhancing one program could only be done by reducing funding from another one of *your* programs, would it be a worthy goal? (If so, which program would you reduce?) If reducing funding for this program could strengthen another area, would that be desirable?

- *If the program scores low in viability/sustainability, be sure to examine the causes behind this rating:* Enrollments may be low in a program because it is not being marketed correctly, or they may be low because there is no market for the program. In a similar way, demand for majors in a particular area may be soft because of demographic trends that are unlikely to change or because of a temporary market saturation that may change very quickly. Effective deans do not simply make a decision because of a declining trend in enrollments or student-credit-hour production. They always seek the reasons for the trend and interpret those reasons in light of the program's overall contribution to the institution's primary mission.

- *Make your best recommendation based on solid, professional judgment, not on how people will react to it:* If you allow your decision to be clouded by the potential outcry from faculty members or students or by whether the decision is what the upper administration wants, you are shirking your fundamental duty to your institution. Remember this essential principle:

> *Effective deans reach decisions not by making the easy choice but by doing what is right for the institution as a whole.*

Someone is always bound to disagree with your decision. At times, these disagreements will be intense, even rancorous. We all tend to fight most fiercely for the things that are dearest to us, and nearly every program is dear to someone. Therefore, you must make the decision that you can justify most rationally, even if it is not the decision that your supervisor or your faculty wants you to make. Ultimately, your deanship will be judged not by whom you pleased but by how you have strengthened your college. Trees are sometimes strengthened by fertilizing, sometimes by pruning. So, too, are academic programs. One of your most important challenges will be to determine when each treatment is most appropriate.

Resources

Barak, R. J., & Mets, L. A. (1995). *New directions for institutional research: No. 86. Using academic program review.* San Francisco, CA: Jossey-Bass.

Burke, J. C., & Associates. (2005). *Achieving accountability in higher education: Balancing public, academic, and market demands.* San Francisco, CA: Jossey-Bass.

Dickeson, R. C. (1999). *Prioritizing academic programs and services: Reallocating resources to achieve strategic balance.* San Francisco, CA: Jossey-Bass.

Eckel, P. D. (2003). *Changing course: Making the hard decisions to eliminate academic programs.* Westport, CT: Praeger.

References

Buller, J. L. (2006). *The essential department chair: A practical guide to college administration.* Bolton, MA: Anker.

Murray, J. P. (1995). *Successful faculty development and evaluation: The complete teaching portfolio* (ASHE-ERIC Higher Education Report No. 8). Washington, DC: The George Washington University, Graduate School of Education and Human Development.

Seldin, P. (2004). *The teaching portfolio: A practical guide to improved performance and promotion/tenure decisions* (3rd ed.). Bolton, MA: Anker.

Seldin, P., & Higgerson, M. L. (2002). *The administrative portfolio: A practical guide to improved administrative performance and personnel decisions.* Bolton, MA: Anker.

34

Policies and Procedures

Every college has its own time-honored ways of making decisions, reaching consensus, or implementing strategies for the future. Unfortunately, in too many cases these policies and procedures exist solely as an oral tradition, with no written record in a printed manual or on a web site. Nevertheless, as institutions become more complex—and as society becomes more litigious—creating written policies and procedures has become more important. At least once in your deanship (and probably far more often), you'll be asked to develop a new policy or procedure for your unit. There may also be times when you decide that you *want* to create a new policy or procedure, not because there is any external reason compelling you to do so, but because you believe it would be more equitable or efficient to have a standardized process in place. No matter whether you are drawing up the policy or procedure yourself or entrusting it to a delegate, committee, or group of advisors, there are several important principles to keep in mind.

Always approach a new written policy or procedure by asking, "What problem are we trying to solve?"

Policies and procedures are never created in a vacuum. They are always the result of an attempt to either fix or avoid a problem. Remember, however, that poor policies tend to be established in response to a single, extremely rare, and isolated event when an individual takes advantage of the system. Although it can be valuable to close loopholes in an existing policy that allow people to violate its original spirit, it is best to avoid developing policies and procedures simply as the result of single, relatively minor situations. (On the other hand, a single *egregious* situation—something that caused a scandal, financial disaster, termination of an employee, or the departure of a large number of students—is a different matter and may well be the impetus for a policy change.) For the most part, if a situation is not of the utmost significance and is extremely unlikely to recur, you don't need a policy. Simply note the lesson about human nature from the bad experience, and move on.

In other words, good policies and procedures are not elaborate filters designed to screen out every conceivable way of abusing the system. Given human nature, people will find a way to turn nearly *any* set of policies and procedures to their advantage if they are inclined to do so. Rather, your college's policies and procedures should be designed so that decisions can be made as efficiently and equitably as possible. So the first questions you must address when developing a new policy are these: What exactly are we trying to achieve, and what are we trying to avoid? Steer clear of the tendency to brainstorm every possible eventuality and then develop a contingency plan for it. Doing so will only extend your process indefinitely and create a cumbersome—even unworkable—document. Your primary purpose will be lost in pages of relatively unimportant additions.

Most of all, remember that a policy or procedure's main purpose is not to make more rules for their own sake, but rather to make people's lives easier. With well-written policies and procedures, everyone knows *what* is expected, *when* it is expected, and *how* decisions will be made about competing priorities. If, in the midst of developing a policy, you find yourself veering from this primary purpose, it is time to stop, step back, and reconsider what you are doing and why.

Look for best practices to adopt.

Another common mistake that deans make in developing policies and procedures is starting from scratch. Almost any conceivable policy matter—from intellectual property disputes to issues of faculty load and overriding enrollment caps—has been explored dozens, even *hundreds* of times on other campuses. (On intellectual property policies, see Chapter 45, "Intellectual Property Disputes.") It is extremely valuable for each college to see itself as distinctive—even unique—when presenting its special advantages to prospective students, donors, and faculty candidates. It can be extremely detrimental, however, for a college to assume that it is so unique that it must create every single policy or procedure out of whole cloth. An Internet search using key words related to the policy that you are trying to create will probably result in more examples of well-designed documents than you or your committee could possibly read. Don't simply cut and paste sections from these documents or adopt another institution's policy or procedure wholesale. Rather, examine what approaches other institutions have taken to similar situations, consider how these ideas can be adapted to your own environment, and explore the ways in which useful approaches from several different institutions can be combined to create the best possible policy for your college.

Begin drafting the new policy or procedure with an eye toward clarity, not rhetorical style.

All of us have opportunities to be creative; to use evocative language to create a memorable, lasting impression; and to amuse readers with our wit, charm, and cleverness. Writing policies and procedures is not one of these opportunities. The hallmark of a well-written policy statement is its lucidity. If you develop an ambiguous statement or one that allows for multiple interpretations, you really have not solved the problem you set out to fix. After completing a draft of your new policy or procedure, reread it sentence by sentence, asking the following questions:

- Is each statement free from ambiguity, capable of being interpreted in only one way, and specific enough that it applies precisely to the situations we are trying to address?

- If you omit one word at a time in each sentence, does each word you leave out significantly change the overall meaning? (If it doesn't, the word is probably unnecessary.)

- Are there adverbs or qualifying phrases—such as "normally" and "in most cases"—that produce undesirable vagueness? An ambiguity that may work in the college's favor may also be used against it in certain situations.

For truly major policies and procedures, always have the document reviewed by both the human resources and legal affairs offices on your campus.

Human resources personnel and your legal affairs staff or university counsel have a great deal of experience in the implications of various policies. They will be able to understand what the repercussions might be under specific conditions. In addition to screening your document for additional ambiguities and multiple interpretations, they will also serve as a good counterbalance against developing *too* simple a policy. As we saw earlier, one of your guiding principles should be to create as minimal and clear a policy as possible. Your human resources and legal affairs offices, on the other hand, will want to make your policy as comprehensive as possible, covering every conceivable scenario and contingency. Out of this tension, you are likely to develop the best possible compromise, a document that is as specific as possible to your college's distinct situation and that covers the most likely contingencies. For instance, you may be the dean of a liberal arts college who wants an intellectual property policy to be as generous as possible, rewarding your faculty for their creativity and scholarship by allowing them to retain ownership of everything they develop at the college. Your human resources and legal affairs offices will probably suggest numerous contingencies—such as the creation of marketable products, patentable inventions, and new biotechnological developments—that are simply inconceivable in your liberal arts setting. Nevertheless, by encouraging you to think of various contingencies and scenarios, this external review will result in a far better policy or procedure. The tension between your desire for simplicity and your reviewers' desire for comprehensiveness is, in the end, extremely healthy.

Develop a formal appeals process for every policy and procedure.

Policies and procedures are frequently adopted to *avoid* appeals. If there previously were numerous ad hoc decisions because no clear-cut policy existed or multiple exceptions requests because an established procedure was too lax, you may think that the new document will remedy this situation. Certainly, a well-designed policy or procedure will reduce unwarranted appeals, but it will never eliminate them. For this reason, it is important to plan for how appeals and exceptions requests will be conducted, who will hear the plea, and on what grounds an appeal may be granted. The last issue is particularly important. You may wish to state in your policy that the individual or group making the decision—such as a department chair, committee, or you, as dean—has final jurisdiction; appeals can be made only when the individual or group did not follow the established procedure or criteria. Such a restriction eliminates the necessity to reexamine the issue from top to bottom with every appeal. It also sends a very strong message to members of your administrative team that you support them and trust their judgment (see Chapter 21, "Searching for and Building a Strong Administrative Team").

Teach faculty, staff, and possibly students about a new policy or procedure, and periodically reteach policies and procedures to everyone.

After the appropriate bodies have approved your document, it is important to teach the new policy to the constituents that it affects. It is not sufficient to post the new policy or procedure on a web site or include it in a new version of the college manual. No one can be expected to reread all existing policies each year, noting any differences from what was previously in effect. Training can occur in a public forum, by email, by paper flyer, or by some other appropriate means—as long as it reaches all the relevant parties. At times, it might be tempting not to make too big a deal out of a policy change because there will be inevitable resistance and opposition. Nevertheless, anything less than perfect candor in such matters is highly undesirable. It is far better to face criticism head-on than to be accused of both deception and poor policymaking. By creating a formal opportunity to teach community members about the new policy or procedure, you have an occasion to explain its rationale, summarize its benefits, and address resistance early on. Moreover, if you have adopted an open and collegial process in generating your proposal, people are unlikely to feel blindsided by a change.

Training members of your college in policies and procedures should not be a single occurrence. All new faculty and staff members should receive comprehensive training in existing policies and procedures, and the entire faculty and staff should regularly receive a refresher course. It is not necessary to review every policy at every training session. The information that is covered in this way is too complex to remember. Nevertheless, taking a few moments at a faculty meeting to review current policies and procedures is time well spent; it should be an ongoing part of every college's development plan for faculty and staff members.

Writing policies and procedures entails a different sort of writing than that used in articles, reviews, letters, and proposals. If your institution has faculty members trained in technical and professional writing, or if your institution maintains a writing center, run a draft of your proposed policy or procedure past these people; they can assist you with structure, clarity, and precision.

Resources

Campbell, N. J. (1998). *Writing effective policies and procedures: A step-by-step resource for clear communication.* New York, NY: AMACOM.

Page, S. (1998). *Establishing a system of policies and procedures.* Westerville, OH: Process Improvement.

Page, S. (2001). *7 steps to better written policies and procedures.* Westerville, OH: Process Improvement.

Page, S. (2002). *Best practices in policies and procedures.* Westerville, OH: Process Improvement.

Wieringa, D., Moore, C., & Barnes, V. (1998). *Procedure writing: Principles and practices* (2nd ed.). Columbus, OH: Battelle Press.

35

A Scenario Analysis on the Dean's Documents

Note: For a discussion of how scenario analyses are structured and suggestions on how to use this exercise most productively, see Chapter 8, "A Scenario Analysis on the Dean's Role."

Case Study

One morning you open your mail to discover that a colleague at another institution has written to you for help. This colleague is new to the deanship, and because of your growing reputation as "the essential academic dean," you have been asked to review two documents this new dean has drafted. The first document you read is an announcement for a new position.

Department of Anthology

Tenure-track position at the rank of assistant professor. Ph.D. required; some teaching experience preferred. Applicants should have a strong commitment to college-level teaching, with experience in the following courses: Introduction to Anthology, Anthology for Nonmajors, Theory and Practice of Anthological Research, Special Topics in the Major, Anthology 202, Proseminar in Anthological Studies, Selection and Collection of Literary Materials, Advanced Thesis Preparation, and Service-Learning Issues in Anthology. Preference may be given to applicants who also demonstrate the ability to use a second language for conducting research (Asian languages preferred), knowledge of advanced statistical methods and their application in anthology, experience with student advising at both the undergraduate and graduate levels, and a willingness to be an active participant in a new, experimental residential living/learning community. Send letter of application, curriculum vitae, a minimum of three recent publications, official transcripts of all college work, and five letters of recommendation to Dr. Spoon River, Assistant

Professor, Department of Anthology, Palatine University, Miscellany, East Virginia, 99999.
Deadline: January 15, 2007. AA/EEO/ADA.

You are just developing a few suggestions about how to respond to your colleague when you find the second document in the envelope. Printed on official letterhead, this item is an annual performance appraisal for a faculty member. Coincidentally, the faculty member who is being evaluated is the chair of the search committee mentioned in the position announcement.

Dr. Spoon River
Assistant Professor
Department of Anthology
Palatine University
Miscellany, East Virginia, 99999

Dear Spoon,

The purpose of this letter is to provide a written evaluation of your performance as assistant professor of anthology over the past academic year, as required by our *Faculty Handbook*.

Your level of instruction last year was excellent. The mean score on your student course evaluations was 4.2563, and students frequently included such comments as "Professor River really knows this stuff!" and "Great professor!"

In scholarship, you attended two conferences, made one presentation, and submitted an article for review by a scholarly journal.

In the area of service, I am primarily concerned by your perceived level of collegiality. Faculty members who served with you on the curriculum committee frequently characterized you as "so disorganized that important materials were often lost," a circumstance that, I am told, you then proceeded to blame on other committee members. You need to do better in the area of service next year, particularly because your review for promotion and tenure is getting close.

Sincerely,
Jan

What advice do you give your colleague after reviewing these two documents?

Considerations

1. How might your advice to the other dean change if you knew the following about that person's institution? (As you conduct this exercise, assume that *only one* of the following statements is true at a time.)

    •   The institution has expressed its commitment to improving the quality of its undergraduate instruction.

    •   The institution is trying to increase the scholarly productivity of its faculty.

    •   The institution is trying to increase the gender and racial diversity of its faculty.

    •   The institution employed a temporary faculty member in the anthology department during the past year. The current search is being conducted on the line occupied by this temporary faculty member, that person is a candidate for the position, and he or she fits the position description exactly.

    •   The institution prides itself on the mentoring and development it provides to its junior faculty members.

    •   The institution is extremely prestigious, having its choice of several applicants who would be eager to work there.

    •   The institution is struggling for recognition and almost unknown outside its immediate area.

2. What additional advice might you give your colleague if you were reviewing the position announcement less than a month before its due date?

3. How might your advice to your colleague change if these documents were not drafts of documents that would appear in the future but copies of documents that had already been distributed?

4. What additional materials might you like to examine before you respond to your colleague?

Suggestions

The documents that you have received are obviously in need of much improvement. Among the suggestions that you might consider making to your colleague are the following.

In the Position Announcement

- The expression "Tenure-track position at the rank of assistant professor. Ph.D. required . . ." restricts the search committee greatly. It means that, at most institutions, the committee will not be able to offer the rank of associate professor or above to a candidate who truly merits it, will not consider any candidate who is ABD or who holds any type of doctorate other than a Ph.D., and will not offer the position to someone on a temporary basis without first closing the search. In certain situations these restrictions may not matter. Nevertheless, in situations where the applicant pool may be small or where diversifying the applicant pool is important, it may be desirable to consider less restrictive language.

- The statement "some teaching experience preferred," although common in search advertisements, is too general to provide any useful information to the candidate or to the search committee. It is better to omit it or to define the type and quantity of experience that is desired (see Chapter 32, "Position Requests and Descriptions").

- The requirements for the position, including experience in a large number of specific courses and a minimum of three publications, are likely to be unattainable for an assistant professor position at all but the most prestigious institutions.

- Although the advertisement requires that candidates have "a strong commitment to college-level teaching," they are never required to document that commitment in their application materials. In fact, there is a profound inconsistency between the focus of the advertisement (which gives a great deal of attention to teaching) and the focus of the materials required for the application (which emphasize scholarship). As a result, the message to candidates is unclear.

- The expectation that the applicant have "experience" in the courses listed is highly ambiguous. Does this statement mean that the candidate must already have taught these courses, had graduate coursework relevant to them, been a teaching assistant in similar courses, or something else? The type of experience desired should be spelled out.

- The list of courses for which the candidate must have experience is confusing. Will these course titles apply to precisely the same courses at different institutions? Also, referring to courses by number rather than title (such as "Anthology 202") is meaningless in a position description because course numbers vary widely from institution to institution.

- The list of preferred qualifications is also quite long and overly specific, particularly because it contains the word "and" rather than "or." The likelihood that a candidate will have experience in all the courses indicated *and* all the preferred qualifications is very remote indeed. If there is an internal candidate (such as the temporary faculty member mentioned in the "Considerations" section) who matches all these criteria, external candidates will suspect that the search is a sham, and the entire process will be liable to legal challenge. If a temporary faculty member is so valuable to an institution that it wants to convert him or her to a tenure-track position, there are almost always alternatives to conducting an unfair national search. Two of these alternatives include conducting an internal search and requesting an exception from the institution's governing board.

- On why it is undesirable to ask applicants for an initial screening to submit such items as publications, official transcripts, and letters of recommendation, see Chapter 32 ("Position Requests and Descriptions"). This requirement will discourage a number of highly qualified candidates from applying.

- The phrase "recent publications," although commonly used in advertisements, is ambiguous. How recent should the publications be? The author's sense of this term is likely to differ from that of the reader.

- The deadline date is also ambiguous: Is this a postmark deadline or a deadline for the applications to be received?

- Ending the advertisement with the letters "AA/EEO/ADA" is not as effective as it could be. Although including this phrase does demonstrate some commitment to affirmative action, equal opportunity (which, for the institution, may or may not be identical to its affirmative action goals), and the Americans with Disabilities Act, the abbreviation doesn't demonstrate a very deep commitment. Everything else in the advertisement was fleshed out in full sentences or complete phrases; why was this last item reduced to an abbreviation? Moreover, the bare sequence of letters does not appear very welcoming to the groups it is supposedly including. Far better would have been a brief statement outlining *why* the institution is committed to diversity and accessibility.

- The advertisement tells the reader nothing at all about Palatine University. A highly desirable candidate will thus not know from this advertisement alone whether he or she would even be interested in applying for the position. If there were several other options, the best possible candidates might decide not to apply for this job. Including information about an institution is essential unless the school is highly prestigious or nationally known.

In the Faculty Evaluation

- A formal document like an evaluation letter is best not opened personally with a casual expression like "Dear Spoon." Titles and given names are more suitable for formal documents. "Dear Dr. River" would have been better.

- If the evaluator is going to cite the faculty handbook, it is better to make a specific citation (including a reference, such as a section or page number). In that way, there is less ambiguity about which requirement the letter is fulfilling. A better phrase would have been something like "as required by Section 13.48 of our *Faculty Handbook*."

- This letter evaluated Dr. River's quality of instruction on the basis of student evaluations alone. Although student course evaluations can provide informative insights into certain aspects of a faculty member's quality of instruction, they should never be regarded as the *only* indicators of teaching excellence. For a complete discussion of how to document excellence in teaching, see Buller (2006, pp. 275–285).

- Because most instruments used for student course evaluations require students to provide answers as discrete data (i.e., 1, 2, 3, 4, or 5) rather than continuous data (i.e., any whole number fraction between 1 and 5), the average score should have been calculated using medians instead of means (see Chapter 31, "Chair Evaluations"). Moreover, if means are the only form that the institution calculates, these data should be examined alongside a measure of distribution, such as standard deviations. Calculating the standard deviation, for instance, will give you a sense of the degree to which students agreed or disagreed with one another in their evaluations. Moreover, even if it were appropriate to calculate the mean, providing this average to the ten-thousandth of a point (4.2563) overinterprets the data. This figure should have been rounded to the nearest 10th of a point (4.3) or, if the number of evaluations was extremely large, possibly to the nearest 100th (4.26) of a point.

- Although it may be clear elsewhere in the college's evaluation policy, it is certainly not clear from the letter itself how average scores on the student course evaluations were calculated. Were all questions considered or only a subset relating to quality of instruction? Without that information, it is extremely difficult to interpret the provided figure. Moreover, because the number does not appear in context (such as "a median score of 4.3 where the median for the department as a whole is 3.8"), it is impossible to tell whether this average is a good or bad score.

- The student comments included in the letter are poorly chosen. Students are not in the best position to know whether a faculty member has kept up with developments in his or her field; that observation is more appropriately made by faculty colleagues. Moreover, generic praise (such as "Great professor!") is far less informative to the reader than a comment indicating *why* Dr. River is a great professor.

- The section on scholarship lists items without evaluating them. As a result, it is impossible for the reader to tell whether this is a high or low level of scholarly activity. We learn later in the letter that the professor is coming up for promotion and tenure, so evaluative language on the extent of the professor's research should definitely have been included. That language should also indicate whether the faculty member is currently on track for tenure and promotion, at least from the dean's perspective. Also, the letter does not indicate whether the venues for the scholarship were highly selective journals and conferences, so it is difficult to gain a sense of the *quality* of Dr. River's scholarship.

- In the section on service, it is unclear how the dean learned the information that led to his or her conclusion. Is there a formal mechanism for evaluating service at the institution? Were these comments hearsay? Had there been a formal complaint? Without this information, it is very difficult to know what to make of the criticism cited.

- No other aspect of the faculty member's contributions to service, other than the tendency for disorganization and blaming others, is mentioned. Had the faculty member expressed an appropriate willingness to serve on committees and to assume other professional duties? Is the criticism cited part of a repeated pattern or a single instance?

- The recommendation to "do better in the area of service next year" is extremely unhelpful to the faculty member. No specific advice for improvement is given. There is no acknowledgment of what standard will be used to note improvement or what action will be taken if that standard is not met. The statement, in other words, fails both as formative advice (because it does not provide appropriate guidance) and as summative evaluation (because it does not specify what the faculty member did wrong, this error's negative effect, or the conclusions to draw from this incident). Indeed, the dean states only that he or she is "concerned" about Dr. River's lack of organizational skills; the dean avoids more definitive language, such as "inappropriate," "unsatisfactory," or "fails to meet the college's standards." Finally, tying this criticism to an observation about a pending promotion or tenure decision implies a threat but without clear guidance about what action the faculty member should take.

- Considering these two documents together, you may wonder why your fellow dean has assigned a faculty member with disconcerting organization and committee leadership issues to take responsibility for a search committee. There may well be reasons, but you will want to ask what they are.

References

Buller, J. L. (2006). Helping faculty members document excellence in teaching. In J. L. Buller, *The essential department chair: A practical guide to college administration* (pp. 275–285). Bolton, MA: Anker.

36

Leadership When Meeting One on One

Some of a dean's most challenging meetings are appointments with individuals. One-on-one meetings might include regular appointments with supervisors; unexpected encounters with a faculty member or student who comes in to lodge a complaint; formal meetings with a parent who wishes to talk to the dean about a serious issue; interviews with a candidate who is being considered for a position; tense sessions with an employee who is being reprimanded or dismissed; and a wide variety of other such meetings. Most one-on-one conversations are relatively routine, a part of a normal day's work. Nevertheless, some of them are extremely stressful, emotion filled, or simply uncomfortable. In certain instances the other person in these meetings may be angry, and the dean may feel threatened by his or her hostility. At other times emotions may be vented more easily because the two of you are alone; the other person may not hold back tears or frustration. In light of all these variations, what is the best way to prepare for and conduct one-on-one appointments? Moreover, how can you demonstrate leadership in such situations, focusing on the issues that are most important to you and your college as you address the other person's concern? Is it even *possible* to demonstrate leadership in the presence of only one other person?

The answer to the last question, at least, is easy. Yes, it *is* possible to demonstrate leadership when meeting one on one. The following guidelines will help you do so.

Whenever possible, plan as carefully for one-on-one meetings as you do for formal presentations before large groups.

There is a tendency to treat one-on-one appointments as somehow less critical than the formal presentations we make before committees, boards, and similar groups. After all, individual meetings occur all the time—how much preparation do we require to *talk* to someone? The fact of the matter is, however, that some of your most important—and anxiety-producing—meetings will take place in one-on-one conversations. Without others present, people tend to say things they would never admit in a public setting. They also feel free to bring up matters that they would be reluctant to broach before groups of people. For this reason, dismissing a one-on-one appointment as a mere conversation is rarely a good idea. At best, you may miss an opportunity to discuss ideas that could truly advance your college. At worst, you may be unprepared for a situation that could become disastrous or at least unpleasant because you didn't take the time to do your homework.

It is probably a bad idea to walk into *any* meeting unaware of the topic of discussion. Issues that reach the dean's level tend to be so important and varied that you'll want some time to refocus from the last topic of concern to the issue at hand. Even more critical, there may be documents or types of information that could clarify matters quickly if you have them with you. Always ask your staff to request a meeting's purpose when scheduling. Even a brief notation such as "10:00 a.m.: Prof. Smith (re: salary concerns)" can help you prepare for the conversation and make the meeting time more productive.

Whenever possible, consider in advance what your basic message will be in the one-on-one meeting. Reflecting on your central theme in advance doesn't mean that you are going to be inflexible, ignoring any valid points and observations your interlocutor might raise. It is merely a way of reinforcing your initial starting point so that the other person's passion or rhetoric doesn't catch you off guard. If we fail to reflect on our central idea, we often fail to have *any* idea at all, and we end up allowing others to set the agenda. A conversation is, of course, always a matter of give and take, and some well-considered reflection on the thoughts you will contribute can make the entire conversation more productive.

When blindsided in a one-on-one meeting, listen carefully, offer little reaction, and then reflect on what has occurred.

Not every conversation, of course, allows you time for preparation. Some conversations occur on the spur of the moment. Others surprise you because their focus is not what you had anticipated. For instance, your calendar reads "10:00 a.m.: Prof. Smith (re: salary concerns)" but the concerns that are raised are not about Professor Smith's *own* salary; rather, Professor Smith feels that clerical salaries have been rising too rapidly. At times, too, someone will make an appointment to discuss one issue only to raise a second, and far more important, issue later in the meeting. Every dean is familiar with the phrase, "While I've got you here, I also wanted to ask you about . . ." In situations like these, unless you are already well prepared to discuss the new issue, your best approach is probably to listen to the ideas being presented, ask questions to make sure you understand them, and respond that you'll get back to the person very soon. As you have probably already discovered, nearly every situation has more than one side to it, and because you were unaware that this particular topic would come up, you had no opportunity to explore those other perspectives. Before making a firm commitment, you'll want to gather some facts, think through the matter carefully, and examine the issue from a broader perspective.

When pressed for an immediate reaction in these situations, it is best to respond in a general, philosophical, or procedural manner. You can say something like, "I haven't looked into your specific salary situation relative to other assistant professors in our college. But let me explain what approach I take when I consider matters of salary inequity . . ." Then take down the particulars of the individual's situation, examine the larger picture, develop a clear plan of action, and get back to him or her. Although being caught off guard in a conversation can be extremely stressful, you can still exert leadership if you remember the following essential principle:

> *You may find that the other person in a conversation has already set the agenda. Nevertheless, if you operate on your principles and core beliefs as an administrator, you can still set the direction for that agenda.*

In other words, don't be forced against your will into making a commitment to any particular course of action without considering the larger picture. By focusing on how you will make a decision in all such cases, you both refine your basic principles and make it clear that, although you consider suggestions or requests when they are made, you do not make private deals.

Remember that demonstrating concern is not the same as committing to a particular course of action.

Frequently, when you are caught off guard in a one-on-one meeting, you and your interlocutor will want entirely different outcomes. The other person will want you to commit to solving a problem or granting a favor. You will want to avoid making any commitment until you learn more about the issue, exploring all the options and carefully considering the implications of each. Yielding to one request for a salary adjustment, for instance, may create an even greater problem of inequity than the other person realizes. Moreover, there may be policy restrictions that prevent you from solving the other person's problem in the manner that he or she wishes. In other words, there may be several very compelling reasons why you do not want to make an immediate commitment. Nevertheless, your promises to "look into it" or to "see what we can do" will frequently come across as cold and indifferent. The person raising the issue may feel that you're simply stalling when all you really want to do is gather information and reflect on the decision's broader implications.

The appropriate middle ground in a situation like this is to demonstrate your full concern for the person who is raising the issue while explaining why you are unable to make a commitment now. You will quickly lose credibility if you adopt this approach as a stalling technique. Be sincere about your desire to get back to the person. Make a note on your calendar, reminding yourself to do so in the next day or two. Gather the information that you need, but understand that the other person is waiting for your reply. What may seem like only a few days to you will be seen as several whole days without any answer to the other person. You will begin developing a reputation as a dean who doesn't get back to people and who pretends to be concerned about people's issues unless you follow through quickly after the initial conversation.

When making a decision or commitment, always do so within the context of your core beliefs as an administrator.

Next to failing to get back to someone after promising to do so, nothing damages an administrator's credibility more than appearing to cut private deals with a small group of favorites. Indeed, one of the most essential reasons for not making an immediate decision when blindsided is to avoid creating greater inequity by granting a request without understanding the larger context. For this reason, you should be very clear that any decision you make as the result of an individual request both adheres to your overall policies and values and is understood as adhering to those policies and values. Be sure to explain your decision—whether positive or negative—in light of your core principles. Don't assume that the other person will automatically make this connection. You may need to explicitly explain how the current situation relates to your overall administrative philosophy. Some examples include:

- *Equity:* "As you know, I try to treat all my department chairs as fairly as possible, understanding that each of their situations is quite different. So, after carefully examining their salaries, their years of experience, the number of people they supervise, how they contribute to the college and the larger institutional mission, and the number of students they serve, I've decided to . . ."

- *Collegiality:* "I've never believed that members of a college all have to agree with one another or even have to *like* one another in the same way that we like our personal friends. But I do believe that we have to work together efficiently and productively, meeting each other's professional needs to the best of our abilities. That's why, in the interests of collegiality, I've decided to . . ."

- *Professionalism:* "In my administrative career, I've come to place a priority on true academic professionalism, by which I mean respecting the importance of confidential information, getting training to keep current in our jobs and to perform our functions effectively, and not letting our personal differences get in the way of doing what needs to be done to achieve our core mission. So, when I considered this matter in that light, I realized that what I needed to do is . . ."

When the other person does not accept your decision, make it clear that the decision is final.

At times, when you follow up with an individual and render your decision, the person will not accept the result as final and will want to keep arguing a point or reviewing matters that you have already considered. This problem is particularly acute at small institutions where the dean is the sole academic officer and the avenues of appeal beyond him or her are limited (see Chapter 54, "The Dean as Chief Academic Officer"). Even in other academic environments, however, a person may be unwilling to accept a negative decision because there are no others present who can reiterate and amplify your arguments, demonstrate to the individual that he or she does not have universal support on the matter in question, or clarify that it is not simply you who is unwilling to grant this request. In private conversations people sometimes feel that, if they keep arguing long enough and passionately enough, you will eventually give in—if only to get such an unrelenting person out of your office. When faced with obstinate interlocutors, resort to the following strategy:

- Make it clear that your decision is final if your mind is indeed made up. Say something like, "I'm sorry, but as I've told you, that's my final decision, and I won't reconsider the matter."

- Adopt the "stuck record" strategy. You may need to repeat yourself over and over until the other person finally understands that the discussion is at an end. "I understand your arguments," you might say, "but as I've said before . . ."

- If no other approach is effective, bring the conversation to a close and mention any recourse that the individual may have. You really do not want to give the impression that you are throwing someone out of your office, but in the most extreme situations, you may need to end the conversation when it is clearly no longer productive. You can do so in a polite and effective manner by saying something like, "I'm sorry, but I can see that my reasons don't satisfy you, even though I've tried to explain them as clearly as I can. I think it's best, therefore, that we simply conclude this meeting. If you feel that you must pursue this matter further, your next step would be to . . ."

We sometimes imagine leadership as taking place only in crises or when we are debating major issues before large groups of people. It is possible, however, to demonstrate leadership in the individual conversations that deans have with constituencies every day. Basing each decision on a compelling set of core principles, and making it clear that our decisions are always firmly grounded in those principles, is one of the most important aspects of decanal leadership.

37

Leadership When Chairing Committees

In the last chapter we saw that one of the best ways for deans to demonstrate leadership in a private conversation is by relating the topic of discussion to a set of core administrative principles. A key goal of administrative leadership, in other words, is making sure that people *understand* the connection between decisions and the administrative standards of the person who makes those decisions. This essential rule also applies when you are chairing committees, councils, or task forces. True committee leadership begins in principled leadership. Sharing your guiding principles with committee members not only makes their work easier (because they understand what to expect and where the committee's work is headed) but also provides an important type of faculty development by demonstrating effective group dynamics. Nevertheless, although basing your leadership on a clear and well-understood set of core principles is an important place to begin when chairing committees, there are several other factors to keep in mind.

Be sure that you are thoroughly grounded in parliamentary procedure.

Even if your committee has an official parliamentarian, as the chair you will need to know more than the rudiments of parliamentary procedure. This knowledge will help you understand whether discussing various matters is appropriate, how to amend or table motions when necessary, and how to vote. Because most faculty members have only a general sense of parliamentary procedure, decisions that should be challenged or debated can be made in haste. For this reason, such materials as Robert, Evans, Honemann, and Balch (2000); Jones (1990); and Sturgis (2000) will give you essential information about conducting meetings and evaluating the priority of various motions.

In addition, there are several web sites that can help you review most aspects of committee procedure and organization. Among the best of these are the Official Roberts Rules of Order Web Site (www.robertsrules.com), Roberts Rules of Order Online (www.rulesonline.com), and an excellent online resource developed by the Student Activities Office of California State University, Chico (www.csuchico.edu/sac/parliament.html). Finally, both the American Institute of Parliamentarians (www.parliamentaryprocedure.org) and the National Association of Parliamentarians (www.parliamentarians.org) offer a wide range of information and training materials, including opportunities for workshops and distance learning, that can provide you with even more detailed knowledge of applying parliamentary procedure.

Organize your meetings to be as task oriented as possible.

Every dean needs to participate in an occasional meeting that is primarily conducted to exchange information rather than to produce results. Getting together for face-to-face updates is one of the ways in which administrators and faculty members stay in touch. Nevertheless, considering your ability to disseminate information electronically and through internal newsletters, be very careful about overusing meetings to update and exchange routine information. One of the most common complaints that people have about meetings is "I'd have time to do all the work that at these meetings we keep saying needs to be done—if only I didn't have to attend all these meetings." For this reason, you'll want to respect busy committee members' time by reducing the number of roundtable updates and by keeping most committee time free for discussing issues, making decisions, and planning.

Before chairing a meeting, you should ask yourself, "What is it that I hope our group will accomplish during this meeting? What should be our 'product'?" If you cannot answer that question clearly and succinctly before you call your meeting to order, you are unlikely to accomplish anything that is worth your members' time. In addition, you are increasing the likelihood that a particularly strong-willed committee member with his or her own agenda will hijack your meeting.

You should prepare for each committee meeting by writing an agenda. Whenever possible, this agenda should be distributed to the other committee members at least 48 hours before the meeting begins. Advance notice of the issues allows the members to think through each one, perhaps even gathering data or supporting materials to bring with them to the meeting. If you have done sufficient advance preparation and identified the meeting's purpose, it is extremely useful to state this purpose right on the printed agenda so that everyone will be fully aware of what they can expect to accomplish and what will be expected of them. In this way, a well-constructed meeting agenda should look something like this:

AGENDA

College Curriculum Committee
November 8
3:00 p.m.
Hunter Classroom Building, Room 302

Purpose
To consider new course proposals for possible approval and to begin drafting a policy on minimum standards for independent study courses.

I.   Call to order.

II. Approval of minutes, meeting of October 15.

III. Old business.

    A. Consideration of new course proposal PARL 101: Introduction to Parliamentary Procedure (carried over from 10/15 meeting due to lack of departmental signatures).

    B. Consideration of renumbering course PEDN 218: Advanced Pedantry to PEDN 318 (carried over from 10/15 meeting due to lack of quorum).

IV. New business.

    A. New course proposals.
       1. PARL 201: Intermediate Parliamentary Procedure.
       2. PEDN 460: Capstone Project in Pedantry.

    B. Development of a policy on minimum standards for independent study courses.
       1. Review of policies in place at peer and aspirational institutions (see materials distributed at 10/15 meeting).
       2. Review of draft policy proposed by subcommittee (B. Rogers, chair; H. David; J. Tompkins).
       3. Development of action plan for 12/1 meeting.

V.   Announcements.

VI. Adjournment (target: 4:00 p.m.).

Remember that the word *agenda* is a Latin term meaning "things that *must* be done." The agenda format just outlined makes it clear what must be accomplished at the meeting and what will result from it (course approvals or rejections, a response to a draft proposal, and creation of a work plan that will help advance the draft proposal for the next meeting). As the committee's chair, you have made your goals clear to members through the agenda, demonstrated your respect for your members' time, and established your own goal of concluding the meeting in a timely manner.

Without clear agendas, meetings often get sidetracked by long discussions about those items that happen to be addressed first. In other words, if committee members do not have a clear understanding of everything that needs to be discussed and the probable time limits for that discussion, the meeting time will likely be used ineffectively and accomplish little genuine work. As the committee's chair, you should remember the following essential principle for demonstrating leadership in committees:

> *Constructive meetings begin with well-constructed agendas.*

Make your agendas clear, easily digestible, and free from more action items than can be accomplished within a reasonable time. If there is more business on hand than can productively be addressed at a single meeting, consider attending to it in order of priority and then carrying over less time-sensitive or critical items to later sessions.

Remember that delegation helps both you and your committee members.

In their haste to get committee work done quickly, accurately, and creatively, many deans assume too many committee tasks themselves. They approach the committee with a draft of a report or proposal that is largely complete and ask, "What do you think?" Although this strategy may be useful in those rare situations when the committee's work needs to be completed in a *very* short amount of time, it is usually counterproductive. Certain committee members may not feel free to express their opinions if you, as dean, assume too great a role in taking charge of the group's work. At the other extreme, certain faculty members may object more strenuously to aspects of your proposal simply because you are the dean. They may be posturing before their peers or they may simply feel disenfranchised by the way in which you've so aggressively taken charge of the process.

Your failure to delegate responsibilities also deprives committee members of the opportunity to develop their own skills as leaders and members of an administrative team. Effective leadership, in other words, involves effective delegation. To delegate tasks appropriately, don't simply assign the duties that you yourself don't want to fulfill. You should delegate tasks to give others experience in leadership, to take advantage of their creativity, and to help your committee function as efficiently as possible. Inevitably, of course, certain committee members will perform their delegated tasks more effectively than others. But never lose sight of the essential principle that was stated in Chapter 2 ("Preparing for the Dean's Role"): Delegation always implies a certain loss of control. The delegated report or decision is unlikely to look *exactly* like what you would have done. However, the committee's review of such a proposal, report, or document—even if it may not be, from your perspective, nearly as good as what you could have created yourself—is actually a very constructive aspect of the committee process. Through it, you may discover that there are alternative ways of approaching an issue or that there is far less consensus about certain matters than you had originally believed. Working through an imperfect draft can be a wonderful exercise for a committee as it develops new suggestions in response to flawed proposals and comes together as a team to sort through complex issues. For this reason, just as you don't expect a student group to get a complex task right the first time, so you should not expect a faculty or staff committee to accomplish its task without experiencing a learning curve. Delegating responsibilities thus helps committee members improve their own leadership, teamwork, and creative problem-solving skills, even as it frees you from the burden of having to complete the entire assignment on your own.

Foster an environment in which all voices are heard and given due consideration.

One of the most important duties of committee leadership is making certain that all the members' perspectives are given due consideration. In fact, of the 10 "General Principles of Parliamentary Procedure" (cited, e.g., at www.csuchico.edu /sac/parliament.html, studentactivities.mscd.edu/modules/org/resources/13.html, and www.gsg.umd.edu/assemb/parliamentary_procedures.html), 4 items deal explicitly with this goal:

• All members have equal rights, privileges, and obligations; rules must be administered impartially.

- The minority has rights which must be protected.

- Full and free discussion of all motions, reports, and other items of business is a right of all members.

- Members must not attack or question the motives other members. Customarily, all remarks are addressed to the presiding officer.

Although in larger, more formal committees, you may wish to enforce the "all remarks are addressed to the presiding officer" rule, that solution is simply not practical for most committees. How, then, do you go about creating a committee environment in which all opinions are heard and given due consideration? Partly, you do this by example, sincerely asking for alternative viewpoints, treating those viewpoints with respect when they are offered, and discussing them on their merits, not as a reflection of the person who introduced them. Partly, too, you do this by insisting on a high standard of collegiality in all discussions, intervening quickly if one or more of your committee members deviate from these standards, and maintaining an atmosphere that rewards individuals for the free exchange of ideas. As committee chair, you will at times need to advocate for or defend a committee member who may be feeling coerced into silence by the more vocal committee members. Part of being a good leader in committee meetings involves ensuring that all perspectives receive a fair hearing, and that goal cannot be achieved if certain committee members intimidate others into silence. In situations where this occurs repeatedly, you may even need to have a quiet conversation with the more aggressive members, explaining how their behavior has been counterproductive to the group's work and reiterating your own commitment to the free exchange of ideas.

There are few things about which college and university employees are more cynical than committee meetings. Chairing meetings effectively can make the time you spend together as a committee more effective, even enjoyable. Doing so is also an important part of your work as a mentor: By chairing effective meetings, you teach others how this important goal may be accomplished.

Resources

Chan, J. F. (2003). *Jossey-Bass academic administrator's guide to meetings.* San Francisco, CA: Jossey-Bass.

Doyle, M., & Straus, D. (1982). *How to make meetings work.* New York, NY: Jove.

Kelsey, D., & Plumb, P. (2004). *Great meetings! Great results: A practical guide for facilitating successful, productive meetings* (Rev. and expanded ed.). Portland, ME: Great Meetings!

Parker, G., & Hoffman, R. (2006). *Meeting excellence: 33 tools to lead meetings that get results.* San Francisco, CA: Jossey-Bass.

Schwarz, R. M. (1994). *The skilled facilitator: Practical wisdom for developing effective groups.* San Francisco, CA: Jossey-Bass.

Smelser, N. J. (1993). *Effective committee service.* Newbury Park, CA: Sage.

Streibel, B. J. (2003). *The manager's guide to effective meetings.* New York, NY: McGraw-Hill.

References

Jones, O. G. (1990). *Parliamentary procedure at a glance.* New York, NY: Penguin.

Robert, H. M., III, Evans, W. J., Honemann, D. H., & Balch, T. J. (2000). *Robert's rules of order* (10th ed.). New York, NY: Perseus.

Sturgis, A. (2000). *The standard code of parliamentary procedure* (4th ed.). New York, NY: McGraw-Hill.

38

Leadership from the Middle

In Chapter 1 ("The View from the Middle"), we learned that deans, because of their position within an institution's administration, tend to see things from a unique perspective. That perspective may differ at times from others' point of view, but it provides deans with numerous leadership opportunities. It is easy to see how such leadership opportunities can occur within the college itself, where the dean stands at the head of the organizational chart. But it can be much more difficult to understand where leadership possibilities exist institution-wide. How, in other words, can deans help lead an entire institution when their position is, by definition, one that falls at the very center of the institutional hierarchy?

To understand how leadership can occur at the middle of an organization, we need to understand what is perhaps the most essential "essential principle" of all:

> *All leadership must be leadership from the middle. When you understand how organizations work, you understand that everybody reports to somebody.*

In other words, on your institution's organizational chart, faculty members report either directly to you or to department chairs. Department chairs, in turn, report to you in your capacity as dean. You report to either a chief academic officer or the president. The president reports to a board. Given this type of structure, if leadership were possible only at the very top of the organizational pyramid, individuals could exert only small changes. But we have all known a president, provost, dean, or department chair whose energy, insight, or personal charm completely transformed an institution. The true academic leader can thus arise at *any* level of the institutional hierarchy.

To begin demonstrating your own contagious, transformative leadership, you need to apply the following strategies at your institution.

Be known for something. Establish a positive reputation.

We saw in Chapter 21 ("Searching for and Building a Strong Administrative Team") how standing for something brings energy and esprit de corps to the work done by the dean's staff. People begin to feel that they're not just making a living but making a difference; they sense that they're on a mission to accomplish something truly important for others. In a similar way, deans can begin to demonstrate leadership not just in their own individual areas but throughout the institution as a whole by being known for something. What you are known for will depend a great deal on your own background and area of expertise. Nevertheless, you might consider developing your distinctive identity at your institution in at least one of the following three areas: expertise, values, or vision. Although there is a great deal of overlap between these categories, they are a useful starting point in analyzing how you can carve out your unique identity:

- *Being known for your expertise:* This area involves developing a level of knowledge or skill in some specific area that distinguishes you from your peers. Because of your great expertise in some particular area, you become the go-to person whenever advice or insight in that area is needed. For instance, every institution needs gurus in technology, assessment, faculty development, course evaluation, fundraising, program review, budgeting, and so on. By developing an expertise, you become known at your institution not just as an effective advocate for your disciplinary area but also as someone who works on behalf of the whole institution. "Oh," people will say, "if your question involves distance learning, you really ought to talk to Dean So-and-so; she's the expert on that." Moreover, by developing an area of expertise that transcends your own college, you will have a platform to speak quite broadly on a host of institutional issues. As such, you will begin to function—and *to be seen*—as a leader beyond the boundaries of the disciplines in your unit.

- *Being known for your values:* This second area means establishing a clear identity based on the principles and practices that you advocate. Some deans are known as "the institution's conscience," framing each discussion with its moral or ethical implications. Perhaps the values that you believe in most involve protecting the environment, looking out for the underprivileged, promoting professionalism, representing the faculty's (or student body's or staff's) interests, supporting collegiality throughout the institution, or exploring creative new solutions to perennial problems. Perhaps your values take you in a different direction, establishing you as an early adopter of new technology or institutional initiatives, the person who always remembers other people's birthdays or sends congratulatory notes when good things happen in their lives, or the advocate for typographic and grammatical perfection in every public document. Whatever values most resonate with you can become the basis for your identity as the institutional specialist in that area.

• *Being known for your vision:* This entails constantly seeing beyond what *is* to imagining what *could be.* As the campus visionary, you would be the person who always thinks in terms of larger possibilities and future directions. Good vision is, of course, not wholly divorced from practicality, so you will need to amass a certain amount of evidentiary support for the vision that you promote. For instance, based on the demographics of your region or enrollment trends at peer institutions, you could be the person who positions your institution to be ahead of the curve when those new developments arise. Students' need for specific services, their attraction to particular majors, and their relationships both with the institution and with their parents change over time. As a visionary leader, you might be the person who is aware of how each new generation of students will differ from its predecessors and who can help your institution prepare for those changes (see Strauss & Howe, 1991, 1997.)

Be the sort of dean who radiates positive energy.

Some of the best administrative advice for deans comes from an unusual source—the actor Cary Grant: "I think that being relaxed at all times, and I mean relaxed, not collapsed, can add to the happiness and duration of one's life and looks. And relaxed people are fun to be around" (Nelson, 2003, p. 25). Certainly, no one can deny that it can be very stressful to serve as dean. There are times when the implications of your decisions, the intensity of the criticism you receive, and the pressure to succeed on a variety of fronts can shake your confidence, resulting in a high level of anxiety. In addition, deans (like many others in positions of authority) sometimes believe that they *should* feel constantly harried, always rushing from one important meeting to the next. After all, if the position weren't stressful, anyone could do it, and then how could you justify the salary and benefits that come with the deanship?

What deans need to realize, however, is that by publicly demonstrating anxiety, tension, or a sense of being overworked, they can actually end up being far less effective in their roles and can undermine their position as a campus leader. As Cary Grant suggested, people naturally gravitate toward others who are relaxed, confident, and self-assured. When leaders are relaxed, they give faculty, students, and staff a sense that, even if matters are difficult now, everything will work out in the end. People thus acquire the confidence they need to *make* matters work out in the end. On the other hand, administrators who function in crisis mode all the time give the impression that they cannot distinguish between truly serious matters—an imminent threat to the life or safety of a member of the campus community, a financial exigency so severe that it threatens the entire institution—from the more routine challenges that colleges and universities face every day. Leadership from the middle, therefore, may begin with nothing more than maintaining a calm and confident attitude when everyone around you is panicking. The pressures of the academic year bring about these periods of *Sturm und Drang* on an almost predictable schedule. As each semester draws to a close and nerves are frayed from the pressure of final exams, grade deadlines, and reports, the mood on campus can change dramatically. Tempers flare. Despair sets in. What seemed insignificant before suddenly seems insurmountable. At times like these, leadership can be demonstrated through a quiet confidence; an attitude that "we can do this, and the result will be fantastic"; and a gentle optimism that even today's momentary frustrations will lead to something exciting.

A dean who exerts leadership on his or her campus is thus likely to be a person who radiates a high level of confidence. Rather than stoking the fires of anxiety, effective leaders approach difficulties as simply par for the course and convey an attitude that solving problems is interesting because it requires creativity. People at your institution—not simply in your college, but university-wide—enjoy being with individuals who reinforce their own confidence through a relaxed and inspiring demeanor. This type of positive energy does not necessarily have to be demonstrated by your president, chancellor, or governing board chair. In fact, if the head of your institution tends not to project a positive and confident demeanor, it is even more important that *someone* at the institution do so. It is this type of leadership that you as a dean can effectively demonstrate from your vantage point at the middle of the institution.

Collins (2001) notes that the highest caliber of "leaders embody a paradoxical mix of personal humility and professional will" (p. 39). Thus, another essential ingredient in leading from the middle is combining confidence that all obstacles will be overcome with an ability to be unassuming, humble, even self-deprecating about your own accomplishments. Strong academic deans tend to be very serious about fulfilling their college's mission, but they rarely take themselves too seriously. Confidence that comes across as arrogance or pretentiousness alienates others; it does not make them eager to follow the dean's charted direction. Deans who insist too often that they must stand on their dignity can end up with very little dignity to stand on. They are more likely to become mere caricatures of a supercilious dean. Everyone's personality is different, of course, but most deans discover that allowing themselves to be seen having a good time on occasion—even if some of the humor is at their own expense—enhances, rather than detracts, from their position's authority.

Look for ways in which you can unite others' dreams and visions with your own.

Leadership is not a matter of getting other people to do what you want. It's a matter of helping people achieve a common goal regardless of whether that goal is a dream of yours. Weak and ineffective leaders insist on taking a unit in a direction that only they see as important; they may seem successful for the moment, but they are unlikely to be very effective at their institutions in the long run. Good leaders help others develop their own shared dreams and visions. They may even be the catalyst for creating that image of an exciting future (see Chapter 4, "Creating a Vision for the College"). These effective leaders see building a shared enthusiasm for the future as an important part of their job, regardless of whether they themselves are given credit as the authors of that vision (see Chapter 5, "Building a Shared Vision for the College"). Deans can best lead from the middle by uniting the visions and dreams of their own colleges with the plans that are being developed or pursued elsewhere at the institution.

Building partnerships with other colleges can be an extremely effective way both of helping your own unit achieve its goals and of developing an entirely new culture at an institution. Because resources are limited, presidents and boards look favorably on proposals that benefit more than one segment of an institution. Because the traditional organization of universities into departments, schools, and colleges tends to fragment institutions, cooperative efforts can help reverse this silo mentality and foster a new culture of cooperation. Mandating this type of institutional change from the top down rarely works; presidents and provosts are often far less effective than visionary deans in getting units to collaborate in new and exciting ways. For this reason, intercollegiate cooperation can be the perfect way to demonstrate the effectiveness of leadership from the middle.

The collaborative effort that you propose is likely to be determined by your institution's individual needs and history. Nevertheless, there are themes that transcend the individual programs. For instance, you might propose a new initiative in creativity, innovation, and entrepreneurship that draws together the arts, sciences, engineering, and business under a single umbrella to explore how people discover what is truly original and to expose others to this discovery. A leadership initiative could combine the theoretical and historical study of major leaders, managers, and visionaries with practical experience in leading on-campus organizations, small start-up businesses, and committees within the university's own hierarchy. Indeed, many important developments in scholarship occur between traditional department divisions: Bioengineering draws on expertise in both biology and engineering; modern publication incorporates studio art, computer information systems, design, printing, and marketing; neuroscience spans psychology, biology, medicine, and philosophy. These interdisciplinary endeavors can themselves prompt the exploration of a new type of intercollegiate cooperation.

Moreover, the very kind of collaborative endeavor that you propose with other colleges could assume a variety of forms. It can range from something as simple as a lecture series or single team-taught course to something as ambitious as a new center, program, or endowed professorship (see Chapter 51, "Consortia, Centers, and Institutes"). Whatever you propose, begin by asking what dreams and visions you already share with other units at your institution, and then think creatively about how you can work together to pursue these common interests.

Seek ways of offering more than you receive.

Deans can demonstrate effective leadership from the middle by focusing on the secret of *all* leadership: working on behalf of those who report to them, not simply making those who report to them work on their behalf. In other words, an effective leader is always motivated by the best interests of those for whom he or she is responsible. Once deans start viewing the whole institution, not merely their own units, as their responsibility, they begin to act more effectively as leaders. For instance, a dean who finds that students from other colleges tend not to be very successful in the service courses offered by his or her own college can respond in several ways. The dean can see this situation as confirmation that "our students are better than the other colleges'," or the dean can do something to help those students. A peer tutorial center, an ad hoc committee that explores potential curriculum revisions to promote student success, or a constructive talk with other deans and department chairs to see what can be done to improve the situation all demonstrate true leadership. Leaders reach out to others to address their needs, and that is a practice that can be initiated anywhere in an institutional hierarchy, not merely at the very top.

As middle managers, deans encounter leadership opportunities on many levels. Deans stand at the very top of the school's or college's organizational structure. To their fellow administrators, deans can serve as peers, mentors, and examples. To the upper administration, they can demonstrate leadership through a willingness to address the institution's needs from a broad perspective while still serving as an effective advocate for their own academic areas. Being at the middle of a hierarchy does not, in other words, restrict their leadership opportunities; it multiplies the number of different *directions* in which that leadership can be demonstrated.

Resources

Kouzes, J. M., & Posner, B. Z. (2003). *Jossey-Bass academic administrator's guide to exemplary leadership.* San Francisco, CA: Jossey-Bass.

Morris, V. C. (1981). *Deaning: Middle management in academe.* Champaign, IL: University of Illinois Press.

Wolverton, M., & Gmelch, W. H. (2002). *College deans: Leading from within.* Phoenix, AZ: American Council on Education/Oryx Press.

References

Collins, J. (2001). *Good to great: Why some companies make the leap . . . and others don't.* New York, NY: HarperCollins.

Nelson, N. (2003). *Evenings with Cary Grant: Recollections in his own words and by those who knew him best* (2nd ed.). New York, NY: Citadel Press.

Strauss, W., & Howe, N. (1991). *Generations: The history of America's future, 1584–2069.* New York, NY: William Morrow.

Strauss, W., & Howe, N. (1997). *The fourth turning: An American prophecy.* New York, NY: Broadway Books.

39

Leadership in Development and Increasing Revenue

Nothing can help transform a college—or perhaps an entire institution—as much as a large gift, grant, or bequest. Often these sources of external funding are large enough that their effect can be felt immediately throughout the unit. This type of transformative funding generates a great deal of excitement, produces a widespread feeling that things are moving in the right direction, and continues to make a difference far outside the area in which the gift was made or the grant received. Deans who help make positive changes in their colleges by aggressively pursuing large gifts and grants are thus frequently regarded as visionary, the very sort of leader who can help improve an entire institution. For this reason, if you truly hope to make a lasting and positive impact on your institution, then demonstrating leadership through development and increasing revenue is one of the best approaches.

How do you begin to lead in development and other aspects of increasing revenue? This chapter assumes that you've mastered the basics of fundraising, as presented in Chapter 18 ("Donors and Potential Donors"), Buller (2006), and Ciconte and Jacob (2005). It also assumes that you've received at least some training in fundraising, such as the excellent Development for Deans workshops that the Council for Advancement and Support of Education (www.case.org) offers each year. You should be familiar with the grant-writing process at your institution and have improved your own skills as a grant writer by consulting such works as Brown and Brown (2001), Hall and Howlett (2003), and Miller (2002). This chapter also assumes that you have a good comprehensive manual of fundraising principles, such as Alexander and Carlson (2005), Greenfield (2002), or Schaff and Schaff (1999). Finally, it assumes that you already have had some practical fundraising and grant-writing experience and have successfully obtained $10,000 or more from an external donor or foundation. With all that as your foundation, you're now ready for more of a leadership role, seeking the big gift that will truly transform your college. In doing so, the following are some principles that will help you lead in development and increasing revenue.

Use your resources.

Sit down with a development officer or member of your research and sponsored programs office and start formulating a list of untapped or underutilized resources with connections to your institution. Your list might include potential donors who have significant private resources and who have not yet made a large gift to your institution, regular contributors to the annual fund who appear to be ready for a major gift request, foundations in your area with a history of supporting institutions like yours, and foundations or government programs that have a focus related to your college's work. If you are relatively new to your position, go through the files to find the names of the people who gave your unit substantial gifts in the past; find out whether they are still living or, if not, the names of their heirs. Remember that your best donors are likely to be people who have had a close connection to your college in the past. Once you've created your list, go through it name by name or foundation by foundation, exploring where there may be a possible overlap between the donor's or grantor's philanthropic interests and your program's focus or needs. An individual on your list may be an alumnus, for instance, or someone who attended another institution but majored in a field represented in your college. He or she may have had a successful career in a profession that relates in some way to the scholarly pursuits of your faculty members. A potential donor who has been active in a field like construction, architecture, or contracting may be approached about a proposal for a new building, with their services donated as an extremely generous gift in kind. There may be a potential donor who is known to have developed new interests later in life, perhaps because of an activity that was important to a spouse, child, or friend. A foundation may be known for philanthropic work in a field that bears some connection to one or more of your college's disciplines. By the time you have completed this review, you will probably notice that a small number (perhaps two to six) of the names on your list have the best possible combination of available resources and an interest related to what you do. These are the resources that you will want to pursue.

Dream creatively.

Gifts and grants that are large enough to transform or reinvigorate a college tend not to be given for ordinary things. Your greatest need from day to day might be a few more computers, extra travel money, or a bit of adjunct support, but these are not projects that will fire large donors' interest or carry your college to its next level of excellence. Truly transformative gifts must be impressive enough to make a statement and must symbolize something essential both about your college and about the donor or foundation that provides it. For this reason, your next step should be to collect a select group of individuals who can help you develop a dream or vision that will inspire donors to make a real difference in your college. As you assemble this group, ask yourself who in your college and elsewhere at your institution has the perspective to dream big enough to be meaningful but not so extravagantly as to be unattainable. Naturally, you'll want your development officer or grant writer to be part of this select group. But who else in your college has the proper mixture of vision and practicality to succeed in this capacity? Working with this group is good preparation for future leaders, so you will not want to restrict the committee to your senior faculty or the usual suspects, who tend to be tapped for every significant role in your college. Just as you will want your group to think creatively about fundable projects, so, too, will you need to be creative in assembling your ad hoc committee.

After the group is formed, explain your task as clearly as you can. Tell the members that you are trying to achieve the following goals:

- Propose a fundable project that addresses both the philanthropic interests of the donor or foundation (after explaining to your group what those are) and the mission of the college as a whole or of one of its parts

- Develop a project on a suitable scale to excite the imagination not only of the people who are already associated with the college but also potential students and faculty members, members of the community, and potential donors

If the foundation's guidelines or your development office's analysis of the donor's giving capacity already has formulated a recommendation for the maximum amount of your proposal, reveal that information to your committee. You might say something like, "We know that we are more likely to be successful if our request is no larger than $100,000, so that's the amount that we're going to be pursuing. The advice I need from you is the sort of project that addresses what the donor [or foundation] is interested in doing and that helps us achieve our overall mission."

To help prime the pump for the committee's ideas, you might mention some of the possibilities for a transformative major gift, such as:

- A new facility or extensive renovation of an existing structure

- An endowed professorship

- An endowed scholarship fund

- A large annual award that recognizes the recipient for contributions made to some particular area
- A high-profile annual conference

Then, using these ideas and the others generated by your committee members, begin to build your core idea into new, more exciting variations. Rather than a simple scholarship endowment, for instance, perhaps your proposal will seek funding for a program that provides a student with a stipend sufficient to pay for tuition and for a paid summer internship so that he or she will graduate with demonstrated practical experience. Rather than a simple annual conference, perhaps you will also seek funding for publishing the best dozen or so presentations each year in a volume that will make a significant contribution to research. Or perhaps you will seek ways of recording each presentation in the conference, producing a DVD, and distributing it free to colleges and universities nationwide. Rather than a simple classroom building, perhaps you will incorporate space for a research center devoted to the field in which the donor or foundation has a particular interest. Challenge your committee to use its creativity so that the proposal is not just one more building or endowed chair but something that will immediately attract attention when people learn of it.

Developing this proposal in concert with an ad hoc committee is far preferable to attempting to do so alone or with only your development officer or grant writer. Although the process may take longer, in the end you'll get better ideas, a group of committed supporters who will help you advance the idea through any institutional committees that may need to review it, and additional help when you present the idea to your potential donor or foundation. Particularly if you're not the sort of person who thinks creatively on your feet, feels comfortable asking others for money, or has the sort of eloquence that may be needed to sell this idea, meeting with your select committee will put you in contact with people who do have these talents. You'll develop a good sense of whom you'd like to have at your side as you begin your cultivation calls with your funding source.

Take full advantage of a leisurely cultivation phase.

Even though your initial proposal has now been developed, it is highly unlikely that you'll get it fully funded with only a single donor visit or grant submission. You must begin the process of getting to know the potential donor well or developing a relationship with the foundation's program officer. Your first visit—even your first several visits—may involve only general discussions of your committee's idea. In many cases you may not even discuss the idea directly at all for the first several conversations, exploring instead those areas where the donor's primary focus corresponds with what you do or hope to do in your college. When you do broach the specific proposal, ask for review, reaction, and guidance; do not immediately ask for funding. Remember the essential principle that we saw in Chapter 18 ("Donors and Potential Donors"): Ask for money, and you will get advice; ask for advice, and you will get money. At this point you should only be seeking recommendations: How can this proposal be strengthened? What would make the basic idea more useful to people? How can we reach a larger audience? Most important of all, remember to *take* the advice you receive. For one thing, it is probably extremely useful guidance because it comes from someone who is used to considering philanthropic requests. For another thing, the donor or program officer is, intentionally or not, guiding you closer to his or her own areas of primary interest.

Remember, as you make these cultivation visits, that your title of *dean* carries with it a great deal of prestige. For many college graduates, the dean was a remote and lofty figure. By having an opportunity to sit down one on one and talk to the dean, many prospective donors feel that they are being given highly privileged access to the upper levels of the university. You should remember, therefore, that the donor may regard your very presence as something valuable during these cultivation visits.

The first document that you will leave with the potential donor or program officer should be a one- to two-page case statement, rather than a long proposal with a complete budget and timetable for implementation. (On case statements, see Chapter 18, "Donors and Potential Donors.") Once the donor or program officer has critiqued the case statement and provided recommendations for its improvement, incorporate these ideas into your full proposal. Within a week of your initial visit, write a personal note, thanking the donor or program officer for his or her time and promising to send a revised case statement in the very near future. Depending on the grant application deadline or the donor's personal style, you may even submit a revised case statement several more times before sharing a full, detailed proposal with your funding source.

Only when you and your development officer both agree that the time is right (or when the grant application deadline is approaching) should you submit the complete proposal. (With certain funding agencies, foundations, and program officers, you may be able to submit a full proposal for review and emendation before the final version is due. If this possibility is offered, *always* take it. The recommendations offered on your proposal greatly enhance the likelihood that your project will receive funding.) Before leaving, arrange a specific time when you will contact the donor or foundation again. Without setting this time in advance, you may well find yourself wondering whether the contact's silence means that:

- The proposal is being ignored.

- The other person is simply waiting for you to call back.

- Future contacts about the proposal will just appear to be nagging.

On the other hand, by prearranging your next contact time, you have a reason to touch base with the person, even if he or she is not yet ready to discuss committing to your project.

Use funded proposals as a way to achieve both primary and secondary goals.

Because your goal is not simply to obtain funding for one discrete project, but rather to transform your college and to demonstrate leadership at your institution, you should think of ways that you can leverage the successful funding of a proposal to attain other goals for your college. For instance, one of your objectives as dean might be to increase the competitiveness of your faculty salaries. Nevertheless, donors rarely contribute funds with the primary purpose of increasing faculty compensation. By strategically developing your funding priorities, however, you may be able to achieve this objective as a *secondary* result of your proposal. The following example illustrates how this idea can be put into effect.

Suppose that you have a faculty member who is about to retire with a salary of $94,000 and that your institution's average rate of benefits approximately costs an additional 24%. With the approval of your provost and president, you could hire an entry-level faculty member on this line at, for instance, $55,000. Taking benefits into account, you would then have $48,360 of salary savings that you could then direct to raising your faculty's salaries. Doing so would be effective deaning, and it's the sort of budgetary redirection that good deans make all the time. (If faculty salaries are not your institution's highest priority, the salary savings could be redirected to any continuing budgetary item, such as travel, research funding, or equipment upgrades.) On the other hand, if you could interest a donor in endowing an eminent scholar position to replace the retiring faculty member, you could achieve your primary goal of enhancing your college's prestige and scholarly reputation through acquiring a distinguished professor of national renown and accomplish your secondary goal of enhancing faculty salaries. Now, with the approval of your provost and president, you have the retiring faculty member's *entire* salary and benefits compensation of $116,560 to redirect toward your salary improvement fund. In addition, because the endowment will probably provide you with an eminent scholar salary that is more than the retired faculty member's, you will have taken an additional step toward making your entire range of salaries more competitive. That's not just effective deaning; that's *visionary leadership.*

As you continue to build your leadership skills in development, an excellent activity for a faculty retreat or start-of-year meeting can be a workshop devoted to strategies for increasing revenue. Have members of your college share with you their ideas for a truly transformative gift. If your college is large, form break-out discussions of 10 or 12 people each. Ask the groups to consider such questions as:

- What would you propose that we do with a $20 million gift to our college? Why should that project matter to someone outside our college?

- What do you regard as our college's single biggest need? Why is that particular need so important?

- If you could look 10 years in the future and conclude, "The entire college was positively transformed by a single gift," what changes would you have seen? How large would the gift have been?

The discussions that arise from these questions are important on several levels. They can help your college develop a shared vision along the lines discussed in Chapter 5 ("Building a Shared Vision for the College"). They can give you excellent ideas that you can use in your own development efforts. And the energy generated by your faculty when they begin to think about exciting possibilities will be contagious, inspiring you as their leader to help secure the donors that will bring these ideas to fruition.

References

Alexander, G. D., & Carlson, K. J. (2005). *Essential principles for fundraising success: An answer manual for the everyday challenges of raising money.* San Francisco, CA: Jossey-Bass.

Brown, L. G., & Brown, M. J. (2001). *Demystifying grant seeking: What you really need to do to get grants.* San Francisco, CA: Jossey-Bass.

Buller, J. L. (2006). What every department chair needs to know about fundraising. In J. L. Buller, *The essential department chair: A practical guide to college administration* (pp. 129–137). Bolton, MA: Anker.

Ciconte, B. L., & Jacob, J. G. (2005). *Fundraising basics: A complete guide* (2nd ed.). Sudbury, MA: Jones and Bartlett.

Greenfield, J. M. (2002). *Fundraising fundamentals: A guide to annual giving for professionals and volunteers* (2nd ed.). New York, NY: Wiley.

Hall, M., & Howlett, S. (2003). *Getting funded: The complete guide to writing grant proposals.* Portland, OR: Continuing Education Press.

Miller, P. W. (2002). *Grant writing: Strategies for developing winning proposals* (2nd ed.). Munster, IN: Patrick W. Miller and Associates.

Schaff, T., & Schaff, D. (1999). *The fundraising planner: A working model for raising the dollars you need.* San Francisco, CA: Jossey-Bass.

40

A Scenario Analysis on the Dean's Leadership

Note: For a discussion of how scenario analyses are structured and suggestions on how to use this exercise most productively, see Chapter 8, "A Scenario Analysis on the Dean's Role."

Case Study

You've recently accepted a position at an institution where you are dean of one of five academic colleges. Although everyone you met during your interviews seemed very upbeat about your college's long-range potential, you discovered a rather different situation after you arrived on campus. The morale of your college's faculty and staff is not just bad—after all, you've dealt with tough morale problems before—it's the worst you've ever *heard* about. Collegiality may be charitably described as nonexistent. The very first faculty meeting you attended became almost unbearably tense, with speech after speech filled with accusations and recriminations. Almost universally, members of your college distrust the administration; even the people who had been gracious to you during your interviews now treat you either coldly or with open hostility because you are now "one of *them*." The internecine warfare in your unit is so bad that the other colleges at your university openly regard it as "a real snake pit" and treat it with contempt. You discover that your fellow deans consider you to be little more than their junior partner because your college is seen as so dysfunctional that it is widely dismissed as ungovernable.

As you explore the reasons for this difficult situation, you discover that much of the rancor is due to a long-standing dispute over faculty salaries. More than a decade earlier, a university-wide salary study concluded that faculty and staff members of your college were underpaid relative to their colleagues at the university and to their disciplinary peers at other institutions in your region. The higher administration and several of your predecessors promised to remedy this situation, but a decade of increasingly tight budgets—due to flat or declining enrollment, a disappointing return on the university's endowment, and an institutional commitment to keep tuition increases low to avoid exacerbating the enrollment challenges—have made this goal unattainable. Your college's faculty and staff openly claim that they have been told lies repeatedly, that promises made to them have been broken, and that there is little reason to trust any statement made by any administrator, including you.

One of the reasons that you were hired is that both the upper administration and the members of the college were impressed by your vision for the unit's future. Now, however, each time you refer to one of the ideas that people seemed so excited about just a few months earlier, you are met with open resistance. "If the university has money to do that," you are asked again and again, "why doesn't it ever have any money to put into faculty salaries?" You've tried on several occasions to explain the difference between one-year expenditures and continuous expenditures (see Chapter 25, "Setting Budgetary Priorities"), with little impact. You've even tried to explain how pursuing some of the goals that you've outlined will help the college increase its revenue base in a way that can alleviate the salary problem, but this suggestion was met with widespread skepticism. Increasingly, you believe that the salary issue is being used as a litmus test of your leadership: If you can't solve this problem, people will not trust you on any other issue. Meanwhile, the upper administration is eager for you to put into effect some of those ideas that you discussed while still a candidate for the position.

The situation comes to a head even before your first year as dean is over. You notice that members of your college are not taking sufficient advantage of a major national endowment that could help fund their research, bring the college some much needed indirect revenue, and help improve the salary situation because part of the grant money could be used as supplementary stipends. You schedule several one-on-one meetings with individual faculty members whom you believe have an excellent chance of submitting a successful grant proposal. Although most of these meetings result in the faculty member expressing either indifference or a lukewarm promise to think about the opportunity, one faculty member shocks you by being openly hostile. After a few sentences in which you explain the grant program, the faculty member interrupts you to present a litany of perceived grievances that the individual allegedly suffered under previous administrations. Most of the complaints deal with failures to meet the faculty member's repeated demands for a higher salary, and you are given what sounds very much like an ultimatum: Either you immediately raise the faculty member's salary by what you quickly calculate to be approximately 40%, or the person says, "You can forget about any of these other proposals you have in mind because none of us are going to support any of them." You reiterate that, although you're committed to doing everything you can to improve salaries, that problem simply cannot be addressed in isolation, and the appointment comes to a hasty and unsatisfactory conclusion.

Matters only get worse at the next faculty meeting when the same individual takes the floor to propose a vote of no confidence in your leadership. "I personally met with the dean," the faculty member says, "and explained in clear and unmistakable detail what the salary situation is, how it developed, and what needed to be done to fix it; and I received no commitment to address what we all admit is the single most pressing issue in our college. Nothing has changed from previous administrations. We get lip service on salaries but no action. It's time for us to take a stand and admit that we made the wrong hire. We'd be better off with no dean at all than with yet another person who promises us one thing during the search but doesn't want to do anything to help us once the position is offered."

Confronted with this situation, how do you best demonstrate leadership?

Considerations

1. Does your reaction change at all if one of the following scenarios occurs? Assume that the faculty members proceed to take a vote of no confidence and . . .

    •   The vote is unanimous against you.

    •   The vote is significantly against you, although it is not unanimous.

    •   The vote is against you, but by a very slim majority.

    •   The vote is in your favor by 58%, with 40% voting against you and 2% abstaining.

    •   The vote is unanimously in your favor except for the individual who proposed the vote and the person who seconded the motion.

    •   The vote is inconclusive because most faculty members believe it's too early to judge your job performance.

2. Does your way of handling the situation change if one of the following possibilities occurs? Assume that you do your own analysis of the salary situation and discover that . . .

    •   The faculty and staff in your college have a very strong case. The situation has deteriorated even beyond what had occurred a decade ago, and salary levels now lag *substantially* behind those of the other colleges at the university and at peer institutions.

    •   Despite claims to the contrary, the salary situation has actually improved quite a bit in your college over the past decade. Equity has been achieved or nearly achieved both with other colleges at the university and with similar colleges at peer institutions.

- The methodology used in the original study was seriously flawed, and there never was a significant salary gap.

3. Is your response any different if you are operating in a unionized environment (see Chapter 52, "The Unionized Environment")?

4. Suppose you discover that previous deans were extremely aggressive in making faculty salaries a high priority but with little effect on overall morale and absolutely no change in the rhetoric used by opinion leaders in faculty meetings. Does this discovery alter your view of this issue's priority?

5. Suppose that neither the president nor the provost regard your college's salary issue to be a high priority. They dismiss it as a red herring and want you to focus on the other initiatives that you discussed during your interviews. How might you react in each of the following situations?

- You are told firmly by the upper administration, "Don't worry about what the faculty thinks. They don't decide on your contract; *we* do. And we think that other issues are simply more important."

- You have good reason to believe that both the president and the provost will leave the institution at the end of your first year.

- You are told, "You can fix this problem if you want to, but you're going to have to find the funding to do that. Frankly, we've got other priorities."

6. In retrospect, is there anything that you could have done either during your interviews or before beginning your deanship that would have prevented this issue from blindsiding you?

7. Suppose you are attending a national conference for college deans who share your disciplinary focus. At a lunch with several of your fellow deans, you are told, "Oh, we have precisely that same situation at our college. Faculty and staff members in our disciplines are *always* claiming that they're oppressed and taken advantage of when it comes to salaries. Look, you're never going to solve this problem. It *can't* be solved. You just have to ignore it and do the job you were hired to do." Does this advice change the way in which you might respond to the situation? Is it good advice?

Suggestions

As uncomfortable as the situation described in the case study may be, it is actually quite similar to what many deans encounter at least once during their tenure. Faculty salary complaints, like parking problems, largely go with the territory of being a dean. So, if you haven't already worked in an environment that bears a striking similarity to the hypothetical situation described in this case study, you probably will in the future. Every dean needs to develop a clear stand on the issue of improving faculty salaries and a plan to do so, if you decide that it is one of your priorities.

Nevertheless, because the situation described in this case study has come to such an impasse, it is probably best addressed head-on rather than handled merely as one of your many administrative objectives. If, after doing appropriate research, you find that the faculty and staff have justification for their complaints (even if the situation is not as severe as they claim), you will want to take positive steps to address their concerns. After all, if you don't take action, then every other initiative that you have is likely to be dead in the water. Your plans for the college will be met by open hostility or passive-aggressive promises to do something, followed by little or no real action. That said, it is probably also inadvisable to put all your plans on hold until you've "fixed" the salary problem. Salary problems are rarely, if ever, fixed in a college: Meeting one set of demands leads to still more demands; meeting all demands creates further insistence that faculty be compensated in some way for years of being underpaid. Thinking realistically, you should understand that you will never completely put this issue behind you, but you should try to address it at the same time that you also pursue other goals for your college.

Your best strategy is thus to make the salary situation a focal point of discussions whenever you meet with faculty and staff members and to seek progress on this front in several different ways. As we saw in Chapter 39 ("Leadership in Development and Increasing Revenue"), foundations and external donors are rarely interested in projects to boost faculty salaries. There are exceptions to this general rule, however, and you should actively pursue this opportunity whenever you discover such an exception. Because of the unlikelihood of solving your problem directly through fundraising, you might consider adopting a strategy of increasing salaries as a *secondary* benefit to a gift or grant. The way to achieve this goal that was discussed in Chapter 39 involved seeking an endowed chair as a replacement for a vacancy and then redirecting the resulting salary savings into your equity pool. There are, however, other variations of this approach that you might consider. For instance, nearly every college has a large number of naming opportunities—chances for donors to name a building, classroom, center, or even the college itself. Most frequently, these opportunities provide the right to designate a name for the facility or entity in perpetuity. Increasingly, however, naming opportunities are being given for set periods, allowing additional investments to be made in the future. Thus, instead of saying, "For a gift of $25 million, you will have the right to name our college," you might consider a proposal like, "For a gift of $10 million, you will have the right to specify the name our college will use for 10 years." You could then use the profit from this endowment to help alleviate your salary situation. An endowment of $10 million, for instance, could provide a 2% draw of $200,000 for salary improvement, leaving the remainder to be used for funding some of your other goals or for reinvesting in the endowment, expanding its size in the future.

Because the large gift that you will need to pursue this strategy is likely to take several years to acquire and to start generating interest, you will also need a short-term strategy to begin making progress on the salary front and to demonstrate good faith to your faculty and staff. If your college is large enough, you could examine the pattern of guaranteed or likely retirements that will occur over the next 5 to 10 years. Estimate the replacement costs for hiring new, entry-level employees on those lines, and negotiate with your upper administration to determine whether you can retain all or part of the resulting salary savings. As you direct the salary savings into making equity adjustments, you will have several options. You can adopt the strategy that a rising tide raises all ships, distributing equity dollars across the board, or you can adopt a more targeted approach, addressing either the easiest cases to fix or the most demanding cases of need. Any of these approaches might be advisable in different situations, and your institutional culture will be your most reliable guide. Nevertheless, you should be aware that across-the-board approaches frequently squander the dean's opportunity to make a demonstrable impact on an individual's salary. In other words, if a person's raise changes from 2% to 2.2% in a given year, that change is likely to be too small to be noticed. But a raise that amounts to $10,000 a year instead of $1,200 a year is large enough to have an immediate effect. You will probably only be able to increase an individual's salary that significantly, however, if you target specific cases rather than provide everyone with a comparable raise.

There are two precautions to keep in mind if you target increases rather than distribute them across the board. The first is that this must only be done as part of a multiyear plan. Multiyear plans are always risky because the budget situation can change dramatically from year to year. As bad as the morale situation is now, it could be far worse if you commit to addressing the entire salary problem but are forced to abandon your plan after one or two years. If you proceed with a multiyear plan of targeting individuals in some priority order, you will need to be able to justify that order and make it your *first priority* each year as you plan your budget. Second, you may be tempted to target first the problems that are easiest to fix rather than those that have the greatest need. For instance, if you have only $20,000 of equity money to distribute, it is a great temptation to adjust the salaries of 40 faculty members who are only $500 below peer targets rather than to adjust the salaries of the 2 faculty members who are $10,000 below peer targets. In the first case, you can make 40 people happy, in the second case only 2. Nevertheless, there are reasons why a targeted approach should always address the worst cases first. To begin with, these are the individuals who have the greatest claim in terms of equity. They are also the individuals who tend to distort your college's average salary calculations the most. Addressing their needs first can, in many cases, make a much greater impact on overall faculty morale than numerous minor adjustments. It will also entitle you to state that you decided to tackle the hardest problems first.

Make no mistake, however: Salary equity issues are rarely ever solved by any dean. No matter how creative and aggressive your plan to address the problem may be, you are likely to encounter the issue repeatedly throughout your deanship. You can run the risk of saying, "This problem is never fixable, so we're just going to move on," but this approach is likely to destroy your chance of achieving many of your initiatives. Leaders cannot lead if nearly all their followers actively resist. You may well find, as one of the scenarios in the "Considerations" section suggested, that the salary problem is not as severe as many people claim or perhaps does not really exist, but failing to address it in some fashion is unlikely to be a successful strategy in the long run.

Resources

Moore, K. M., & Amey, M. J. (1993). *Making sense of the dollars: The costs and uses of faculty compensation* (ASHE-ERIC Higher Education Report No. 5). Washington, DC: The George Washington University, School of Education and Human Development.

Sutton, T. P., & Bergerson, P. J. (2001). *Faculty compensation systems: Impact on the quality of higher education* (ASHE-ERIC Higher Education Report Vol. 28, No. 2). Washington, DC: The George Washington University, School of Education and Human Development.

41

Terminating a Faculty Member

The most difficult situations that administrators face involve making negative personnel decisions. Turning someone down for promotion, hiring another candidate for a position, and refusing a request for a salary adjustment all present significant challenges and can result in unpleasant, even confrontational, discussions. Of these cases, however, there is none more challenging for deans than terminating a faculty member. In most situations the decision to terminate a faculty member falls into one of the following six categories:

- The faculty member receives annual contracts, and his or her services are simply no longer needed.

- The faculty member receives annual contracts and is not being renewed for reasons other than because his or her services are no longer needed.

- The faculty member receives annual contracts but is being terminated "for good cause" before the expiration of a contract.

- The faculty member is tenured and is being terminated "for good cause."

- The institution is facing severe financial exigency and is thus eliminating an entire program or class of employee to help ensure its overall survival.

- The faculty member's program is being phased out for reasons other than financial exigency.

Each of these situations involves different considerations and may well require different actions from the dean.

Terminating an annual contract holder because his or her services are no longer required

At most institutions faculty members on annual or noncontinuing contracts include all part-time or adjunct faculty members, individuals with nontenure-track or temporary appointments, and probationary faculty members who are on the tenure track but who have not yet been granted tenure. Some institutions and systems also permit hiring nontenure-earning instructors who may have heavier teaching responsibilities than their tenure-earning colleagues but who also have lower service and research commitments than tenure-track faculty members. In the vast majority of cases, when the services of annual contract holders are no longer required, the institution has significant lead time to notify the individuals. For instance, if there is a plan to collapse several part-time positions into a single tenure-track line for which a national search will be conducted, the dean will have ample opportunity to notify the part-time faculty members of the institution's intentions so that they can either apply for the full-time position or make other arrangements for their employment. Similarly, faculty members who are hired as sabbatical replacements or to fill other short-term needs should understand that the nature of their employment is necessarily confined to a specific period after which they will need to seek employment elsewhere.

Terminating an annual contract holder for other reasons

Aside from no longer needing that person's service, the most common reason for terminating an annual contract holder is that the employee's work has not been suitable in one way or another. Perhaps you can point to a demonstrated cause, such as insubordination, misuse of funds, or the failure to follow established procedures. Perhaps there is no demonstrated cause other than the person is a bad fit for the position or you think you can find a more appropriate person. The most important thing that deans need to know about this type of termination is that no reason is required when you are not renewing an annual employee's contract. Indeed, some institutions and university systems will not even permit you to provide the employee with the reason for nonrenewal. Furthermore, even if you are permitted to do so, you should not state the reason or put it in writing. Why? Stating a reason for nonrenewal does little more than open the door to a legal challenge that could easily have been avoided. Think of it this way: An annual contract is a self-contained, self-limiting contract, much like the contract that you might give someone to build your house or paint your kitchen. The builder or painter works for the duration of the contract and, when that task is complete, has no right to expect any future employment from you unless you explicitly offer a new contract. If you are not satisfied with the work, you do not owe that person a reason for hiring someone else the next time; you simply do so. Even more, you may hire someone else in the future for any reason or for no reason at all. The contract with the original worker was fulfilled, and you are free to do whatever you like in the future. Those same rules apply to annual contract employees at a college or university. When you do not renew someone's annual contract, providing a reason is not required. Doing so can cause unnecessary problems.

Terminating an annual contract holder for good cause before the current contract's expiration

Situations where it is necessary to break a contract before it expires tend to be far more complicated than simple nonrenewals at the end of a contract. In these cases you will need to provide a reason for the dismissal and, in many instances, allow the individual some recourse for appeal or due process. Breaking a contract must never be done lightly. In anything but the most extreme situations, it is usually better to endure inferior performance until the contract reaches its stated term or to reassign the individual to tasks where he or she can make a more positive contribution. Nevertheless, there are situations where termination for good cause is fully warranted. According to *West's Encyclopedia of American Law*:

> [Good cause] is legally adequate or substantial grounds or reason to take a certain action. The term *good cause* is a relative one and is dependent upon the circumstances of each individual case. . . . An employee is said to be dismissed for good cause if the reasons for the termination are work related. However, if the employer simply did not like the employee's personality, this would not ordinarily constitute good cause, unless the employee held a position, such as a salesperson, for which a likable personality was required. (Lehman & Phelps, 2005, p. 186)

At many colleges and universities, faculty handbooks or human resources manuals state that individuals may be dismissed before the expiration of a contract *for cause*. Use of the phrase "for cause," while common, is inadvisable for several reasons. To begin with, court-established definitions of the phrase deal almost exclusively with removing individuals from public office (see Nolan & Nolan-Haley, 1990, p. 644). Therefore, as we have seen, the more correct definition for what colleges and universities mean, as established by legal precedent, is *for good cause* (see Gifis, 1996, p. 220; Nolan & Nolan-Haley, 1990, p. 692). Most institutions of higher education recognize incompetence, gross immorality, felony, insubordination, violation of contract terms, and failure to follow stated policies as among the reasons for which an individual may be terminated before his or her contract expires. At other institutions the precise definition of "for good cause" is left undefined but generally involves extremely serious violations of a faculty member's responsibilities as a teacher, scholar, or colleague. These violations may include plagiarism, violating the rights of protected classes, contributing to an atmosphere that diminishes an individual's rights of free inquiry and expression, and abusing one's position for inappropriate personal gain.

Dismissals for good cause are almost always contentious matters and must be preceded by careful planning, analysis, and consultation. In each instance you should be sure that you have both adhered to your institution's internal procedure and consulted all the appropriate offices, such as human resources and legal affairs. In addition, you should remember to follow these three important steps:

- *Maintain proper documentation:* It is in your college's best interests for you to compile a clear paper trail that leads up to this dismissal. In the best possible scenario, you will have a series of performance appraisals that indicate the employee was informed of needed improvements, a timetable by which to take these actions, and indications that the required improvements have not occurred. Many annual contract employees do not have performance appraisals; the individual may have been under contract for too short a time to have been evaluated, or the contract renewal itself may have been regarded as the performance appraisal. Even in these situations, however, it is extremely useful to document conversations in which someone spoke to the employee about concerns with his or her performance, email messages illustrating the problems for which the employee is being dismissed, time cards or attendance records suggesting the employee's failure to perform the full functions of the position, or other clear and written evidence that will suggest, to a reasonable observer, that you were justified in terminating the employee before the contract expired.

- *Give all notices of termination with at least one witness present:* It is always advisable to have a third party present when you are dismissing someone. The third party's testimony can be extremely useful if there is ever a question later about specifically what was said, promised, and done. Particularly in cases where you and the employee are of different genders, sexual orientations, racial backgrounds—or where there has been a history of tension and animosity—a witness can verify that the proper policies were followed and that nothing inappropriate occurred behind closed doors. When selecting a witness, it is best to recruit someone from your institution's human resources or legal affairs office who has dealt with other terminations and can offer you guidance about precisely what to do. Meet privately with the witness before joining the employee to plan your strategy, go over precisely who will say what, decide whether a written dismissal notice will be given to the employee on the spot or at a later date, and remind one another of the importance of discretion and common courtesy in matters of this sort.

- *Confirm that the dismissal does not violate a protected employee's right to be discharged:* There are many different laws and statutes that protect certain classes of workers from being discharged. These laws and statutes change from time to time. For this reason, begin by consulting the summary of laws relating to protected classes that appears in Anglim (1997, pp. 447–448), and then consult with legal counsel to determine whether any modifications to Anglim's list have occurred.

Terminating a tenured faculty member for good cause

Despite popular beliefs to the contrary, tenure does not offer faculty members lifetime job security. Tenured faculty members need to fulfill their contract terms, demonstrate that they remain competent in their disciplines, and refrain from violating any of the standards that would make them liable to dismissal for good cause. Before the abolition of mandatory retirement ages at colleges and universities, an institution would occasionally endure a tenured faculty member's lack of productivity or ineffective performance for a time, knowing that at age 65 or 70 the individual would be compelled to retire by university policy. Now that mandatory retirement ages are forbidden, institutions are often compelled to initiate agonizing and often unsettling processes to revoke the tenure of senior faculty members who are no longer performing their responsibilities at an acceptable level. The implementation of post-tenure review procedures at many institutions have helped make evaluating tenured faculty members somewhat more equitable. With post-tenure review *every* tenured faculty must undergo a periodic review of his or her performance, not just individuals who are suspected of incompetence or dereliction of duty. Some tenured faculty members see the handwriting on the wall when they receive an unsatisfactory post-tenure review and volunteer to retire. Nevertheless, there are occasional cases in which a tenured faculty member must be dismissed. Even with a well-designed review process in place, revoking any faculty member's tenure for good cause is likely to involve a high degree of acrimony and difficulty, making it one of the most challenging situations that deans face.

Although tenure is not the lifetime boon that popular media makes it out to be, it does provide a faculty member with two things that a nontenured faculty member cannot expect: the right of being told the reason for a dismissal and access to some form of due process. When you give a tenured faculty member a reason for dismissal, you will probably adhere to the standards of dismissal for good cause that were discussed in the previous section. The due process that you make available to the faculty member must be established in advance of the particular case and should offer at least some opportunity for the faculty member to dispute the grounds for the dismissal. One important fact to observe is that due process need not always involve a formal hearing, but most institutional policies do equate their interpretation of due process with an in-house hearing of some sort. If this is the case at your institution, be certain that your procedures address the following:

- *Who will be involved in the hearing or other form of due process?* Does the faculty member get to choose any of the committee members who will render the decision? Is the faculty member entitled to legal counsel or some type of advocate or representative? Is the session open to other observers or closed? Who is allowed to speak at the hearing? Is it possible to call witnesses and to cross-examine the testimony of those who speak at the session?

- *When must the request for due process be received?* Is a process to review the decision automatic, or must the faculty member request it? Are there restrictions on how soon the hearing must take place? How long are records kept after the hearing?

- *Where can an appeal be directed if the due process results in upholding the tenure revocation?* Where are the official records or transcripts of the hearing stored?

Needless to say, revoking tenure is an *extremely* serious action for an institution to take. If you become involved in a matter of this sort, you should experience it only once or, at most, twice during your tenure as dean. If you discover that you are facing tenured faculty members' dismissals more frequently than that, it is an indication that something is seriously wrong with your college's tenure policy, post-tenure review procedure, or treatment of its senior faculty.

Terminating a faculty member because of financial exigency

Although it rarely happens, an institution's financial situation may become so precarious that it must reduce staffing to prevent an economic disaster. The time to plan the steps to take in a financial exigency is not, of course, in the midst of the crisis itself but well in advance, so that planning can be done in a well-considered and dispassionate manner. The strategies commonly used by institutions to reduce staffing during periods of extreme financial exigency include:

- *Last in, first out:* In this system, seniority provides a certain degree of job protection. The most recently hired faculty members are released first in difficult financial times, with the order of reductions proceeding from the least senior to the most senior employees.

- *Reduction by contract type:* In this system, types of employment status are placed in a hierarchical order, with reductions determined by that order. Usually, this means that part-time faculty members are reduced first, full-time temporary faculty members second, tenured associate professors third, and tenured full professors last.

- *Reduction by program demand:* With this approach, academic programs are ranked according to some measurable standard, such as number of student credit hours generated per academic year or average number of majors who graduate during an academic year. Programs that are in less demand according to this standard are phased out first.

Regardless of the system used, it is important that the financial exigency policy be established and discussed long before there is a need to implement it. If not, there is likely to be a perception, whether justified or not, that the system was fabricated to eliminate certain individuals from the faculty. Reductions because of financial exigency cause a great deal of tension and distrust—even in the best of cases. These problems are only exacerbated if the institution is perceived as inventing policies out of retribution or as a way of targeting the most highly paid faculty.

Terminating a faculty member due to a program elimination

Programs are also eliminated for reasons other than financial exigency. At the conclusion of a program review, for instance, it may be determined that a given program is no longer viable because of enrollment trends or projected demands for its majors, incompatibility with institutional mission, or an irremediable lack of quality. Additionally, institutions may shift their programmatic emphasis as part of a strategic planning process, mandate from a state legislature, or revised institutional mission as determined by the governing board. When eliminating programs for reasons of financial exigency, most institutions attempt to reassign tenured faculty members and other long-term employees.

No matter how congenial your relationship with a particular employee has been, it is important to realize that termination will be extremely stressful for that individual. As a result, you will want to extend as much courtesy, respect, and professionalism as you can bring to the situation. When you think about how you will approach the situation, ask yourself how you would wish to be treated if you were ever in a similar position. Remember, too, that our tendency to want to alleviate a painful encounter can lead us to say things that we don't really mean. Because of a terminated employee's tears or anguish, we may start to praise aspects of the person's performance that we might not otherwise regard as particularly high in quality. It is important not to send mixed messages that can end up complicating your task. Be clear and direct in stating what you had planned to say, but do not be unnecessarily heartless in either your phrasing or demeanor. The goal, in other words, is to be clear and direct but also humane.

Resources

Buller, J. L. (2006). How to let someone go. In J. L. Buller, *The essential department chair: A practical guide to college administration* (pp. 25–31). Bolton, MA: Anker.

Covey, A. (2000). *The workplace law advisor: From harassment and discrimination policies to hiring and firing guidelines—what every manager and employee needs to know.* New York, NY: Perseus.

Falcone, P. (2002). *The hiring and firing question and answer book.* New York, NY: AMACOM.

Fleischer, C. H. (2004). *The complete hiring and firing handbook: Every manager's guide to working with employees—legally.* Naperville, IL: Sphinx.

Horowitz, A. S. (1999). *The unofficial guide to hiring and firing people.* New York, NY: Macmillan.

Levin, R., & Rosse, J. (2001). *Talent flow: A strategic approach to keeping good employees, helping them grow, and letting them go.* San Francisco, CA: Jossey-Bass.

Repa, B. K. (2000). *Firing without fear: A legal guide for conscientious employers.* Berkeley, CA: Nolo.

Weiss, D. H. (2004). *Fair, square and legal: Safe hiring, managing and firing practices to keep you and your company out of court* (4th ed.). New York, NY: AMACOM.

References

Anglim, C. T. (1997). *Labor, employment, and the law: A dictionary.* Santa Barbara, CA: ABC-CLIO.

Gifis, S. H. (1996). *Law dictionary* (4th ed.). Hauppauge, NY: Barron's Educational Series.

Lehman, J., & Phelps, S. (Eds.). (2005). *West's encyclopedia of American law* (2nd ed.). Farmington Hills, MI: Thomson Gale.

Nolan, J. R., & Nolan-Haley, J. M. (1990). *Black's law dictionary* (6th ed.). St. Paul, MN: West.

42

Replacing a Chair

The relationship between the department chair and the dean can be critically important. Deans rely on their chairs for advice, maintaining good relationships with academic departments, early warning about possible problems, and a host of other key issues. But what do you do when, for whatever reason, a chair is not working out? How do you replace a department chair? Under what circumstances *should* you force a chair to step down? And how do you help an academic department continue to make progress during what will probably be an extremely difficult period of transition? These are among the questions that every dean must answer at least once during his or her tenure, and answering them correctly is often essential to the success of both the academic department and the dean.

What are the first things you need to consider when you suspect that a chair is not working out?

Some of the individuals who report to you will do their jobs more effectively than others. Your group of department chairs will unlikely all have equally superior people skills, equally superb records of meeting both students' and faculty members' needs, and equally admirable strategies for helping their disciplines prosper. In addition, you will probably feel a greater affinity to certain chairs than others. Perhaps because of their personalities or management styles, certain chairs will always remain individuals with whom, if the necessities of the job didn't force you together, you'd prefer not to associate. These situations are not problems. The real difficulty usually arises in response to a question like this: When is a chair actually causing harm to a program? What harm is the person doing? If you can't point to specific concerns you have about opportunities that are being missed, work that is not being performed, or successes that are not being achieved, then you really need to reconsider whether you have an ineffective department chair or a simple personality conflict. We all encounter people in the work environment whom we don't like or who do things differently from our preferred approach. Nevertheless, if you cannot make a compelling case about the damage that a chair's personality, management style, or decisions have made, then the situation may not be as bad as you had initially believed. It may even be possible that *you* are the leading contributor to the personality conflict; some candid reflection and self-assessment may be in order before you decide to take any action. Remember: The problem isn't always *them;* sometimes it's *us.*

Nevertheless, if you do decide that the department chair is causing serious problems for the unit that he or she supervises, you should evaluate the situation in light of the following considerations:

- *Is the problem fixable?* Can the chair be given guidance or support that will eliminate the situation or reduce the problem to a manageable level? Is it reasonable to expect the chair to change behavior and to act in the way that you hope?

- *Is the problem unfixable but endurable?* If the situation, for whatever reason, cannot be improved, is it something that is better off simply tolerated until the chair's term is over? Which would cause the greater harm: waiting out the chair's term or dealing with the disruption that would result from replacing the chair now?

- *What do you hope to achieve by replacing the chair?* Does that advantage more than compensate for the disadvantages that would arise by making this staff change now? Is it likely that the department will be able to attain some goal under new leadership that it cannot attain under the current chair?

The degree of disruption that replacing the chair would cause will depend greatly on the department's history, the duties of chairs in your college, and the personalities involved. The most important thing is to consider what outcome you'd like to see in the situation, whether that outcome will occur with appropriate guidance, and where the department will head if the chair does not significantly change his or her behavior.

Under what circumstances should you replace a department chair?

Even in situations where you conclude that the chair is causing difficulties for the department and that his or her behavior is unlikely to improve significantly, you will not always want to replace the chair. Regardless of whether the chair was elected, appointed, or hired into the position, removing a chair is always disruptive. The key question must be, will the resulting improvement be sufficient to justify the inevitable disruption? Such disruption occurs in a department when a chair is removed from office before the expiration of his or her term because these situations are always perceived, at least in the beginning, as demotions. Although in many cases such chairs will ultimately be assigned duties that they can perform more successfully and be freed of the frustrations that led to their removal, there is almost always an initial resistance to the loss of authority (and often salary as well) that accompanies the reassignment. To make the situation more palatable, many deans have allowed the former chair to retain the administrative stipend, rolling it over into his or her annual salary. Although this approach may ease the immediate situation, it can cause more serious problems in the long term. If successful chairs who return to the faculty after several well-respected tours of administrative duty are not rewarded in the same way, you can end up giving the impression that you only recompense chairs for *poor* service. The ultimate impact on morale is usually not worth the short-term benefit that this approach offers.

Another potential disruption occurs elsewhere in the department. Almost every chair, no matter how ineffective, has at least some support base. Only in extremely rare cases is every department member united in wanting the chair removed. In fact, all too often one of the problems caused by an ineffective chair is departmental factionalism, with cliques either siding with the chair or becoming members of a departmental insurgency. In these situations replacing the chair will convey the impression that you have taken sides in the departmental dispute, declaring one faction the winner and the other side the loser. Unless you believe that one bloc is definitely in the right—and are prepared to defend this perspective both to the department itself and to the rest of the faculty and administration—you should reflect long and hard on the implications of this decision. You should forgo other, less drastic alternatives—such as meeting regularly with the department yourself to mediate disputes and to ensure that arguments do not degenerate into unprofessional and personal attacks—only if you are absolutely convinced that extensive or irreparable damage to the department will be done unless you remove the chair. Offering the department access to mediation, providing faculty development training in conflict resolution and constructive group dynamics, and assigning an appropriate mentor to the department chair are often much more desirable solutions than a staff change. At the very least, you may want to try these approaches before resorting to dismissing the chair.

Admittedly, however, there are situations when replacing a chair is the most appropriate course of action. Examples of situations when you should dismiss a chair include the following:

- *Budgetary mismanagement:* It is not always a department chair's fault that a discipline consistently exceeds its allocated budget (see Chapter 26, "Supervising a Budget"). Nevertheless, you may notice a pattern where consistent shortfalls can be traced to a chair who has failed to provide suitable oversight to departmental allocations. Perhaps the department was regularly within its budget until the start of the chair's term, or perhaps a change in budgetary practice begun by the chair has led to excessive expenditures. If, after suitable guidance and warning, the chair proves incapable of managing the department's budget effectively, you may best be served by appointing a replacement.

- *Serious failure to follow institutional policies:* If a chair does not adhere to established procedures and subsequently harms the institution—such as by creating a lawsuit, causing a search to be aborted late in the process, prompting a highly valued employee to resign, or causing many students to transfer out of the institution—aggressive intervention is needed. If you believe that the chair's mismanagement, negligence, or incompetence caused the problem (particularly if the chair does not appear to have learned anything from the situation), you may need to look for a replacement.

- *Other types of problems that can cause severe or ongoing harm to the discipline:* Other problems do not neatly fall into any category. You can't really regard them as failure to follow a procedure because they involve situations for which no policy was ever established. They don't really qualify as insubordination, fiscal mismanagement, or violation of contract terms. Nevertheless, the lack of professionalism demonstrated by the department chair so undermines his or her continued effectiveness in the department or so irreparably destroys your confidence in him or her that you believe a replacement is essential. These situations will be among your most trying challenges as a dean and will test your administrative acumen to the utmost.

When drastic actions are necessary, how do you replace a department chair?

Naturally, there are likely to be formal policies in place at your institution or in your college that outline the steps to replacing a chair. In most cases these policies will tell you the people you need to consult, the notification you need to provide, and the procedure you must follow in electing, appointing, or hiring a new chair. What your written policy is unlikely to give you, however, is the following important advice:

- *Be direct:* It does not benefit you, the department, or the chair whom you're replacing when you operate behind the chair's back once you've made your decision to seek a replacement. Make a special appointment with the chair to discuss your decision. If you are asked the reason for the meeting and don't want to give too much away in advance, describe the meeting as "planning for the future" or "matters of staffing for next year." Once the appointment begins, state clearly and directly your reasons for deciding to replace the chair. Be specific in saying that the decision has been made and that this is not an issue for further discussion or debate. Outline your plans for the next steps in the department's future.

- *Be charitable:* If the chair is being forced to step down as the result of a disciplinary matter or an egregious failure, you have very few options for making your decision more pleasant. In fact, you may well not wish to do so. The individual has failed in the position's responsibilities, and you do not want the chair to dismiss this failure as a minor matter. Other situations often call for a gentler touch. The chair who is simply in over his or her head, who has been assigned the wrong responsibilities, or who is basically a very good person but the wrong person for the job is best treated with all the compassion and generosity that you can muster. In certain cases allowing the chair to step down voluntarily is an appropriate face-saving measure. In other situations offering a new assignment that better suits the individual's talents will ease this transition. In each case praise what you can honestly regard as the person's successes, being careful not to overplay your hand and end up sending a mixed message.

- *Be transparent:* Rumors spread quickly throughout a university community. Meet with the chair's department as soon as possible after informing the chair of your decision. If too much time elapses, the department may end up believing a distorted version of the decision. Morale will suffer, and the entire situation will soon get out of control. Moreover, do not convey this news first via memo or email: Meet face to face with department members. They will have questions—some of which you will be able to answer, others of which you will need to defer. In any case, state without extensive elaboration the result of your meeting with the chair. If you have offered the possibility of a resignation to the chair, say nothing that will undermine this face-saving measure. If you have forced the chair out, say so in clear terms, but avoid revealing any information that would be regarded as personal or confidential for personnel purposes. Focus the meeting on what will take place in the future, not on reliving the past.

- *Be quick:* The transitional period between chairs is often difficult. A very dynamic department may lose some of its momentum. A highly polarized department may find that its wounds cannot heal until new leadership is in place. A truly dysfunctional department may even be reduced to anarchy or open hostility before the entire matter is resolved. For this reason, you will want to have a new permanent chair in place at the earliest possible opportunity. If a national search must be conducted, take the steps necessary to get this process under way as soon as possible. If an internal candidate will be elected or appointed, do not allow a long interval to pass before completing the process. Move with appropriate thought and planning but with some dispatch. A long delay will only make an unsatisfactory situation even worse.

How do you keep an academic department working together effectively during this difficult period?

Because the purpose of replacing a chair is always to improve a department, you don't want the transitional period to cause the department to lose momentum or to fragment even further. How you approach this situation is likely to depend on whether a new chair is appointed immediately or after a more time-consuming process, such as a search or an election. If the new chair is appointed immediately, you will want to give this person an opportunity to establish himself or herself in the department and to develop his or her own identity in this new role. Don't visit the department too frequently, particularly in a formal capacity, because your frequent visits may be regarded as undermining the chair's authority, checking on things that you don't trust the new chair to do properly. Rather, give the new chair the freedom to act independently, meeting occasionally with you in your office just so that you can get updates, lend support, and *if requested,* provide advice. When the transition from an old chair to a new chair occurs immediately, in other words, the best thing that you can do is to provide that new chair with a little bit of space.

The situation is different, however, in cases where there is a clear transitional period between chairs. For instance, the department may be under the direction of an acting chair for a few months. There may be a national search to hire a new chair. The department may need to vote for a new chair, with the outgoing chair remaining in office until this election can be completed. In these situations you will want to meet with the department regularly, perhaps every week or so. These visits will help demonstrate that the department is not being forgotten during its change in leadership, that there is still a high-ranking administrator in place who can help the department achieve its goals. You may even want to use this transitional period to redirect the department more formally. For instance, this may be a good time to revise the departmental mission statement, establish a departmental code of conduct (see Buller, 2006), or update the department's strategic plan. Your goal, in other words, is to keep the department's energies focused on the future: Where can we go from here? How can we assist the next chair in understanding who we are by reaffirming our core values? What do we hope this department can become in the next 5 to 10 years? These questions are far more productive than continually revisiting the past and asking, "What went wrong?"

Perhaps the most difficult scenario in replacing a chair occurs when you and the department are in clear disagreement over the next step. For instance, you may require a chair to step down after years of budgetary mismanagement that has been disastrous for the college but fairly invisible to the department itself. You hold an election for the next chair, and, to your great disappointment, the former chair is reelected by a sizable majority. What do you do in such a case? Nearly every institution has some type of policy in place that allows deans to override a departmental vote to elect a chair. You may well need to take this step in such a situation, but it will require some additional effort on your part. You should explain to the department members as candidly as possible (without revealing information that is regarded as privileged under your institution's personnel guidelines) why you cannot accept the situation and why they must either reconsider their vote or accept your appointee. You must also lend the new chair additional support because that person may well meet resistance from the faculty, perhaps to the point of being dismissed as your toady. And you will need to do all this in a manner that does not come across as merely obstinate or authoritarian, but as genuinely in the department's best interests. If, on the other hand, you decide to accept the department's vote, you should establish some unmistakable parameters for the chair's performance and make it clear to the department and chair alike what consequences will occur if these guidelines are not met.

A good department chair has an almost incalculable effect on a unit's morale, efficiency, and productivity. Nearly every dean is surprised to find a department that seemed completely dysfunctional improving dramatically after the introduction of a new chair. Conversely, it is not uncommon for even the best department to become fractious and unmanageable simply because a new chair has been ineffective. The most important thing you can do is to gauge your chairs, not on the extent to which you like them or they reflect your own administrative style, but on the degree to which they add to a department's ability to fulfill its central mission of teaching, scholarship, and service.

References

Buller, J. L. (2006). Departmental ethics and politics. In J. L. Buller, *The essential department chair: A practical guide to college administration* (pp. 208–214). Bolton, MA: Anker.

43

Responding to Emergencies

In Chapter 38 ("Leadership from the Middle"), we saw how important it is to distinguish truly serious matters—an imminent threat to the life or safety of a member of the campus community, a situation of financial exigency so dire that it threatens the entire institution—from the more routine challenges that colleges and universities face all the time. Deans who function in crisis mode too frequently are ultimately far less effective when actual emergencies occur. They can give the impression that they regard a disagreement among the clerical staff and the death of a student as somehow similar in importance. They diffuse their own energy and credibility when genuine crises arise.

There is one thing that every dean can count on: Emergencies do occur. Hurricanes, floods, earthquakes, fires, or tornadoes unexpectedly destroy facilities. Faculty and staff members are charged with serious crimes. An armed intruder is discovered in one of the college's buildings. A student is hospitalized after a drug overdose, car accident, or injury during a laboratory experiment. A campus visitor is assaulted. Bomb threats are issued against college buildings. Suspicious packages are discovered. Dangerous materials go missing from a laboratory. A student threatens or commits suicide. A terrorist attack on a nearby community affects the campus. These are trying events for any campus. But what do deans need to know about responding to these types of emergencies?

Have a disaster plan already in place, and follow it scrupulously throughout the emergency.

The most important step in handling emergencies is to have already developed an effective disaster preparedness plan. It is impossible, of course, to create a plan so comprehensive that it covers *every* contingency that may occur. One of the reasons why emergencies are so stressful is simply that most of them are unforeseen and thus tax the institution's abilities to respond. Nevertheless, a good disaster preparedness plan takes into account the most likely emergencies and also remains flexible enough to provide guidance even when the unpredictable happens.

Most institutions have already created such a plan. Your task as dean, therefore, is to know your institution's existing procedure (because, in an emergency, others will be turning to you for advice), to make sure that as many people in your college as possible are aware of the plan, and to ensure that copies of the plan are available both online and on hard copy (in the event that it must be consulted during a power failure) at numerous convenient locations throughout your facilities. Also, it is possible that your college may be in charge of facilities, equipment, or supplies that make it more susceptible to certain emergencies than other areas. For these situations, you should work in harmony with your faculty (who know the nature of your facilities, equipment, and supplies the best), your security office, and your environmental safety officer or department to develop more specialized emergency response plans for these contingencies.

You may also be in that rare situation where your institution does not have an existing plan for emergencies or where the current plan is inadequate, confusing, or out of date. Most common of all is the situation where *multiple* emergency response plans exist—at the institutional, collegiate, and departmental levels—with little consistency or coordination. If this is the case, exert some decanal leadership, and help improve this potentially dangerous situation (see Chapter 38, "Leadership from the Middle"). There is absolutely no need to start this process from scratch: Henderson (2004) provides useful examples of plans that can be adapted to your institutional needs, and many other colleges and universities have posted their own procedural manuals online. Whatever way you begin this process, be sure to serve as an advocate for a disaster preparedness policy that:

- *Begins with a single, short, easily understood first step:* When an actual emergency occurs, people will not have the time or mental focus needed to review an extensive or complex policy. Each disaster preparedness policy should thus be prefaced with a very brief initial course of action (that can perhaps be expressed in one or two steps, in bold print, on a web page or at the front of a manual), telling the reader what to do first. Typical initial instructions might be "Dial 911 and report the nature and location of the emergency." You might instead instruct the individual to call campus security (so provide both on-campus and off-campus numbers), to select someone to wait outside for the emergency responders, and to remain on the telephone until help arrives.

- *Provides clear hyperlinks or page references to what to do in the case of different types of emergencies:* Because the reader will need to respond to different crises in different ways, provide various kinds of information. But, once again, keep the initial instructions as short, simple, and clear as possible. Provide a sidebar (on a web site) or a simplified table of contents (in a printed manual), giving the reader information about what to do next. An excellent example of this type of crisis management plan may be found at the University of Minnesota Duluth's emergency preparedness web site (www.d.umn.edu /ehso/emergencies/general.htm). Other good policies may be found at Arizona State University (www.asu.edu/uagc/EHS/emresponseguide.htm) and Seattle Pacific University (www.spu.edu/info/emergency/index.asp). Remember that the person who will be reading the procedures is likely to be extremely anxious or distraught. Keep all these policies straightforward, without the need for further cross-referencing. For instance, anytime instruction is given to call or contact someone, provide *all* the contact information the reader will need. Don't force the reader to recall an emergency number or to page through an appendix in search of contact information.

- *Contains a contact tree for emergency notifications:* After calling 911 or campus security, who else should the reader alert to the emergency? In which order? What crises are so important that the president should be notified regardless of the time of day or his or her schedule? At what point and by whom is the campus relations office notified? Unless clear thought is given in advance to whom should be notified for which type of campus emergency, mistakes are likely to be made in the heat of the moment. At the very least, one of your supervisors or colleagues may be offended because he or she wasn't notified and had to learn about the situation from the evening news. Even more serious, however, is the likelihood that further loss of life or damage may be done by not contacting the appropriate individuals in a timely manner.

During an actual emergency, make your first priority the safety of everyone involved.

When an actual emergency happens, it is likely that a thousand different thoughts will occur to you. None of these considerations will be as important as this one: What needs to be done *immediately* to make sure that everyone's all right? Make your first priority securing people's safety, providing the emergency treatment that they need, and reducing the likelihood of further injury or trauma. Facilities, if damaged, can be restored. Feelings, if hurt, can be repaired later through apologies and explanations. Actual physical harm to someone is the one thing that you should avoid or alleviate. For this reason, even if it means that someone else will end up looking more heroic or decisive than you, be absolutely certain that your first thought in every emergency is "How can people be protected?" rather than

"How will I or the college be seen by others?" You will have many opportunities during your deanship to put your unit's image first and to receive praise for your creativity and initiative. This is not one of them. Do not even begin to consider other factors until you know that everyone's safety has been secured.

Act with composure, compassion, and decisiveness.

Everyone responds differently in a crisis. It is possible that, as the emergency unfolds, you will be extremely tense, nervous, and uncertain what to do next. Despite this very natural feeling, however, it is important for you to remember that, during crises, people turn to their leaders for decisiveness and comfort. If you are excessively flustered or convey an attitude of despair, it can complicate the emergency even further. Panic is contagious, so remain as calm as possible, even if everything and everyone around you appears to be falling apart.

Conveying an attitude of strength does not, however, imply that you should come across as coldly indifferent or dispassionate to others' suffering. Your goal should be to reflect composure, decisiveness, and compassion. Particularly in cases where a student is killed or seriously injured, your expressions of compassion to the student's parents and siblings are of the utmost importance. Those conversations or telephone calls are the hardest that you will ever make, but they are essential to the healing process of those to whom you demonstrate concern. At times, parents may even unleash their anger toward you as a representative of the institution that "let" this happen. You must allow the individual to vent his or her anger and then express your compassionate understanding of the person's suffering without admitting liability. As we saw in Chapter 36 ("Leadership When Meeting One on One"), demonstrating concern is not the same as committing to a particular course of action. There will be plenty of time later for responsibility to be assigned and corrective action to be taken. But do not allow the necessity for a thorough and cautious review of the situation prevent you from the humane treatment of those affected by this disaster.

Be extremely cautious when confronted by the media.

Reporters will sometimes appear on your campus while an emergency situation is unfolding or shortly after it has been resolved. They have a duty to report the news, and crises that occur on university campuses are frequently regarded as major news, at least for the local community. You will want to assist the media in carrying out these duties responsibly. At the same time, you will want to avoid being distracted from your own, more immediate response to the crisis or answering a reporter's questions while still in a state of high emotion. For this reason, you should *always* defer the media's questions to your institutional public relations office and follow scrupulously all the procedures that we will discuss in the next chapter, "Dealing with the Media."

Every emergency will be different. In the end, one of the best possible preparations is to brainstorm or role-play possible responses to a crisis situation during a mini retreat or focused meeting of your department chairs (see Chapter 13, "Department Chairs"). Not only will that preparation better help them develop their own responses to an emergency, but you will also learn from them useful techniques that you yourself can use when that inevitable crisis occurs.

Resources

Augustine, N. R., Sharma, A., Kesner, I. F., Smith, N. C., Thomas, R. J., Quelch, J. A., et al. (2000). *Harvard Business Review on crisis management.* Boston, MA: Harvard Business School Press.

Dreshman, J. L., Crabb, C. L., & Tarasevich, S. (2001). *Caring in times of crisis: A crisis management/postvention manual for administrators, student assistance teams and other school personnel.* Chapin, SC: YouthLight.

Fink, S. (2000). *Crisis management: Planning for the inevitable* (Rev. ed.). Lincoln, NE: iUniverse.com.

Warner, D., & Palfreyman, D. (2003). *Managing crisis (managing universities and colleges).* Philadelphia, PA: Open University Press.

Zdziarski, E. L., Dunkel, N. W., & Rollo, J. M. (2007). *Campus crisis management: A comprehensive guide to planning, prevention, response, and recovery.* San Francisco, CA: Jossey-Bass.

References

Henderson, D. (2004). *Crisis management protocols for colleges & universities: A crisis management template* [CD-ROM]. Brookfield, CT: Rothstein Associates.

44

Dealing with the Media

Nearly every dean interacts with the media in some way or other. As chief administrators of our units, we want to develop positive media relations to publicize our events, convey our college's message effectively, and reach potential students and donors. On the other hand, when problems arise at our institution—particularly problems that seem serious enough or scandalous enough to have high news value—we may need to deal with the media when we'd much prefer to be left alone. Any dean who has been interviewed on several occasions has experienced the discomfort of being misquoted, misunderstood, or quoted out of context. These situations can cause a great deal of tension between the dean's office and the upper administration. Even worse, misleading or inaccurate news stories can do serious damage to enrollments, donations, and recruiting and retaining the most desirable faculty members. For this reason, every dean needs at least a little preparation in the area of press relations. The following information is intended to serve as something of a primer on the most important guidelines to keep in mind when interacting with the media.

We'll begin our discussion of media relations with one essential principle that you should remember in every situation involving the press, radio, or television:

> *Never interact with the media without having first contacted your institution's public relations office.*

In the vast majority of cases, media inquiries are best turned over to the public relations office. You can save yourself a considerable amount of frustration and regret by answering every request for a statement or interview with "I'm sorry, but my policy is to channel all our college's information solely through our public relations office. Let me get you their number, and then I'll forward your call directly to them. Hold a moment, please." The professionals in that office are trained in how to deal with reporters, know precisely what the institutional message is on just about any issue, and understand how best to delay a request for information if the institution is not yet ready to go public on an issue. Even if it turns out that an interview with you is absolutely essential, the public relations staff can help you prepare for your interview, make the appropriate arrangements, and even participate in it with you, amplifying or clarifying any information where necessary. In situations where you find yourself ambushed by a reporter or are otherwise caught unawares, contact public relations as soon as possible. Someone from that office may be able to contact the reporter or redirect the focus of the story, provide more complete background information, or otherwise assist you in telling your college's story.

In addition to this one cardinal rule, the other guidelines that you should follow in dealing with the media fall into several major categories.

Guidelines to follow in all situations that involve the media

- *Try to provide only factual information:* Reporters will frequently want you to speculate on the reasons why a particular situation occurred. Although you will often have opinions on the matter, it is unwise to share them with the media. Your speculation may well be proved incorrect later, or it may contradict an equally valid alternative explanation favored by your upper administration. You are far safer sticking to the facts and will have less to retract if you do so.

- *Never answer a question spontaneously:* If you are asked a question to which you have not given careful consideration in advance, defer answering it whenever possible. As difficult as it may be to say, "I simply don't know," that admission may be your wisest answer. Don't allow repeated iterations of the same question goad you into providing an answer about which you are unsure. If you absolutely must answer an unanticipated question, say either "Let me think about that for a moment" or "Give me some time to consider that question, and we'll come back to it later." A glib or unconsidered response increases the likelihood that the story will embarrass you when it appears in print.

- *Stay on message:* As deans, we are good at listening carefully to questions and at providing clear and appropriate answers. Many of us, in fact, were offered our positions because, unlike other candidates, we actually *responded to* the questions asked at our interviews. Nevertheless, a press interview is not at all like an employment interview. Nor is it a final examination: No one is going to grade you lower for not answering a question. For this reason, you should take the opportunity that interviews offer to get out your message even if it is utterly irrelevant to the question you are asked. Remember that your ultimate audience is not the reporter but, rather, the community at large. What message do you want the community to hear? Prefacing sentences with the phrases "Well, the most important thing is . . ." and "As I said earlier, the really critical idea to keep in mind is . . ." reinforce the central message that you are trying to convey.

- *Do not fill silences:* Silent pauses are awkward, and we're often tempted to keep on speaking to fill them. In these situations you are more likely to reveal something that you do not wish to reveal or to make a comment that will be misunderstood. The reporter is not there to evaluate your social skills. When you've said all that you mean to say, be silent and allow the silence to continue as long as necessary.

- *Use clear and accurate statistics whenever possible:* If there is an issue that you are eager to have reported, include a few carefully chosen and accurate statistics. Reporters like to quote quantitative information in their stories—it makes the story seem more researched—and, by offering the reporter something that he or she can easily use, you will increase the likelihood that the information you would like to see reported ultimately appears in the final story.

- *If you have additional information to provide to the reporter, follow up with that information as soon as possible, but do so only once:* Particularly in situations where you have had to answer a reporter's question with "I don't know," you may wish to follow up later with the information desired. Do so as soon as you can so that this additional information reaches the reporter before his or her deadline. But don't allow yourself to be drawn into an additional interview about matters that you are not prepared to discuss. Provide only the information that you promised (email and voicemail are extremely useful for this purpose). Also, don't keep contacting the reporter with *multiple* additional clarifications or amplifications. You will find that repeated calls only cloud the issue and make it appear as though you are defensive or trying to conceal something.

- *Do not use disciplinary jargon:* Even if you readily use the technical terms of your discipline, remember to define them or rephrase them in ordinary language for the reporter. Outside of academia, people do not always understand the difference between an assistant professor and an associate professor, computer science and computer information systems. You should never use terms that you are not absolutely certain are clear to both the reporter and the general public. If you sense that you need to define a term, do so in the course of the conversation: "Well, the most important thing for us to remember is that we didn't actually fire this person. The matter was a nonrenewal of contract, and here's the critical difference between those two concepts . . ."

Guidelines to follow when you have time to prepare for an interview

- *Ask the reporter the story's purpose or focus:* With student newspapers, you may even be able to demand a list of the questions you will be asked in advance of the interview. Say something like, "My policy, whenever I'm interviewed by a student newspaper, is always to make the process as educational for the student as possible. For this reason, I require that I be shown all the questions that I'm going to be asked at least 24 hours in advance, so that I can be certain that they adhere to proper journalistic standards." You will rarely be accorded this privilege with a professional newspaper. Nevertheless, this ploy does work from time to time, and it never hurts to ask, "Can I be sent the questions in advance so that I can have all the information at my fingertips when you get here?" At the very least, you will want to know the general subject of the story so that you can prepare for the interview adequately.

- *Plan for the interview by establishing talking points:* By knowing what message you wish to convey in the interview, you will be more likely to direct its focus to issues that benefit your college. If necessary, you can place a notepad, single index card, or printed sheet with bullet points on the table or desk in front of you to glance at from time to time. Preparing your ideas will also help you in the situation discussed earlier where you may need to answer the question you wished you were asked rather than the question actually posed by the reporter.

- *Conduct a practice interview if you are not experienced in dealing with reporters:* It can be extremely beneficial to ask a colleague to help you prepare for your interview by asking you potential questions, even grilling you on uncomfortable issues. You will feel more at ease in the interview itself, and your colleague may be able to suggest ways in which, by providing information differently or by slightly altering your vocabulary, you will be more successful in your efforts to remain on message.

- *Prepare a few sound bites to use in the course of your interview:* The reporter is likely to include short, pithy, and catchy remarks in the printed article or broadcast because they are quickly understood and appreciated. Few of us are creative enough to think of something quotable on the spur of the moment. Because you have time to prepare for your interview, devote some of your creativity to developing a few memorable sound bites that will help you tell your story most effectively. Drop these phrases casually into the conversation, but never use the same sound bite more than once in the same interview.

Guidelines to follow when a reporter ambushes or blindsides you

- *Always defer the discussion if you have any opportunity to do so:* As we saw earlier, the best possible strategy is to direct the reporter to your institution's public relations office. When this is not possible, you should still try to delay the interview until you can compose yourself, think about the message that you wish to convey, and develop an overall strategy for your conversation. Saying something like "I'm terribly busy right now, and I have a meeting that I simply have to prepare for. Is there a time later when I can call you or when we can meet?" will at least give you an hour or two to prepare. In that time you can contact your public relations officers and strategize with them how you will proceed at the interview itself.

- *Remember that news often involves matters that are controversial, scandalous, or embarrassing:* We might wish that reporters would only communicate our successes, but that is simply unrealistic. The vast majority of news is *bad* news, and reporters will inevitably be interested in anything negative that occurs on your campus. The negative issues that may be reported could run the gamut from an enrollment decline to the death of a student, from consistently poor attendance at an event "paid for by the public" to the most personal details surrounding a staff member's dismissal. Refusing to speak at all to the media on these topics will not make the stories disappear. In fact, it can end up looking even worse for the college if a story says something like, "Despite repeated contacts, no one from the university returned this reporter's calls." For this reason, it is important for you and the public relations staff to know the message you wish to convey. Perhaps an internal investigation is continuing so that tragedies of this kind may be prevented in the future. Perhaps the institution is committed to ensuring that all personnel decisions are made in an equitable and appropriate manner and to discovering whether this high standard was followed in the current situation. Whatever response you or your public relations office must give in a difficult situation, you will want to focus on the positive efforts that are under way and to demonstrate both compassion and professionalism.

- *Never reply "no comment"; instead, offer the reason why you are unable to comment:* In certain situations it would be improper or unwise for you to provide the media with information. Frequently, these situations arise when confidential personnel matters are involved or when student records are protected by the Family Educational Rights and Privacy Act (see Chapter 10, "Parents"). Stating a simple "no comment" to a reporter is usually an ineffective strategy. It makes you look as though you have much to conceal. It can even lead to speculation that is far worse than the actual situation. For this reason, it is far preferable to say something like this: "Well, unfortunately, our institutional practice is not to discuss publicly the reasons behind personnel decisions. We find that that helps protect the individual's privacy and serves that person's best interest in the long run. What I *will* tell you, however, is that we have a detailed policy on how these types of decisions are made and that, in this case, we followed that policy to the letter. In fact, I can get you a copy of the procedure that we used. It's in the public domain and is even posted on our web site . . ."

Guidelines to follow when you wish to gain publicity or initiate contact with the media

Sometimes it is not a reporter who is pursuing you; it's you who are pursuing the media. You may wish to publicize an event or be recognized for a success. In these cases there are also several guidelines to follow:

- *Work with your public relations office to prepare a short and compelling press release:* Your press release should be no longer than a single-sided page, but it should contain enough detail to be the basis for a good story. Put the most interesting or eye-catching information first; if the press release does not interest the recipient after a brief glance, it will probably be ignored. Include several short quotes that could be inserted into an article or paraphrased during a broadcast. Attach a good photograph that could be used as part of a print article or as a background during a television report.

- *For an event, think of arrangements that will make it as easy as possible for members of the media to attend:* In addition to free tickets to the event itself, include maps that indicate where to go, passes for special parking arrangements, and a schedule of when it might be possible to have a private conversation with the speaker, performer, or special guest. Identify in advance a few good locations for photographs or video footage to be taken.

Deans frequently find dealing with the media very frustrating. Only a fraction of what we say appears in the final report. Often the fraction that does appear is, in our minds, the least important part of the story. Despite our best attempts to provide the media with facts, errors all too often appear in the final story. Despite these frustrations, however, good media relations are an important component of every deanship. Try to maintain cordial and ongoing relations with the journalists in your area. Don't set your expectations too high. And most important, never say *anything*—even off the record or in a private conversation—that you don't want made public.

Resources

Bonk, K., Griggs, H., & Tynes, E. (1999). *The Jossey-Bass guide to strategic communications for nonprofits: A step-by-step guide to working with the media to generate publicity, enhance fundraising, build membership, change public policy, handle crises, and more!* San Francisco, CA: Jossey-Bass.

Hoffman, J. C. (2004). *Keeping cool on the hot seat: Dealing effectively with the media in times of crisis* (Rev. ed.). Highland Mills, NY: Four C's.

Stewart, S. (2004). *Media training 101: A guide to meeting the press.* Hoboken, NJ: Wiley.

Wade, J. (1992). *Dealing effectively with the media: What you need to know about print, radio and television interviews.* Mississauga, ON: Crisp Learning.

Walker, T. J. (2004). *Media training A–Z* (3rd ed.). New York, NY: Media Training Worldwide.

45

Intellectual Property Disputes

For many of the issues that we have considered so far, your institution really *should* have a detailed written policy on how to deal with the matter. For questions of intellectual property, however, it is *imperative* that your institution develop a clear, well-considered written policy. Several accreditation bodies, such as the Southern Association of Colleges and Schools (www.sacs.org), require that institutions submit an approved policy on intellectual property to qualify for accreditation. Why, we may wonder, is intellectual property such a central issue for colleges and universities? Because nearly everything we do in higher education concerns intellectual property in some form or another. As academics, we live in a world of ideas, discoveries, research, and innovations, and it is sometimes unclear who holds the rights to a development that is made by an individual (or a specific group of individuals) on institutional time, using institutional facilities, and as a result of an institutional investment.

Intellectual property may be defined as any creation or product of human invention, creativity, or innovation that has commercial value. The key phrase in this definition is "that has commercial value." A faculty member's discovery of a more effective way to explain the ablative absolute or a novel interpretation of the Siege of Berwick may well be a wonderful "product of human invention, creativity, or innovation," but these ideas' commercial value is not altogether clear. Certainly, if someone were to present these contributions as his or her own or to make use of them without acknowledging their sources, we would regard that person as guilty of plagiarism and scholarly misconduct. Nevertheless, without a compelling reason for believing that the innovations have significant commercial value—which may be the case if the new method of teaching the ablative absolute were the distinctive feature of a widely adopted new textbook or if the reinterpretation of the Siege of Berwick were integral to a faculty member's bestselling historical novel about Edward Balliol—the institution's intellectual property policy would probably not apply.

One of the challenges in dealing with disputes regarding ideas and innovations is that, from a legal perspective, the term *intellectual property* is extremely amorphous:

> Intellectual property is an umbrella term that includes a num-
> ber of federal and state legal regimes, including trademarks,
> copyrights, patents, and trade secrets. . . . The IP spectrum
> also includes rights of publicity, rights in ideas, and unfair
> competition. (Nard, Barnes, & Madison, 2006, p. 1)

For this reason, most instances of intellectual property legislation involve not
one federal or state statute but a whole range of existing laws that address copy-
right, patents, trademarks, unfair competition, or trade secrets (see Lehman &
Phelps, 2005, pp. 183, 186; McJohn, 2006, pp. 2–4). Examples of intellectual
property issues that might occur at the collegiate level would thus include the
new melody for an alma mater that has been copyrighted, the discovery of a new
medication that has been patented, or the design for a new college mascot that
has been issued a trademark. Unfair competition or the use of trade secrets
occurs far less commonly in an academic setting. If, for example, a for-profit
institution were to choose a name extremely similar to that of an existing college
or university, operate from a mail drop in the same town, and create a web site
using the same colors and fonts as those adopted by the existing college or university, there may be an issue of unfair competition because a prospective student or donor could reasonably confuse the two institutions:

> A trade secret is information that has economic value from not
> being known to or readily ascertainable by those who could
> gain value from its use or disclosure, and is the subject of rea-
> sonable security measures. Typical trade secrets are customer
> lists, manufacturing processes, computer programs, and blue-
> prints for machines, where such information is kept secret
> using reasonable security measures. (McJohn, 2006, p. 4)

The laws governing trade secrets thus protect the proprietary use of "any formula, pattern, device, or compilation of information that provides a business
advantage over competitors who do not use or know of the formula, pattern,
device, or compilation of information" (Lehman & Phelps, 2005, p. 186.) If
Extraordinary University constructed a truly innovative facility for teaching a
specific discipline and this facility was demonstrably different from and superi-
or to that used anywhere else for teaching that discipline, Extraordinary
University may have cause to seek damages against another institution that
copied the facility without permission. Given academia's long-standing commitment to the free exchange of ideas, a formal lawsuit is probably unlikely in
such a case, but it is not wholly beyond the bounds of possibility.

Matters of intellectual property are most easily addressed when they fall into one of the following two categories:

- *Work for hire:* Work for hire occurs when an institution specifically assigns, directs, or funds someone to develop a piece of intellectual property. In these cases, the institution should specify that ownership rights will remain with the institution. For instance, if an individual is paid a stipend or bought out of part of his or her contract to develop a written strategic plan for an institution, that plan becomes the institution's property, and the author may not sell it to any other institution.

- *Sponsored programs:* Frequently, the terms of an externally sponsored research program or a third-party funding agreement allocate to the institution specific rights for any intellectual property that results from the contracted activity. Because this arrangement was agreed on as part of the contract itself, ownership of the product is clear. For instance, if a foundation sponsors medical research at a university, it will often specify that any patentable discoveries arising from the research will be the institution's property, not the researcher's.

Nevertheless, not all intellectual property matters are as clear cut as these two categories. For instance, who owns the rights to the book that a faculty member wrote while on sabbatical if the book suddenly proves to be extremely popular and profitable? Who owns the course module created for a classroom management system that a faculty member developed on university time and with university equipment? Who owns the painting that a faculty member created on university-purchased canvas with university-purchased paint as a demonstration in a course taught by that faculty member? It is this type of question that your institutional policy will need to address.

Be sure that your institution's written policy has a clearly stated appeals procedure that refers requests for administrative review to an authorized group, not to an individual.

Most institutions' intellectual property policies will grant faculty members ownership rights to both traditional works of scholarship (including articles, books, artwork, musical compositions, and scripts) and traditional instructional aids (including course syllabi, classroom materials, examinations, course web sites, and other items that assist the instructors' pedagogical purposes). Nevertheless, each institution's policy needs to set forth its official position on this issue and, most important, who ultimately decides whether something falls into the categories of traditional works of scholarship or traditional instructional aids. The who in this case should be some formal body, such as a standing or ad hoc committee, rather than an individual. Matters of intellectual property cover too many disciplines and have too many implications (technological, legal, administrative, and philosophical) for any one person to have mastered all perspectives of the wide variety of cases that may emerge. Moreover, because intellectual property is, as we have seen, a fluid term involving potential discoveries, inventions, and media that have not yet been conceived, it is difficult to identify any single person who would be the perfect arbiter on all issues.

The key questions to consider in any dispute involving intellectual property are:

- To what extent was this particular item of intellectual property supported by the institution?

- To what extent were institutional resources significantly involved in the item's creation?

- To what extent were institutional resources essential to the item's creation?

- To what extent is the individual who created the item profiting directly from a development that was only possible due to institutional investment?

In other words, these questions help clarify such situations as when a faculty member writes an article in his or her office and explain why most institutions would exert no ownership rights over a traditional work of scholarship of this kind. After all, someone might argue that the article represents the institution's intellectual property because:

- The article was written on institutional time.

- The article was written using institutional resources (computer, electricity, paper, toner, etc.).

- The article was only possible because the faculty member had access to institutional facilities (such as the library and the databases that he or she consulted while researching the article).

Nevertheless, these issues will not cause the resulting article to be regarded as a piece of intellectual property owned by the institution *in most cases.* To begin with, institutional resources were not substantially involved in or essential to the writing of the article. Using one's desktop computer to perform word processing entails a far lower level of institutional investment than, for instance, using a specially built laboratory for formulating a new medication. The faculty member *could* have written the article on his or her own time, using his or her own equipment; the scientist *could not* have fabricated the medication without the special laboratory. Moreover, the article's commercial value is likely to be extremely limited. Although the faculty member may benefit indirectly from it (for instance, by gaining a promotion, tenure, and invitations to lucrative speaking engagements), there is likely to be little direct profit from the article itself. The medication, on the other hand, may well have significant potential for direct profit.

The group that delineates between the creator's rights and the institution's rights will need to work its way through issues like these for each disputed intellectual property claim. The clearer a written policy is, the easier this group's task will be. For instance, disputes can commonly occur when individuals on sabbatical create works that prove to be highly profitable. Because the institution invested in the individual by buying out his or her time to work on the activity, does the institution have a right to share the profits? This can be a particularly challenging question when someone has submitted a sabbatical proposal that was approved specifically so that the project could be accomplished. To what extent is that project then to be regarded as work for hire? The degree to which each institution's policy on intellectual property and sabbatical leave clarifies these issues in advance will reduce the number of difficult interpretations that an appeals committee will need to make at a later date.

Remember students' role in intellectual property matters.

When institutions create intellectual property policies, they always give special attention to faculty members' rights and obligations because this group will be most actively involved in intellectual property matters. Institutions almost always give attention to staff members because staff members also create intellectual property, although many of these products constitute work for hire. Nevertheless, the group that too many institutions do not address in their intellectual property discussions is the student body. This omission can cause significant problems because a student's understanding of his or her ownership rights regarding creative works and items of scholarship may be significantly different from the institution's. On the other hand, certain intellectual property matters involving students are far clearer:

- Most institutions would claim no right of ownership over traditional works of scholarship produced by students when they are working on their own.

- Students who contribute to a project that is governed by a contract or agreement to which the institution is a party will be bound by the terms of that contract or agreement.

- Students who perform work that is compensated by the institution will be subject to the provisions governing work for hire.

Other types of student products fall into categories that are less clear cut and that should be addressed by an institution's intellectual property policy:

- *Papers and theses:* If an institution wishes to retain copies of student papers and theses for archival purposes or as part of a permanent student portfolio, it should clarify this intention. The most desirable solution is to make the institution's right to retain copies of student papers and theses a condition of matriculation.

- *Class notes:* The institution should specify that any notes taken by a student who is enrolled in a course are for that student's personal use only. It should be clearly stated that paying tuition fees does not entitle a student to disseminate for commercial purposes notes or video or audio recordings made in a course.

- *Internships:* Most institutions should state that, even for unpaid internships, all intellectual property created during the course of an internship is owned by the corporation, agency, or organization where the internship is performed, not by the student.

- *Projects involving substantial use of institutional resources:* As is the case with faculty and staff members, it may be desirable to state in your intellectual property policy that student products involving substantial use of institutional resources (i.e., situations in which the institution's resources were significantly involved in or essential to the production of the intellectual property) are subject to institutional ownership.

Intellectual property policies exist for the dual purpose of:

- Encouraging creative activity by rewarding those responsible for developing the intellectual property

- Protecting the investment rights of the person or organization whose resources made the intellectual property possible

Inevitably, there will be situations in which the two components of this dual purpose come into conflict. Deans should *never* be sole arbiters in these matters. Rather, a well-informed review committee, guided by the principles outlined in this chapter, should assist deans in making the best possible decisions in complex and ambiguous situations.

Resources

Kaplin, W. A., & Lee, B. A. (1995). The college as research collaborator and partner. In W. A. Kaplin & B. A. Lee, *The law of higher education: A comprehensive guide to legal implications of administrative decision making* (3rd ed., pp. 945–961). San Francisco, CA: Jossey-Bass.

Merges, R. P., & Ginsburg, J. C. (2004). *Foundations of intellectual property.* New York, NY: Foundation Press.

Merges, R. P., Menell, P. S., & Lemley, M. A. (2006). *Intellectual property in the technological age* (4th ed.). New York, NY: Aspen.

References

Lehman, J., & Phelps, S. (Eds.). (2005). *West's encyclopedia of American law* (2nd ed.). Farmington Hills, MI: Thomson Gale.

McJohn, S. M. (2006). *Intellectual property: Examples and explanations* (2nd ed.). New York, NY: Aspen.

Nard, C. A., Barnes, D. W., & Madison, M. J. (2006). *The law of intellectual property.* New York, NY: Aspen.

46

Addressing Differences with Other Administrators

All deans hope to have a harmonious relationship with the other administrators at their institutions. They want to work with their peers in an environment of mutual respect, valuing one another's contributions for the way in which they advance the college's or university's overall mission. When disagreements occur, deans hope that the dissent will be over alternative visions or perspectives, not about personalities. They hope that an occasional difference of opinion with a colleague will ultimately strengthen the college and university by breaking down groupthink and allowing both sides to explore even more creative ways of educating students, discovering new ideas, and serving the profession.

There are institutions, of course, where administrators do go about their work relatively untrammeled by personal differences. More commonly, however, there will be administrators with whom we must work but with whom we cannot avoid some degree of conflict. At times, our administrative styles are just too different from others'. Perhaps we try to focus on the truly big ideas that will make our units successful for years to come, whereas one of our colleagues annoys us by focusing on petty details that don't strike us as particularly important. Perhaps we have to work with someone who is openly contemptuous of the disciplines that we represent. Or perhaps we tend to see things differently than another administrator, always emphasizing teaching when that person emphasizes scholarship or advocating for lower student-to-teacher ratios when that person defends higher levels of productivity.

In other words, interpersonal conflict is inevitable in most deanships. Such conflict can be challenging enough when it involves someone who reports to you, but how do you handle these situations when they involve another dean, an administrator at some other level of the institution, or someone to whom *you* report? In Chapter 15 ("Other Deans"), we discussed the most important first step in addressing a difference with one of your peers: In situations where there is a serious or chronic impasse with a fellow dean, have a private, closed-door meeting to clear the air and seek a new beginning. This approach is certainly a good starting point for addressing a conflict with *any* administrator. Choose neutral territory—neither your office nor the other person's office—and address the matter candidly. Note that you sense an ongoing tension or hostility in your interactions, are troubled by it, and would like to know what you may have been doing to exacerbate the situation. Pose your questions, and then truly listen to the answers. Don't retreat to defensiveness. Learn what you can about the other person's view of the matter, and explore what you can do together to rectify the situation. Then try to end the meeting with a commitment to better relations in the future.

That approach will not always be successful, however. So what can you do if you've reached out to the other administrator and found that little, if anything, has improved?

Understand the difference between constructive and destructive conflict.

The first thing to do is to ask yourself candidly and objectively, "What harm is being done by this ongoing conflict? If the only answer is "It makes me feel uncomfortable" or "I don't like it when other people don't seem to appreciate what I do," then it may be time for you to reconsider the seriousness of the situation. Our work in higher education gives us a tremendous opportunity to change people's lives and to improve the world through discovering important new knowledge; the purpose of our jobs is not to make us comfortable. There will always be people who don't like or appreciate us; it goes with the territory of being a dean. You can't allow the fact that you've been unable to win all the hearts and minds at your institution to distract you from your job. Just as a faculty member cannot be expected to be the idol of every student in every single course, so will there be those people at your institution who dislike you, for whatever reason. At times, a professor is fortunate enough to hear from a former student who was openly hostile years ago while enrolled in a course but who now appreciates everything that the faculty member did. Your experience on the administrative level may be somewhat similar. The important thing is to remind yourself that the conflict is causing no real harm. Your work is still being performed at a high level, and so is that of the other administrator. You're a big enough person to endure a little bit of discomfort.

There may even be situations in which you find that you are involved in a *constructive conflict.* Perhaps the other person's excessive attention to detail causes you to double-check documents so that they are perfect, simply because you want to avoid the other person's ridicule. Perhaps the frequent challenge that that person makes to the very existence of your disciplines forces you to think of new and creative ways to justify your contributions to the institution. Perhaps his or her self-righteous attitude after landing yet another multimillion-dollar donation has caused you to redouble your own development efforts. It may well be that demonstrable good has resulted from the conflict. If that is the case, then you should actually be grateful to your fellow administrator, as difficult as that may be. Just as the pressure from a coach or personal trainer can make someone reach new levels of athletic success, so can constructive conflict cause you to become an even better dean.

The real challenge arises when you realize that you're in a situation of *destructive conflict.* This problem can occur if the institution is missing out on collaborative opportunities because you cannot work with another individual. It may be that, because of a personal disagreement with you, another administrator is becoming less cooperative about providing all the seats your students need in a service course or scheduling a section of the course at a time that does not conflict with your students' schedule. How should you approach the situation if you notice that the conflict is causing real harm and that your attempts to resolve the matter amicably are not working? The following strategies may help you deal with this destructive conflict.

Remember that differences with other administrators should never be visible to students or external constituents.

Deans sometimes feel that it's hypocritical, or at least not completely honest, to conceal their differences with another administrator when speaking to students, parents, or potential donors. "I just can't be two-faced like that," a dean might say. "An academic community respects honesty and standing up for what you believe in. I'm not going to act as though I can tolerate So-and-so because that would be insincere." This attitude is ultimately both self-serving and destructive to the college. Students don't care about whom you like or don't like, what your disagreements with colleagues may be, or who makes your job more difficult by being rude and unreasonable; students *are* interested in getting a good education and in being treated with professionalism. Parents, donors, and board members likewise will not respect you or your institution more if you impose your professional disagreements on them. In fact, they are likely to lose respect not for the person about whom you are complaining but for *you* because you are airing your dirty laundry in public. Every college and university will have interpersonal tensions lurking just below the surface. Sometimes these tensions are petty; at other times they're extremely serious. At no time, however, should these rifts be visible to students or external constituents. This is a case where brutal honesty does not serve you well; it only makes matters worse. After all, it is always possible that you and your administrative colleague will resolve your differences. If that occurs, it will be very difficult to reverse the negative impression already formed in the minds of those who were aware of the conflict.

Don't let how another administrator treats you determine how you treat that administrator.

Differences and conflicts always flow in two directions. It's difficult to see when you are in the middle of a conflict, even though it may be abundantly clear to external observers. "But they started it," we often say, unaware of how juvenile this sounds. "Yes, but it's up to you to resolve it," someone needs to remind us in these cases. Fighting hostility with hostility, coldness with coldness, or contempt with contempt only escalates differences. To overcome a difficulty with another administrator, you frequently have to be the bigger person and defuse a situation that you did not create. You may find it unpalatable time and again to have to endure someone else's rudeness or pretend that nothing happened after a fit of pique dissipates. Nevertheless, as a dean, your first priority is the effective operation of your college, and occasionally that priority involves tolerating the unpalatable.

It is perfectly natural to say things like "He infuriates me so!" or "She makes me feel about two inches tall, and I can't take it anymore!" The truth is that no one can make you feel angry, hurt, or ashamed. You always have more choice than you realize about how to respond or even *whether* to respond. Have you ever noticed someone shrug off or smile in mild amusement at another person's anger, rudeness, or insults, even though many others would have reacted with outrage? For whatever reason—and it may only have been that the first person happened to be in a particularly good mood that day—he or she was able to view the experience objectively, not subjectively. "That person's anger does not have to become my anger," he or she may have said or thought. "This behavior is not about me; it's about that person. Maybe the person has had a bad day or has difficulty with anger issues or was reminded of a terrible experience from the past. In any case, I don't have to be rude just because I've been treated rudely." It's surprising the number of conflicts that we can resolve with other administrators simply by refusing to contribute to someone else's negativity.

In certain situations, when you can't figure out any other way to end a difference, you can make progress by "killing them with kindness." Sometimes deans are reluctant to adopt this approach because they feel that it'll make them appear weak or not authoritative. This fear is almost always misdirected. As a strategy, repaying rudeness or hostility with kindness tends to be effective simply because it's difficult to keep a disagreement going if you refuse to play along. More important, this approach will both decrease your stress as an administrator and help you model a more effective interpersonal style to others. You will have chosen not to get angry or offended, electing instead to be guided by Abraham Lincoln's essential principle:

> *People are just about as happy as they make up their minds to be.*

In other words, you've made up your mind to be happy and to refrain from continuing the conflict. If you continue this approach long enough, the other person may eventually make the same choice as well.

If you feel that you must discuss the matter with the upper administration, do so only on rare occasions. When you do, discuss the matter to seek advice, not resolution.

There is no magic formula to resolve every interpersonal dispute or difference. Some situations will remain problematic even though you've made the first move by candidly addressing the situation with the person behind closed doors, acting with professionalism in front of others, and responding to repeated hostility with warmth and generosity. You may be tempted to discuss the conflict with your supervisor or, depending on your individual situation, that person's supervisor. If you elect to follow this plan, do so only on rare occasions and only for mentoring and advice. Make it clear that you're not asking the person to fix the problem or to intervene in any way. Third-party intervention can be very effective in conflict resolution if the mediator is viewed as an honest broker, usually because he or she is a peer of some sort. As soon as a supervisor intervenes in matters of interpersonal relations, the dynamic of the disagreement changes radically. At best, this type of mediation will backfire. You may be perceived as "running to daddy or mommy," and the other party will probably resent you even more. At worst, the supervisor may now regard you as not capable of solving your own problems, particularly if you've brought more than one such situation to his or her attention. A supervisor can give you general advice about conflict resolution, discuss your formal mediation options, and, in certain cases, give you helpful insight into the other person's reasons for responding as he or she has done. But you should never expect your supervisor to solve the problem for you or leave the impression that you want your supervisor to take your side in the dispute.

Give the same consideration to conflicts with your own supervisor.

If you find yourself having a serious conflict with your president or provost—or if you routinely end up at loggerheads with a supervisor—you should begin by following the same strategies. Discuss the matter candidly. Act professionally at all times. Repay coldness or hostility with kindness. In addition, you should also answer the following questions as objectively as possible:

- In the grand scheme of things, how important is this issue?

- Is there a particular time or event you can point to when the relationship began to break down? For instance, did you have excellent relations with a previous president but difficulties after a new president arrived? Did the provost begin treating you differently after you openly disagreed with him or her on some issue?

- To what extent is this difference making your job more difficult to do effectively?

If, after considering these questions, the disagreement seems truly serious, have a second candid discussion with your supervisor. Explore what outcome he or she would like to see in this situation. If the proposed outcome is both non-negotiable and completely unacceptable to you, you'll know that your relationship with this person has broken down irrevocably (see Chapter 56, "Knowing When It's Time to Go"). In most cases, however, you'll discover that you are offered a solution that can restore a satisfactory working relationship. Even if the two of you never become close friends or see eye to eye on every issue, it is entirely possible for you to continue to function together professionally in a manner that places priority on the best interests of both the institution and your college.

Conflicts with other administrators arise over many different issues. Sometimes our personalities seem to be perennially at odds with those of our peers. Sometimes genuine differences of opinion become personal. Sometimes, too, after objectively considering the entire matter, we realize that *we* are the ones who, because of something in our demeanor or a statement that we have made, are responsible for the rift. In these cases never underestimate the power of looking someone straight in the eye and uttering a direct, clear, and sincere apology. When doing so, always apologize for what you have *done;* don't just say you're sorry that the other person feels bad. Taking responsibility when it is due is an important aspect of leadership and a key component of deaning.

Resources

Bolton, R. (1979). *People skills: How to assert yourself, listen to others, and resolve conflicts.* New York, NY: Simon & Schuster.

Cloke, K., & Goldsmith, J. (2005). *Resolving conflicts at work: Eight strategies for everyone on the job* (Rev. ed.). San Francisco, CA: Jossey-Bass.

Cupach, W. R., & Canary, D. J. (2000). *Competence in interpersonal conflict.* Prospect Heights, IL: Waveland Press.

Edelmann, R. J. (1993). *Interpersonal conflicts at work.* Leicester, UK: British Psychological Society.

Kaye, K. (1994). *Workplace wars and how to end them: Turning personal conflicts into productive teamwork.* New York, NY: AMACOM.

Pickering, P. (2000). *How to manage conflict: Turn all conflicts into win-win outcomes* (3rd ed.). Franklin Lakes, NJ: Career Press.

Wilmot, W. W., & Hocker, J. L. (2005). *Interpersonal conflict* (7th ed.). New York, NY: McGraw-Hill.

47

A Scenario Analysis on the Dean's Challenges

Note: For a discussion of how scenario analyses are structured and suggestions on how to use this exercise most productively, see Chapter 8, "A Scenario Analysis on the Dean's Role."

Case Study

The Department of Dichotomy and Discord has long been something of a problem for your college. Not only is it highly factionalized, but in recent years it has become an increasing drain on the rest of your unit's budgets. Despite frequent conversations with and even warnings to the chair, the department has continued to end each year with significant budgetary overruns. You've done everything you can think of to solve the situation. You've analyzed the department's budget with similar departments at your institution and comparable departments at peer institutions; you can find no indication that the department is underfunded. Reluctantly, you've come to the conclusion that the reason for most of the department's problems can be traced to the current chair. Not only did the shortfalls begin almost immediately after the current chair's election, but you've also noticed that the chair has an abrupt and dismissive style that tends to fuel the flames of this already incendiary department. You've tried mentoring the chair yourself. You've assigned a successful, experienced chair as an additional advisor. None of your remedies seems to work. It is bad enough that the department always appears on the verge of an open revolution, but this year an even worse situation has arisen. The institution's budget has been extremely tight because of low enrollment and its poor-performing investments. Despite repeated discussions of the need for fiscal restraint, the chair of the Department of Dichotomy and Discord has allowed deficits to mount. The situation has become so severe, in fact, that you may need to divert a significant amount of money from other departments' budgets to meet this shortfall. The current chair is eligible for reelection to one more term, but you've concluded that continuing on the current course is not in the best interests of either the department or the college. You've followed all your institution's procedures, and the department is now about to select a new chair.

That's when the problems really begin.

   The Department of Dichotomy and Discord has become so factionalized that there is no clear candidate to serve as the next chair. In the entire department only three individuals are eligible to serve, and you have strong misgivings about each of them:

- Candidate A is one of the department's most senior members. Widely liked, this candidate is also extremely weak willed and not regarded as the department's most astute member. You've heard rumors that certain department members want Candidate A to be the next chair because this person "can be controlled." Your own concern is that this candidate is too weak to make the hard choices required to solve the budget problem.

- Candidate B recently returned to the Department of Dichotomy and Discord after several years as associate provost. This candidate was forced out of the associate provost position by the president, based on this person's improper handling of several budgetary items and the widespread suspicion (never, however, proved) that this candidate had an inappropriate relationship with the provost.

- Candidate C, although eligible for the position, is the area's newest faculty member whose career, you believe, could be damaged by the chair position. Many of the department's most difficult personalities will be voting on this candidate's future promotion. If this candidate confronts those responsible for the spending that has led to the current budget crisis, you are afraid that there will be retribution in the future. Nevertheless, if the candidate plays politics with these faculty members, the budgetary problem will either continue or grow worse.

   The procedure in place at your institution is that, when more than two individuals are eligible to serve as chair, multiple ballots are conducted, with each vote several days apart. After each vote is taken, the candidate receiving the fewest votes is dropped from the next ballot, until only two candidates remain. In this way, the chair who is eventually elected always receives a clear majority, not simply a plurality, of the votes. As dean, you have the right to overturn this decision, even to appoint someone as chair who was not on the final ballot, but this option has rarely been exercised. Department members would view such an action as a clear statement that you have no confidence in their ability to select their own representative. Even in cases where you may privately feel this way, you realize that intervening in the department's election would make your relationship with it far more difficult and may even doom your appointed chair to failure.

   Because there are only three eligible candidates, there will be two rounds of voting. You're uncomfortable with all three choices but have gradually concluded that you can live with Candidate A. You will need to provide this candidate with a great deal of support and mentoring, but you do not see any other options. Candidate B has been even more abrasive and divisive since returning to the department; not only would the budget situation likely worsen under Candidate B's leadership, but you also share the president's discomfort with this individual's budgetary decisions while working in the provost's office. Candidate C provides you with no better alternative; you've come to the conclusion that the Department of Dichotomy and Discord is so fractious that this individual's future promotion possibilities could not sustain a term as chair. Moreover, you worry that, when push comes to shove, Candidate C may not be any stronger than Candidate A when tough budgetary decisions need to be made.

Having reached your decision with so much difficulty, you are distressed to learn that Candidate A has been dropped by the department after the first ballot. Even worse, you hear reports that the provost has been talking with several department members, urging them to support Candidate B. Such meddling would be troubling in any case, but it is particularly unacceptable in light of the suspicions about the provost's inappropriate relationship with Candidate B. In addition, because Candidate B and the provost opposed you in several important strategic decisions in the past, you are extremely uncomfortable with the prospect of this individual as chair. Your concern reaches new heights, however, when the provost calls you in for an unexpected meeting. "I think we've got a real problem with the chair election in that Department of Dichotomy and Discord of yours," the provost tells you. "A couple members of that department have told me that your associate dean has been canvassing votes on behalf of Candidate C. Well, *pressuring* people to vote on behalf of Candidate C would be a more accurate description. I think the whole process has been corrupted now. The only choice you've got, because the department clearly didn't want Candidate A, is to declare this election invalid and simply appoint Candidate B as the new chair. The sooner you do that, the better it'll be for everyone."

What do you say to the provost, and how do you handle the selection process for the chair of the Department of Dichotomy and Discord?

Considerations

1. Do you confront the provost with the reports that you have heard about the provost's own electioneering on behalf of Candidate B?

    *   If so, what do you do if the provost flatly denies these reports? "If you pursue this matter any further, I'll regard it as your public declaration

that I'm a liar," the provost then tells you, "and I would consider that a very severe accusation indeed."

- If so, what do you do if the provost responds, "That's completely irrelevant. I'm not a faculty member in your unit, so I can support anyone I want. But your associate dean is responsible for performance appraisals in that department. That's a direct implication of coercion that we just can't have."

- If not, do you make any other use of this information? Do you convey it to the president? Do you investigate it further to determine whether it is accurate?

2. Even if you don't tell the president about the reports that the provost may have been exerting inappropriate influence on the election, is there any other way in which you involve the president in this election?

- If so, at what point do you begin to involve the president? What do you say, and what action do you hope the president will take?

- If not, do you keep the president out of the loop because you regard the matter as too insignificant for the president's concern?

- If not, do you keep the president out of the loop because you do not want the president to think you are incapable of handling your own affairs?

3. Do you allow the departmental election to proceed?

- If so, how do you handle the provost's objections to this strategy? How do you treat the possibility of inappropriate involvement in the election by both the provost and your associate dean?

- If not, do you call a new election, taking steps to avoid the irregularities that occurred in the current election?

- If not, do you revert to appointing a chair?

4. Do you consider placing the department in receivership and appointing someone from outside the department to act as chair for a year or two until some of the conflict can be resolved and the budgetary problems fixed?

5. If the election is allowed to continue, what do you do if . . .

    •   Candidate B is elected?

    •   Candidate C is elected?

6. Do you accept the department's decision or overturn it? If you overturn the vote, do you appoint . . .

    •   The other candidate in the final election?

    •   Candidate A?

    •   Someone else?

7. Do you decide that, despite all your problems with the current chair, allowing this chair to continue in the position is better than any of your other choices? (Remember that this chair is still eligible for an additional term.) If you do make this decision, do you . . .

    •   Call a new election, allowing the current chair to run?

    •   Simply appoint the chair to an additional term? (If so, how do you explain your decision to remove the chair and then reappoint the chair only a few weeks later?)

8. Suppose that for whatever reason—your own appointment of the individual or the department's election—you ask Candidate C to be the chair. This individual is highly reluctant to accept the position, however, because of the possible future repercussions. You then proceed to persuade Candidate C to serve as chair by saying, "Don't worry, I've got your back. Don't forget that all promotion recommendations come to me. If I even suspect that the department has voted against you for the wrong reasons, I'll overturn its decision in a heartbeat." Then, less than a year later, you find yourself offered your dream job at another institution. If you turn this job down now, you know that you'll never again have the opportunity to make this career move. What do you do?

    •   Do you turn down your dream job out of your commitment to assist Candidate C when the promotion vote is taken, still two years away?

    •   Do you try to leave a paper trail for your successor, even though you know that your successor is under no obligation to follow your recommendation?

- Is your choice complicated or made easier if you know that, should you leave the institution, the provost will appoint Candidate B as the next dean, effectively eliminating any chance that Candidate C may have had of promotion?

- Do you simply accept the job offer, thinking that "these things happen, we're all adults here, and no one can ever really promise us a promotion anyway"?

Suggestions

This case study, like several others that we have considered, causes deans to confront the lesser of several evils. In fact, from one perspective, what you really have in this scenario are *two* options, one of which allows you several additional suboptions. From this perspective, you may prefer that the next chair is:

- Someone whom you do not believe would be strong or effective enough to solve the severe budgetary crisis afflicting the Department of Dichotomy and Discord (i.e., the outgoing chair, Candidate A, and Candidate C).

- Someone about whom you have serious reservations on many different fronts, including disagreement with this person's previous budgetary practices, suspicions of an improper liaison with the provost, and the likelihood that your own position will be undermined if you were to be sandwiched between this person and the provost (i.e., Candidate B).

Your handling of this case study is likely to be based on which of these two alternatives you find more unpalatable. Most deans would probably choose to strengthen a potentially weak chair rather than deal with a consistently hostile and potentially treacherous chair. Moreover, if actual evidence of an illicit relationship between the chair and provost came to light, most deans would not want to answer questions about what they knew and when they knew it. In any case, your own administrative style and tolerance for confrontation will be your best guide in this matter. Some deans prefer outright resistance to weakness and indecision—at least they know where they stand—whereas others don't.

There are many reasons in the current scenario why you might prefer taking a more passive role to an active one, allowing the election to play itself out and hoping for the best. The sheer divisiveness in this department's history ensures that, if you intervene with an appointment too soon, your appointee's effectiveness will be diminished from the start. You have already intervened in departmental matters by compelling the previous chair to step down. Any additional action that causes the faculty members to think that their next chair is *your* person, not *their* person, will make all the department's challenges much harder to resolve. Because there is not a clear and obvious best choice in this scenario, you may be wiser to save intervention for situations in which you have better alternatives.

As for discussing the situation with the president, this matter is sufficiently serious and complex that most presidents would want at least a heads-up. Conduct your conversation not as tattling on the provost or attempting to plead your own case before the situation becomes worse, but rather for informational and mentoring purposes. If your president is an experienced academic administrator, he or she may be able to give you some effective guidance on the best approach to the problem given the personalities involved and your institution's history. Don't expect the president to intervene directly in a departmental matter or to deal with the provost. Rather, provide information, ask for advice, and be understanding if your president decides that there are bigger fish to fry than the departmental election.

48

The Honors College

In this section, "The Dean's Unique Opportunities," we'll explore seven situations and challenges that do not apply to every academic deanship. The opportunities that we'll be considering are special circumstances that you may need to address, for instance, if you are the dean of a graduate school, the chief academic officer of your institution, someone who works with a unionized faculty and staff, and so on. The opportunities that you will have in these cases may be substantially different from what other academic deans encounter. In the current chapter we'll begin our discussion of the dean's unique opportunities by examining the special circumstances that surround the dean of an honors college.

In their quest to recruit and retain high-ability students, many colleges and universities are developing, expanding, or redesigning honors programs and honors colleges. Although these two terms are sometimes used interchangeably, an *honors program* is a specially designed group of curricular, cocurricular, and extracurricular enhancements that enriches the undergraduate experience of academically gifted students. On the other hand, an *honors college* should significantly surpass what is possible in an honors program by having a more highly developed administrative structure, a comprehensive academic program (in which a larger proportion of a student's courses are taken at the honors level), and a role in such matters as recruitment, advising, faculty development, its own curriculum, and institutional governance—just as other colleges at the institution do. According to guidelines approved by the National Collegiate Honors Council (NCHC) in 2005, a fully developed honors college should represent as many of these characteristics as possible:

- A fully developed honors college should exist as an equal collegiate unit within a multi-collegiate university structure.

- The head of a fully developed honors college should be a dean reporting directly to the chief academic officer of the institution and serving as a full member of the Council of Deans, if one exists. The dean should be a full-time, 12-month appointment.

- The operational and staff budgets of fully developed honors colleges should provide resources at least comparable to other collegiate units of equivalent size.

- A fully developed honors college should exercise increased coordination and control of departmental honors where the college has emerged out of such a decentralized system.

- A fully developed honors college should exercise considerable control over honors recruitment and admissions, including the appropriate size of the incoming class. Admission to the honors college should be by separate application.

- An honors college should exercise considerable control over its policies, curriculum, and selection of faculty.

- The curriculum of a fully developed honors college should offer significant course opportunities across all four years of study.

- The curriculum of the fully developed honors college should constitute at least 20% of a student's degree program. An honors thesis or project should be required.

- Where the home university has a significant residential component, the fully developed honors college should offer substantial honors residential opportunities.

- The distinction awarded by a fully developed honors college should be announced at commencement, noted on the diploma, and featured on the student's final transcript.

- Like other colleges within the university, a fully developed honors college should be involved in alumni affairs and development and should have an external advisory board.

In other words, if the unit responsible for honors education at your university bears more similarities to the college of arts and letters or the college of business administration than to those entities on your campus that have *program* in their titles (such as the community service-learning program or the leadership development program), then it probably is a true honors college. If it doesn't, then it may be better designated as an honors *program*. If, as dean of an honors college, you hold a rank comparable to deans of other academic colleges, control your own budget in the way that they do, and make decisions alongside them as an equal member of an academic council or provost's council, then you may regard this as a clear indication that your institution has developed a true honors college structure.

Nevertheless, as helpful as these general guidelines may be, there is still an almost bewildering range of differences between units that are legitimately labeled as "honors colleges." For instance, some honors colleges have their own faculties; most do not. Some are degree-granting entities within their institutions; most are not. Some honors colleges cover all four years of the traditional undergraduate program; others do not. It is from these distinctions that the unique opportunities and challenges of the honors college dean will arise. For instance, honors college deans who do not have their own faculties may face the difficulty of having to beg for sections of courses from other deans. Other deans may be reluctant to surrender faculty members to teach for a program in which they do not receive the student credit hours generated. Moreover, even when these credits are assigned to the faculty member's home college, honors courses—which typically have lower student-to-faculty ratios than other courses—do not seem very attractive to deans when credit hour production drives budgetary decisions. Also, even when funds exist to buy out from the home college a faculty member who is teaching an honors course, these buyouts are often made at adjunct rates. A dean may not want to reassign a highly distinguished senior faculty member to teach in the honors college when all that his or her college will receive in return is the equivalent of an adjunct instructor's salary (usually without benefits) for teaching one course.

For all these reasons, most honors college deans prefer to have their own faculty members in much the same way that the deans of the college of engineering and the college of education each have their own faculty members. Nevertheless, this scenario, too, can present certain challenges. Having faculty members dedicated to the honors college can isolate these individuals from their disciplinary counterparts elsewhere in the institution. For example, does a faculty member who teaches chemistry and who is assigned to the honors college have full faculty rights and privileges in the college of science? If so, won't this "dual citizenship" create resentment with the rest of the science faculty, potentially endangering the faculty member's chances when it comes time for tenure and promotion? If not, isn't there a danger that the science curriculum in the honors college will increasingly diverge, in undesirable ways, from the curriculum followed by the college of science? How does one handle, particularly for accreditation purposes, the existence of two tracks or degrees in the same discipline? Moreover, because honors colleges are usually rather small entities, it is extremely difficult to offer a full range of curricular choices at a very high level with only a few full-time faculty members. Do you then need to limit the honors college's curricular offerings (decreasing its attractiveness to students); rely on adjuncts to supplement the curriculum (potentially making it weaker than that offered by the institution's non-honors colleges, which have more full-time faculty members); or end up begging faculty members from other deans anyway?

Because honors college deans have so many unique opportunities and challenges, there are two central principles they may wish to follow to make their students' experience as rich as possible.

Seek a truly distinctive focus for the honors college.

Honors education is not only more rigorous and accelerated than typical undergraduate work, it also seeks to enrich the educational experience of high-ability students in an exceptionally meaningful way. After all, honors students are not distinguished from other students because they are more capable in this or that academic subject. (We already have a commonly accepted term for students who are more capable than others in a specific field. We call them "majors.") Honors students are distinctive because of their greater talent at a *broad range* of academic disciplines. The opportunity and challenge of the honors college dean is, therefore, to make the best use of honors students' exceptional strength in all, or nearly all, disciplines; to see connections between areas of study at a very sophisticated level; and to understand how the methods of one discipline may be applied to an entirely different intellectual pursuit.

For this reason, honors college deans are frequently eager to help their units discover the program features that makes those units truly distinctive. Besides greater intellectual challenge, what do students gain from fulfilling their general education coursework in the honors college? If the college offers upper division coursework or partners with other colleges for this purpose, what does an honors student in, say, psychology gain that would not be true of a student who completed his or her major with nonhonors courses through the psychology department? The honors college's unique theme or focus should be compelling enough to provide a clear identity for the unit but not be so specific that it fails to attract a broad range of students. Topics of contemporary interest may be attractive because they are perceived as being on the cutting edge; within a few years, however, what had once seemed progressive and fashionable may seem passé. As you continue to develop your honors college's distinctive theme, therefore, keep in mind some of the following general themes:

- *Interdisciplinarity:* Honors college students frequently see connections between ideas where other students may not. A college rooted in interdisciplinarity would reflect this approach in its curriculum, offering or requiring several team-taught courses as well as courses that fall between the boundaries of traditionally defined disciplines. Students would be required to complete a senior thesis or an equivalent capstone experience that reflects the highly interdisciplinary nature of their honors experience.

- *Direct sources of knowledge:* Honors students would have greater access to primary sources, laboratory and studio experiences, service-learning, multiple internships, and other learning approaches that took full advantage of direct sources of knowledge, producing not merely one original work of research at the program's end but several significant research projects along the way.

- *Leadership:* An honors college built on the theme of leadership would not only provide academic insight into leadership theories and management techniques but also require students to participate in multiple practical leadership experiences, such as in student government, community affairs, ROTC, corporate internships, and campus organizations.

- *Creativity, innovation, and entrepreneurship:* The development and marketing of an original discovery can also provide a central theme for an honors college. Too often people tend to associate creativity only with fine arts programs. Innovation, however, transcends all academic disciplines and can provide a useful focal point for uniting the methods adopted by many fields of study.

- *Civic engagement:* Civic engagement, community service-learning, and social entrepreneurship have become such common themes on college campuses that adopting them as signatures of the honors college may not be sufficiently distinctive. Nevertheless, if your institution does not emphasize civic engagement, honors students' proclivity for service and community involvement may form the basis of an appropriate theme.

- *Collaboration:* Because of honors students' academic talent and commitment to learning, their endeavors in collaborative work are largely free of the problems (poor communication, vastly unequal contributions, procrastination, etc.) that tend to plague team-based studies. An honors college that focuses on developing collaborative research skills can provide students with a distinctive advantage for their future work in graduate or professional school, as well as in the workforce.

- *Site-specific themes:* Your institution's location may give it certain advantages that can be developed into a distinctive theme. Rural institutions might use the environment as the basis of a theme (see, e.g., Green Mountain College's honors program, which is organized around the Environmental Liberal Arts Program: www.greenmtn.edu/learning/honors.asp). Urban institutions might base an honors college on the individual character of the cities in which they are located (see, e.g., the honors program at Wayne State University, where the first year is devoted to "community and the urban experience": www.honors.wayne.edu/why.php and www.honors.wayne.edu/culturalpassport.php).

Track appropriate indicators to make the case for the importance of honors education.

Honors colleges are frequently challenged because of their high cost per student credit hour generated. To include a great deal of writing and discussion in their courses, most honors colleges cap class size at 15–40 students. At institutions where the average class size may be several times this figure, the cost of the honors college may seem extremely high compared to how the institution benefits from it. One of the honors dean's unique opportunities is to make the case that neither cost nor revenue per student credit hours generated is the only—or even the *best*—indicator of a unit's productivity. When examined from other perspectives, the benefits an honors college produces for an institution can look very great indeed:

- *Admissions data:* Honors colleges frequently attract the sort of students that enhance the institution as a whole. Track the following data to see what your institution would look like if honors college students were omitted:

    - Number of high school valedictorians

    - Number of National Merit Scholarship finalists

    - Number of Advanced Placement and International Baccalaureate credits transferred in

    - Average SAT/ACT scores

    - Average weighted high school GPAs

    Moreover, can you determine how many students came to the institution *because* of the honors college? (A survey completed by recently admitted students should be able to provide you with this information.) These data will also help you make a very strong case for the institutional contribution of the honors college.

- *Graduation data:* In a similar way, graduates who have participated in an honors college almost always have a profile that sets them apart from other graduates. The institution's reputation is based, at least in part, on the success of these high-ability alumni. What would the following data be if honors college students were omitted?

  - Freshman to sophomore retention rate

  - Lower division to upper division retention rate

  - Graduation rates

  - Placement rates for graduate or professional schools (does the honors college contribute to the institution as a whole by placing a significant number of its alumni in the university's own graduate programs?)

  - Annual fund contribution rates (most institutions find that honors program/college graduates contribute to the annual fund twice as much as other graduates)

- *Data on persistence in the area:* Are you able to demonstrate that honors college students remain in your state or region at a higher rate than students with a similar academic profile who choose institutions outside your state or region?

Honors college deans are frequently resented by other deans, who believe that programs for high-ability students skim the academic cream from the student body, consume resources at a higher rate per capita than other colleges, and are inherently elitist. For honors college deans, even more than for other deans, it is often necessary to reach out to fellow administrators (see Chapter 15, "Other Deans") and to demonstrate the ways in which their programs serve the institution's interests. Honors college deans who reinforce the negative stereotype of privilege and elitism only make this task that much harder. Taking the initiative to maintain excellent relationships with their colleagues is an important opportunity and challenge for all honors college deans.

Resources

Green, S. M. (2006). *A study of academic achievement among freshmen gifted female honor college students versus academic achievement of freshmen gifted female non-honor college students at a southern public university.* Ann Arbor, MI: ProQuest/UMI.

Long, A. (1995). *A handbook for honors administrators.* Lincoln, NE: National Collegiate Honors Council.

Otero, R., & Spurrier, R. (2005). *Assessing and evaluating honors programs and honors colleges: A practical handbook.* Lincoln, NE: National Collegiate Honors Council.

Schuman, S. (2006). *Beginning in honors: A handbook* (4th ed.). Lincoln, NE: National Collegiate Honors Council.

References

National Collegiate Honors Council. (2005). *Basic characteristics of a fully developed honors college.* Retrieved July 13, 2007, from www.nchchonors.org/basic.htm

49

The Professional School

Professional schools or colleges are those institutions (or subunits of an institution) that prepare students for direct entry into a profession other than teaching and conducting research at a college or university. As such, professional schools may be distinguished both from vocational schools (which prepare students for careers that are not generally regarded as "professions") and schools of the liberal arts and sciences (which prepare undergraduate students for entry into a graduate program or professional school and, at the graduate level, produce scholars qualified for teaching and research at a college or university). Some professional schools operate at the postgraduate level only (such as law schools and medical schools); others have both undergraduate and graduate programs (such as most colleges of business administration, education, nursing, architecture, and engineering). Beyond this general distinction, however, a more precise distinction between professional schools and other colleges is futile due to the large number of exceptions that can arise. For instance, consider these facts:

- Some professional school graduates do go on to teach and conduct research at institutions of higher education, thus blurring the distinction between professional schools and colleges of the liberal arts and sciences. Moreover, liberal arts and sciences graduates may at times enter professions rather than proceeding to graduate school, professional school, or postsecondary teaching.

- Conservatories, art schools, and theater schools further complicate the notion of what constitutes a professional school. Although music, art, and theater are generally classified as liberal arts, many programs in these areas aim at *professional* musicians, artists, actors, directors, and set designers.

For all these reasons, we might consider the designation "professional school" as a flexible term that should be tied more to a unit's primary mission than to the specific group of disciplines it contains. If you are dean of a college that regards its central goal as preparing students to enter the workforce in a field that requires an undergraduate or graduate degree, then you may be considered the dean of a professional school and can expect to encounter both the opportunities and the challenges explored in this chapter.

In an analysis written for *BizEd* ("Challenges for Deans at Professional Colleges," 2006), four business school deans—Ron Bottin of Missouri State University, Linda Garceau of East Tennessee State University, Diane Hoadley of Eastern Illinois University, and Bob Rogow of Eastern Kentucky University— identified many of the challenges faced by deans of professional programs. These challenges included:

- Solving personnel issues, such as the discrepancies in tenure and promotion standards between departments

- Addressing the salary disparities that may arise from such factors as market equity and institutional history

- Keeping up with standards for multiple accrediting bodies

- Determining resource allocation

- Creating a cohesive faculty

These challenges are so common in professional schools that they are best addressed in some detail.

Personnel issues and the professional school

Part of the deans' challenge is that they deal with disciplines that tend to have distinctly different pedagogical methods and forms of scholarship from those found in other academic units. For instance, law schools and business schools generally teach through the case study method. Medical schools often use rounds in a teaching hospital to assist interns in the techniques of diagnosis and prescribed treatment. Teachers in conservatories rely on individual coaching and instruction more than professors in many other fields. Colleges of education use student teaching as a structured and highly supervised internship. Just as all these pedagogical methods differ from the traditional lecture-and-discussion format still adopted by most disciplines, so, too, do the types of scholarship in colleges of nursing, architecture, or business differ from the peer-reviewed articles and books prepared by scholars in other academic disciplines.

Frequently, these differences do not cause problems within the academic unit itself. Musicians know what good instruction, scholarship, and creativity look like in their field, as do physicians, lawyers, architects, nurses, teachers, and engineers. It is usually only with individuals *outside* the immediate academic field that misunderstandings arise. This problem can occur even before a recommendation for promotion leaves the college itself. Deans of fine and performing arts frequently discover that theater faculty members may not understand why the credit hour production of their colleagues in music is so low or why the adjudication process so common in their own discipline has not been used to assess creative activity in the other arts. Even worse, outside the college, tenure and promotion committees that are used to easily quantified results (such as the number of students who were accepted into graduate programs or the number of pages published in peer-reviewed journals) may not immediately recognize the quality of teaching or research in fields where pedagogy and scholarship assume demonstrably different forms.

To help overcome these obstacles, professional school deans may find it useful to:

- Work with the disciplines in their areas to develop clear mission statements that clarify their unit's central goal, how that mission relates to the institution's overall purpose, and why that mission is critically important to the institution's constituents and service areas.

- Develop explanations that will be readily understood outside individual disciplines of why certain forms of pedagogy or scholarship are both essential and appropriate to their individual areas' missions. These explanations may include descriptions of why a particular teaching technique is essential to that discipline's educational mission or what type of research, preparation, and reflection must be completed before the production of a painting, set of blueprints, musical score, or the like.

- Propose equivalencies, wherever possible, between the forms of pedagogy and scholarship used in their disciplines and more widely recognized forms found elsewhere in academia. The accrediting bodies of individual disciplines can help you establish these equivalencies. How can contact hours for disciplines with extremely low student-to-faculty ratios be translated into equivalencies to student-credit-hour production? How does an applied project in a discipline relate to scholarship in more theoretical disciplines? How is quality assessed in the scholarship of disciplines where it is impossible to have a work peer-reviewed before its public appearance?

Salary discrepancies

Professional school deans must frequently deal with salary discrepancies both inside and outside their units. For instance, business school deans may be challenged about why their economics professors' salaries lag so far behind those of their accountancy professors. Medical school deans may encounter widespread envy because the salaries commanded by their faculty members are so high, whereas education deans may be under pressure from their own faculties because average salaries in their units are so low. The most important thing that deans can do in all these situations is to help put matters of faculty salaries into their proper context:

- The College and University Professional Association for Human Resources (generally known as CUPA-HR or simply as CUPA) conducts an extensive annual survey of faculty salaries by discipline and rank in public and private four-year colleges and universities (see www.cupahr.org /surveys/salarysurveysinfo.html). The results of these surveys can provide you with a general benchmark to compare your disciplines' salaries with those of other disciplines. Because your institution will differ from the national average in certain respects (e.g., the cost of living in your area may be extremely high or extremely low, or your institution's faculty may be, on the average, far more senior or more junior than the faculty elsewhere), this information will provide you with a *general* comparison.

- Further information on a broad range of faculty matters can be obtained from the National Center for Education Statistics (see http://nces.ed.gov/ surveys/nsopf). For example, the center's National Study of Postsecondary Faculty includes information on faculty members' sociodemographic charac- teristics; academic and professional background; field of instruction; employ- ment history; current employment status, including rank and tenure; workload; publications; job satisfaction and attitudes; and compensation.

- You can also track data internally to help you place your unit's salary pic- ture in a broader context. How many faculty members has your unit lost within the past five years to higher salaries elsewhere? How many of these individuals took positions outside academia because they were able to earn higher salaries in other lines of work? How many potential faculty members have you lost in searches because you could not meet their salary expecta- tions? How many times have you had to resort to second- or third-choice candidates (or even had to abandon a search) because you could not meet your applicants' salary demands?

Tracking the number of faculty members who leave the institution for higher salaries elsewhere is particularly useful because it is often argued that market equity is important at the time of hiring but is not important later when salary increases are distributed. In other words, people understand that recruiting a management professor may require a higher salary because the institution has to compete with private industry; nevertheless, many academics believe that this same argument cannot be made year after year when raises are assigned. "But once we choose to enter higher education as a profession," people say, "we're all on the same playing field. Certain disciplines should not get 5% salary increases while other disciplines receive only 2%." For this reason, if you can legitimately demonstrate that you are losing faculty members because other institutions' salaries or private businesses' salaries rise more rapidly than yours, you may well have a compelling response to this common argument.

Multiple accrediting bodies

Professional school deans are more likely than their colleagues in colleges of liberal arts and sciences to be caught between the competing demands or standards of multiple accrediting bodies. Not only do professional school deans face the regional accreditation challenges imposed on all of us by such bodies as the Middle States Association of Colleges and Schools, the New England Association of Schools and Colleges, and the North Central Association of Colleges and Schools; but they also have to follow the guidelines of numerous specialized accrediting boards, such as the Association to Advance Collegiate Schools of Business, the Accreditation Board for Engineering and Technology, the Council for Interior Design Accreditation, and the National Council for Accreditation of Teacher Education. Each of these groups may have individual requirements for faculty load, student-to-faculty ratios, facilities, and the like—which can trap deans in a complicated web of conflicting standards. There are no perfect solutions to this predicament, but the following approaches should always be kept in mind:

- Whenever possible, correlate institutional program review and external accreditation processes, including the timetables and standards for both. If the timetables are different, departments find themselves continually conducting self-studies, writing reports, and analyzing assessment data, without the time to implement the results of these studies, reports, and data. If the standards are demonstrably different, disciplines find themselves trying to serve two masters and ultimately satisfy neither. For this reason, professional school deans should serve as advocates for aligning review processes to whatever degree their institution allows.

- Analyze the cost-benefit ratio of specialized accreditations. How many students or faculty members would you lose (or never be able to recruit) if a discipline lacked its specialized accreditation? How would your placement rate into jobs or graduate programs differ if the discipline lacked specialized accreditation? In some cases you may actually discover that it is impossible to justify the expense and extra effort required for discipline-specific accreditation. In these situations you should redirect these resources into areas where they are more likely to make a difference. In other cases you may be able to demonstrate that an accredited status is itself the distinctive feature that helps set your college apart from its peers.

Determining resource allocation

In matters of resource allocation, professional school deans need to make the case that *equity* is not the same as *equality*. Because of the differing missions, pedagogical methods, and forms of scholarship that we discussed earlier, disciplines will have distinctly different budgetary needs. Certain disciplines are equipment intensive. Others cannot attract students without significant scholarship support. Still others may need specialized facilities or a great deal of space. One important goal for the professional school dean must always be to relate the discipline's individual mission directly to the college's and institution's overall mission. Be able to provide data that explain or put into context any information that may seem unusual or anomalous. For instance, if one discipline's cost per student credit hour generated or per square foot of facility space occupied is significantly higher than another discipline's, can you also demonstrate that that discipline *contributes* disproportionately to the institution in some other way? Does it attract a larger number of National Merit Scholarship finalists or valedictorians to the institution? Are faculty members more productive in scholarship or more active in national organizations? Do the faculty's or student body's activities bring positive attention to the institution in ways that are not possible in other disciplines? Is there an element of institutional diversity that would be lacking if it were not for your unit's contributions? Are the career or graduate school placement rates higher for this discipline than the institutional average? How can you demonstrate that the seemingly disproportionate levels of resources actually produce disproportionate results?

Creating a cohesive faculty

Faculty unity is often easier to achieve in units where there is some homogeneity of academic disciplines than in professional schools, which can house a wide variety of fields for no other reason than administrative convenience. In these situations the dean may need to take an active role in promoting a more cohesive faculty and sense of identity. Creating a college-wide mission statement or creed—a statement of the values shared by all the college's disciplines—can be an important first step in developing the esprit de corps that your college needs.

What do you do better than other colleges of your kind? Besides teaching cours-es and generating scholarship, what goal do your disciplines share? Perhaps you stress the importance of internships, international travel, civic engagement, cre-ative development, communication skills, or some other value-added factor that sets you apart even from the other colleges at your institution. Remember two of the factors that we considered in Chapter 21 ("Searching for and Building a Strong Administrative Team"): Stand for something, and never underestimate the power of celebration. These approaches also work in transforming an entire college into a strong team. If your college becomes the college of "100% Placement in First-Choice Graduate Schools," then this goal becomes both an important identifying factor for your unit and an immediate cause for celebra-tion. Explore your disciplines' core beliefs, and you'll be amazed to discover unexpected sources of unity and focus among seemingly discrete fields of study.

Professional school deans are frequently frustrated by the simultaneous envy and contempt they receive from other deans. They are envied because their units' salaries are frequently higher, students and parents tend to be interested in their program's career focus, their alumni giving rates are often higher, and their placement of students into jobs and graduate programs is often high. They are treated with disdain because their disciplines deal with practical matters of pro-fessional training rather than the more theoretical focus of fields specializing in "pure research." Neither the envy nor the scorn is likely to subside anytime soon. Nevertheless, the more skilled professional school deans become at explaining the relationship of their missions to that of the institution as a whole, the easier it will be for them to overcome the special challenges that they face both inside and outside their colleges.

Resources

Austin, M. J., Ahearn, F. L., & English, R. A. (Eds.). (1997). *New directions for higher educa-tion: No. 98. The professional school dean: Meeting the leadership challenges.* San Francisco, CA: Jossey-Bass.

Bennis, W. G., & O'Toole, J. (2005, May). How business schools lost their way. *Harvard Business Review, 83*(5), 96–105.

Lee, A., & Hoyle, E. (2002, November). Who would become a successful dean of faculty of medicine: Academic or clinician or administrator? *Medical Teacher, 24*(6), 637–641.

Quell, T. T. (2006). *Job satisfaction in the role of the academic dean in schools of nursing*. Ann Arbor, MI: ProQuest/UMI.

References

Challenges for deans at professional colleges. (2006, July/August). *BizEd, 5*(5), 8–9.

50

The Graduate School

Graduate school deans share many challenges with honors college and professional school deans (see Chapter 48, "The Honors College," and Chapter 49, "The Professional School"). For example, like their colleagues in honors colleges, graduate school deans may not have faculties of their own (they staff their courses with the same professors whose positions "belong" to academic colleges under other deans), are pressured to justify a comparatively high cost per student credit hour generated, and have frequent opportunities to engage students in academic work at an advanced level or accelerated pace. Like their colleagues in professional schools, graduate deans may face challenges when they try to develop a clear identity for their graduate school, whose mission must be more than to serve as a collection of disciplines committed to post-baccalaureate education. Certainly, all graduate schools are similar to professional schools in their effort to prepare students for careers, and they hope to achieve an excellent placement record. Nevertheless, graduate school deans also face several challenges of their own. These unique problems include dealing with questions that involve graduate faculty status, harmonizing the graduate school's combined mission of research and advanced education, and reassessing the role of graduate education in modern society.

Graduate faculty status

In most colleges it's fairly easy to determine whether a particular individual is a member of that unit's faculty. The field in which he or she teaches, the department offering most of his or her courses, and even the location of his or her office all provide some sense of the faculty member's identity and disciplinary affiliation. But how do you determine whether someone is a graduate faculty member? Is this even a meaningful designation? And how do you decide whether a particular individual has the appropriate credentials to teach at the graduate level? Institutions answer these questions in different ways based on their individual missions and histories. Some schools make no distinction at all between members of the graduate and undergraduate faculty; if you're teaching a graduate course, you're regarded as a graduate faculty member for the duration of that course, even if you never again teach students beyond the undergraduate level. Other institutions grant graduate faculty status to anyone who holds a terminal degree; the right to teach graduate students was, these schools argue, one of the prerogatives that traditionally fell to those who held the doctorate or its equivalent. In other words, this approach has the weight of historical precedence. Still other institutions, prompted by the increasingly rigorous standards of accrediting bodies, have instituted a more formal type of graduate faculty status for which individuals must apply and be approved.

The idea behind a distinctive graduate faculty status is that individuals who have demonstrated significant contributions to scholarship beyond the terminal degree, a commitment to graduate education, and the capacity to supervise advanced research (such as research that leads to a thesis or dissertation) are best qualified to provide the academic experience that graduate students need. Certain institutions may even refine this concept further, distinguishing associate graduate faculty status from full graduate faculty status. For instance, at North Carolina State University (NCSU), for a faculty member to qualify for full graduate status, he or she must demonstrate distinction in graduate education and research that goes far beyond possessing a terminal degree. "Evidence of such distinction is indicated by a number of significant publications, by service as chair of the advisory committees for several Master's students or as co-chair of the advisory committees for doctoral students, and by excellence in graduate teaching" (NCSU, 2006). Members of the graduate faculty with associate status may:

- Teach courses carrying graduate credit;

- Participate as a member of advisory committees in planning graduate student programs;

- Chair Master's advisory committees upon recommendation of Director of Graduate Programs (DGP) or Department Head;

- Co-chair doctoral advisory committees when committee chair holds full Graduate Faculty status; and

- Serve as Graduate School Representative when requested by Graduate School. (NCSU, 2006)

These individuals must either "hold a doctoral degree, [or] there must be demonstrable evidence that the candidate possesses the experience, knowledge, and capability in the area of intended participation in the graduate program of the university" (NCSU, 2006). If the faculty member demonstrates the additional qualifications to warrant full status on the graduate faculty, he or she may also chair doctoral advisory committees.

Similarly, at Ball State University (n.d.), individuals who hold *associate* graduate faculty membership may:

- Teach graduate-level courses

- Serve as a committee member on a master's thesis or creative project

- Chair a master's thesis, creative project, or research project

Those individuals who hold *regular* graduate faculty status may serve in all those roles and also may:

- Serve as a committee member for a doctoral committee

- Serve on or chair a specialist committee (Ball State University, n.d.)

At the University of Memphis, this structure is further refined, with full, associate, affiliate, adjunct, adjunct research co-mentor, and adjunct-teaching statuses—each with its own set of criteria and roles in graduate education (see http://academics.memphis.edu/gradschool/gradfactable.html).

As a dean of the graduate faculty, you will wish to review from time to time whether your current policy on graduate faculty status is adequate or in need of modification. As you do so, keep the following principles in mind:

- *What is your institution trying to accomplish by this policy?* Determining who is a member of the graduate faculty can be a time-consuming and cumbersome process. This process will be made all the more difficult if you add unnecessary levels to your schema of graduate faculty with different roles, criteria, and designations. For this reason, no institution should ever have a more complex graduate faculty structure than it absolutely needs to achieve its purpose. If your institution is relatively small, and if it is relatively easy to justify to accreditation bodies that your faculty members are fully qualified to teach at the graduate level, you may not need a distinct graduate faculty status at all. Nevertheless, if your institution is more complex and there is good reason to screen faculty members' credentials before assigning them to graduate courses or thesis committees, or if it would be unduly burdensome to determine eligibility to serve on a graduate council (discussed later) or dissertation committee without a screening and certification process, or if you are trying to increase participation in graduate education and wish to give greater prestige to the faculty members who are actively involved in it, then some type of graduate faculty distinction may be desirable. Be sure, however, not to complicate the system beyond your ability to implement it effectively.

- *What criteria for graduate faculty status are really meaningful?* Institutions all too frequently adopt criteria for graduate faculty status that are either overly specific or overly vague. An example of overly specific criteria would be a policy that requires such accomplishments as "a minimum of five peer-review articles." (Are articles the *only* acceptable product of scholarship at the institution? Do five 1-page articles carry the same weight as five 50-page articles, provided that they are peer reviewed? Do you automatically exclude the faculty member who has only four peer-reviewed articles but who would be an excellent mentor for graduate students? What value does this particular criterion add to the individual's ability to teach at an advanced level and to supervise the writing of a thesis?) Overly vague criteria include policies that require "a strong commitment to graduate education." (How do you measure strength of commitment? What sort of documentation would be acceptable to demonstrate a strong commitment? Is a teacher with a commitment to graduate education necessarily the same as an *excellent* teacher at the graduate level?)

- *When must a graduate faculty status be renewed?* Some faculty members are active in graduate education for a short time in their careers because they are interested in working on a research project with a particular student. Others will seek graduate faculty status as a résumé builder or because they are interested in accruing academic recognition. For graduate faculty status to be meaningful, it should be subject to reevaluation at set intervals, such as every three to five years. If a faculty member has not taught a graduate course during that time or has had only minimal involvement with graduate education, his or her status as a graduate faculty member should not be renewed.

Harmonizing research and advanced education

When a graduate program works as intended, its twin mission of producing scholarship and educating students at an advanced level will be in perfect balance. Students will develop their skills in creating new knowledge. They will make appropriate progress toward their degrees in a timely manner. A new generation of students will follow in their steps, and the entire process will continue. In actual practice, however, there is much that can go wrong with this system. Graduate students can stall in their programs, becoming so-called career students because they lack the courage to face what awaits them after graduation, their research programs take far longer than they had originally anticipated, or they become so distracted by teaching or serving as research assistants that they do not make adequate progress in their own scholarship. Faculty members can become so caught up in their own research that they don't provide adequate supervision for the students in the program. Situations also occur where graduate students prove to be such valuable research assistants—at so low a cost—that faculty members assign them a large amount of research activity, causing the students' own progress toward their degrees to slow down or stop. Moreover, grant activity, although important for the income and prestige it brings to the institution, can distract faculty members from their other duties. As a result, teaching and service responsibilities fall disproportionately on relatively few full-time faculty members or must be assigned to adjuncts.

To meet these challenges and to help harmonize the graduate school's missions of research and teaching, graduate deans should:

- Develop a strategic plan for graduate education that allows each graduate program the flexibility it needs to pursue unforeseen opportunities. Nevertheless, the plan should also guide programs to seek grants and other forms of external support that truly advance their educational mission.

- Implement a rigorous and formal review process by which student research proposals are evaluated not only for their originality and appropriate use of methodology but also for their completion within an acceptable period of time.

- Set limits on the amount of time (or the number of successive terms) that students may be awarded research or teaching assistantships so that they can have the uninterrupted time they need to complete their theses or dissertations.

- Impose stricter time limits on graduate programs as added inducement for students to complete their degrees. These time limits should not be developed on the assumption that everyone who is enrolled in a program will necessarily be a full-time student, but rather, they should be designed to discourage *unnecessary* delays in progress toward a degree.

- Institute a sign-off process for all externally funded grants, if such a process is not already in place. A formal sign-off procedure gives everyone affected by the receipt of a grant the opportunity to meet together in one room and determine how courses would be covered, student projects supervised, matching funds obtained, and essential committees staffed *before* a grant proposal is submitted.

- Think creatively about new possibilities for interdisciplinary or multidisciplinary graduate programs that are based on issues, topics, or problems rather than on traditional academic disciplines. By approaching graduate education from a new perspective, deans can help students break the trend of becoming overly narrow in their focus or approach, opening up to them new methods and viewpoints from a wide variety of disciplines (see Golde & Gallagher, 1999).

Reassessing the role of graduate education

Why do institutions of higher education devote substantial resources to graduate education in the first place? If the programs cannot sustain themselves through tuition and external support, are there still reasons for their existence? Aside from preparing students to perform independent research at an advanced level, is there any particular focus or theme that characterizes the graduate programs at a particular institution? As higher education continues to emphasize accountability (to trustees, to legislatures, to students, to donors), graduate deans increasingly need to be able to answer these questions and to justify the role of graduate education at their institutions.

Graduate programs that have a clear focus and rationale are much more likely to pass the scrutiny of legislators, donors, and other proponents of accountability. For this reason, a graduate program can no longer afford to be a mere aggregate of advanced coursework, followed by exams, followed by the production of a significant piece of independent research. The new generation of graduate programs should have a clear shape and identity, a philosophy that outlines what the program seeks to accomplish, how it intends to achieve that goal, and why that particular mission is important. One of the graduate dean's chief allies in reassessing this new role for graduate education should be the membership of the institution's graduate committee or graduate council. Too frequently, graduate councils serve unnecessarily narrow functions. They approve new courses for graduate credit. They offer advice on the development of new graduate programs. They elect new individuals to graduate faculty status. The larger philosophical considerations—what should be the role and mission of graduate education *here?* what is the distinctive feature of *our* approach to graduate education?—are often left unaddressed or relegated to individual programs. Few people, aside from the graduate dean, seek to consider graduate education from the institutional perspective and to ask the questions that can truly make a difference in the quality of graduate education.

Graduate school deans should, therefore, use their graduate committees as true advisory councils, developing a distinctive and visionary mission for graduate education across the institution as a whole. Doing so can actually be a great impetus for creating successful and truly significant grant proposals or development activities. For instance, if an institution were to agree that all its graduate programs must prepare students for advanced research from a global perspective, new opportunities for external funding would become available. It would be possible to approach foundations and donors that have international interests, even if they do not have a history of supporting graduate education. In addition, a clear and distinctive mission for graduate education encourages students and faculty members to select that particular program over others because of its unmistakable identity within an increasingly crowded academic marketplace.

Using your resources

The Council of Graduate Schools (CGS; www.cgsnet.org) regularly runs an institute for deans of graduate programs. If you're new to your position, this institute's workshop can be an excellent opportunity for you to learn in a short amount of time many of the most important recent developments in graduate school administration. The CGS institute is also a good way to meet peers at other institutions, discuss common challenges, and learn about ideas to strengthen your graduate program. In addition, CGS maintains a useful online bookstore and provides electronic access to the organization's newsletter, the *CGS Communicator.* A quick glance at back issues of the *CGS Communicator* is another very effective way to learn about policy changes affecting graduate education, new initiatives, and other information that is difficult to obtain elsewhere.

The reputation of an institution frequently rests on the quality of its graduate programs. It is in these programs that truly innovative scholarship tends to be developed, important discoveries made, and significant research funding obtained. Despite these possibilities, however, graduate programs too frequently have an ill-defined mission. If you contribute nothing more than bringing some degree of clarity to this mission and a renewed commitment to the importance of graduate education, you will have fulfilled a very important role as a graduate school dean.

Resources

Anderson, M. S. (Ed.). (1998). *New directions for higher education: No. 101. The experience of being in graduate school: An exploration.* San Francisco, CA: Jossey-Bass.

Baird, L. L. (Ed.). (1994). *New directions for institutional research: No. 80. Increasing graduate student retention and degree attainment.* San Francisco, CA: Jossey-Bass.

Glazer-Raymo, J. (2005). *Professionalizing graduate education: The master's degree in the marketplace* (ASHE Higher Education Report Vol. 31, No. 4). San Francisco, CA: Jossey-Bass.

Page, R. N. (2001, June/July). Reshaping graduate preparation in educational research methods: One school's experience. *Educational Researcher, 30*(5), 19–25.

Weidman, J. C., Twale, D. J., & Stein, E. L. (2001). *Socialization of graduate and professional students in higher education: A perilous passage?* (ASHE-ERIC Higher Education Report Vol. 28, No. 3). San Francisco, CA: Jossey-Bass.

References

Ball State University. (n.d.). *Procedures for application for graduate faculty status.* Retrieved July 13, 2007, from www.bsu.edu/gradschool/media/pdf/gradfacprocedure.pdf

Golde, C. M., & Gallagher, H. A. (1999). The challenges of conducting interdisciplinary research in traditional doctoral programs. *Ecosystems, 2*(4), 281–285.

North Carolina State University. (2006). *Membership in the graduate faculty.* Retrieved July 13, 2007, from www.ncsu.edu/policies/academic_affairs/faculty_grad/REG02.40.1.php

51

Consortia, Centers, and Institutes

Consortia, centers, and institutes all offer deans the opportunity to build on their institutions' special strengths while simultaneously complementing areas where resources may be scarce. All three types of cooperative arrangement share certain features, though the terms are not synonymous. For instance, consortia tend to have more of an outward focus, creating a link between a college and other institutions to achieve a certain economy of scale or to supplement resources. Centers preserve more of an inward focus, crossing boundaries within a particular college or university to address a specific area or problem. Institutes tend to be the most flexible arrangement of all, usually combining aspects of both consortia and centers while adding several important features of their own.

Because this terminology may be unfamiliar to many deans, our discussion will begin with detailed definitions. Although these terms may be used in different ways at different institutions, the following definitions tend to be most common:

- *Consortium:* A consortium is a collective effort made by several entities to achieve some common purpose. Academic consortia generally fall into two overlapping categories: economic consortia and educational consortia. An *economic consortium* is a cooperative agreement made to achieve a financial goal that would be beyond the ability of each member independently. For instance, institutions might form an economic consortium to negotiate a better rate for business-related travel or to make bulk purchases, such as computer equipment, supplies, textbooks, and office furniture. An *educational consortium* is formed when institutions jointly offer an academic program or a research opportunity that no single member could support independently. Common types of educational consortia include associations made to offer study-abroad opportunities, service-learning projects, or environmental studies programs. These types of consortial agreements draw faculty members, students, and facilities from each participating institution.

- *Center:* A center is a cooperative arrangement that serves as a basis for research, scholarship, or service. Most centers are devoted to a single topic or clearly defined focus. Many of these topics tend to be interdisciplinary or multidisciplinary. The center thus provides an administrative home for issues that cannot easily be confined within an institution's traditional departmental structure. Although in most cases, the term *center* refers to a physical location, such as an office or a building, centers may be intellectual constructs rather than specific places.

- *Institutes:* Institutes are often more formal or elaborate cooperative efforts than centers. Although some schools use the terms *center* and *institute* interchangeably, the most common distinction is that institutes are allowed to offer courses for credit; centers are not. There are also a few more subtle differences between centers and institutes that we'll explore later.

The establishment of a consortium, center, or institute can open possibilities for new ideas that would lack strong advocacy within the traditional departmental structure. These initiatives are also extremely useful when the college wants to offer students or the community opportunities that cross disciplinary boundaries. As part of a strategic plan, creating a consortium, center, or institute can provide a framework for moving a college in a new direction or building on a widely recognized strength (see Chapter 6, "Launching Initiatives").

Consortia

It's common for institutions to use the term *consortium* inconsistently. They fail, in other words, to distinguish those arrangements that exist for educational purposes from those that exist for economic purposes. This inconsistency can cause problems because accrediting agencies usually assume that a consortium is a credit-producing agreement and thus expect each consortium to have a high degree of curricular oversight and quality control. For example, the Southern Association of Colleges and Schools (SACS) specifies under Comprehensive Standard 3.4.7 that, to qualify for accreditation, "the institution ensures the quality of educational programs/courses offered through consortial relationships or contractual agreements, ensures ongoing compliance with the comprehensive requirements, and evaluates the consortial relationship and/or agreement against the purpose of the institution" (Commission on Colleges of the Southern Association of Colleges and Schools [COC], 2004, p. 23). The rationale for this standard is then explained in the association's resource manual:

> A consortial relationship typically is one in which two or more institutions share in the responsibility to develop courses and programs that meet mutually agreed-upon standards of academic quality. A contractual agreement typically is one in which an institution enters an agreement for receipt of

courses/programs or portions of courses or programs (i.e., clinical training, internships, etc.) delivered by another institution or service provider. The institution is responsible for ensuring the quality of all such coursework included on its students' transcripts as credit earned from the institution and for ensuring that the quality of such programs meets the standards required of similar programs.

An evaluation process that delineates the responsibility and role of all parties to the agreement is basic to the institution's ability to ensure the quality of the educational programs and courses covered by the agreements. Regular evaluation and comparison of program and course offerings against the institutional mission are also important in establishing educational quality. (COC, 2005, p. 42)

It is clear from these guidelines that SACS assumes that all consortia exist for the purposes of expanding *academic* programs. As we've see, however, consortia can be created for many other purposes. The institution can avoid this problem by developing its own highly focused definition of *consortium* and then publishing that definition prominently on its web site and in its printed materials. This is the approach that has been taken by the University of Oklahoma (1997):

A consortium is defined as a group of at least four (4) industrial, private or other non-federal, non-state agencies which provide, on an annual basis, at least $10,000 each or which provide a set dollar amount such that the annual funding totals at least $50,000 toward the general support of a specific, well-defined independent internal research program at the University of Oklahoma. These full members of a consortium should be full participating members and must contribute the amount each year that has been set for that particular consortium. In addition to the minimum of four full members, a consortium may include associate members who contribute a reduced amount and receive reduced services.

To encourage the formation and leveraging of member funds by these consortia, the University will:

• direct cost all budget lines

- charge a general and administration fee of 26 percent on all other direct cost items in the program budget except equipment items.

These sustaining funds are expected to be leveraged by each consortium to produce a significant multiplication of consortia support through acquisition of externally-funded grants and contracts for which the consortia recover maximum allowable indirect costs.

Another way of avoiding ambiguity is to restrict the use of the term *consortium* to credit-bearing agreements (because that is how accrediting bodies tend to use the term) while applying a separate term—such as *cooperative, partnership,* or *syndicate*—for arrangements of an economic or political nature.

Centers

There is a certain degree of institutional variability in how the term *center* is used. For instance, at Rowan University (2003), the purpose of a center is "to provide predefined services to a specific population. Centers are created for an indefinite period of time, and may or may not generate revenue. If they generate revenue, they may be fully or partially self-supporting."

That description differs in several ways from the following definition that appears in the *Academic Affairs Handbook* of the University System of Georgia:

A "center" provides an organizational base for research in a given academic area or closely related areas. It often provides a vehicle for interdisciplinary research in a given area involving faculty and students from a variety of internal administrative structures. It may be involved in the offering of continuing education activities related to its area(s) of interest. The "center" structure may facilitate efforts of the college or university to obtain extramural funding in specific areas. It serves as a formalized link between the academic community and the professional community in the area(s) of focus. A "center," however, is not an autonomous structure within the internal statutory organization of a college or university. It is administratively most often an appendage of one of the traditional administrative structures, such as a department. A "center" is not involved in the independent offering of credit course or degree programs. (Board of Regents of the University System of Georgia, 1986)

Furthermore, there may be even other uses of this term, such as at Duke University (1997), where a center is defined as "an interdisciplinary unit, with a temporary lifetime, with an educational and/or research mission, which can make non-tenured (but not tenure-track) faculty appointments if authorized by the Provost."

Nevertheless, despite the wide range of what institutions regard as a center, all these definitions share several common features:

- Centers—like all the arrangements that we are considering in this chapter—are created to serve purposes that not easily addressed through an institution's regular organizational structure.

- Although centers may exist for an indefinite period of time, they are usually regarded as somehow less permanent than such units as academic departments and institutes.

- Although centers have an educational and/or research mission, they also tend to exist for specific economic reasons, such as soliciting support from private donors, external sponsors, or foundations.

- Unlike consortia and institutes, centers rarely offer their own credit-bearing courses.

- Unlike institutes, centers are less likely to hire faculty members whose primary locus of appointment is the center itself.

Centers frequently publish journals, sponsor web sites, hold conferences, offer noncredit-bearing workshops, and apply for grants to support their mission. For this reason, centers may be good short-term options for deans who wish to bring visibility to an area of interdisciplinary prominence without the prolonged commitment that might occur by establishing a new department or institute.

Institutes

As we saw earlier, some institutions regard centers and institutes as essentially the same thing. This is the case, for instance, at the University of Alabama at Birmingham (2002), where:

A "center" or "institute" focuses and concentrates efforts, usually multidisciplinary in nature, toward meeting a specialized need or dealing with a current issue. Most centers and institutes provide an umbrella organization for efforts directed toward a common goal. Some provide a central, visible focal point to enable individuals from the state and community to take advantage of the research and service opportunities of the University.

This approach is quite different from the policy of the University System of Georgia, where institutes differ from centers primarily in terms of their organizational structure and ability to offer credit-bearing courses:

An "institute" shares the center's focus on research, provision of opportunity for interdisciplinary activity, involvement in continuing education activities, value in facilitating efforts to obtain extramural funding, and service as a link between the academic and professional communities. It is, however, a far more formalized structure and may be equivalent to an autonomous unit within the internal structure of the college or university such as a department, division, school or (university level) college. It will, unlike a "center," be involved in the offering of credit courses and may offer degree programs. (Board of Regents of the University System of Georgia, 1986)

Many schools require that an institute be self-supporting. Others allow institutes to hire their own faculties, develop their own curricula, and present their own budget proposals for possible funding. Still other universities anticipate that all centers will eventually evolve into institutes if there is a long-term reason for their existence.

Despite these possible differences, institutes share with centers the possibility to deal nimbly and creatively with topics that can benefit from the perspectives of many disciplines. In certain cases institutes may even generate revenue for a college through the consultation fees that it charges or the services that it provides. An institute may also be established through a partnership with a corporation, foundation, or agency, broadening the college's service mission and creating new possibilities for student internships. Moreover, like centers, institutes provide an excellent opportunity for enhanced development activity, attracting the support of donors and foundations that have a special interest in topics addressed by the institute.

There is a temptation to create a consortium, center, or institute for nearly any topic that happens to have the support of a small but vocal group of faculty members. Creating agreements that are little more than paper entities can, however, do serious damage to a college's credibility and end up costing resources that are more appropriately channeled elsewhere. Certainly, no consortium, center, or institute should be so dependent on the personality of a particular director that it cannot be sustainable once that director leaves. Nevertheless, a highly select number of well-designed special agreements can play a valuable role in enhancing a college's service mission, vision for the future, and access to external funding.

Resources

Dotolo, L. G., & Strandness, J. T. (Eds.). (1999). *New directions for higher education: No. 106. Best practices in higher education consortia: How institutions can work together.* San Francisco, CA: Jossey-Bass.

Florida International University. (2002). *Academic affairs policies and procedures manual, section 13: Centers, institutes, and special offices.* Retrieved July 13, 2007, from www.fiu.edu/provost/polman/sec13web.html#1320

Leverty, L. H., & Colburn, D. R. (Eds.). (2000). *New directions for higher education: No. 112. Understanding the role of public policy centers and institutes in fostering university-government partnerships.* San Francisco, CA: Jossey-Bass.

References

Board of Regents of the University System of Georgia. (1986). *Academic affairs handbook* [Section 2.15: Centers and institutes]. Retrieved July 13, 2007, from www.usg.edu/academics /handbook/section2/2.15.phtml

Commission on Colleges of the Southern Association of Colleges and Schools. (2004). *Principles of accreditation: Foundations for quality enhancement.* Decatur, GA: Author.

Commission on Colleges of the Southern Association of Colleges and Schools. (2005). *Resource manual for the principles of accreditation: Foundations for quality enhancement.* Decatur, GA: Author.

Duke University. (1997). *Minutes of the regular meeting of the academic council.* Retrieved July 13, 2007, from www.duke.edu/web/acouncil/minutes/ 1996-97/5-15-97.htm

Rowan University. (2003). *Guidelines for centers, institutes and/or special projects.* Retrieved July 13, 2007, from www.rowan.edu/provost/downloads/Centers_InstTaskForceReport_%20 Final%20514.pdf

University of Alabama at Birmingham. (2002). *Establishment of centers and institutes.* Retrieved July 13, 2007, from www.iss.uab.edu/Pol/CentersCtab.pdf

University of Oklahoma. (1997). *Consortia policy—University of Okalahoma Norman Campus.* Retrieved July 13, 2007, from http://research.ou.edu/about/Consortium_Policy.html

52

The Unionized Environment

There are two fundamental rules that deans must always remember about organized labor and its relationship to higher education. First, working with a unionized faculty and staff can simplify matters greatly. Second, working with a unionized faculty and staff can complicate matters to an almost unimaginable degree. The real difficulty arises because these two rules are both equally true *simultaneously.* In other words, there is much about the dean's relationship with the faculty and staff that becomes much clearer when one is dealing with a union. Workload considerations, salary increases, evaluation standards, and the like tend to be addressed through highly systematic and organized processes in a unionized environment. So many factors are specified by contract terms that you frequently know exactly where you stand in matters of job responsibilities, understand clearly what you can and cannot ask of those who report to you, are aware of which standards must be used in performance evaluations, and have guidance about where to go to arbitrate differences. Nevertheless, a unionized setting can also complicate a great deal about our working relationships. For instance, your ability to launch new initiatives may be severely restricted. You may not have the freedom you would like to modify workloads and free up certain individuals for tasks that you regard as important to the institution's future. You may be limited in the way in which you can reward an employee for a job particularly well done, just as you may not be free to choose the ways in which you can impose sanctions against underperformers. In addition to the challenges you will always face when terminating a tenured faculty member (see Chapter 41, "Terminating a Faculty Member"), firing an employee who is protected by a union contract can be even more complicated.

Above all, deans often discover that the unionized environment can make their relationship with faculty members adversarial—and more challenging. After all, most deans tend to view their relationship with faculty members as supervisory, but not in a traditional labor management sense, the type of relationship more commonly found in factories and large corporations. Almost all deans were themselves once faculty members and still think of themselves largely as faculty leaders. For this reason, the dichotomy of "us versus them" that can arise in unionized environments may strike deans as incompatible with the collegial, consensus-based approach of shared governance that they hope to develop. Unfortunately, other than understanding the inherent complexities of working with organized labor, there are relatively few guidelines that can make this type of employment relationship any less complicated. However, the following are suggestions that should be considered by every dean who is called on to serve in a unionized environment.

Consult with your legal affairs staff or campus attorney regularly—especially if a union is involved.

According to Kaplin and Lee (1995):

> The mix of factors involved, the importance of the policy questions, and the complexity of the law make collective bargaining a potentially troublesome area for administrators. Heavy involvement of legal counsel is clearly called for. Use of professional negotiators, or of administrators experienced in the art of negotiation, is also usually appropriate, particularly when the faculty have such professional expertise on their side of the bargaining table. (p. 169)

In other words, deans should *never* presume to engage in negotiations directly with a union unless they have the full support of legal counsel, prior experience in negotiations (at least to the point of having sat in on previous negotiations as an observer), and a clear mandate from their institutions to do so. Even beyond this, however, deans must be alert to the gray areas that may fall into the general domain of negotiation with the union or contract modification. For instance, workload changes that free a faculty member to spearhead a new initiative may be construed as improperly delegating management responsibilities to nonmanagement employees. Particularly in situations where department chairs are regarded as first-level managers or as serving "out of unit" for contract purposes, developing new assistant chairs, directors, program supervisors, or project coordinators can have unforeseen contract implications. Previous court decisions have shown that faculty members cannot be required to assume labor and management roles simultaneously. For this reason, you may have limited options if you wish to assign a faculty member a responsibility that requires supervisory or managerial responsibilities. Be certain, therefore, that you refer to your college counsel or the legal affairs office whenever you contemplate any change that would affect someone's workload.

Naturally, any action that negatively affects an employee (ranging from a mild sanction, such as a reprimand, to a severe sanction, such as termination) should also be discussed thoroughly with both an attorney and the human resources office before it is implemented. There may well be initial steps or timetables that must be followed before you can proceed with the sanction. Proper guidance will prevent you from taking a step that, at best, could embarrass you if it has to be reversed. At worst, an improperly implemented negative decision could threaten *your* position if it appears that you violated policy, acted irresponsibly, sought retribution, or violated the rights of a member of a protected class.

Remember that issues of academic freedom, while complicated at all higher education institutions, are more complex in a unionized environment.

In an excellent survey of the issue, Ronald Standler (2000) notes that the concept of academic freedom in American higher education has long consisted of two not wholly synonymous principles (see also Kaplin & Lee, 1995, pp. 299–300):

1. *Individual academic freedom* protects an individual professor.

2. *Institutional academic freedom* protects universities from interference by government, a right that applies to the community of scholars, *not* to individual faculty.

As Louis Menand (1998) has noted, these ambiguities have obfuscated the discussion of academic freedom at colleges and universities. Administrators and legislatures frequently use the term in the sense of what Standler calls "institutional academic freedom." Unions and certain professional organizations, such as the American Association of University Professors, frequently assume that the term is identical to individual academic freedom. Therein lies the problem.

Much of the case law involving this issue—see especially *Regents of the University of Michigan v. Ewing* (1985), *Edwards v. California University of Pennsylvania* (1998), and *Urofsky v. Gilmore* (2000)—has concluded that the First Amendment rights involved in academic freedom apply only to institutions, not to individuals employed by those institutions (see Rabban, 2001, pp. 16–20). Despite this development, faculty unions occasionally take on the role of defending individual academic freedom, even in instances where that right may come into direct conflict with legally established rights of institutional academic freedom. As Poskanzer (2002) notes:

> In upholding a faculty union's statutory right to consult with administrators on matters of college governance (and conversely denying parallel rights to individual faculty outside the union), the Supreme Court noted that it had "never recognized a constitutional right of faculty to participate in policymaking in academic institutions." Indeed, both line academic administrators (chairs, deans, provosts, and presidents) and nonacademic officials (vice presidents for human resources, student affairs professionals) will rightly assert that they are the ones charged with responsibility for managing the affairs of the institution and that—both by knowledge and by breadth of perspective—they are much better suited to do so than faculty (who, perhaps out of self-interest, often resist change and efforts at increased accountability).
>
> In light of such tension, the answer to the question of who benefits from academic freedom in intra-university affairs depends almost entirely on whose claim of autonomy prevails. Faculty gain stature and influence over college and university operations if their bid for independent speech and action is upheld; administrators will be the direct beneficiaries if claims of *institutional* autonomy are honored. (pp. 105–106)

Therefore, in a unionized environment even more than in other institutional settings, the dean has to differentiate the *type* of academic freedom that is under discussion. Moreover, as a middle manager, the dean should never serve as the voice of the institution on matters of individual academic freedom in a unionized environment because this right will be defined and protected almost exclusively by that individual institution's history, not, as many deans and faculty members wrongly believe, by clearly established case law.

Work to establish clear lines of communication with the union, even if you disagree with its stand on certain issues.

Conflicts between unions and administrations tend to be most severe when both sides communicate only to negotiate contracts or solve a problem. An adversarial relationship naturally arises when the bulk of the issues dealt with concern conflicting views about salary and benefits, workload, difficult evaluation matters, and termination appeals. Deans can develop a far more constructive relationship with the union on these and other issues if they meet with the union regularly even when there is *not* an obvious conflict. Allow union representatives to state their hopes and concerns. Build in an opportunity to discuss your own initiatives. As we saw earlier, you should avoid giving any impression that these discussions are either unofficial negotiation sessions or that you are improperly ceding to the union the right to make decisions that are more appropriately made at the administrative level. These conversations should be more informal, an outgrowth of what Poskanzer (2002) called "a faculty union's statutory right to consult with administrators on matters of college governance" (p. 105). By providing some regular venue for informal consultation, you will have an opportunity to demonstrate that your initiatives have significant value, that they are not merely the administration's stance during times of negotiation. Conversely, you will learn, more clearly than during contract negotiations, how problems affect your employees' quality of life and the mission of education and research that is so vital to your institution.

Unionized environments, like most aspects of higher education, can vary considerably. What is a congenial and amicable relationship at one university may become a fractious and confrontational environment at another school. Too often administrations and unions lose sight of the fact that both parties in this relationship simply want what they believe to be in the best interests of the institution and its constituents. They tend to view alternative ways of achieving similar goals with unnecessary hostility and to regard the other party's viewpoints as though they were mere bargaining chips. As a dean, you are well positioned to begin improving this situation through increased communication, genuine effort to understand different perspectives, and candid assessment of the type of change that may be possible.

Resources

Arnold, G. B. (2000). *The politics of faculty unionization: The experience of three New England universities.* Westport, CT: Bergin & Garvey.

Duryea, E. D., & Fish, R. S. (1973). *Faculty unions and collective bargaining.* San Francisco, CA: Jossey-Bass.

Hutcheson, P. A. (2000). *A professional professoriate: Unionization, bureaucratization, and the AAUP.* Nashville, TN: Vanderbilt University Press.

Johnstone, R. L. (1981). *The scope of faculty collective bargaining: An analysis of faculty union agreements at four-year institutions of higher education.* Westport, CT: Greenwood Press.

Wheelan, S. A. (2004). *Faculty groups: From frustration to collaboration.* Thousand Oaks, CA: Corwin Press.

References

Edwards v. California University of Pennsylvania, 156 F.3d 488 (3rd Cir. 1998).

Kaplin, W. A., & Lee, B. A. (1995). *The law of higher education: A comprehensive guide to legal implications of administrative decision making* (3rd ed.). San Francisco, CA: Jossey-Bass.

Menand, L. (Ed.). (1998). *The future of academic freedom.* Chicago, IL: University of Chicago Press.

Poskanzer, S. G. (2002). *Higher education law: The faculty.* Baltimore, MD: Johns Hopkins University Press.

Rabban, D. M. (2001, November–December). Academic freedom, individual or institutional? *Academe, 87*(6), 16–20.

Regents of the University of Michigan v. Ewing, 474 U.S. 214, 226 n. 12 (1985).

Standler, R. B. (2000). *Academic freedom in the USA.* Retrieved July 13, 2007, from www.rbs2.com/afree.htm

Urofsky v. Gilmore, 216 F.3d 401 (4th Cir. 2000).

53

Promoting Diversity

Deans can play a vital role in increasing their colleges' diversity at both the faculty and student levels. Although nearly every college and university has developed a plan for enhancing its diversity, these plans may be overly general and difficult to implement effectively when recruiting students or faculty members into a specific academic area. Moreover, it is important for deans to understand that, although institution-wide diversity plans are common, no two are identical. In fact, they may not even share the same philosophical basis.

For instance, if you examine the diversity plans in place across the country, you will discover at least three different philosophical principles by which institutions justify their quest for diversity and the ways in which they pursue it:

- At some institutions the need to increase diversity is tied primarily to the school's instructional mission. Because students need to succeed in a highly diverse world, we are told, it is part of the institution's pedagogical duty to expose students to that environment before they graduate.

- At other institutions diversity tends to be tied more closely to the scholarly or research mission. One of the most important aspects of higher education, it is argued, is that students are exposed to a variety of competing ideas, compelling them to work their way through different perspectives of the world and its problems. Without encountering the points of view held by individuals of different cultures, races, socioeconomic classes, genders, nationalities, and sexual orientations, the students' scholarly context—and the perspectives that faculty members and other scholars develop—is not sufficiently rich.

- Still other institutions see their commitment to diversity as arising out of their service mission. American colleges and universities have long played a role in improving their communities. One of the hallmarks of higher education, some institutions will argue, is that it not only studies but also transforms society by increasing its students' knowledge, skill levels, or worldview. By reaching out to groups that were formerly underrepresented in American higher education, colleges and universities are thus continuing their traditional roles as society's change agents.

These three bases for diversity plans in higher education often overlap. Nevertheless, even when they do, different assumptions about diversity's importance can lead institutions to fulfill their diversity goals in various ways. For instance, schools that base their commitment to diversity largely on their service missions tend to develop plans that emphasize admissions strategies or faculty and staff recruitment. Schools that tie diversity more to their pedagogical or scholarly missions may pay more attention to curricular development or faculty and student services. In the discussion that follows, we'll explore several ways that deans can help move from their institution's lofty but general goals to diversity plans that are specifically tied to their individual college's mission.

Make it a habit, when discussing diversity, to explain the reasons why this goal is important to your college. Do not make the mistake of focusing only on the techniques you will adopt for attaining diversity.

People are much more likely to pursue a goal energetically if they understand why that goal is important *to them*. For instance, few faculty members in your college are likely to devote their time to a new initiative if they don't understand the importance of the problem it is trying to address (see Chapter 6, "Launching Initiatives"). Few faculty members are going to contribute to the college's annual fund if they don't understand why participation rates are important to donors (see Chapter 18, "Donors and Potential Donors"). In the same way, you are likely to get only modest support for your diversity goals unless you explain *why* your college's diversity should be important to every student, faculty member, parent, staff member, and donor whom you serve. We saw earlier that the philosophical basis for promoting diversity may differ from institution to institution and that these rationales tend to fall into three categories. Once you yourself fully understand the reasons behind your institution's diversity plan, you'll be in a much better position to help that plan succeed. You'll be able to convince people to make the extra effort because you'll know why those efforts are important and be in a good position to explain the situation to others.

This task is not one that you can attempt once and then assume is complete. Stressing the way in which your college's mission benefits from increased diversity is something that you will need to consider every time you and others meet to plan a student recruitment strategy, develop a job description, write a search announcement, or review your curriculum. In each of these cases, there is likely to be someone present who understands that achieving diversity is important to the institution but who really hasn't internalized the benefits of this pursuit.

At times, the person will say something like, "Why can't we just try to attract the best possible people into the pool and let diversity take care of itself?" More frequently, someone will think these thoughts without expressing them. By taking the initiative and making certain that people are always aware of the institution's overall diversity plan and the plan's philosophical basis, you will be much more likely to see energetic and committed follow-through on your college's diversity efforts.

Examine your policies and procedures to overcome existing obstacles to diversity.

We saw in Chapter 32 ("Position Requests and Descriptions") that institutions may claim to be strongly committed to diversifying their faculty and staff, but they then create job advertisements that unintentionally narrow the applicant pool. They focus on areas of interest or qualifications that women or minority group members are least likely to have, request application materials that are of little value to the search committee and that discourage candidates from applying, and mistakenly believe that abrupt phrases like "AA/EEO/ADA" or "Women and minorities are encouraged to apply" will demonstrate a strong institutional dedication to diversity.

In much the same way, there may be other policies in place at your college that unintentionally undermine the diversity you are trying to create. Ask yourself the following questions about your college's policies:

- Are your class attendance policies and personal leave policies flexible enough to address the needs of students or employees who may be members of religious faiths that are not dominant at your institution?

- Does the food served in the dining hall, in the faculty club, and at major college-sponsored events take into account the dietary preferences of members of various faiths, as well as those with food allergies or dietary restrictions based on philosophical beliefs?

- Have you worked with the benefits office to ensure that employee benefits accommodate nonmainstream lifestyles and households?

- Do your employment plans include such family-friendly measures as a tenure stop-clock policy, spousal placement policy, and residence assistance plan (see Chapter 11, "Faculty")?

- Do you have a committee that regularly reviews all faculty, staff, and student policies to identify the problems any given policy might cause someone who is less than full-time?

- Do you allow flexible work hours for every position for which there is no compelling reason to require fixed hours?

- Do you review your course schedule to ensure that those who wish or need to pursue degrees at nontraditional times are able to graduate in a timely manner?

- Do you provide as much coursework as possible through alternative delivery means (such as online courses and asynchronous distance learning) so that people may attend your institution even if they have complex work schedules or alternative learning styles?

- Do you have a forgiveness policy for students whose academic work is negatively affected by a circumstance beyond their control (such as military mobilizations and family illnesses)?

Certain people in your college may be reluctant to consider revising these policies, assuming that doing so lowers standards or allows everyone to do whatever they want. Nevertheless, if you explain that diversity comes in all forms and involves respecting each person's individual needs, you can better explain how removing unnecessary obstacles can actually create a richer mix of people at your institution. After all, if we assume that everyone has the same needs, we will be more likely to recruit only students, faculty, and staff members who have the same needs and outlook that we do. If, on the other hand, we develop policies that compensate for individual differences, we develop a community that deeply respects others' contributions to our community.

Provide the necessary services that will allow all community members to achieve their maximum level of success.

Institutions tend to devote a large amount of resources to recruiting a diverse student body and applicant pool for searches. They tend to be a lot less effective in following through and addressing employees' and students' needs once those people are on campus. As a result, many of the individuals who have been recruited at such effort by the institution leave after a short time. They may experience loneliness because they feel that they simply don't fit in with the rest of the institution. They may have hoped to find accommodations for their individual learning styles or a more flexible work environment. Whatever the reason, they may sense that they were warmly recruited and welcomed by the institution, only to be deserted once they arrived.

If attrition rates are a problem at your institution—particularly if these rates are higher for faculty, minority students, or members of other protected groups—you can take steps to remedy this situation. But don't assume that you can figure out on your own what people need. Every institution is different, and the specific needs of your faculty, staff, and students may vary from what you regard as most important. One of the best ways to start addressing this situation, therefore, is to hold a series of conversations, either one on one or in small groups, to discover what needs are not currently being met or what problems have arisen. With faculty and staff members, you can probably do this best through informal conversations every few weeks, coupled with several small discussion groups built into your regular faculty and staff training program. With students, it is probably better to gather information through peer-conducted support groups or regular discussions that are part of an introduction to college, orientation, or other threshold course. Allow the issues to emerge naturally in these conversations or discussions. The person in charge of the event should ask general questions such as these: How have things been going? Is there anything that seems to be getting in the way of your satisfaction or success here? Are there any resources you wish you had access to? The answers to these questions are not likely to arise immediately. Don't be surprised if the initial answer is "Everything's fine. I don't need anything." No one, after all, wants to be perceived as weak or a failure. If you keep probing, however, you may eventually reach some problem areas. The event mediator could ask, "Do you feel as though you're fitting in? Have you found a group of friends that you meet with regularly? Do you have someone to talk to if you have a problem?" If, in response to these questions, you discover that the individual does have an unmet need, you can either help the person get in touch with appropriate resources that are already available or start planning services that could help address these unmet needs.

Be holistic in your approach to diversity.

In addition to services that your institution may not currently provide, begin to look at other aspects of the entire experience encountered by all the members of your community. Think in the broadest possible terms of those groups that you would like to attract and retain among your students, faculty, and staff. What type of diversity are you most lacking that would provide a richer experience for everyone who lives and works at your institution (e.g., gender, racial, socioeconomic, ethnic, sexual orientation, physical capability, religion, age, political views, family situation)? Then, once you have identified the groups that appear to be underrepresented in your college, ask yourself:

- How would my college's curriculum look to members of these target groups? Do we offer the sort of courses and programs that would appeal to a broad range of students, or are we unintentionally alienating some of the very groups we say we're trying to attract?

- Do our cocurricular and extracurricular activities appeal to our target audience? Do our public lectures, organizations, and institutional celebrations speak broadly to the full range of students we are trying to attract?

- Is there curriculum already in place that would attract a diverse faculty to my institution? Have I taken steps to ensure that my reward structure and recognitions encourage newer faculty members (who, because of the institution's past practices, may be significantly more diverse than the senior faculty)?

Seek to address diversity through long-term strategies as well as through short-term fixes.

Institutions sometimes lament that competition for highly qualified graduate students and faculty members from minority groups is so intense that they have difficulty making progress. Although many institutions exist in service areas where the local population is 25%–30% non-white, they discover that fewer than 5% of many disciplines' doctoral graduates each year are non-white. Rather than simply giving up when faced with odds like these, institutions sometimes seek to "grow their own." In other words, because the student body is likely to be more diverse at the undergraduate than the graduate level, they explore the possibility of granting scholarships that will bring them a diverse and talented group of faculty members or graduate students. For instance, they may seek a donor who will fund all or part of a student's graduate program elsewhere—if that student then returns to the institution as a faculty member for a specified time after graduation. Moreover, some of the postdoctoral instructors financed in this way will be so talented that they will be *highly* competitive candidates when tenure-track positions become available. (In fact, because this approach provides them with several years of guaranteed full-time experience after completing their graduate programs, they may well be highly competitive compared to other candidates.) Even those instructors whom you cannot retain (or do not wish to retain) indefinitely will increase your staff's diversity for a time, probably also increasing their dedication to your institution because of the opportunity you gave them. None of these strategies will pay off immediately, of course. Nevertheless, if you are dedicated to promoting diversity for the long term, they can be important tactics in your overall diversity plan.

Too frequently, promoting diversity at colleges and universities occurs solely in the effort to recruit rather than to retain a broader spectrum of individuals. By knowing why your institution is committed to diversity, focusing on services and other holistic approaches, and planning for the long term rather than just the immediate future, you will be far more successful than other deans in creating a truly diverse faculty and staff.

Resources

Adams, M. (Ed.). (1992). *Promoting diversity in college classrooms: Innovative responses for the curriculum, faculty, and institutions.* San Francisco, CA: Jossey-Bass.

Adams, M., Bell, L. E., & Griffin, P. (Eds.). (1997). *Teaching for diversity and social justice: A sourcebook.* New York, NY: Routledge.

Cooper, T. L. (2006). *The sista' network: African-American women faculty successfully negotiating the road to tenure.* Bolton, MA: Anker.

Flowers, L. A. (Ed.). (2004). *Diversity issues in American colleges and universities: Case studies for higher education and student affairs professionals.* Springfield, IL: Charles C. Thomas.

Goodman, D. J. (2001). *Promoting diversity and social justice: Educating people from privileged groups.* Thousand Oaks, CA: Sage.

Hale, F., Jr. (Ed.). (2003). *What makes racial diversity work in higher education: Academic leaders present successful policies and strategies.* Sterling, VA: Stylus.

Johns, A. M., & Sipp, M. K. (Eds.). (2004). *Diversity in college classrooms: Practices for today's campuses.* Ann Arbor, MI: University of Michigan Press/ESL.

Smith, D. G., Wolf, L. E., & Busenberg, B. E. (1996). *Achieving faculty diversity: Debunking the myths.* Washington, DC: Association of American Colleges and Universities.

Turner, C. S. V. (2002). *Diversifying the faculty: A guidebook for search committees.* Washington, DC: Association of American Colleges and Universities.

Watson, L. W., Terrell, M. C., Wright, D. J., & Associates. (2002). *How minority students experience college: Implications for planning and policy.* Sterling, VA: Stylus.

Wood, P. (2004). *Diversity: The invention of a concept.* San Francisco, CA: Encounter.

54

The Dean as Chief Academic Officer

Although much of the discussion in this book has assumed that the dean is reporting to a chief academic officer (an administrator who usually holds the title of *provost* or *vice president for academic affairs*), there are also many institutions where the dean is the chief academic officer. For instance, deans will often serve as chief academic officers at small or private institutions where they may be given such titles as *dean of the faculty, dean of the college,* or *academic dean.* At times in these organizations, department chairs or division directors will perform various administrative tasks on the dean's behalf; these individuals may have direct supervisory authority over the faculty members in their areas, or they may serve in a more collegial role as simply "first among equals." At times, every faculty member will report directly to the dean. Whatever structure exists, whenever a dean functions as a chief academic officer, he or she will encounter different challenges and opportunities than colleagues in institutions with more complex hierarchies.

A conflation of roles

Institutions that establish the chain of command through the department chair, dean, chief academic officer, president, and governing board achieve a certain degree of predictability because each of these positions comes with its own role and expectations:

- *The department chair:* The chair is expected to advocate for an individual discipline.

- *The dean:* The dean, on the other hand, is expected to advocate for a group of disciplines that share a common methodology, history, or pedagogical approach.

- *The chief academic officer:* This person is expected to arbitrate between these competing needs and also advocate for the academic mission of the institution as a whole.

- *The president (or chancellor):* The president (or chancellor) is expected to arbitrate between the institution's competing needs and also advocate for the institution as a whole.

- *The governing board:* This entity is expected to approve institutional policies, ratify the strategic plan, supervise the overall management of the institution, provide fiscal oversight, review essential operations, and make the final decision in certain appeal cases. Most governing boards also appoint and evaluate the president.

Whenever several of these levels are conflated, it can become much more difficult for the person placed in that combined role to meet expectations. For example, when deans also serve as their institutions' chief academic officers, they may be torn between advocating for the academic programs they supervise and protecting the fiscal integrity of the entire academic program. Combining these roles also can send mixed messages to the faculty. "Why are you refusing to fund this project?" the dean ends up being asked. "I thought you were our advocate." This situation is only exacerbated when the institution does not grant true supervisory or line authority to department chairs or division directors. In such a case, the dean may feel as though he or she has to switch roles constantly—serving at one moment as the chair of a discipline, the next moment as the dean, and the next moment as the vice president for academic affairs—and possibly pleasing no one in the process.

Deans who also serve as chief academic officers should thus make an effort to explain to others (both those to whom they report and those who report to them) the complexity that results from filling these multiple roles. They may need to say to faculty members regularly, "Of course, I'm your advocate, and I want your program to flourish. But I also know that this goal would be impossible if we end up having to make a lot of budget cuts next year because we exceeded our allocation. We could fill only two full-time positions this year, and as the college's chief academic officer, I had to make the hard decision to assign those positions to other areas. Sometimes the need to take the whole academic picture into account means that I don't have all the resources I'd like to devote to your area. But I do have a plan for achieving our goals for your discipline. Here's what I think we need to do . . ." Conversations of this sort help remind others of the difficult dual role that deans play when they also serve as vice president for academic affairs. They begin to distinguish between what one *needs* to do in arbitrating numerous competing needs and what one *plans* to do as an advocate for the discipline in question.

A conflation of decision and appeal

One other challenge that deans can face when their institutions lack multiple administrative levels is the pressure that arises when faculty members or students have limited venues of appeal. In more complex institutions many decisions are made by faculty members themselves or by department chairs. If a student or faculty member believes that a chair's decision was unfair or violated the institution's procedures, an appeal can be submitted to the dean. The dean's decision can then be appealed in turn to the provost or vice president for academic affairs. These multiple layers of appeal are valuable in terms of both principle and practicality. From the standpoint of principle, they protect the person affected by the decision from the arbitrary judgment of one individual. From the standpoint of practicality, multiple levels of appeal usually result in a more smoothly functioning institution. Why? When individuals have had their cases considered at several previous levels, they often think that the matter has been sufficiently reviewed, even if the provost, president, or board eventually denies the appeal. These multiple reviews make the appellant feel that his or her voice has been adequately heard. (There are, of course, exceptions to this principle, and that is precisely why appeals sometimes reach all the way to the institution's governing board.) Nevertheless, when one or more administrative levels are removed, the intensity of the appeals process can increase dramatically. The individual making the request may view the offices at which the decision is made and to which the decision should be appealed as identical. After all, where else is there to go to seek redress? Moreover, because several individuals have not each independently reached the same conclusion, the appellant may think that the dean's stubbornness or inability to understand the seriousness of the issue has prevented the "correct" decision from being made. The result, all too familiar to deans who also serve as chief academic officers, is that the faculty member or student simply refuses to accept the dean's decision, appeals the decision on the spot, appeals the result of the appeal, becomes increasingly adamant, and refuses to leave the office until being granted what he or she wants.

Because of this situation, deans who are also chief academic officers need to develop stellar communication, persuasion, and counseling skills. Whereas at other institutions a decision can often be justified by referring to precedent, this practice is rarely possible at schools with a flat administrative structure. The dean will immediately be challenged to justify the precedent, exhorted to decide on the basis of justice rather than history, and tested to the utmost of his or her rhetorical skills. Emotions tend to ratchet up very quickly in these situations because the individual knows that there are no other opportunities for appeal. Moreover, if there does exist another venue for appeal (such as the president and governing board), the individual may think that these levels are impossibly remote and likely to reaffirm the dean's decision. For this reason, the dean must be patient, explain the basis for the precedent, and clarify whenever possible how his or her decision is ultimately in the individual's best interests. As we have seen repeatedly, *all* deans need to have superior people skills. Nevertheless, deans at smaller institutions must have those skills perfected on the very first day on the job because of the environment in which they will be required to make and communicate their decisions.

Balancing workload

An academic administrator's workload tends to be voluminous. Serving on committees, addressing constituents' needs, answering letters and other forms of communication, attending meetings, and writing reports can be an all-consuming job. Nevertheless, when an institution has fewer administrative levels, this workload will be even higher. Rather than having a provost who serves on the president's cabinet, the dean must also fill this role. Rather than having department chairs or other directors who can handle responsibilities, the dean must take on these duties. Although logic might dictate that the larger and more complex an institution is, the heavier and more difficult the dean's workload would be, the reverse is frequently the case. Deans at small institutions are regularly pulled in several directions at once, emerging from a meeting unable to accomplish the tasks the committee has decided were essential because there is yet another meeting to attend and no one else to take on those tasks.

In addition to balancing competing demands at work, deans need to balance their professional duties with their personal lives, scholarly work, and the frequent expectation to serve in organizations, church groups, or volunteer activities. Although no one solution fits each dean's personality and individual situation, the following recommendations usually provide some relief when the pressure of responsibilities becomes too great:

- *Plan your time carefully and wisely:* Too often the activities that end up consuming our time are not those that are most productive or even the most important to our institutions. Although a carefully constructed calendar or day planner should never become your master, it can be your best asset in effectively using your time. Build in time for your own scholarship, walking around and talking to people, getting off campus occasionally, and just having some quiet time to think. Block these periods out on your calendar before other demands arise. If you don't plan time for the really important activities from the very beginning of the academic year, other responsibilities will consume your days.

- *Don't be embarrassed to ask for help if you need it:* Deans sometimes think that requesting additional staff members or delegating responsibilities to others is tantamount to admitting that they're not up to the job. These fears are almost always unfounded. Presidents expect deans to be candid about their workload and would prefer duties to be reassigned than allow important work to slip through the cracks or replace a dean who leaves the institution because of job dissatisfaction.

- *Say no (politely) when you need to:* Many deans also regard it as a matter of pride to chair every committee they are asked to serve on, agree to every speaking engagement they are invited to attend, and travel to every conference for which they are eligible. Nevertheless, taking on too many obligations increases the likelihood that few of these obligations will receive the dean's full attention. It is perfectly acceptable to decline a few responsibilities to focus more on others. Remember that, all too frequently, no one but you expects you to accept every responsibility you are offered.

- *Take real vacations:* Deans who serve on 12-month contracts earn vacation time. Use it! It's true, there is no good time for a dean to be away from campus. Even when classes are not in session, significant planning must be done. Nevertheless, it's in your institution's best interests for you to be fresh and focused when you perform your duties. So, although it may be difficult, make it a practice to take a week or two off at a time. With enough warning, the institution can plan to do what needs to be done while you are away. Moreover, be sure that it is a real vacation: Attending a conference or checking in by phone or email several times a day does not give you the leisure you need to unwind and recover all your energy. Delegate your responsibilities to others while you are away, check in (if you must do so at all) no more than once a week, and leave your laptop and wireless personal digital assistant locked in your desk.

Getting perspective

Earlier we saw that, at institutions with relatively flat administrative structures, deans may be accused of being stubborn or not really understanding an issue when they fail to grant someone's request. The other side of this coin is that the dean truly *is* being stubborn or not really understanding an issue. All of us have our blind spots, and without multiple levels in the reporting relationship both above and below us, there's no one who can keep us honest, serve as the devil's advocate when we are working our way through complex issues, or simply challenge us to see an issue in a different light. Deans who are also chief academic officers thus need to work even harder to gain perspective on issues. Unless their institution is so small that it doesn't even have department chairs, working with the council of chairs as a sort of dean's cabinet or internal advisory council can be an extremely effective way for deans to broaden their perspective on several significant issues (see Chapter 13, "Department Chairs"). Gradually changing the focus of meetings that used to be devoted to sharing information will both help manage your workload (because you may discover that there are less time-consuming ways of disseminating information than roundtable discussions) and give you access to a group of invaluable advisors. Try reducing the frequency of routine announcements, distributing a written agenda in advance, and devoting a sizable portion of the meeting to expressing views, not just information, on a topic of mutual concern. At the very least, you may gain the others' respect because you took the time to ask their opinions. Even better, you may find that issues you believed to be one sided or clear cut are actually far more complex.

Maintaining a good relationship with the president

We saw in Chapter 16 ("Upper Administrators") that all deans should interact with their presidents with candor, collegiality, and confidentiality. This principle becomes even more important when the dean is also the chief academic officer. In these situations your relationship with the president is your most critical professional relationship at the institution. A good rapport with the president can make all the difference between success and diminishing job satisfaction. For this reason, you should take steps to help build this relationship, particularly in situations where the president is off campus frequently because of development responsibilities or does not have the sort of personality that leads to warm relationships with colleagues. Set aside time for one-on-one meetings where the two of you can just get to know each other as people. Get off campus together at least once a month for a breakfast or lunch. Offer to drive when attending off-campus meetings to give yourselves time to catch up and perform an attitude check. Above all, don't use these meetings as opportunities to advance your personal agenda or make additional requests. Doing so will change the purpose of the meeting and may even make the president reluctant to experience a sequel. The chief academic officer and the president must be members of a close and harmonious team, and it may well be up to you to prepare the groundwork for this relationship to flourish.

Serving simultaneously as dean and as chief academic officer is the best possible illustration of the following essential principle:

> *Nearly every institution of higher education has the same committees. The only difference is that, at smaller schools, fewer people are available to serve on those committees. The result is that everyone ends up wearing multiple hats.*

A corollary to this principle is that many of the same tasks that, at more highly stratified institutions, would be assigned to department chairs, deans, and provosts will all fall to the chief academic officer at smaller schools. As compensation for the higher workload and stress level, the dean who also serves as chief academic officer has a greater potential for making a real difference at his or her institution and gaining experience in a wide variety of important administrative functions. Particularly if you are hoping someday to serve as the president of a college or university, this position can be an excellent training ground.

Resources

Diamond, R. M. (Ed.). (2002). *Field guide to academic leadership.* San Francisco, CA: Jossey-Bass.

Krahenbuhl, G. S. (2004). *Building the academic deanship: Strategies for success.* Westport, CT: Praeger.

Martin, J., Samels, J. E., & Associates. (1997). *First among equals: The role of the chief academic officer.* Baltimore, MD: Johns Hopkins University Press.

Wolverton, M., Gmelch, W. H., Montez, J., & Nies, C. T. (2001). *The changing nature of the academic deanship* (ASHE-ERIC Higher Education Report Vol. 28, No. 1). San Francisco, CA: Jossey-Bass.

55

A Scenario Analysis on the Dean's Unique Opportunities

Note: For a discussion of how scenario analyses are structured and suggestions on how to use this exercise most productively, see Chapter 8, "A Scenario Analysis on the Dean's Role."

Case Study

One day a delegation of students and faculty from your college comes to see you in your office. The group wishes to discuss with you both a concern that its members share and a proposal that it believes will address this concern. All the students and faculty are from the same ethnic heritage. They note that, for the past decade or so, their cultural heritage has been expanding in visibility throughout your institution's service area. Their festivals have been growing each year. Restaurants catering to this ethnic group have greatly expanded in number. Several prominent members of local and state government have shared this heritage. As a result, the delegation believes that it is time for the institution to take a more active role in studying the culture and historical contributions of this population, which, at least nationally, remains a minority. Moreover, the delegation is concerned that neither your college nor any other institution in the area has a program of studies devoted to this group's history or culture, a conference dealing with issues of special concern to it, or even a sufficient number of individual courses that address the part of the world from which the ethnic group comes. The delegation is requesting that this problem be resolved in some appropriate way, beginning in your college.

The challenge is that, due to declining enrollment and other budgetary constraints, you are under a great deal of pressure to consolidate academic programs, not to expand them. In fact, one of your president's most important strategic goals has been "Focus the number of academic programs to reduce the overall cost per student credit hour generated and improve the institution's reputation. In the future the institution will provide fewer but stronger academic programs." From previous discussions with the president, you know that your upper administration is likely to respond that the delegation's idea may be well and good but that the current fiscal situation makes a new program—or even a few additional courses—impossible at the present time. You begin to explain this situation to the delegation, but they state, politely but firmly, that they are interested in action, not the reasons why action is impossible. The group makes no threats and issues no ultimatum. In fact, the entire meeting is extremely cordial. Nevertheless, you become increasingly concerned because the group repeatedly refers to a press conference that it is planning for the following week. In response to your questions about the press conference, you are told that the delegation wishes to make its concerns known more publicly and was hoping to be able to announce the institution's response—or at least its *plans* for a response—at that event. The students and faculty members who are meeting with you merely want to show you the courtesy of letting you know their intentions so that you can be ready if you are asked questions following the press conference.

With your promise to continue discussions with this group, the meeting draws to a close, and the delegation leaves. What is the first thing you do? What do you do in the week that you have before the press conference? What do you intend to do in the longer term?

Considerations

1. What factors do you consider as you deliberate on your response?

   - Do you already have enough information that you feel compelled to launch a new initiative of some kind?

   - If you do not think you have enough information, what else do you need to know? How will you try to obtain this information?

   - If you have already decided that this situation does not call for a new initiative, what factors led you to that conclusion?

2. How might you address this opportunity through a consortium, center, or institute?

   - If you were establishing a consortium, who might you contact at other schools or organizations to begin this process?

   - If you were establishing a center or institute, how might you attempt to accomplish this goal at little or no cost because budgetary factors are a major consideration?

3. How might you address the delegation's issues by enlisting the support of . . .

   - The honors college dean (or director of the honors program)?

- The graduate dean (or director of graduate programs)?

- The chair of the faculty union?

- The officer in charge of diversity programs?

4. Assume that this scenario occurs at a smaller institution where you are both dean and chief academic officer.

   - What additional factors would you have to consider that you would not need to consider if you were dean of one of several colleges at a university?

   - Does this modification to the scenario make your ability to act easier or more complicated?

5. How might your response change if your institution's strategic plan contained one of the following statements? (As you do this exercise, assume that *only one* of the statements may be found in the strategic plan at a time. Reconsider your priorities in light of each statement.) "Reflecting its core principles as an institution of higher education, this plan commits all of us to . . ."

   - "Devote our resources to those programs in which we find common ground in our shared beliefs, avoiding fragmentation and factionalism whenever possible."

   - "Explore the rich diversity of our community and celebrate the complex variety of the human experience."

   - "Exert the utmost fiscal restraint as we examine not only the benefits but also the costs of expanding into new areas."

6. Suppose that you decide to respond to the group's request with an initiative.

   - First, if you can only do so by redirecting funds from one of your existing programs, what process do you use to identify the program that will be reduced or eliminated?

   - Second, if you can only do so by identifying a new external funding source, what steps do you take to raise these funds?

7. Are there ways in which you can begin addressing the group's concerns through a conference, symposium, festival, or lecture series without incurring the expense of a major new program? How would you launch this type of activity?

8. The delegation told you that a press conference would take place in about a week.

    •   Under what circumstances might you advise against this idea or even take steps to have it canceled?

    •   If the press conference does take place, is it better for you to attend or to stay away?

9. Is your response likely to differ if you yourself were a member of the same ethnic group as the delegation? Would this situation make you proceed more cautiously? Would it open new opportunities for you?

    •   Would your response differ if the president or the chair of the governing board were a member of this ethnic group?

    •   Would your response differ if you were aware that members of this ethnic group had been discriminated against in the past by the institution's unwritten policies?

10. Would you feel less obliged to address the delegation's concerns if you knew that another institution in your area were on the verge of announcing a major new program to study this ethnic group's history and culture?

Suggestions

Unlike several other case studies that we have considered, the current situation provides you with an opportunity, not a challenge or a problem. Although few deans enjoy meeting with a delegation that has come to lodge a serious complaint, the group described in this scenario "makes no threats and issues no ultimatum," presenting its case in a highly collegial matter. For this reason, you should approach the information that you've been given not as a situation calling for damage control but as a chance to do something truly beneficial for your institution.

Your initial impulse after the delegation left is a good indicator of how you view the situation. The first two people you should probably call are your direct supervisor and your office of institutional relations, but the *order* in which you make these calls is revealing. If your first reaction is to call the office of institutional relations, you are probably regarding this situation as a potential problem that must be handled. If you call your direct supervisor first, you are more likely to regard the situation as a possibility for constructive action. Only when you have a clearer idea of the institution's overall response would it be appropriate to bring in the media professionals. In other words, place *content* ahead of *message*.

One important way in which this case study presents you with an opportunity is the observation that no other college or university "in the area has a program of studies devoted to this group's history or culture, a conference dealing with issues of concern to it, or even a sufficient number of individual courses that address the part of the world from which the ethnic group comes." In other words, the situation allows your institution to achieve a certain degree of distinction in your service region, while at the same time meeting the needs of an increasing segment of the population. In fact, that observation gives you an important choice. You can go it alone by developing a response only at your institution, thus setting it apart from other schools in the area. Alternatively, you can pursue the possibility of a multi-institutional consortium, sharing the credit and the expenses of the initiative that you develop. Each of these alternatives has its own advantages. You will want to choose the appropriate path based on the severity of your institution's financial challenges, the likely benefit of having a unique program in this area, and the possibility of a more comprehensive solution by partnering with several schools and other organizations.

In the short term you could meet with your unit's chairs and directors, apprising them of the meeting you have had and developing a strategy for an immediate and demonstrable response. In the longer term you will want to consider a more holistic approach, perhaps modifying curriculum and programs, establishing annual or biennial events, and offering curricular and cocurricular activities. Because there are festivals already celebrating this ethnic heritage in your area, are there ways in which your college can participate in them? Because several ethnic restaurants were mentioned in the case study, could they assist you in sponsoring an event that would both serve your students and be a form of advertisement for them? Because "several prominent members of local and state government have shared this ethnic heritage," can they be contacted as possible speakers at college events or even approached as possible donors for a more significant initiative?

In most cases you will not want to take any action that can be construed as trying to silence the group, including canceling the proposed press conference. Rather, in the week before the event, hold several meetings to discuss possible approaches, gauge the upper administration's readiness to embrace this cause, and develop a few ideas about how to proceed. It is not necessary to rush the creation of an entire new curriculum or even to submit new course proposals. Instead, set some preliminary goals so that, if contacted by a reporter as a result of the press conference, you will be able to say, "In fact, we've been having several meetings about this very issue. Let me outline for you a few of the ideas that have been proposed so far . . ." Most important of all, be sure to follow up on those ideas in a timely manner. Otherwise, you will give the impression that you are the sort of administrator who makes promises when confronted by a group of concerned students and faculty members but who reverts to inactivity once the pressure is gone.

Because this case study involves limited resources, you will need to fund any initiative either through redirecting current resources or developing new ones. The large number of individuals in your area who share the ethnic heritage of concern to the delegation offers you a clear fundraising opportunity. One possibility, therefore, is to ask the upper administration not for permanent funding but for temporary seed money to get an effort under way while grants are written and donors solicited. Remind the president or provost that the indirect funding resulting from a grant could defray the institution's initial investment. Conceivably, because the initiative would be unique in your service area, your development office could even tap into a lucrative new source of community support. Alternatively, if you need to shift resources temporarily from one of your existing programs, be sure that you have a clear and compelling rationale for doing so. Be able to demonstrate that you are not simply greasing a squeaky wheel but addressing a need that is significant in your service area. Reallocate funding according to a clear and easily understood principle. Otherwise, you will find yourself confronted by another delegation—this time consisting of faculty members, students, and alumni from the reduced or eliminated programs—in the very near future.

56

Knowing When It's Time to Go

The average dean serves for about 5 years in his or her position. Like most averages, however, that figure conceals as much information as it reveals. We've all known deans who have served 15, perhaps even 20, years at a single institution; and we've all known the administrator who, for whatever reason, left the position after only a year or 2. Besides, knowing the tenure of the average dean really tells us very little about our individual situations. After all, who wants to be an *average* dean? The length of time that you'll serve in your position may depend on your own personality and goals, your institution's needs, and changes in the staff with whom and for whom you work. Nevertheless, there are several clear warning signs that suggest it may be time to explore other career opportunities. Let's look at several of them and discuss why each situation may indicate that it's time to go or, at least, that you should reflect seriously on why you should stay.

A sense of staleness

As we saw in Chapter 2 ("Preparing for the Dean's Role"), there are many *bad* reasons for becoming a dean, including a desire to increase your salary, reach a position where you can advance your own discipline to the detriment of others, and enjoy the many benefits that can accompany administrative positions. Nevertheless, we also saw that several excellent reasons to serve as dean have attracted some fine scholars into administrative roles. These individuals have a passion for making a difference in the quality of higher education, a commitment to creating an environment in which both students and faculty members can grow with intellectual freedom, a capacity to understand the needs of higher education on a large scale while still advocating for one's own college, and a delight in communicating with a broad range of constituents about the successes, challenges, and possibilities of the college's disciplines. Reflect for a moment on the reasons why you first became a dean or accepted your current position, and then ask yourself:

- Am I still motivated by the same opportunities and challenges? Do I still think that I have important contributions to make in these areas?

- If not, have I found *other* major opportunities and challenges that I can pursue in my current position? Have I found new ways in which I can make a positive difference at my institution? Are these new ways exciting to me?

- Do I find my work to be challenging enough to engage me but not so challenging as to be a continual source of frustration?

- Do I look forward to returning to my position after I've been away from work for a weekend or longer?

- Do I still see myself happily working in this position five years from now? Two years from now?

- As I think of my college's goals for the next 5 to 10 years, do I find them interesting?

- Do I regularly have new ideas to share with my college, or am I mostly implementing and building on my past ideas?

In other words, do you still find meaning and a desirable level of challenge in your current position? As Lev Vygotsky demonstrated long ago with his theory of "the zone of proximal development," most people learn best and achieve the greatest satisfaction when they are sufficiently challenged to stretch their abilities but not so overwhelmingly challenged that they feel frustrated and discouraged (see Vygotsky, 1986, pp. 187–189, 1978, pp. 86–89). If you think that there are still important contributions for you to make in your job and that the opportunity to make these contributions is both interesting and rewarding, then there may be no compelling reason at the moment for you to explore a different position. As we'll see in Chapter 57 ("Changing Institutions"), a new position that may look enticing from the outside is sometimes fraught with disappointments once you accept it. If you still enjoy the work that you're doing and have ideas to explore in the future, consider yourself fortunate. Many people in the world are not that lucky.

If, on the other hand, you find yourself getting stale—answering the same questions and attending the same meetings year after year—then it may be time to think about moving on. Lack of challenge isn't good for you because it can lead to boredom and ultimately to you resenting an institution and career you once loved. Perhaps even more important, it isn't good for your college because someone else with fresher ideas or a higher degree of energy may better help your disciplines achieve a new level of success. If that is the case, the best contribution you can make to your institution now is to seek a new assignment.

A lack of fit

At other times deans may find that it is not their position's continuing challenge that concerns them but rather their specific environment. You may not be the right person for your current job, or the job may not be the right opportunity for you. Several factors may make your current position a bad fit for you:

• *The level of the position:* Some people become dissatisfied as deans because they think that they are misplaced at this level of the institution. The position may allow them too little time for teaching or research. They may miss the close interactions with students that they had as faculty members. They may think that they were more effective representing one particular discipline as a department chair. Or the dean's position may not offer them a broad enough canvas for the initiatives they'd like to pursue, opportunities that may only be possible at the level of a provost, president, or chancellor.

• *The focus of the position:* Other people may find that they enjoy their work but that their current position seems wrong for their talents and temperaments. Perhaps they assumed a role as dean of an honors college or graduate school when their real passion was in the arts and sciences, business administration, or education. Perhaps they took a position as the head of one of these academic units at a large university when they were better suited for a role as the sole dean at a smaller liberal arts college. For whatever reason, it is not being a dean that feels wrong but being *this type* of dean.

• *The specific institution*: Other people discover that they are incompatible with their institution's goals and mission. Although this experience is most common for individuals who are hired in from other institutions, those who rise through the ranks of an institution may begin to see things from a new vantage point—and feel uncomfortable with what they observe. They may not agree with their institution's plan to balance its budget through expanded enrollments rather than through cutting faculty positions. They may be philosophically committed to community service and civic engagement when their institution's new strategic plan places a higher priority on individuals' rights. They may find that they cannot adequately express their religious beliefs at a secular institution or that their humanistic outlook seems stifled at a private institution whose outlook is growing increasingly fundamentalist. In other words, they still enjoy their jobs; they simply don't enjoy the environment in which they must perform those jobs.

- *The people:* Every job entails working with an irritating individual or two. Even the best deanship will occasionally confront you with students, faculty members, parents, other deans, or bosses who will annoy, frustrate, or offend you. The section of this book called "The Dean's Constituents" deals precisely with what to do when you find yourself in these difficult or stressful situations. Nevertheless, there are times when deans find themselves in increasingly uncomfortable situations because the *vast majority* of the people with whom and for whom they work seem to be unbearable. At times, this annoyance is a sign of burnout: One of the indications that we have been at a task too long is that we lose sympathy for the people we work with. At other times, deans may attribute their own dissatisfaction with their position or the institution as a whole to the people around them. Moreover, it is always possible that others have a different personality or outlook than the dean. All these factors may cause deans to consider whether their current positions are right for them. If you find yourself out of harmony with many people at work, keep the following essential principle in mind:

> *When everyone else seems annoying or the source of frequent problems, stop and evaluate the situation as objectively as you can. In most cases you will find that the real problem isn't them; it's you.*

When you do discover that you are the one responsible for your irritation, frustration, or dissatisfaction, you have options. You can try to correct your attitude. You can explore the root cause of your discontent. Or, if the relationship between you and your constituents has broken down irreparably, it may be time to reconsider whether you should remain in your current position.

A clear lack of support

Leadership, even leadership from the middle, requires colleagues who are willing to be led. Discovering an exciting destination for a college means little if no one wants to go there. And no matter how visionary a particular dean may be, his or her vision will remain little more than a dream unless it is shared and actively pursued by the college as a whole. For this reason, one of the factors that may cause deans to think that it is time to look elsewhere is that they lack strong support from chairs and other faculty members. A formal vote of no confidence is, of course, the most obvious expression of this lack of support. But there are plenty of other, less dramatic signals. The frequency with which one's proposals are voted down, one's recommendations ignored, or one's opinions hotly refuted in meetings are all indications that support from below is waning or absent. Make no mistake about it: There will always be opposition to a dean, and the mere occurrence of disagreement is not a guarantee that support may be in decline. To the contrary, new deans may well experience a honeymoon period during which they receive widespread endorsement for nearly every idea that they have. Nevertheless, after some time has elapsed, the vast majority of deans will begin to experience greater resistance to some of their initiatives, a greater willingness to debate publicly their new proposals' merits. This change does not necessarily indicate the absence of faculty support; to the contrary, it usually indicates that members of the college are beginning to feel more comfortable with the dean, less likely to treat the dean as a guest, and more likely to regard the dean as a member of the family. Moreover, opposition is not in itself something to be avoided. Difference of opinion can prevent colleges from making mistakes through groupthink, and a certain amount of conflict can produce tension that allows for genuine progress.

The fact is that a true loss of support simply feels different from the constructive sort of give and take that every college should have. Engaging seriously with a person's ideas implies that one is giving those ideas the respect and scrutiny that they deserve. By contrast, dismissing a dean's ideas out of hand, ridiculing them without permitting them the benefit of genuine analysis, or simply ignoring them entirely are all signs that the faculty's backing for the dean is gravely lacking. When you've redoubled your efforts to argue persuasively on behalf of a certain measure with little or no difference, you have to question your effectiveness in your position. You can tough it out, discuss the matter with your supervisor, and conclude that as long as the person who is issuing your contract is satisfied with your work, you can get through the difficulties. You can also try to learn from some of the faculty opinion leaders what accounts for the mood change and try to address those issues head-on. At times, these approaches will solve the problem; at other times, they will make little difference. When you get to the point that you cannot easily answer why you're continuing in the position, you should probably consider seeking another position.

Serious incompatibility with the president or provost

The dean's relationship with the president or provost tends to be the most critical relationship in terms of the dean's success, happiness, and job satisfaction. A dean may endure long periods without strong support from the faculty and chairs. Frequently, these rough patches occur when an institution is resisting the pain of a necessary change, but people will eventually come around. Nevertheless, without upper administration's constant support, a dean's long-term success is impossible. If you report to the president through a provost or vice president for academic affairs, either of those administrators may play the most important role in your overall success. For some deans, it is the relationship with the provost that is vital because the president tends to focus primarily on off-campus responsibilities, such as development and community relations. In other cases, however, the chief academic officer may function more as a manager of the deans, with the president providing the institution's visionary leadership and guidance for how its colleges are to develop. If the president's strategic initiatives seem to be taking the institution in a different direction from (or to be based on values wholly incompatible with) the dean's own core principles, it may be impossible for the dean to accomplish the tasks that he or she thinks are essential to the college's success. For all these reasons, this dean-and-provost or dean-and-president combination must be harmonious. Although it is certainly possible for your institution to move ahead, your individual college to flourish, and your job satisfaction to be high when there is no particular chemistry or even a meeting of the minds between you and your direct supervisor, your task will be all that much harder. You will have to make up your own mind whether the challenges you face will, in the end, be worth it.

These concerns notwithstanding, it is not at all essential—it may not even be *desirable*—for the dean and the provost or president to be in complete agreement on every issue, have the same general management style, and approach challenges in precisely the same way. One of them may be a big-picture person, and the other is best when handling details. One of them may be gregarious and a member of several different community organizations, whereas the other is most content working behind the scenes. These differences in style are less important than differences in fundamental beliefs about where the institution is going, how students and employees are to be treated, and what the dean's basic priorities for his or her college should be. The Myers-Briggs profiles of you and the provost or president need not be the same, as long as you are not in serious disagreement about the nature of your mission. In fact, a dean whose abilities and outlook *complement* those of his or her direct supervisor is likely to work with that person extremely well, as long as they share core beliefs about the purpose of higher education and their institution.

When deans discover, for any of the reasons outlined in this chapter, that it's time for them to leave their current positions, they can:

- Seek a comparable position at another institution

- Return from administration to a teaching or research position within their own college

- Move to a higher administrative role, perhaps as a provost or president

It is also possible to pursue some combination of these goals, such as returning to the faculty at another institution or making a lateral move (e.g., from dean of arts and sciences to graduate dean) within their own institution. Nevertheless, because each of these possibilities comes with its own distinctive choices and preparations, let's devote the next three chapters to an extended analysis of these alternatives.

Resources

Basalla, S., & Debelius, M. (2001). *So what are you going to do with that? A guide to career-changing for M.A.'s and Ph.D's.* New York, NY: Farrar, Straus and Giroux.

Edwards, P., & Edwards, S. (2001). *Changing directions without losing your way: Managing the six stages of change at work and in life.* New York, NY: Tarcher/Putnam.

Holloway, D., & Bishop, N. (2002). *Before you say "I quit!"* Gretna, LA: Wellness Institute.

Jansen, J. (2003). *I don't know what I want, but I know it's not this: A step-by-step guide to finding gratifying work.* New York, NY: Penguin.

Martin, R. H. (1997, May/June). A graceful (but risky) goodbye. *Trusteeship, 5*(3), 20–23.

McDaniel, T. R. (2002). A dean's demise. In T. R. McDaniel, *Dean's dialogue* (pp. 47–48). Madison, WI: Magna.

Rubin, G. N. (2003). *Quit your job and grow some hair: Know when to go, when to stay.* Manassas Park, VA: Impact.

References

Vygotsky, L. S. (1986). *Thought and language* (Rev. ed., A. Kozulin, ed.). Cambridge, MA: MIT Press.

Vygotsky, L. S. (1978). Interaction between learning and development (M. Lopez-Morillas, Trans.). In M. Cole, V. John-Steiner, S. Scribner, & E. Souberman (Eds.), *Mind in society: The development of higher psychological processes* (14th ed., pp. 79–91). Cambridge, MA: Harvard University Press.

57

Changing Institutions

Deans may decide to change institutions for any number of reasons. They may be seeking a higher administrative role than any currently available to them. They may be returning to teaching or research but do not wish to do so at the same schools where they were deans. They may wish to continue in the deanship but want to apply their skills elsewhere, perhaps because they lack the support of their faculty and chairs or perhaps because they do not have a satisfying relationship with their upper administration. Or they may wish to continue as deans but are seeking greater challenges, a different sort of deanship, or the experience of working at a different kind of institution. In this chapter we'll explore the challenges and opportunities that arise when deans hope to continue work as deans or in very similar roles at other institutions, leaving for the next two chapters the experiences likely to face those who wish to return to the faculty or seek a higher administrative role at their own or another institution.

Changing institutions can help revitalize deans who fundamentally enjoy their work but find that their current positions are getting stale or repetitive. You may (and, in fact, probably *will*) encounter many of the same challenges in your new position as in your old job. But at least the personalities involved will be new, and your ideas may not have been tried before, so they will *seem* new to your new institution. Keep in mind, however, the old adage about the grass seeming greener on the other side of the fence. It is not uncommon for deans to look with envy at other institutions where the faculty seem more harmonious, the funding more generous, and the upper administration more enlightened, only to discover the same old problems exist in an altered form at the new institution. If you have spent most or all of your professional life in the private college setting and are tempted to expand your experience by seeking a deanship at a public university (or vice versa), you should not make any binding decisions until you have come to grips with the following essential principle about changing institutions:

> *People who work at private institutions often assume that budgets are better at public institutions. People who work at public institutions often assume that budgets are better at private institutions. Both groups are wrong.*

This principle surprises many people unless they have extensive experience in these two settings. Many faculty members and administrators at private institutions assume that, if they only had access to "all that state funding," they would be far better off. At the same time, many faculty members and administrators at public institutions assume that, if they could take advantage of higher tuition rates and large endowments, they would have all the resources they need. In fact, operating budgets at public and private institutions tend to be almost identical for institutions of similar *size,* whereas salaries at public and private institutions tend to be extremely comparable for institutions of similar *prestige.* For this reason, if you want access to a higher salary and a larger operating budget, then your goal should be to apply to a larger, more prestigious institution, regardless of whether it is public or private. Before you make this choice, however, you need to understand that, if you succeed, you will be even busier than you are now, under a great deal more stress, and confronted with significantly more pressure from students, faculty, and the upper administration. In addition, many of the problems that you encounter now will be duplicated at your new institution. Nevertheless, your salary and budget are likely to increase. It's simply a matter of what is most important to you.

The reason why it is an institution's size and prestige that matter far more than its status as a public or private institution is not difficult to understand. Whereas public institutions receive state funding, they also tend to have far lower tuition rates for in-state students, qualify for fewer grants from private foundations, generally have lower contribution rates to their endowments and annual funds, and often manage endowments that are much smaller than those of similarly sized private institutions. At many public institutions the cost of each student's education can be divided into three *approximately equal* parts: that paid for by tuition and externally funded scholarships; that paid for by the state; and that paid for by all other sources, including contributions, proceeds from the institution's own foundation, and internally funded scholarships. Compare this situation to that of private institutions: They almost always charge much higher tuition and generally have larger endowments but receive little or no state money, must heavily discount the sticker price of tuition so that students can actually afford the cost of attendance, and frequently maintain a lower student-to-faculty ratio (with the result that each faculty member's salary must be supported by correspondingly fewer students). Out of all these factors, discounting tuition is usually the most costly expense at private institutions. The catalogs of private colleges may state that tuition is approaching $40,000, but few, if any, students are likely to pay full freight. A tuition discount rate of 30%–60% is not uncommon, and many scholarships offered by private colleges do not involve actual transfers of money but rather simple reductions to what the student must pay. As a result, at many private institutions the cost of each student's education may be divided into two parts: roughly 40% revenue from tuition and roughly 60% resulting from externally funded scholarships, contributions, and proceeds from the endowment. The important factor to observe is that the total return to the private institution from those two sources will be approximately equal to what a public institution of comparable size and prestige receives from all three of its sources.

The real difference occurs, therefore, when one institution is larger or more distinguished than another. A larger institution is more likely to have a higher student-to-faculty ratio. Because the total revenue available to the institution will be very similar regardless of whether the school is public or private, if you increase the number of students who are enrolled in each course, you can increase the size of the operating budget used to support that course. Similarly, if you increase the number of students per faculty member at the institution, you can increase the overall budget that is available for salaries. Likewise, if you attract students to your institution because of its prestige and desirability, you will not need to discount tuition as heavily at a private institution or offer as many internally funded scholarships at a public institution. In either case you will have more money available for operating budgets and salaries.

Learn all you can about a new institution before committing to a job.

As a result of the connection between the type of institution and its financial resources, deans should research a new institution carefully before accepting any offer. Among the questions that you should always raise before changing institutions are those that deal with:

- *The nature of the position:* As we have seen repeatedly, the responsibilities that fall under the dean at one school may be quite different from those performed by the dean at another. If you are used to a great deal of independence in your current job, you may be frustrated working at an institution where the dean functions more as a manager, implementing policies developed by the upper administration rather than actively participating in the formulation of those policies. Also, the very area in which you have the greatest strength, such as program review or faculty development, may be handled at an entirely different level of your new institution.

- *The flexibility of the budget:* Deans are frequently in charge of fairly large budgets, but they may actually control extremely small budgets. The reason for this paradox is that 95% of most academic budgets tends to be devoted to personnel costs. At institutions where a large portion of the faculty is tenured—and where an even greater portion of all employees are in stable positions (because they are either on tenure track or in secure staff positions)—the dean may have very little flexibility in how this budget can be used. For this reason, you will want to find out the size of the dean's operating and discretionary budgets at the school you are considering; compare these figures not only to the size of your current budgets but also to those at institutions of a similar size and mission. Your key question, then, should be this: If an opportunity or problem arises, how much budgetary flexibility will I have to address it?

- *The interaction with other administrators:* Your relationship with your new colleagues will play a major role in your job satisfaction. As we saw in Chapter 56 ("Knowing When It's Time to Go"), your ability to develop a good working relationship with your president or provost will be critical for your college's success and for your ultimate success in your new position. But the way in which you will interact with your department chairs and fellow deans will also factor into your effectiveness in your new position. See whether you can determine why the deanship you are seeking is currently available. If it has been vacated for any other reason than retirement or the previous dean's acceptance of a highly desirable position, ask a few questions about the dynamics that existed between the dean and others at the institution. You may be inheriting a situation that is more complicated than it appears initially.

Be prepared to learn a great deal in your new position.

Although you have already served as a dean and know much about college administration, you should never assume that you have all the answers to administrative questions. Matters at your new institution will involve a completely different institutional history and new personalities that may make an approach that worked admirably in one environment less successful in another. For this reason, you should arrive at your new job with a readiness to appreciate what makes this deanship both similar to, and different from, your former position and keep the following essential principle firmly in mind:

As much as possible, never begin sentences with the expression "back at my old institution." Eliminate this phrase completely from your vocabulary.

In your new environment there will be a great temptation to relate many experiences back to your previous situation. You will be particularly tempted to do so if your new deanship is only the second or third institution at which you worked. All of us become familiar with a certain way of addressing issues, implementing policies, and making decisions, and we use that experience to guide us in new situations. Effective deans learn, however, that there are numerous "right" ways to do things, any one of which may be more effective or more appropriate at one institution than another. Just as we expect our students to develop skills at coping effectively with an unfamiliar environment, to expand their horizons by encountering different ways of thinking, and to question their own assumptions, we must learn to do the same as administrators. Feel free to ask, "Why do we do such-and-such the way that we do?" but always be willing to learn from the answer. Under no circumstances should you resort to nostalgic recollections of "Well, when I was at Wistful Memories State . . ." For the first six months of your new position, people will probably grudgingly accept a *few* backward glances. But as you begin to approach a full year in your new position, these statements will increasingly backfire. At best, people will assume that you have no fresh ideas. At worst, people will conclude that you are contrasting your former institution's expertise with their own regrettable incompetence. Deans can *never* afford to give the impression that everyone at their new school was inept until they came along, much less that they have arrived to "save" the college. In fact, you should go out of your way to speak of how you are building on the strong foundation that you discovered when you arrived. Even if you were brought to the institution to solve some serious problems, remember that the college would not have lasted as long as it has if the people there were doing everything wrong. Lavish praise widely. Be particularly generous in extending praise to your predecessor and long-term faculty members. Discover procedures to admire. Replace the phrase "Back at . . ." with "One more reason why I'm glad I'm here is . . ." Most of all, be willing to learn as much as you can from your new deanship—that is one of the most important reasons why you took the job.

Finally, keep in mind the lesson that we learned in Chapter 6 ("Launching Initiatives"): Few, if any, institutions are ever ready for as much substantive change as faculty members may say they want. During your interviews for your new position, you may have been told repeatedly, "We need some new ideas. We need to change the way things work around here. We want you to be bold, to take some risks." Because you have already been a dean elsewhere, you may even have been preferred over other candidates precisely because you have the type of experience that can take the college in a new direction. Nevertheless, be very careful about regarding any of these statements as a clear mandate for radical change. Learn how the institution and the college work before you begin changing things. Colleges are like ecosystems: Introducing significant change into an environment can harm the delicate balance that allows the system to survive. After all, you can't fill one pond without draining another. Just as in the wild, the law of unintended consequences applies when you introduce something new to your college's environment (see Chapter 6, "Launching Initiatives"). Certainly, you will want to consider some necessary improvements and to make a positive difference in your new position. You will only want to embark on a dramatically new direction, however, when you truly understand how the local environment works. For this reason—between proceeding too cautiously or forging ahead too recklessly—caution is always less destructive unless the college is so dysfunctional or in danger of financial ruin that immediate, substantive change is imperative. These situations are quite rare.

When you move from one institution to another, you'll find that some things are both stranger and more familiar than you had anticipated. Problems that you thought were unique to your former institution have a tendency to arise at the new institution as well. Procedures that you had assumed were standard in academia turn out to be quite different at your new school. Transfer your decanal skills— your ability to identify the causes of problems, your communication skills, your critical judgment—to your new job, and leave behind "The way we did things back at my former institution . . ." After all, you left there for a reason.

58

Returning to the Faculty

After spending some time in an administrative role, many deans either choose or are asked to return to the faculty. If the choice is made by the deans themselves, it may be that they miss making a direct contribution to teaching and research or that decanal work no longer holds as much interest for them. Moreover, an increasingly common option for deans is to return to the classroom for a year or two before retirement, rounding out their academic careers by rediscovering what had brought them into the profession in the first place. If you are considering this option, you will need to explore your institution's policies on your right to choose to return to the faculty. Most schools are quite flexible in allowing the deans themselves or the upper administration to decide that it is appropriate for deans to return to a faculty role. The assumption in these cases is that the institution will not be well served by an administrator who is either no longer happy in his or her position or not demonstrating the desired level of success. Making it as easy as possible for someone to return to teaching, research, and service thus serves everyone's best interests in the long run. Nevertheless, not every institution is flexible in allowing administrators to initiate this move whenever they wish. Unions may create impenetrable boundaries between management and labor, or the institution may allow deans to return to the faculty only when positions are available. The latter situation is the case at Amarillo College (2006):

> A full-time administrator who does not have tenure at the College but desires a faculty appointment shall be given preference for any vacant position for which he or she is qualified and is recommended by his or her administrative supervisor. . . . Tenured faculty who accept an administrative position shall retain their tenured status in the area (discipline or program) in which they were tenured. However, their return to the tenure area will be subject to need (determined by the administration) and availability of funds. In no case shall another tenured faculty [member] in the same area be released to accommodate this move, even though such person was tenured last. However, a probationary or temporary appointed faculty [member] may be

released if necessary to accommodate the transfer. If all faculty in the area are tenured and there is no need for an additional person, then the administrator has no recourse except to be retained in the administrative position or be released from employment at the discretion of his/her administrative supervisor. Any faculty member who accepts an administrative position prior to the receipt of tenure forfeits any progress made toward tenure.

Moreover, although returning to the faculty is an attractive option for many deans, it can be a difficult task to accomplish without some advance preparation. For this reason, it is necessary for deans who are contemplating such a move to consider several factors before they make their decision and to prepare appropriately if they decide to pursue this option.

Consider very carefully what it would be like to no longer be in charge.

Everyone reacts differently to the reality of no longer being the boss. To some, the transition is quite easy; they can yield authority to others without a qualm, immediately settling back into a role that frees them from the burdens of leadership. To many others, however, the transition is more difficult, perhaps even *far* more difficult than they anticipated. They are used to being asked for their opinion on a variety of issues and to having that opinion matter to many people. They miss being introduced whenever dignitaries arrive on campus. They have come to value knowing about important matters before everyone else, being able to make decisions independently, and having the authority to solve many kinds of problems. For these deans, giving up the job responsibilities that they long took for granted, moving to a smaller office, losing the perquisites of their position, and no longer being consulted about important issues turn out to be a greater sacrifice than they envisioned.

In addition to your own feelings on this matter, you will need to take into account how other faculty members will perceive you when you return to their ranks. Ask yourself the following questions:

- *What sort of relationship do you currently have with the faculty members in the discipline where you will be working?* Discovering that you have no relationship with your future colleagues should be just as much of a warning sign as finding that you have a poor one. If you think that you have not developed a good rapport with members of you future department, you may end up being resented as a person who has not paid your dues or who assumes that you can walk into the department and take whatever you want. You will need to build some bridges before you can smoothly rejoin the faculty in this case.

- *Have you regularly attended departmental meetings to become apprised of issues that are of recent concern to the department?* As the dean, it may have been awkward or impossible for you to attend departmental meetings of your academic discipline. You will probably want to remedy this situation once the announcement is made that you are returning to the faculty. Make it clear that your reason for attending these meetings is not in any official decanal capacity, but rather to learn as much as you can about topics of current concern to your discipline and to ease your transition back to the faculty ranks.

- *When you return to the department, are you likely to be perceived as being given advantages that you didn't earn?* In other words, if your teaching schedule is lighter or composed solely of desirable courses, your research space larger than that of your colleagues, or your on-campus duties arranged for your own convenience, members of your department may resent you. As you return to the faculty, be sure to accept the whole faculty experience, including inconvenient class times, introductory courses, committee assignments, and cramped quarters. If you don't do your part, rejoining your discipline will more likely be an uncomfortable experience. You will also not have a genuine faculty experience, increasing the likelihood that it will be a long time before you are regarded as a real colleague. Don't be surprised, too, if there is a question about where your real loyalties lie: with the department or with the administration. It may be quite some time before this doubt subsides.

Remember that most deans require some time to prepare for resuming their roles as faculty members.

Unless you have served as dean only for a year or two, you will discover that you will need a good deal of preparation before returning to a faculty role. Most deans either do not teach at all or teach at most one course per semester or year. As a result, new scholarly developments will have to be reflected in many of the courses that the dean will teach. There may also be new elements of pedagogical technology that the dean may not have used firsthand and that will require some time to master. It is also quite likely that, during their tenure as deans, most administrators have not pursued an active scholarly agenda in their discipline. They may have published works on higher education administration, but deans' time commitments make it extremely difficult to continue research in their academic field. Reestablishing an active program of research may also take a long time and careful preparation.

For all these reasons, deans should request from the upper administration a sufficient time to retool for their return to a faculty role. A semester- or yearlong sabbatical or educational leave can be extremely important for making this transition effectively, particularly if the dean has been out of full-time teaching and research for five or more years. These periods of retraining are valuable for the deans themselves, but they can also be important for the institution. They allow students and faculty members a break between seeing the same person as the dean and as a faculty member. They provide an opportunity for the new or interim dean to establish his or her own identity in the college without the daily presence of the former dean to complicate everyone's impression of who's really in charge. This period of retooling can actually benefit the new dean as well because, when the former dean is less visible for a semester or so, everyone (*including* the new dean) will be less likely to ask that person how this or that policy is implemented. The new dean thus has both the opportunity and the necessity to begin making his or her own decisions and helping the college move in a new direction.

The following are a few guidelines to keep in mind if you believe you may return to a faculty role at the conclusion of your deanship:

- *If you are not thinking of returning to the faculty immediately, begin laying the groundwork for your eventual return through incremental measures:* Your transition from administration back to the faculty will be easier if you begin your return to teaching and research gradually. Certainly, most deans' workload makes this added effort difficult, but the sacrifice will be worthwhile in the end. If you have not taught for several years, begin discussing with the department chair of your discipline whether there is a teaching assignment that could serve both the department's needs and your own. For instance, an evening course or a section that meets very early in the morning may be an unpopular time for most faculty members, but it could fit your schedule far more easily than a course that meets midday. Similarly, a survey course may not be many faculty members' first choice; nevertheless, teaching at the introductory level may require the least amount of preparation from you. In the area of scholarship, too, you might begin to ease back into a more challenging research agenda by simply attending a conference in your discipline without making a presentation yourself or by offering to chair a session or serve as a discussant. Volunteering to review books for a journal can reacquaint you with recent developments in your discipline while at the same time give you a short, easily managed opportunity for publication. Finally, making a presentation or publishing an article on pedagogical or administrative issues in your field of study can help you take advantage of your expertise both as a dean and as an academic with a specific disciplinary focus.

- *Try to negotiate a period of educational leave or retraining into your contract:* Because of the advantages that will result from your being fully prepared to resume your role in teaching, scholarship, and service, many institutions will grant you a formal period of paid leave during which you can better prepare for your new duties. At times, there will even be formal policies that outline this possibility. For instance, the University of North Texas's "Policy on Tenured Administrators Returning to Full-Time Academic Status" (2002) states: "Any development leaves granted by the University to an administrator immediately prior to his or her return to full-time faculty status shall be at the determination of the President and at the salary level as determined [by institutional policy] and in accordance with Section 51.105 of the Texas Education Code." Even at institutions without formal policies, however, it is frequently possible to negotiate either an educational leave or a sabbatical, particularly if you have served your college well for an extended period as dean.

- *If a developmental leave is not possible, explore other ways in which you can effect a more gradual reentry into your faculty role:* At some institutions you will not be able to receive a leave before rejoining the faculty because of restrictions on the availability of sabbaticals to administrators or because of budgetary limitations. In these cases it may be possible for you to ease back into your faculty role by adjusting your schedule and load for the first year or two. A reduced teaching assignment, a larger number of introductory courses (which may reduce your preparation time), multiple sections of the same course (which will reduce your number of weekly preparations), adjustments to your service obligations, and the like will help provide you with the time you will need to reestablish a full research agenda, update course materials, and accomplish other tasks required to be a successful faculty member. Just remember that these special favors could well be resented by those peers who have to maintain full teaching loads with multiple preparations while still remaining active in scholarship and service.

Never lose sight of the fact that, once you return to the faculty, the new dean is now *your* dean.

It can be extremely difficult to accept seeing a different person in a role that was once yours, particularly when you see that person making ill-advised decisions, allowing crucial tasks to go undone, or charting a course that you do not regard as in the college's best interests. It is important for you to remember—as challenging as this can be—that you must give your successor the freedom that he or she will need in this position, the same freedom that you once hoped to have. Avoid the temptation to second-guess the new dean. Everyone has a unique style of leadership, and what the new dean is attempting may not have worked for you but may well work under new leadership. People may frequently ask your opinion of decisions that the new dean has made, presentations that the new dean has given, or the new dean's general performance. Being less than supportive benefits no one. Criticizing the new dean can undermine his or her chances for success and ultimately make you seem petty or bitter. Your status as a former dean does not entitle you to any special privileges with regard to the position you once held. Your role is now the same as any other faculty member, except that you have an obligation to be generous to someone who is attempting to do a job you know to be tough. Even if all the other faculty members disparage the new dean, you will need to temper your own remarks. A statement that may be innocuous coming from another faculty member could easily seem mean spirited and uncalled for if it comes from you.

You should also be highly reluctant to serve on the college's advisory board for several years after you leave the deanship. Placing yourself in an advisory role to your successor creates an awkward position for that person and encourages others to continue seeing you as the dean, with the new dean merely filling in for you temporarily. A clean break from your former administrative role is desirable and will give you the time you will need to refocus your energies on your faculty responsibilities.

Some deans even find it preferable to change institutions when resuming faculty roles. At an entirely different school, they are less likely to see themselves or to be seen by others as the dean. They have an opportunity to create a new identity for the next phase of their careers among new colleagues. In fact, leaving a deanship for a position as a distinguished professor or eminent scholar of one's discipline can provide comparable visibility with an entirely new level of opportunity and challenges.

Deans frequently believe that a transition back to a faculty role will be easy for them because they were once highly successful as faculty members and because they have spent a number of years assisting faculty members' own development. Nevertheless, in the years spent away from full-time teaching and research, the students have changed, classroom technology has changed, and the disciplines have changed. Preparing to return to the faculty is just as essential as preparing for the dean's role, and it must be approached with a similar amount of care and prior thought. Returning to the faculty is a desirable option for many deans, but those deans need to be ready both for their new tasks and for how they will feel after returning to a role they once left behind.

References

Amarillo College. (2006) *Administrators returning to/or seeking faculty appts.* Retrieved July 13, 2007, from www.actx.edu/president/index.php?module=article&view=92&page_num=5

University of North Texas. (2002). *Policy on tenured administrators returning to full-time academic status.* Retrieved July 13, 2007, from www.unt.edu/policy/UNT_Policy/volume3/15_1_10.html

59

Planning for a Higher Administrative Role

After serving successfully as academic leaders, it is not uncommon for many deans to wonder whether they may be suited for a higher administrative role. Particularly for deans who have moved up through the administrative ranks— first as a department chair or president of the faculty senate, next as an assistant or associate dean, and finally as dean of a college or special program—continuing this progression to a term as a vice president, provost, or president may seem logical, possibly even inevitable. Nevertheless, the very skills that made you most effective in one role—fierce advocacy for your area, a distinguished reputation as a scholar, or a tendency to view a university's academic mission as its essential function—may be impediments to advancing to a new role. Even the sphere in which you attained your success may work against you. For instance, you may have established such a reputation as the dean that others have a hard time imagining you in any other capacity. So, if you are considering whether the challenges of upper administration might be an appropriate next step, what issues do you need to consider and preparations do you need to make?

Recognize that not all upper administrative roles are alike.

Being a provost or vice president for academic affairs is not the same as being a dean writ large. Similarly, being a president is not the same as being a provost at a higher level. In fact, transitioning from the deanship to one of these two administrative levels is very different from transitioning from a department chair to dean. Moreover, if your ultimate goal is to serve as the president of a university, your best choice might be *not* to seek a position as vice president for academic affairs; taking a position as chief academic officer can, in certain circumstances, actually hurt your chances of being offered a presidency, as we shall see. For this reason, you need to ask yourself:

- What do I see as my long-range administrative career path?

- Why do I believe that that particular path is right for me?

- What additional skills and experiences do I need to acquire *now* to be prepared for where I eventually want to be?

At an increasing number of institutions, the provost or vice president for academic affairs fills a position that looks inward to the institution. The vice president for academic affairs is the person who is responsible for making sure that the institution's academic programs function effectively, that the institution is providing a superb curriculum, and that faculty members are being hired and developed in fulfillment of the institution's instructional, scholarly, and service goals. To be sure, the term *provost* is often used as a synonym for *vice president for academic affairs*. Nevertheless, the provost should be the administrator to whom all the institution's vice presidents report for the smooth internal operation of the college or university. The provost is, in other words, the chief executive officer for the day-to-day management of the campus; the president or chancellor is the chief executive officer for external affairs. In certain situations the provost and vice president for academic affairs may even be different individuals. When this is the case, the provost serves as "first among equals" for the other vice presidents, and the vice president for academic affairs supervises the institution's instructional and scholarly missions.

On the other hand, the president of an institution more frequently has an external role, looking outward from the institution toward the community. The president thus serves as the institution's chief fundraiser, liaison with the governing board or state legislator, and representative of the institution to service organizations, including the chamber of commerce and other community bodies. For this reason, moving from a dean's role, which usually has both an internal and an external function at an institution, to serve as a provost can actually deprive you of an area of experience that's necessary to become a college president. It is simply no longer the case that the vast majority of presidents were once provosts or vice presidents of academic affairs who rose through the faculty's ranks to lead an entire institution. Particularly at private colleges and universities, only about a fifth of the presidents who are hired each year come to that position directly from service as a provost or vice president for academic affairs. The majority of private college presidents have immediate prior experience in development, advancement, or public life outside academia. Even at state institutions where it is more common for presidents to have served recently as a provost or vice president for academic affairs, the number of individuals who rise to head institutions from fundraising backgrounds, alumni affairs, or political appointments is substantial.

For this reason, you need to consider carefully where ultimately you want to go in higher education. If service as a president interests you, you should at least consider moving from your deanship into one of the following, rather than seeking a position as a chief academic officer:

- *A larger and more challenging deanship:* Because deans often have stronger records raising funds and winning grants than do vice presidents for academic affairs, your next move might be to serve as dean of a very large college, perhaps as large as an institution where you would eventually like to be president. In this role you can point to your advancement successes, document that you have supervised a large number of people, and develop a strategic plan for your college that will prepare you for many of your future responsibilities as president.

- *President of a small college:* Any executive role, even one at an institution far smaller than you may wish to lead someday, can better prepare you for further executive roles than another stint as middle management. In fact, you may find it easier to move from serving as dean of a college to serving as president of a college than to move from a provost position to any sort of executive role. Leading a small college or one campus of a multicampus university will give you opportunities to develop leadership skills in such areas as athletics, student life, housing, and auxiliary services, which would unlikely report to you in academic affairs.

- *A nonacademic vice presidency:* You can also develop some breadth in your administrative portfolio if you seek a different sort of vice presidency, such as a position as vice president for development, advancement, or alumni relations. After all, you've already proved your academic leadership during your tenure as dean. By gaining experience more broadly across the institution, you can both improve your understanding of how other units of the university function and accumulate a portfolio of successes that will serve you well in your applications for presidencies.

There are also many good reasons for seeking a position as a provost or vice president for academic affairs. You may have found that you receive your greatest satisfaction from dealing with matters of curriculum, program development and review, faculty hiring and evaluation, and a solid academic program. You may have a personality that best suits you for making meetings more productive and championing causes within an institutional setting rather than across the full range of external constituents. Or you may have other, more personal reasons for wanting to seek a provost's position, such as the fact that provosts frequently do not have to be on duty 24/7 in the way that presidents almost always are. The most important thing for you to realize is that you don't *need* to seek a position as chief academic officer if your ultimate goal is a presidency. In fact, there are other positions that can help you achieve that goal much more efficiently.

Once you have determined your long-term administrative goals, begin seeking experiences that will get you nearer to those goals.

If you have decided to seek a presidency, the single most critical area of experience to have is development. Look for opportunities that will help you secure multimillion-dollar gifts from private individuals and grants from foundations. As you pursue a presidency, you will receive questions about your single biggest "ask," whether you were successful in obtaining that gift, and your role in cultivating that gift. If you cannot document several substantial gifts that resulted either in new facilities or in major increases in support for the endowment or foundation, you will have a far more difficult time making a positive impression on presidential search committees. Take advantage, therefore, of every fundraising opportunity you can. Participate in training workshops offered by your institution's development office. Explore the possibility of attending national or regional workshops on fundraising for deans (see Chapter 18, "Donors and Potential Donors," and Chapter 39, "Leadership in Development and Increasing Revenue"). See whether you can be assigned, through the development office, your own portfolio of prospects to cultivate. These efforts will benefit your college by increasing revenue for its academic programs' many needs; they will also have the long-term effect of improving your résumé and making it seem more presidential.

In addition to fundraising, however, you will also want to gain other types of institution-wide experience. These other areas include:

- *Athletics:* As a president, you will be expected to know something about the business of athletics. For this reason, offer to serve as a representative to the athletics committee, as an institutional representative to the National Collegiate Athletic Association (or your institution's athletic association), or on a search committee for the next athletic director or major coach.

- *Alumni relations:* As a president, you will have to represent the institution at numerous alumni gatherings and before other groups. Start now by offering to speak at regional or national meetings of your institution's alumni association, initiating or revitalizing an affinity group for your college within your institution's alumni association, and serving as an institutional representative on committees involved in homecoming and other alumni activities.

- *Physical plant and business operations:* As a president, you will need to know how to preserve an institution's fiscal health and maintain a complex physical plant. If you have not been involved in developing a new facility at your college, offer to serve as a member of a planning committee for a structure in another college or area of the university. Because you will need to make the case that you have solid fiscal experience, be sure that you can document sound budgetary management for your own unit. Be prepared to describe the course of action you took if any departments under you faced serious financial challenges or mismanagement.

- *Cocurricular activities:* As a president, you will be responsible for student life, housing, judicial affairs, study abroad opportunities, service-learning, and internships. Explore ways of familiarizing yourself with each of these. Participate in search committees in these areas to learn about the issues that professionals elsewhere in the university must face and the types of training that helps them succeed. If you do not have a strong student affairs background, for instance, offer to serve on an appeals committee for a judicial offense, an exemption to the residency requirement, or a violation of the honor code.

In a similar way, if you have decided to seek a position as a vice president for academic affairs or provost, you will want to begin accumulating the types of experience that you will need to succeed at that level of the institution:

- *Broad academic experience:* As a chief academic officer, you will be asked how you have demonstrated support and advocacy for academic areas beyond your own field of specialty. Serving on an institution-wide curricular committee, establishing grant opportunities that transcend your college's own disciplines, chairing search committees for deans of other colleges, and adjusting your course offerings to provide more service courses for other units will all help you make a more compelling case.

- *Tenure and promotion issues:* As a provost or vice president for academic affairs, you will need to understand some of the challenges faced by individuals seeking tenure and promotion in disciplines outside your area. Volunteering for a university-wide tenure and promotion committee or agreeing to serve on an appeals committee at the institutional level can provide an excellent background in the complexity of these larger institutional issues.

- *Post-tenure review:* As a dean, you have probably reviewed several tenured faculty members in your area, providing them with guidance when it was needed and praise when it was warranted. For the next level of academic administration, you will need experience in how these decisions are made in disciplines other than your own. Service on an institution-wide post-tenure review committee (or even a committee that examines the adequacy of existing post-tenure review procedures) can provide a wealth of information that will broaden your perspective.

Investigate opportunities for networking and advanced administrative training beyond your campus.

The American Council on Education (ACE) sponsors several important training activities that can help you decide on the appropriate next steps in your administrative career. These programs change periodically; the best way of obtaining up-to-date information is by visiting the ACE web site on leadership programs (www.acenet.edu/Content/NavigationMenu/ProgramsServices/Leadership /Leadership_ACE.htm). At the present time the programs sponsored by ACE that may interest you are:

- *The ACE Fellows Program:* Founded in 1965, the ACE Fellows Program allows administrators to spend a significant period of time on another campus, working directly with a president and other important mentors. In addition to the practical information that the fellows gain through workshops and discussions, the experience also gives them a national network of individuals to whom they can turn for advice, career support, and information.

- *Advancing to the Presidency: A Workshop for Vice Presidents:* A more condensed experience than the fellows program, this multiday workshop exposes those who are considering an academic presidency to the issues involved in upper level university administration, the techniques for searching for a presidency, and a constructive critique of one's application materials and interviewing style.

- *Institute for New Chief Academic Officers:* In this workshop a group of approximately 35 chief academic officers (all in their first three years in the position) meet three times over the course of a single academic year to learn about leadership issues facing vice presidents for academic affairs, the role of their units in strategic planning, and budgetary challenges that confront chief academic officers.

In addition, in Chapter 2 ("Preparing for the Dean's Role"), we saw the usefulness of volunteering for an accreditation review committee. If you have not worked in this capacity for some time, serving as a member of an on-site or off-site accreditation review board is an excellent way to gain some quick insight into different institutions' approaches to solving various academic problems. At the same time that you perform a valuable service, you'll also expand your own knowledge of how budgets are prepared, curricular proposals are reviewed, student problems are addressed, and strategic initiatives are selected.

No single administrative path is right for everyone. You should never feel pressured by others—or even by yourself—to seek a higher administrative role simply because it is the logical next step. Many highly effective deans have made very poor provosts and presidents largely because different qualities and skills are required in these positions. Seek out opportunities where you can get to know several presidents and chief academic officers. See whether they are the type of person you would like to be. Do they lead lives that offer the challenges and opportunities that would compel you to go into work every morning? Just as only the worst deans seek their positions because of salary and privileges, so is the case with presidents and provosts. Prepare for a higher administrative role if that kind of position seems to be your calling. If it is not, remember one final essential principle:

> *It is far better to be an effective dean than to be a frustrated provost or president.*

There are many administrators who fail to heed this advice. Never aspire to a different administrative role without reflecting on what you want and what you are best suited to do.

Resources

Bornstein, R. (2003). *Legitimacy in the academic presidency.* Westport, CT: Praeger.

Ferren, A. S., & Stanton, W. W. (2004). *Leadership through collaboration: The role of the chief academic officer.* Westport, CT: Praeger.

Kouzes, J. M., & Posner, B. Z. (2003). *Jossey-Bass academic administrator's guide to exemplary leadership.* San Francisco, CA: Jossey-Bass.

Martin, J., Samels, J. E., & Associates. (1997). *First among equals: The role of the chief academic officer.* Baltimore, MD: Johns Hopkins University Press.

Martin, J., Samels, J. E., & Associates. (2004). *Presidential transition in higher education: Managing leadership change.* Baltimore, MD: Johns Hopkins University Press.

Report of the Commission on the Academic Presidency. (1996). *Renewing the academic presidency: Stronger leadership for tougher times.* Washington, DC: Association of Governing Boards of Universities and Colleges.

60

A Scenario Analysis on the Dean's Next Step

Note: For a discussion of how scenario analyses are structured and suggestions on how to use this exercise most productively, see Chapter 8, "A Scenario Analysis on the Dean's Role."

Case Study

You are now serving in your ninth year as dean of one of seven colleges at a large university. For about the first five or six years in your position, things seemed to be going extremely well. You liked your work. You felt that you were accomplishing many of the goals you had set out for your college. You enjoyed your faculty colleagues and had a good collaborative relationship with your fellow deans. Unfortunately, beginning in your seventh year as dean, you began feeling decidedly less satisfied. It's been harder to come up with new ideas. A new president has arrived at the institution, and you just don't seem to have the affinity you had with the president who hired you. Worst of all, you are faced with a faculty situation that drains all your time and energy. The details of this most pressing problem are as follows.

Late in your sixth year as dean, your college experienced a very difficult tenure review that led to appeals at each level of your institution and finally resulted in a lawsuit. The institution's decision not to tenure the professor was upheld, the lawsuit was dismissed by the courts, and the faculty member has now been gone from the institution for quite some time, but you still feel that this incident caused a significant change in mood at your institution. Four of your tenured senior faculty members have become increasingly hostile toward you. Several of your proposals were voted down when considered by your full faculty, with the four ringleaders heading the opposition. You have tried meeting individually with these faculty members, but to no avail. They appear to have concluded that you are the enemy, and they are stirring up as much trouble for you in the college as they can. You have come to think of these faculty members as the Gang of Four.

What has you most concerned now is that several key items will be up for discussion by your college in the near future. Your institution is about to enter a two-year cycle for reaccreditation. It is time for the strategic plan to be updated. Several more difficult tenure cases are on the horizon. The deteriorating relationship that you have with the Gang of Four leaves you concerned about these pending issues. Moreover, after years of strong evaluations from your faculty, the problems that you have been facing seem to be taking their toll. Your evaluation scores slipped this year from among the best of the deans to near the bottom. In written comments several faculty members described you as "Increasingly out of touch with faculty concerns" and "Losing a sense of direction." There has been a change of mood in your college that you can feel.

Based on what you know so far, is it time to reconsider staying on as dean? If so, what sort of timetable would you set up for your next step? If not, what efforts would you make to improve this situation?

Considerations

1. If you do not feel that you know enough to make a reliable decision in this situation, what additional information do you want to have?

2. Suppose that you report via a provost to the president of the university. Does your response change at all if the provost says one of the following to you?

   - "Oh, this is just the sort of bump in the road that happens to all of us occasionally. Two years ago you had your 'seventh-year itch,' as I call it. I wouldn't take those four faculty members too seriously. You know you have my full support. And the president was just saying to me yesterday that you certainly didn't deserve the kind of grief these people were giving you. So don't lose any sleep over it. This, too, shall pass."

   - "Are you sure that you're still able to be effective after all that's happened? I mean, I know you've done great things for the college. But how do you feel about the future, particularly with that reaccreditation coming up? Do you have a plan for getting through all this?"

   - "I don't want to add to your headache, but the president's really concerned about what's going on in your college. Personally, I think you're doing a great job, and I think we all know that people are upset for reasons that don't really have anything to do with you. But it sounds to me as though you've got some fences to mend with the president."

3. Do you respond any differently if you are . . .

   - Dean of a very small college, and the Gang of Four represents a third of your entire faculty?

   - Dean of a very large college, and the Gang of Four represents barely 1% of your faculty?

   - Within five years of retirement?

   - Likely to have your faculty take a vote of no confidence in you? (Is the mere fact that a vote of no confidence will occur the most important factor in your decision? Does your decision only change if the vote of no confidence goes against you?)

4. Does it matter to you if the Gang of Four is widely regarded as a group of . . .

   - Opinion leaders among the faculty?

   - "Cranks, whiners, and crackpots," as another member of the faculty regularly calls them?

   - So closely associated to the faculty member who failed to receive tenure that their opinions are highly suspect?

   - Likely to leave the institution within a year or two?

5. Suppose that, during your years of service as a dean, you have developed an excellent reputation among the students of your college and are strongly supported by them.

   - Does this factor alter your decision about whether to stay in your position or to move on?

   - If you have decided to leave your current position, does this factor help you decide what your next step should be?

6. Of all the pieces of information in this case study, which do you regard as the biggest red flag (i.e., which concerns or disturbs you the most)?

7. The case study mentioned that your faculty evaluation scores had declined precipitously this year. If the institution where you work now (i.e., not the one in the case study, but the institution where you currently serve as dean)

conducts a formal faculty evaluation of you, how do you interpret the results? Do you . . .

- Compare them, whenever possible, to the scores received by other administrators to see how well you are performing in the context of the entire administration?

- Find yourself often becoming fixated on negative scores and comments even when the overall evaluation is positive?

- Forgo interpreting any of the results until you can review them with your supervisor?

- Regard the evaluations primarily as constructive and formative, scanning them for advice on ways in which you can do your job even better?

- Dismiss negative results on the basis that the faculty can't really understand what your job is like?

8. In a formal faculty evaluation of you where you work now (i.e., not the institution in the case study, but the institution where you currently serve as dean), what would you regard as a clear message that, in faculty's opinion at least, you have not been successful in your position?

- Is there a particular percentage of negative responses or comments on your evaluation that you would regard as a clear red flag?

- Is there a ranking among your fellow administrators, such as "bottom half" or "lowest fifth," that you would regard as cause for great concern?

- Are there particular types of comments that, if more than one or two faculty members made them, would cause you to rethink your position?

- Are there particular types of comments that, if even one faculty member made them, would cause you great concern?

- If your institution uses some type of Likert scale on its evaluations (see Chapter 30, "Faculty Evaluations"), is there a particular score level or ranking that you would regard as cause for concern?

Suggestions

The decision to leave one's current position is an extremely personal one. Some deans regard abandoning any job situation as an admission of failure and will redouble their efforts until they can make things better. Other deans will ask themselves, "And just why am I putting up with this?" as soon as frustrations begin to build and decide to get out while the getting is good. Most deans fall somewhere in between. In general, the three questions that deans need to ask themselves in situations such as those outlined in this case study are:

- Can I still be effective in my position?

- Can I still receive the satisfaction that I need from my position?

- Is remaining in my current position the best thing for my college and institution?

Let's consider each of these questions individually.

Can I Still Be Effective in My Position?

There may be situations whose dynamics prevent the dean from being effective. The dean may need to spend a lot of time on his or her personal life (because of a complicated divorce, caring for a chronically sick relative, or the lingering shadow of questionable ethical decisions), and he or she can no longer give the college and institution the attention that they deserve. The dean's support from the faculty and staff, the upper administration, or both may be so diminished that the college no longer has the leadership it requires to fulfill its fundamental mission of instruction, scholarship, and service. In the situation described by this case study, you should decide whether you have reached this point. Certainly, there are several developments that should concern you. The shift in your faculty evaluation scores could be an indication that your effectiveness as a faculty leader has been irretrievably lost. With a reaccreditation visit and difficult tenure cases coming up, you should at least reflect on whether you still are effective and can represent your college during those important processes.

Can I Still Receive the Satisfaction that I Need from My Position?

Even in situations where deans can still provide effective leadership for their colleges, they may discover that, on a personal level, their current positions are not right for them. It may be that decanal work in general is no longer the proper role for them in academic life. It may be that the institution where they are right now is a bad fit for them. Or it may be that, after a period of satisfaction and success, they're feeling burned out on the job or asking themselves, "Is this all there is?" In the current scenario one of the phrases that should have attracted your attention was "you've been feeling decidedly less satisfied." It appears that, even beyond the challenges of the disputed tenure case, you've sensed that you've already contributed your best ideas to your college and could benefit from some new challenges. Nine years is a rather long tenure in a deanship, and if the prospects ahead no longer seem as rewarding as they once did, this may well be the time to reevaluate your career.

Is Remaining in My Current Position the Best Thing for My College and Institution?

There are also situations in which a dean's effectiveness may have declined significantly and his or her job satisfaction may be low, but it is in the unit's best interests for the dean to remain in the position—at least temporarily. For instance, if both the president and provost were planning to leave the institution at the end of the current academic year, a dean may decide that, regardless of all other factors, it is better to stay on in his or her position for a short period to provide some stability for the near future. In the case study the institution's pending reaccreditation and the college's difficult tenure cases may well complicate your decision. If you are thinking of leaving anyway and the self-study portion of the reaccreditation effort has not yet begun, it may be in the institution's interests for you to hand over your position to someone who can see that process through from start to finish. On the other hand, if the self-study or compliance report required for reaccreditation is already far enough along, you may decide to endure your current situation (even if it is less than desirable) until that entire process is complete. Similarly, you will have to assess whether remaining in your position plays a constructive or a harmful role in the tenure reviews that lie ahead. If you think that your involvement in the previous case has either affected your own objectivity or reduced the impact of your judgment throughout your college, it may be prudent to step down before those cases arise. Nevertheless, if there are several valuable faculty members for whom you are the best possible person to make a strong case, it would be in the best interests of your college to remain in place a bit longer.

Can This Deanship Be Saved?

Certainly, nothing outlined in this case study would suggest that you are indisputably in a position that would call for your resignation. What you decide to do will depend on many of the factors and considerations just summarized, as well as your own personality, career goals, and ability to snatch victory from the jaws of defeat. One thing is certain: All deans will have periods of unpopularity or reduced support. You simply cannot fill an administrative position without meeting some resistance—from your faculty, the upper administration, or both.

Remember the essential principle that we learned in Chapter 33 ("Program Reviews"): Effective deans make decisions not by making the easy choice but by doing what is right for the institution as a whole. One encouraging factor in this case study is that, although your faculty evaluations have suffered for the current year, they were extremely positive for all preceding years. It may well be, therefore, that you are experiencing one of the inevitable glitches that afflict every dean on occasion. By focusing on good communication, mending some fences, openly acknowledging anything you may have done to contribute to current problems, and persevering, you could put the current problem behind you. In addition, although you do not have the same rapport with the current president that you had with the former president, nothing in the case study would suggest that your relationship with him or her is irretrievably broken. This may well be a situation in which you will need to go the extra mile and discover ways to improve your working relationship with the president. At the very least, if you decide to remain in your current position, seeking a closer relationship with him or her is a strategy that you should consider.

The real question thus becomes "Do you *want* this deanship to be saved?" If you think that, after nine years, you have contributed all that you can to the college, are no longer satisfied in your position, and are unlikely to be effective for several more years, it is probably time to consider your options. Although it may be difficult to move to another deanship or a higher administrative role from a position where you are not as successful as you would like, such a move is not impossible. Certainly, you have at least six to eight years of accomplishments to report, and it should not be difficult to find references who can address the positive differences you have made at the institution. Alternatively, if you have maintained a solid record of teaching and scholarship, particularly if you believe that you have preserved an excellent reputation with students, returning to a faculty role could also be an attractive option.

The important thing to remember is what we saw in Chapter 59 ("Planning for a Higher Administrative Role"): There is no single career path in academic life that fits every person. Although many individuals move from faculty member, to department chair, to assistant or associate dean, to dean, to provost, to president, that pathway is not as inflexible as the old Roman *cursus honorum*. Sometimes in our travels the best experiences occur on our side trips, unexpected detours, or when we double back to retrieve something we forgot at a previous location. A dean's administrative career can be much the same. Only you can decide what next step is best for you, and in most cases only you can decide when you are ready to take it. Don't make the mistake of assuming that your academic and administrative life must follow the preset itinerary of a packaged tour. Essential academic deans know that, in their own careers as in the service they provide to others, the goal is not to do what is easy, popular, or expected, but to do what is right. The principles that we have explored in this book will assist you. In the end, however, your own experience and conscience will be your most reliable guide.

Epilogue
A Checklist for the Essential Academic Dean

We have seen repeatedly that being an effective dean does not require any single type of personality or administrative style. Good deans come in all kinds and varieties. Nevertheless, most deans will find that they have the greatest success and receive the most satisfaction in their jobs when they adhere to the following principles:

- *The essential academic dean is accessible.* Good deans know their constituents. "Managing by walking around," having impromptu conversations with students and faculty members, eating regularly in the dining halls, and creating a culture of openness allow deans to understand their colleges' key issues and how these issues may be most appropriately addressed. The best deans are those who can make each person they meet feel as though they have all the time in the world just to interact with that one individual.

- *The essential academic dean keeps things in perspective.* Not every challenge is a crisis. Not every battle is worth fighting. Sometimes, when the vote goes against the dean, the best policy is simply to accept the decision and move on. Good deans tend to focus their energy on what truly matters, not on winning every argument or proving that they were right all along. Letting go of disappointments is not a sign of weakness; it's a sign that you know your priorities.

- *The essential academic dean cares for and respects the people in his or her college.* Deans who speak dismissively of students or faculty members as though they were obstacles to effective administration, rather than the true focus of the institution, have forgotten what colleges and universities are all about. Good deans value students and faculty members—as well as parents, trustees and legislators, donors, and members of the community—because these deans understand that the institution is there to serve these people. Good deans do not cater to students because students are customers of the institution or yield to every faculty whim because it makes their jobs easier. Nevertheless, they demonstrate consistently that they respect the people whom they serve even when they cannot agree with those people.

- *The essential academic dean delegates effectively.* Appropriate delegation does not consist simply of foisting off on others the responsibilities that the dean does not care for. At the other extreme, effective administration also does not mean doing everything yourself, micromanaging, or stifling others' creativity and initiative. Good deans understand that they cannot do everything by themselves, that others' contributions and perspectives are valuable, and that shared governance is a fundamental strength of American higher education.

- *The essential academic dean demonstrates quiet confidence.* People are more likely to be persuaded by leaders and managers who have a sense of assurance that most administrative challenges are all in a day's work and that even serious problems will eventually be overcome. Approaching your job with cheer, conveying an attitude that "we can do this," and taking a justified amount of pride in a job well done will make people *want* to work with you and help you achieve the college's goals.

- *The essential academic dean neither ignores nor becomes preoccupied with details.* A dean who pays no attention to the fine points of budgets, policies, and procedures can end up doing a great deal of harm to both the college and the institution. On the other hand, deans who lose all sight of the big picture because they worry about every minor arrangement and decision are not providing the leadership their colleges really need. There should always be a balance between healthy respect for details and a capacity to look beyond them to more global issues. Spending too much time down in the weeds is just as destructive as spending too much time with your head in the clouds. The best deans respect details, but they don't become obsessed by those details.

- *The essential academic dean preserves a good work-life balance.* Good deans are good people, first and foremost. They cannot serve their constituents effectively if they do not keep their lives in balance. Family, private interests, scholarship, and efficient administration must all be a part of the essential dean's life. Essential deans take vacations, read books unrelated to their jobs, have healthy relationships beyond the confines of the campus, and develop a full range of interests.

- *The essential academic dean has a sense of humor.* Good deans laugh. Occasionally, they even laugh at themselves. They know their own foibles and understand that not everything they do is all that momentous. Deans should feel free to share lighthearted moments with faculty members, particularly in public meetings where lifting the mood can be more effective than approaching every issue with solemn earnestness. Essential deans do not confuse being dignified with being dour. At the same time, they do not make light of every situation to such an extent that they are regarded as superficial or heartless.